THE
J
CURVE

A New Way to
Understand Why
Nations Rise and Fall

IAN BREMMER

———

SIMON & SCHUSTER   New York   London   Toronto   Sydney

SIMON & SCHUSTER
Rockefeller Center
1230 Avenue of the Americas
New York, NY 10020

For information about special discounts for bulk purchases,
please contact Simon & Schuster Special Sales at
1-800-456-6798 or business@simonandschuster.com

Designed by Dana Sloan

Manufactured in the United States of America

10   9   8   7   6

Library of Congress Cataloging-in-Publication Data
Bremmer, Ian, date.
    The J curve : a new way to understand why nations rise and fall / Ian Bremmer.
        p.   cm.
    Includes bibliographical references and index.
    1. Political development—Case studies.   2. Political stability—Case studies.
3. World politics.   4. Authoritarianism—Case studies.   5. Democratization—
Case studies.   6. United States—Foreign relations.   I. Title.
JC489.B74   2006
320.3—dc22   2006040339
ISBN-13: 978-0-7432-7471-5
ISBN-10: 0-7432-7471-7

Contents

THE J CURVE

Foreword

T his book offers a new framework with which to answer the following questions: How can we better understand the natural processes that erode the power of authoritarian regimes and nourish open governance? In an age when political instability can produce nuclear terrorism, severe economic disruption, and the transnational movement of crime, refugees, drugs, and disease, how can we more accurately forecast the moment when isolated states descend into chaos? How can the international community help these states manage their transitions toward greater harmony with the world around them? How can U.S. policymakers create a more effective foreign policy?

Over the next six chapters, we will visit several countries. Some are police states. Others are authoritarian regimes that are open, to a limited extent, to outside political, economic, and social influences. Some of these states have faced chaotic instability. A few have built relatively stable societies based on open governance. Most are countries of great interest for the United States. All illustrate how policymakers can better understand the potential sources of change (positive and negative) within these states, how those changes influence international stability, and how policymakers can use a new set of tools to achieve the outcomes they seek.

Twelve countries will be examined in depth. In each case, I will offer a modest amount of history intended to reveal both the special circumstances that make each foreign-policy challenge unique and the diversity of opportunities and dangers these states pose for the United States and the international community. I will also examine how U.S. policymakers have

1

approached these opportunities in the past and how they can address them in the future.

In the final chapter, I'll offer suggestions about how decision-makers in states with stable and mature governance can use the tools described in this book to protect their individual national interests and to help the citizens of authoritarian states begin to build dynamic open societies.

CHAPTER ONE

Stability, Openness, and the J Curve

On February 10, 2005, North Korea's state-run Pyongyang Radio informed its captive audience that the president of the United States had developed a plan to engulf the world in a sea of flames and to rule the planet through the forced imposition of freedom. In self-defense, the newsreader continued, North Korea had manufactured nuclear weapons.

That evening, Rick Nieman of the Netherlands' RTL Television asked U.S. Secretary of State Condoleezza Rice to respond to Pyongyang's assertion that North Korea needed nuclear weapons to cope with "the Bush administration's ever more undisguised policy to isolate . . . the Democratic People's Republic of Korea." Rice countered: "This is a state that has been isolated completely for its entire history. . . . They have been told that if they simply make the decision . . . to give up their nuclear weapons and nuclear-weapons program, to dismantle them verifiably and irreversibly, there is a completely new path available to them. . . . So the North Koreans should reassess this and try to end their own isolation."[1]

That's the official U.S. policy on North Korea: If North Korea submits to the complete, verifiable, irreversible dismantlement of its nuclear program, Washington will end North Korea's isolation and support the integration of Kim Jong-Il's regime into the international community. If, on the other hand, North Korea persists in developing its nuclear capacity, Washington will "further deepen North Korea's isolation."

To many, this policy is grounded in common sense. If North Korea begins to behave as Washington wants, the United States should reward the regime. If it does not, Washington should further seal it off. If Kim will quiet the relentless drumbeat of war and renounce his campaign to build an arsenal of the world's most destructive weapons, Washington should allow North Korea to escape its wretched isolation. If, on the other hand, North Korea insists on causing trouble, bargains in bad faith, ratchets up tensions in East Asia, violates its agreements, and perhaps even sells the world's most dangerous weapons to the world's most dangerous people, the regime must be swiftly and soundly punished. Kim Jong-Il and those who administer his government must be persuaded that his broken promises and misdeeds doom his regime to perpetual quarantine.

If this policy is properly applied, so the thinking goes, the message will be received far beyond North Korea. Common sense demands that Washington demonstrate that America stands ready to achieve its foreign- and security-policy goals with the sweetest carrots and sharpest sticks available. So the thinking goes.

But, as we'll see in the next chapter, this approach has failed to help Washington achieve its goals in North Korea. In fact, it has produced policies that have had virtually the opposite of their intended effects. Of course, U.S. foreign policies that produce the reverse of their intended consequences are not limited to either North Korea or the George W. Bush administration. Policy failures over many decades in Iraq, Iran, Cuba, Russia, and many other states demonstrate that policymakers need an entirely new geopolitical framework, one that captures the way decision-makers within these states calculate their interests and make their choices—and one that offers insight into how more effective U.S. policies can be formulated.

There is a counterintuitive relationship between a nation's stability and its openness, both to the influences of the outside world and within its borders. Certain states—North Korea, Burma, Belarus, Zimbabwe—are stable precisely because they are closed. The slightest influence on their citizens from the outside could push the most rigid of these states toward dangerous instability. If half the people of North Korea saw twenty minutes of CNN (or of Al Jazeera for that matter), they would realize how egregiously their government lies to them about life beyond the walls. That realization could provoke widespread social upheaval. The slightest improvement in the ability of a country's citizens to communicate with one another—the introduction of telephones, e-mail, or text-messaging into an authoritarian state—can likewise undermine the state's monopoly on information.

Other states—the United States, Japan, Sweden—are stable because they are invigorated by the forces of globalization. These states are able to withstand political conflict, because their citizens—and international investors—know that political and social problems within them will be peacefully resolved by institutions that are independent of one another and that the electorate will broadly accept the resolution as legitimate. The institutions, not the personalities, matter in such a state.

Yet, for a country that is "stable because it's closed" to become a country that is "stable because it's open," it must go through a transitional period of dangerous instability. Some states, like South Africa, survive that journey. Others, like Yugoslavia, collapse. Both will be visited in Chapter Four. It is more important than ever to recognize the dangers implicit in these processes. In a world of lightning-fast capital flight, social unrest, weapons of mass destruction, and transnational terrorism, these transformations are everybody's business.[2]

The J curve is a tool designed to help policymakers develop more insightful and effective foreign policies. It's meant to help investors understand the risks they face as they invest abroad. It's also intended to help anyone curious about international politics better understand how leaders make decisions and the impact of those decisions on the global order. As a model of political risk, the J curve can help us predict how states will respond to political and economic shocks, and where their vulnerabilities lie as globalization erodes the stability of authoritarian states.

J curves aren't new to models of political and economic behavior. In the 1950s, James Davies developed a quite different curve that expressed the dangers inherent in a gap between a people's rising economic expectations and their actual circumstances. Another J curve measured the relationship between a state's trade deficit and the value of its currency. The purpose of the J curve in this book is quite different and much broader. It is intended to describe the political and economic forces that revitalize some states and push others toward collapse.

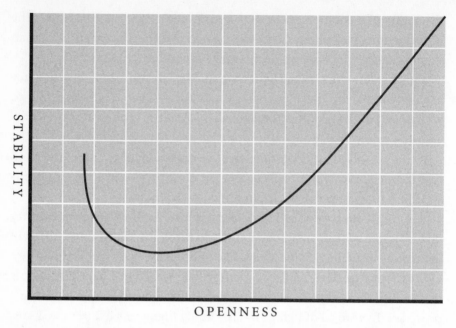

STABILITY

OPENNESS

The J Curve: Nations to the left of the dip in the J curve are less open; nations to the right are more open. Nations higher on the graph are more stable; those that are lower are less stable.

What is the J curve? Imagine a graph on which the vertical axis measures stability and the horizontal axis measures political and economic openness to the outside world. (See figure above.) Each nation whose level of stability and openness we want to measure appears as a data point on the graph. These data points, taken together, produce a J shape. Nations to the left of the dip in the J are less open; nations to the right are more open. Nations higher on the graph are more stable; those that are lower are less stable.

In general, the stability of countries on the left side of the J curve depends on individual leaders—Stalin, Mao, Idi Amin. The stability of states on the right side of the curve depends on institutions—parliaments independent of the executive, judiciaries independent of both, nongovernmental organizations, labor unions, citizens' groups. Movement from left to right along the J curve demonstrates that a country that is stable because it is closed must go through a period of dangerous instability as it opens to the outside world. (See figure on page 7.) There are no shortcuts, because authoritarian elites cannot be quickly replaced with institutions whose legitimacy is widely accepted.

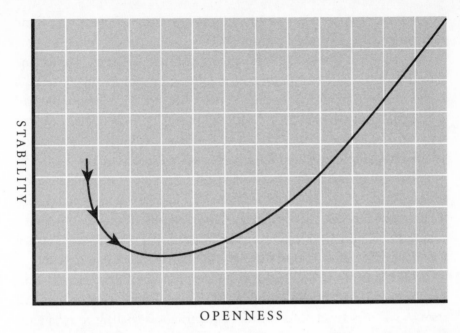

Movement Along the J Curve: Movement from left to right along the J curve demonstrates that a country that is stable because it is closed must go through a period of dangerous instability as it opens to the outside world.

"Openness" is a measure of the extent to which a nation is in harmony with the crosscurrents of globalization—the processes by which people, ideas, information, goods, and services cross international borders at unprecedented speed. How many books written in a foreign language are translated into the local language? What percentage of a nation's citizens have access to media outlets whose signals originate from beyond their borders? How many are able to make an international phone call? How much direct contact do local people have with foreigners? How free are a nation's citizens to travel abroad? How much foreign direct investment is there in the country? How much local money is invested outside the country? How much cross-border trade exists? There are many more such questions.

But openness also refers to the flow of information and ideas *within* a country's borders. Are citizens free to communicate with one another? Do they have access to information about events in other regions of the country? Are freedoms of speech and assembly legally established? How transparent are the processes of local and national government? Are there free flows of trade across regions within the state? Do citizens have access to, and influence in, the processes of governance?

"Stability" has two crucial components: the state's capacity to withstand shocks and its ability to avoid producing them. A nation is only unstable if both are absent. Saudi Arabia remains stable because, while it has produced numerous shocks over the last decade, it remains capable of riding out the tremors. The House of Saud is likely to continue to absorb political shocks without buckling for at least the next several years. Kazakhstan is stable for the opposite reason. Its capacity to withstand a major political earthquake is questionable but, over the course of its fifteen-year history as a sovereign state, it hasn't created its own political crises. How Kazakhstan might withstand a near-term political shock, should one occur, is far more open to question than in Saudi Arabia, where the real stability challenges are much longer-term.

To illustrate how countries with varying levels of stability react to a similar shock, consider the following: An election is held to choose a head of state. A winner is announced under circumstances challenged by a large number of voters. The nation's highest judicial body generates controversy as it rules on a ballot recount. That happened in Taiwan in 2003 and Ukraine in 2004. Demonstrations closed city streets, the threat of civil violence loomed, local economies suffered, and international observers speculated on the continued viability of both governments.* Of course, similar events erupted in the United States in 2000, without any significant implications for the stability of the country or its financial markets.

Stability is the capacity to absorb such shocks. Anyone can feel the difference between a ride in a car with good shock absorbers and in one that has no shock absorbers. Stability fortifies a nation to withstand political, economic, and social turbulence. Stability enables a nation to remain a nation.

LEVELS OF STABILITY

A highly stable country is reinforced by mature state institutions. Social tensions in such a state are manageable: security concerns exist within ex-

---

* Despite the turmoil, Ukraine rose to the occasion. A court ordered a new election, the opposition candidate won, and the majority of citizens accepted the result.

pected parameters and produce costs that are predictable. France may suffer a series of public-sector strikes that paralyze the country for several weeks. When these strikes occur, no one fears that France will renounce its commitment to democracy and an open society. Nor do they fear these shocks might generate a challenge from outside the country. No one worries that political battles within France might tempt Germany to invade—as it did three times between 1870 and 1940.

States with moderate stability have economic and political structures that allow them to function reasonably effectively; but there are identifiable challenges to effective governance. When Jiang Zemin passed leadership of the Chinese government, the Communist Party, and the People's Liberation Army to Hu Jintao, very few inside China publicly questioned the move's legitimacy. If any had—if Chinese workers had taken to the streets as French workers so often do—the state would have moved quickly to contain the demonstrations. Whether China's rigid, political structure can indefinitely survive the intensifying social dislocations provoked by its explosive economic growth is another matter.

Low-stability states still function—they are able to enforce existing laws and their authority is generally recognized. But they struggle to effectively implement policies or to otherwise change the country's political direction. These states are not well prepared to cope with sudden shocks. As an oil-exporting nation, Nigeria benefits from high energy prices. But its central government is unable to enforce the law in the Niger Delta region, where most of Nigeria's oil is located. A group called the Niger Delta People's Volunteer Force has repeatedly threatened "all-out war" against the central government unless it grants the region "self-determination." The rebels briefly shut down 40 percent of Nigeria's oil production in 2003 and forced President Olusegun Obasanjo to negotiate with them. The problem flared again in 2005 and 2006.

A state with no stability is a failed state; it can neither implement nor enforce government policy. Such a country can fragment, it can be taken over by outside forces, or it can descend into chaos. Somalia fell apart in 1991, when several tribal militias joined forces to unseat the country's dictator, and then turned on each other. Since then, warlords have ruled most of the country's territory. Their rivalries have probably killed half a million and made refugees of another 750,000. More than a dozen attempts to restore order, mostly backed by Western benefactors, have failed. Any Somali leader who intends to restore Mogadishu's authority over all of Somalia's territory will have to disarm tens of thousands of gunmen, stop the steady stream of arms trafficking, set up a working justice system, and revitalize a stricken economy. Meanwhile, there are warlords, extremists, smugglers, and probably terrorists with a clear interest in scuttling the process. And while political conflicts in France don't encourage Germany to invade, there are clear threats to any future stability in Somalia from just across the border. One of the few African nations offering to send peacekeeping troops to help Somalia reestablish civil order is Ethiopia, a neighbor with a long history of troublemaking there. The arrival of any foreign troops, especially Ethiopians, could reignite Somalia's civil war.

In August 2005, South Africa went public with concerns that its neighbor Zimbabwe stood on the brink of becoming just such a failed state. Representatives of South Africa's government said a sizable loan designed to rescue Robert Mugabe's country from default on International Monetary Fund obligations might be conditioned on Mugabe's willingness to include the opposition in a new government of national unity. South Africa has good reason for concern. When state failure strikes your neighbor, the resulting chaos can undermine your stability as well, as refugees, armed conflict, and disease spill across borders.

DEMOCRACY AND STABILITY

Democracy is not the only—or even the most important—factor determining a nation's stability. To illustrate the point, consider again the U.S. presidential election of 2000. Did America sail through the political storm with little real damage to its political institutions simply because the United States is a democracy? Taiwan is a democracy too, albeit a less mature one, but its citizens felt the jolt of every pothole on the ride through its electoral crisis. In Turkmenistan—not a democracy by any definition—the open rigging of presidential elections produces hardly a ripple, nothing like the unrest produced in Taiwan. Much of Turkmenistan's stability is based on the extent to which its authoritarianism is taken for granted; a rigged election is not the exception. Democratic or not, countries in which stability is in question are more susceptible to sudden crises, more likely to unleash their own conflicts, and more vulnerable to the worst effects of political shock. Yet, for the short term, authoritarian Turkmenistan must be considered more stable than democratic Taiwan.

At first glance, the J curve seems to imply that democracies are the opposite of authoritarian states. The reality is more complicated. In terms of stability—the vertical axis on the J curve—police states have more in common with democracies than they do with badly run authoritarian regimes. In other words, in terms of stability, Algeria has more in common with the United States than it does with Afghanistan. Consolidated democratic regimes—Germany, Norway, and the United States—are the most stable of states. They can withstand terrible shocks without a threat to the integrity of the state itself. Poorly functioning states—Somalia, Moldova, or Haiti—are the least likely to hold together. But consolidated authoritarian regimes—Cuba, Uzbekistan, and Burma—often have real staying power.

THE ELEMENTS OF STABILITY

A nation's stability is composed of many elements, and while one of these elements may be reinforcing the state's overall stability, another may be undermining it. On the one hand, Turkey's possible entry into the European Union enhances the nation's political and social stability. So long as Ankara remains on track for EU accession, Turkey's government has incentive to implement the reforms the Europeans require—reforms that strengthen the independence of the nation's political institutions, increase media freedoms, decrease the army's influence in politics, and protect the rights of minority groups, such as Turkish Kurds, who might otherwise provoke unrest. The accession process also binds Turkey more closely to European institutions.

On the other hand, the presence in northern Iraq of militant members of the Kurdistan Workers Party heightens concern that instability there could spill over into Kurdish communities in southeastern Turkey and threaten Turkey's security. Ankara is also concerned that, if Iraqi Kurds achieve greater autonomy, they may seek to regain control of the oil-rich northern Iraqi town of Kirkuk, in order to create the financial base for a future independent Kurdish state with claims on Turkish territory.

History, geography, culture, and other factors give each state its own particular strengths and vulnerabilities. As a consequence, each state has its own J curve, though each curve retains the same basic shape. North Korea's J curve is much lower than Saudi Arabia's, because North Korea lacks the resources, like oil, that can raise stability at any given level of openness. When oil prices rise, a country like Saudi Arabia, Venezuela, or Nigeria brings in more revenue and can use the extra cash to create jobs, buy a new weapons system, fund a social safety net, hire more people to monitor Internet traffic, or any number of other measures that increase short-term political stability. India's J curve is higher than Pakistan's because its history of multiparty politics allows it to better absorb shocks to the system than the more brittle governments of its neighbor, where the military has a well-established history of intervention and suppression of dissent. Government crackdowns enhance stability in the short run, but overreliance on them for peace and tranquillity breeds underlying social tensions that must be continually managed. Over time, the management of these tensions saps government resources and energy.

SHOCK

If stability is a measure of a state's capacity to implement government policy in the instance of shock, how do we define "shock"? There are natural disasters—a drought in Sudan, an earthquake in Japan, a tsunami that destroys lives in Thailand and sends floodwaters raging across coastal Indonesia. There are man-made shocks—the assassination of an influential Lebanese politician, a terrorist bombing in the Philippines, a flood of refugees in China, a secessionist crisis in Mexico. There are shocks that originate inside a country—a government default in Argentina. There are shocks that come from outside—the 9/11 attacks.

No country, stable or unstable, has the capacity to prevent all shocks from happening. But less stable states are more likely both to produce their own shocks and to experience shocks from beyond their borders. Shocks in an unstable state are also more likely to be larger in magnitude—ill-considered environmental policies make weather extremes more likely;

inadequate health care provokes more frequent outbreaks of infectious disease; poor economic planning raises youth unemployment.

It's important not to confuse shocks with instability. Over the next five to ten years, reasonably stable left-side-of-the-curve states like Syria, Venezuela, Iran, and Russia may be forced to absorb a number of shocks. Syria may face serious divisions within its ruling elite. Venezuela could experience a return to widespread labor unrest. Iran may wander into military confrontation with Israel. A drop in the price of oil could punch holes in Russian, Venezuelan, and Iranian coffers and produce civil strife. But the effects of these potential shocks are likely to be limited. Syria remains one of the most effective police states in the world. Venezuelan President Hugo Chávez remains popular enough to fend off direct challenges to his presidency. Iran's security apparatus remains loyal to the ruling religious conservatives, and Russia has yet to produce a viable and dynamic political opposition. Serious cracks may appear in the foundation of any of these countries ten years down the road. They're all vulnerable in the long term to challenges to their immature political institutions. But none of them are headed for real unrest this year or next. For now, stability in each of these states is relatively high.

If the worst shocks don't materialize, unstable countries can survive for a surprisingly long time. They just have to be lucky. Take Ukraine: before the election crisis in late 2004, Ukraine's stability was never hit with a large enough wave to sweep it away. In the turbulent years in which Leonid Kuchma held the presidency, a series of low-level controversies rattled the country. Ukraine endured widespread social discontent and substantial poverty, with living conditions little improved from Soviet times. Demonstrations demanding Kuchma's resignation and parliamentary no-confidence votes were common. Russia regularly interfered in Ukraine's domestic politics—even threatening at times to cut off most of the country's supply of natural gas. Despite all this, Ukraine avoided the big one—the shock substantial enough to push Ukraine's government out to sea.

The Berlin Wall once seemed the world's most formidable barrier. It was an illusion. In their haste to build the Wall literally overnight, East German soldiers added pebbles to low-quality cement to make the Wall sturdier. It stood for more than a quarter century as a symbol of the impenetrability of the Communist world for those on the western side and the futility of hoping for a better life for those to the east. But in 1989, a few blows with a hammer and chisel brought down the Wall with the same stunning speed with which the nations of the Warsaw Pact slid down the steep left side of the J curve toward irreversible change. Without the swing of the hammer, the Wall might still stand. But once the shocks of 1989 began, the Berlin Wall was no match for even a single solid blow.

Unchallenged instability does not necessarily lead to crisis. But the probability of state failure is highest when governments have the least political capital with which to respond to turmoil—the very moment when these states are most unstable. Think of state failure as the pull of a magnet under the J curve. As a country approaches the bottom, one sudden shock will have a destabilizing effect and can easily lead to collapse. An August 1991 coup attempt against Mikhail Gorbachev failed. But his government never recovered from the blow to its legitimacy produced by the fact that it was Boris Yeltsin and other reformers, not Gorbachev, who faced down the coup plot. Four months later, the Soviet Union ceased to exist.

The nation-state that replaced it—the Russian Federation—narrowly missed some serious political shocks of its own in the early and mid 1990s. The 1993 standoff between the Kremlin and the Russian Duma ended only when Boris Yeltsin shelled his country's parliament building. A war with Chechen rebels turned disastrously costly and had to be abandoned. Despite all this, the country avoided the series of earthquakes that were devastating the former Yugoslavia. Russian markets were chugging along with the high confidence—if not quite irrational exuberance—of international investors.

But then Russia's luck ran out when a real shock hit. In August 1998, a newly appointed, out-of-his-depth prime minister, Sergei Kiriyenko, made a political decision to simultaneously devalue the Russian ruble and default on the government's debt. Investors quickly discovered that Russia's calm had been the eye of a hurricane. Only a deliberate climb up the left side of the J curve toward more authoritarian, less transparent governance ultimately helped Russian elites restore political and economic stability.

This raises an important point about the shape of the J curve: the left side of the curve is much steeper because a little consolidation and control can provide a lot of stability. It is faster and easier to close a country than to open it. It's more efficient to reestablish order by declaring martial law than by passing legislation that promotes freedom of the press. Nations with little history of openness and pluralism have a habit of responding to turmoil with a centralization of state power; that habit is a hard one to break. The Kremlin's recent moves toward authoritarianism are therefore not surprising. Russia's government committed itself to democratic reform only in 1991—following a thousand years of authoritarianism.

Russia's crisis makes another point about stability: it takes a lot more than money to build it. Filling the world's deepest pockets of instability with cash will not by itself protect a state from the worst long-term effects of a political shock. The Marshall Plan to rebuild countries devastated by World War II was a success because it quickly mobilized resources to help restore normalcy to nations with a history of stable governance. Not all states have such a history.

Most developing countries have no experience of stable normalcy to return to. Throwing money at social and political problems in order to finance the construction of new infrastructure ignores the problem revealed by the J curve: developing countries become less stable before they become more so. It's one thing to build a new parliament building. It's quite another to populate the building with legislators dedicated to pluralist governance. The latter takes time, and before it can be achieved, the process of building an open state requires a period of significant instability.

Finally, some kinds of shock can be minimized. A nation can avoid unnecessary and destabilizing actions that bring a state into conflict with other nations or with its own citizens. Visionary leaders like Mustafa Kemal Atatürk and David Ben-Gurion, for example, limited their new states' territorial ambitions when failure to do so might have compromised their ability to build stability at home.

CAPITAL MUST BE SPENT

Economic reform—especially reform to begin a transition from a centrally planned to a market economy—creates enormous social dislocations. Inefficient industries have to be closed; workforces have to be "downsized." This downsizing swells the rolls of the unemployed, lowers living standards, decimates aspirations, and may well provoke dangerous unrest. The most volatile moment for any emerging market—and the time when the reform process is most likely to fail—is precisely at the inflection point between the two systems. Governments have a finite amount of economic capital at their disposal to maintain a functioning state. Reforms require the expenditure of that capital. That's why economic reform is destabilizing.

The same holds true for political reform. Political capital—the consent, or at least the acquiescence, of the governed—is as precious as economic capital. Movement from a command political structure to a consolidated, effective democracy requires that this capital be spent. As a government undertakes political reform—either voluntarily or as the result of processes beyond its control—the account risks running into deficit. An example: Russian President Vladimir Putin recognizes that his country's social safety net is fiscally unsustainable. Because his popularity rating has long been at 70 percent, he has some capital to spend on reforms that, among their least desirable consequences, sharply undermine the purchasing power of pensioners. Once those reforms are implemented, Russia's senior citizens feel the pinch, and some of them take to the streets. Putin blames others for the reform program's worst effects, but his popularity falls. Street demonstrations encourage Russia's would-be opposition to challenge the now-less-popular president on other issues. Investors express concern that other needed reforms may now be postponed as Putin seeks to refill the Kremlin's political coffers with new capital.

Brazil's President Luis Inácio Lula da Silva is swept into power by previously disenfranchised voters who hope the country's first "left-wing" chief executive will aggressively spend government revenue to reduce the wealth gap between Brazil's richest and poorest citizens. But because Lula is enormously popular, he has a war chest of political capital to spend on another urgent priority—a demonstration to international investors that he will honor the promise of his predecessor to reserve a preestablished percentage of Brazil's government revenue for the repayment of international debt. Lula has the political capital to spend on this unpopular move—and he spends it.

Bowing to pressure from within and without, Egypt announces it will hold a multicandidate presidential election. Egypt's rulers have not historically felt obliged to factor domestic approval ratings into their decisions as directly as the presidents of Russia and Brazil now do. But they too have domestic constraints to consider as they create policy. They must let off pressure for change in increments to avoid unrest—even a political explosion.

The world's most authoritarian leaders hold significant political capital. Kim Jong-Il, Fidel Castro, and Belarusian President Alexander Lukashenko have full control over their countries' levers of authority: the police, army, legislature, and judiciary. As long as that remains true, very little threatens the continued rule of these regimes. As authoritarian leaders spend political capital and institute reform, political opposition groups may gain the capacity to mobilize and challenge the existing system. The countries become less stable. That's why leaders like Kim, Castro, and Lukashenko don't institute political or economic reforms unless they believe their survival may depend on it.

THE PRECIPICE

The left slope of the J curve is much steeper than the right side because a country that is stable only because it's closed to the outside world can fall into a deep crisis very quickly. Weeks after Romanian dictator Nicolae Ceauşescu basked in the glow of the nearly hour-long standing ovation that marked the "re-election" meant to extend his forty-year rule, governments across Eastern Europe (East Germany, Poland, and Czechoslovakia) began to crumble. A Ceauşescu speech from a balcony overlooking a public square in Bucharest was, for the first time in decades, interrupted by hecklers. Days later, following a brief public trial, his bullet-ridden corpse was tossed into a ditch. When such regimes finally fall, they fall hard.

As mentioned before, the reverse is also true: a closed country can substantially reinforce its stability—and become even more authoritarian—through the implementation of measures that further isolate the nation's people. When the king of Nepal wants to sack his prime minister's government and reestablish his own personal authority, he cuts international phone lines, shuts down Internet access, and closes other media outlets. Castro jams antiregime radio broadcasts from Miami. When hard-line Soviet conservatives launched the ill-fated 1991 coup against Gorbachev's government, early word of the putsch created a race by both sides to television and radio stations. The coup plotters wanted to control the airwaves;

opposition groups wanted journalists to continue broadcasting news to the outside world. In 1991, openness triumphed over the attempt to stifle dissent. Unfortunately for Russia, that wasn't the last time soldiers with rifles entered a Moscow television station.

In any left-side-of-the-curve state, it's easier to close a country than to open it. But once mature political institutions are fully constructed and embraced by a nation's people, they are a lot more durable and do far more to protect the viability of the state than any police state tactic can. And communications technology can't be controlled forever. In February 2005, Chinese citizens celebrated the Lunar New Year by sending and receiving a total of 11 billion text messages. If text-messaging had been as readily available in the spring of 1989, the demonstrations in Tiananmen Square might well have ended differently. What happens the next time a spontaneous large-scale demonstration in China takes on a life of its own? That question may already have been answered in the Philippines. Text-messaging there helped topple a government in 2001. Opposition organizers used text messages to direct 700,000 demonstrators to Manila's People Power shrine to demand the removal of then President Joseph Estrada.

In moments of acute crisis, which the Tiananmen Square protests might have become, staying on the curve and avoiding the total collapse of the state requires a resolute move up the curve—in one direction or the other. A regime may try to stabilize the state by closing it as quickly as possible. That's the logic that led Deng Xiaoping to order tanks to crush the prodemocracy demonstrations. Or a government may try to reform its way toward the right side of the curve by increasing democracy, transparency, and openness to the outside world. South Africa's governing African National Congress allowed for the creation of a well-publicized "truth and reconciliation commission" whose sessions were open to the public and the media in order to prevent fear and thirst for revenge from becoming the primary drivers of the nation's politics. Following each of modern Turkey's military coups, the army quickly passed executive authority back into civilian hands, honoring the Turkish tradition of civilian rule. Left or right, the state must move away from the dip in the curve. If it doesn't, the state will collapse and fall off the curve into chaos.

Some economists assume movement along the curve is one-way only, left to right, "developing" to "developed." They refer to developing states as "emerging markets" (ever heard of a "submerging market?"), with the underlying presumption that hunger for progress and modernity and the invisible hand of international markets push these countries toward maturity and their political structures toward greater degrees of independence. A state, they believe, may hit bumps along the long road toward freedom and prosperity, but the market will prevail and the country will ultimately develop.

But emerging markets need not emerge. If their political leaders don't have enough economic capital to carry out the process, they may be forced to abandon it. That's the fear of international investors in Brazil whenever Lula loses a domestic political battle. They wonder if he still has the popularity and political will to tell his people that money sitting in the Brazilian treasury can't be used to build new hospitals and factories in the countryside because it's needed to pay off debt to the IMF. The Treuhandanstalt, a commission set up in the newly reunified Germany to enable inefficient East German industries to privatize with a minimum of social dislocation, was constantly buffeted by political controversy. It made progress in fits and starts, and pressure to slow—or even backtrack on—forced privatizations sometimes carried the day.

Political development works the same way. Just as economic capital is a necessary but insufficient condition for state development, leaders must be willing and able to spend political capital to bring about reform. Even before his death in 2004, it was clear Yasir Arafat would be remembered as a man with a genius for steering the ship of the would-be Palestinian state through storms. But he is also remembered as a man who lacked the political will to finally bring that ship into port. To have political capital is not enough. You have to spend it. Otherwise, an emerging democracy may never emerge.

It's a lot safer on the left side of the J curve than at the bottom. A leader may take the vessel out of the harbor, by instituting real reforms to bring pluralism into government and entrepreneurial energy into the economy, only to lose his nerve as the first threatening waves of instability crack over the bow. That's what happened in Burma in the early 1950s. One of Asia's most promising developing countries completely cut itself off from the outside world. A little over half a century later, it is one of the world's most repressive. The regime is reasonably stable, but its long-term position becomes more precarious as the world outside its borders changes. And, of course, leader X may know that political reform is, for himself at least, political suicide. If China becomes a genuine democracy, its current political leadership will be swept aside. The same is true for Kim Jong-Il, Fidel Castro, the clerics who rule Iran, the Saudi royal family, Bashar al-Assad, Hosni Mubarak, the Burmese military, Alexander Lukashenko, and many others. Only those who believe they might survive reforms are likely to genuinely pursue them.

All states are in constant motion on the J curve. In left-side-of-the-curve states, there is a constant tension between the natural pull toward greater openness and an authoritarian state's efforts to continually reconsolidate power. Street protests and widespread strikes open a country to both greater communication among opposition activists and international media attention, and move the country down the curve toward instability. The state responds by declaring martial law and a news blackout to increase stability by closing the country. Even in a right-side state, unrest in a volatile region and the state's response to it can produce movement in both directions along the curve.

In addition, the J curve itself is in motion up and down. When, for example, a natural disaster strikes, a nation's entire J curve may slip lower. Such a shift indicates that, for every possible degree of openness, there is less stability. The curve can also shift higher. If a state's economy depends on oil revenues, and the global price for oil moves higher, the added revenue increases stability at every possible level of openness. (See figure below.)

When a powerful tsunami hit Indonesia in December 2004, its horrific effects pushed the country's entire J curve lower. But the massive inflow of international humanitarian relief aid shifted the entire curve higher again, because, once the money arrived, the country became more stable at every level of openness.

There are many factors that can suddenly and powerfully shift a state's J curve up or down. Drought conditions in India, a substantial move in energy prices that alters Nigeria's growth prospects, an IMF loan for Argentina, or an earthquake in Pakistan can all provoke a sudden shift in these countries' stability at every level of openness.

Clearly, some states are more vulnerable to these shifts than others. Hurricane Katrina had less effect on U.S. stability in 2005 than the tsunami had in Indonesia a few months earlier. That's in part because the United States enjoys a much higher level of economic, social, and political stability than Indonesia and is far less vulnerable to shocks. A country with a smaller

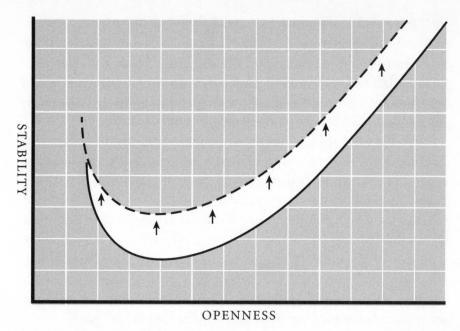

OPENNESS

Shifts of the Entire J Curve: The J curve itself is in constant motion up and down. When a shock occurs, a nation's entire J curve may slip lower. Such a shift indicates that, for every degree of openness, there is less stability. If an event occurs that reinforces stability at every level of openness, the curve shifts higher.

economy is more vulnerable to economic and social shocks than one with a larger economy.

Finally, a country whose economic growth depends too much on the revenue produced by one commodity will face J curve shifts that occur more often and with greater effect. A drop in oil prices will destabilize Venezuela far more than it will a better-diversified oil-exporting state like Norway.

POLICY

If consolidated authoritarian regimes tend to be more stable than democracies in transition, and if stability is critical to averting disaster in today's world, why not drop the whole question of reform and bolster those closed authoritarian regimes? Many have accused the United States of precisely that approach. We'll look closely at policy challenges in the final chapter but one question in particular is worth briefly addressing here. Why push for political reform in Saudi Arabia, Pakistan, Egypt, Russia, and other states on the left side of the J curve that are at least somewhat friendly to U.S. interests? In the interests of global stability, why not encourage them to consolidate domestic political power? There are several reasons.

First, the most stable authoritarian regimes are obviously the world's most repressive. The dynamism necessary to survive in the modern world comes from the intellectual energy and freedom to innovate of a nation's people. In addition, dictatorships can't last indefinitely. The costs of protecting a consolidated authoritarian state from cataclysmic instability can't be sustained forever. These states will eventually collapse under their own repressive weight and the energy released will send them hurtling down the left side of the J curve without brakes—or a steering wheel. In an age of weapons of mass destruction and transnational terrorism, the damage such states can do on the way down is unprecedented in human history.

Authoritarian states are only as stable as the hold on power of an individual leader or group of oligarchs. The viability of such states has little to do with stable institutions. In Cuba, Fidel Castro *is* the revolution. Loyalty to the Cuban government is loyalty to Castro himself. When he dies, the chances are good that the Cuban Communist Party will have to work hard to establish new political capital with the Cuban people. It can be done. The Bolshevik movement survived the death of Lenin in 1924—although the Communist Party preserved his body to help preserve its legitimacy and Stalin's methods might now be difficult to duplicate.

Individual personalities—cult of personality or no—are far less durable than institutions. As a consequence, authoritarian states tend to be much more volatile. The process of political succession is dangerous for an authoritarian state's stability, because much of the political capital vested in an individual dies with him.* Maintaining stability in a closed society requires quick reflexes. Time for strategy is a luxury dictators can rarely afford. Following Egyptian President Anwar Sadat's assassination, Hosni

---

* In some cases, a successor may inherit *some* of his predecessor's legitimacy, as Stalin did following Lenin's death. Stalin took great pains to (falsely) portray himself as Lenin's designated heir.

Mubarak assumed power and moved to limit political volatility by jailing as many of his and Sadat's enemies as he could. It was not Egyptian law that determined the nature of the regime; the regime dictated the law. Mubarak protected Egypt's stability by jailing senior members of the Muslim Brotherhood—those he considered most dangerous to his government.

Consolidated authoritarian regimes shouldn't be bolstered, but that doesn't imply that the correct policy is "regime change"—certainly not in the military, statue-toppling sense. The right approach to closed states is usually inducement and containment. Societies can be persuaded to accept policies that open the country incrementally to the outside world and build a dynamic and financially independent middle class capable of changing society from within. That's why the United States is right to help promote Chinese and Russian membership in the World Trade Organization and might do well to offer support for eventual membership even for North Korea. None of these governments wants to empower potential opposition groups by allowing them independent control of financial resources, but all want to dynamize their economies. Egypt has been induced to increase trade ties with Israel through deals that open American markets to Egyptian goods made with a fixed percentage of Israeli inputs. That will profit an Egyptian middle class that will one day provide the engine for change in Egypt. If Pakistan's middle class were as vibrant as India's, the country might not have a military ruler or so many young religious extremists.

Where inducement fails, containment can prevent behavior that destabilizes states, regions, and the world. The only viable approach to North Korea's nuclear program is probably aggressive enforcement of the Proliferation Security Initiative, a quarantine on weapons and weapons technology entering or leaving the country. In the most extreme case, air strikes may prove the only way to slow the development of Iran's nuclear-weapons capability until change from within alters the way Iran defines its national interest.

Thus, the developed world should neither shelter nor militarily destabilize authoritarian regimes—unless those regimes represent an imminent threat to the national security of other states. Developed states should instead work to create the conditions most favorable for a closed regime's safe passage through the least stable segment of the J curve—however and whenever the slide toward instability comes. And developed states should minimize the risk these states pose the rest of the world as their transition toward modernity begins.

The J curve provides the ordering principle for this book. The next four chapters will focus on individual states—their place on the J curve and the direction they may be headed. This structure is meant to give the reader a framework with which to understand the pressures and motivations that guide these countries' leaders and, as a consequence, how policymakers should interpret the challenges these countries pose for the effective implementation of policies toward them.

The chapters that follow bring together countries that pose vastly different kinds of challenges for the United States and the world. Some countries' policy choices are critically important for the future of American foreign policy, and the actions their leaders take have global significance, as in North Korea, Iran, and India. Some, like Cuba, have very little direct impact on global security, but illustrate what the J curve can teach us about the effective formulation of foreign policy. Some states, like Russia and China, already test the wisdom and resourcefulness of U.S. foreign policy and play vitally important roles in global politics. Others, like Saudi Arabia and Israel, are unlikely to alter the global order for several years, but will eventually reach a moment of truth in their political evolutions that demand foresight from all whose futures they might change. An analysis of policy toward Saddam Hussein's Iraq demonstrates how costly ill-considered strategies can be and how counterintuitive some of the solutions are to the world's most intractable foreign-policy problems. There are two other historical cases, South Africa and Yugoslavia, which provide important examples of what happens when states slide all the way down the curve into the most dangerous levels of instability.

Chapter Two is devoted to three countries near the peak of the left side of the J curve: North Korea, Cuba, and Saddam Hussein's Iraq. Chapter Three examines states that remain on the left side of the J curve but risk an eventual slide toward instability: Iran, Saudi Arabia, and Russia. Chapter Four moves down the slope into the dangerous central section of the curve for a look at two countries that have been there: South Africa and the former Yugoslavia. Chapter Five features three countries on the right side of the curve, examines how they got there, and considers what factors will determine whether they stay: Turkey, Israel, and India. Chapter Six is devoted to a single country, the state whose political, economic, and social development and whose potential for instability pose the greatest challenges for the United States and the world over the next generation: China. The seventh and final chapter will offer some policy conclusions and a few ideas about the future of stability and globalization.

CHAPTER TWO

The Far Left Side
of the J Curve

*Dictators ride to and fro upon tigers which they dare
not dismount.*

—Winston Churchill

Each of the three countries in this chapter is stable only because its ruling elite has sealed off its citizens from the outside world in order to monopolize power and resources in the hands of the regime. North Korea, Cuba, and Saddam Hussein's Iraq (which fell only to an invasion) have defied expectations of collapse for decades. They are all consolidated authoritarian regimes. Each has benefited from the international community's tendency to produce shortsighted policies that help them stay that way. These are the states perched high atop the far left side of the J curve.

The far left side is the most counterintuitive section of the J curve: states that are often among the most destitute and retrograde are surprisingly stable. It's obvious that consolidated authoritarian states are considerably less stable than well-established liberal democracies. But the most durable of these closed countries enjoy a higher degree of stability than other left-side-of-the-J-curve states which have some limited openness to the outside world. North Korea, Cuba, and Saddam's Iraq are more stable than Iran, Saudi Arabia, and Russia, at least in the short term, because Saddam, Castro, and Kim have a surer grip on their countries' resources and tighter control of how their citizens communicate both with one another and with the world beyond their borders.

The ease and speed with which people, information, ideas, goods, and services now cross international borders may well eventually render these police states obsolete. In fact, openness to the outside world poses the greatest immediate danger to these regimes. But the tyrants who control states like North Korea, Cuba, and Saddam's Iraq are well aware that their near-term survival depends on maintaining the walls that insulate their people from the rest of the world. So they develop sophisticated techniques to keep their people uninformed and under control. The fatal weakness of these states is that any crack in the façade, no matter how small, allows in the ideas and information that stimulate hunger for change.

The left side of the curve is much steeper than the right, and the momentum of destabilizing events can quickly propel left-side states down the curve into dangerous instability. A strike by workers in Uzbekistan is a far greater threat to the Uzbek government than a similar strike in the heart of London would be for Britain. However unhappy British teachers may seem during a demonstration, they know they enjoy a stake in the system, a share of Britain's prosperity, and political allies who will speak for them in the corridors of power. As became clear in the spring of 2005, protest in Uzbekistan frightens Islam Karimov's regime, and he answers it with blunt-force repression. Many Uzbek citizens feel they have little to lose by attacking their government—and little hope for relief from their misery if they don't.

These closed regimes are also at risk because a huge portion of their resources must be used to maintain the country's isolation. A closed country must build an "ideological immune system," because airwave-borne viruses of foreign influence can produce a fast-spreading effect on the population that an authoritarian government can't control. Maintenance of that immune system costs a lot of energy, man-hours, and money. The relative availability and low cost of increasingly sophisticated tools of communication make it harder for even the most repressive regimes to completely seal off their citizens. When the residents of China's Jilin and Liaoning provinces get new cell phones, they earn extra cash by selling the old ones to North Koreans. The North Korean government lacks the resources to do much about it. And the impact of foreign ideas is much larger in a nation whose people aren't used to them.

That's why the J curve isn't a U curve. There aren't many regimes left that can maintain old-style isolation, because the democratization of information makes it hard to keep an entire nation in the dark. It's not an easy thing to convince millions of people, as Enver Hoxha once did in Albania, that despite obvious hardship, they're living in a worker's paradise. Nor is it easy to convince them life is harder abroad than it is at home. In the 1970s, the Soviet daily newspaper *Pravda* ran a front-page photograph of New Yorkers waiting in line on a Saturday morning for Zabar's delicatessen to open. The photo was captioned with the words "Look. Bread lines in America, too." Attempts to convince today's Muscovites that America faces economic depression are considerably less likely to succeed.

Another reason such states are so fragile: their stability depends largely on individual leaders or families, rather than on institutions. Because the legitimacy of these governments isn't supported by a system based on independent institutions in which the citizenry has confidence, the death of the supreme leader can spell the end of an authoritarian regime. Yugoslavia did not long survive the death of Tito. The passing of Francisco Franco in 1975 paved the way for democratic change in Spain. Joseph Stalin's demise was kept a state secret for several days to allow Communist Party officials time to prepare for the possibility that Soviet citizens might demand fundamental political change.

Yet, even though it is now much harder to maintain secrecy and isolation, there are still a number of states trying gamely to pull it off. When a devastating tsunami struck South Asia on Christmas Day 2004, information on the disaster's effects poured in quickly from a dozen countries. Yet Burma, which was directly impacted by the disaster, maintained near-total radio silence. After Nepal's King Gyanendra sacked his entire government in February 2005, his first order was to shut down his country's telephone and Internet contact with the outside world. In Sudan, the state does all it can to prevent the international community from investigating the ethnic bloodshed in its Darfur region. Zimbabwe's President Robert Mugabe works overtime to keep international monitors away from his country's bogus elections and to bully and terrorize voters into supporting his government.

And then there's Turkmenistan, a bizarre, totalitarian, Central Asian police state in which an absolute dictator has taken isolation and control of the population to both comic and tragic extremes. The country's self-appointed dictator for life, Saparmurat Niyazov, has pronounced himself

Turkmenbashi, or "father of all Turkmen." There is a portrait of Niyazov on nearly every street corner, and, although many of the portraits don't look alike, those who see them know whom they're meant to represent. Travel into the country from outside is tightly restricted; travel abroad for nearly all Turkmenistan's citizens is impossible. The local KGB has changed its acronym but not its methods. Niyazov has maintained the country's Stalinist character like a shrine to an aging silent film star. In the center of the capital city of Ashkhabad, a triumphal, three-pronged arch, combined with a 220-foot victory column, serves as pedestal for a massive, pure-gold statue of Niyazov, rotating a full 360 degrees every twenty-four hours.[1]

To mold his people's political thought, Turkmenbashi announced in the late 1990s that neither the Koran nor the Bible offered his people the spiritual sustenance they needed.* To fill the gap, he authored *Ruhnama,* or "The Answer to All Questions," a work that has now replaced much of the nation's previous primary-school curriculum. Every government office, school, and university in Turkmenistan features public readings of the pink-covered book. Attendance is mandatory for all workers and students. Niyazov has renamed days of the week and months of the year after himself, his family, and *Ruhnama's* most colorful characters. He has also indulged in show trials and forced public self-criticism sessions worthy of Stalin or Mao. These spectacles air live on giant video screens in Ashkhabad's public squares. Police patrol every street.[2]

Niyazov's faithfulness to many of Mao and Stalin's most effective methods of repression and control demonstrates that the relationship between stability, control, and isolation from the outside world is timeless. But in an age of increasingly fast-paced political and economic instability, terrorism, and weapons of mass destruction, insights provided by the J curve into how these regimes maintain themselves—and how quickly they can slide into chaos—are now more relevant than ever.

These states are brittle, but they are more stable than authoritarian states that allow a more open political discourse with the outside world. These closed authoritarian regimes offer a special challenge to the international predictability that policymakers and international investors seek, because their leaders often understand their interests in profoundly counterintu-

---

* Nearly 90 percent of Turkmenistan's population is Muslim. Virtually all the rest are Eastern Orthodox Christians.

itive ways. Why did Saddam refuse to cooperate with UN resolutions when to do so would have lifted sanctions on his country and made an American invasion far less likely? Why does Castro revel in antagonizing the neighboring superpower? Why does North Korea seem to invite a military conflict it can't possibly survive? Because their leaders believe the international community will respond by giving their governments what they want most: deeper isolation. International political crises serve their purposes. Dictators produce instability abroad to maintain stability at home.

As North Korea continues to demonstrate, even a small isolated state can disrupt global politics and markets in frightening ways. In this case, where North Korea's nuclear deterrent makes the use of brute force against Pyongyang not only dangerous, but increasingly inconceivable, it's essential to understand how these states on the left side of the J curve sustain themselves—and how they might fall.

NORTH KOREA AND WHY IT MATTERS

The Democratic People's Republic of Korea (DPRK) is a small, isolated country with a population of 20 million to 22 million and few natural resources beyond the slave labor of its people. Its economic system does not allow for the efficient exploitation of the limited mineral wealth it does possess. Most of the world's governments treat North Korea as a pariah. Its only real ally, China, keeps the DPRK leadership at arm's length. In short, North Korea doesn't enjoy the natural advantages of some other isolated states: it has no reliable friends, no oil or gas to sell; it will never be a hot tourist destination; no one is dying to try North Korean cigars.

Yet, North Korea is geopolitically important because it is a heavily militarized police state with a million soldiers, several million malnourished citizens, and an arsenal of the world's most dangerous weapons.* On either side of the small demilitarized zone that separates North and South Korea stands the highest concentration of military force anywhere in the world.

North Korea is also important because it maintains a ballistic-missile capability that threatens South Korea and Japan. The regime has sold mis-

---

*About 5 percent of North Korea's people serve in the military.

siles in violation of international law. It could do the same with weapons of mass destruction and related technology. It also traffics in illegal drugs and counterfeit currency. It's a country close to the brink of economic ruin and large-scale starvation, which threatens to send refugees by the millions into neighboring countries, particularly China. This flow of refugees could, in turn, produce severe food shortages in neighboring states, breed communicable disease, provoke environmental crises, and create chaos in global financial markets. In other words, North Korea is important because of the wide range of threats it poses for the international community. Its instability is everybody's business.

Some History

Three days after issuing the general order for Japanese surrender in August 1945, President Harry Truman, fearing the Soviets might attempt to occupy the entire Korean Peninsula, authorized the U.S. military to divide Korea. The dividing line was set at the 38th Parallel. The Soviet Union and the United States installed client regimes on either side of the divide, with the northern half under Communist domination and the southern half directed by a series of authoritarian regimes sponsored by Washington. Immediately after the Second World War, Stalin dispatched Kim Il-Sung, a young Korean officer from a specially trained unit of the Soviet Army, to close the northern half of the Korean Peninsula to the outside world and to construct a stable, Soviet satellite state.

Despite a United Nations plan for Korea-wide elections, the two de facto Korean states, the DPRK in the north and the Republic of Korea (ROK) in the south, were politically and economically separated. This separation produced a natural rivalry between the two Koreas and the instability that comes with it. Following the division, the leaders of the northern and southern regimes each pressured their respective superpower patrons to help them to militarily reunify the peninsula. In early 1950, Stalin agreed to support a North Korean invasion of the south with the aid of an army of Chinese "volunteers." The United States moved to defend its South Korean allies, and for the next three years, war surged up and down the peninsula, destroying much of both nations' infrastructure and creating millions of refugees.

By the end of the war in 1953, 10 percent of all Koreans—almost 2 million people—were dead; 6 million were wounded or missing. More than 900,000 Chinese and almost 37,000 Americans were killed. The north was essentially flattened by near-continuous bombing by the U.S. Air Force. Once the armistice—little more than a ceasefire—was signed, the two sides drove white posts into the ground to create a military demarcation line just north of the 38th Parallel. Legally, a state of war still exists on the Korean Peninsula. A half-century after the armistice, the unfinished Korean War still threatens regional stability.

Under the leadership of Kim Il-Sung, and with the aid and support of the Soviet Union, North Korea grew into a self-sufficient, industrial economy, which, at first, outperformed postwar South Korea. The DPRK developed heavy industry on foundations laid by Japanese occupiers in the 1930s. Agriculture was collectivized and output quickly rose as modern techniques were introduced to what had been a Japanese-dominated feudal society. North Koreans built schools and hospitals, produced enough to eat, and enjoyed the basic labor rights of a developing socialist state.

But by the end of the 1970s, the structural limitations of North Korea's economy began to assert themselves. By 1979, North Korea's per capita GNP had fallen to a third that of South Korea. As in the Soviet Union, the DPRK's ability to expand its industrial base reached natural limits: there was no incentive structure within its economic system to develop the new technology necessary to expand productivity. To safeguard the DPRK's self-sufficiency, the state ordered unsustainable agricultural projects that eventually did tremendous damage to the nation's arable land. Stagnation led to hardship, hardship produced famine, and North Korea was unable to innovate its way out of a deepening economic crisis. With the collapse of the Soviet Union, North Korea—like Cuba—suddenly found itself without the benefactor that enabled it to feed its people without joining the global economy.

North Korea's economy remains the world's most centrally planned and isolated. Industrial capital stock is, for all practical purposes, beyond repair after decades of underinvestment and shortages of spare parts. A lack of arable land, three generations of inefficient collective farming, an inhospitable climate for agriculture, and chronic shortages of fuel and fertilizer have produced severe food shortages. The food that is produced goes to the Communist Party leadership and to the million-man military. Whatever is left feeds some of North Korea's people.

The DPRK's military capability is the regime's guarantee of protection against invasion. The loyalty of the military and security services is the regime's guarantee of protection against its own people. This power and loyalty ensure that North Korea's armed forces have first access to whatever the government can produce or purchase. In fact, the military enjoys a parallel economy, with its own farms and factories. Estimates are that anywhere from one-fifth to one-third of North Korea's GDP goes directly to the army.

Kim Jong-Il

Kim Jong-Il, or "the Great Leader," as he is more commonly known by his subjects, is the world's greatest political and artistic genius.* He was born under a double rainbow atop a sacred Korean mountain. His brilliance extends well beyond his leadership of Communism's first dynasty. Kim is the author of six operas, each more beautiful than any in the history of music. His first visit to a golf course resulted in five holes-in-one and a world record for best score in a single round of eighteen. In fact, Kim eclipsed the previous world mark by twenty-five strokes and has witnesses to prove it. Kim's personal genius is the DPRK's organizing principle.

There is, of course, a more prosaic version of Kim Jong-Il's story. In it, Kim was born in 1941 in a Korean refugee camp in Siberia. A would-be film director—in a country with no film industry—Kim Jong-Il began to take on some modest leadership responsibilities in the 1970s. At age twenty-three, Kim assumed the role of guidance officer in the Cultural and Propaganda Department of the Communist Party Central Committee. In 1980, he was made a full member of the Central Committee, the Politburo, and the Military Committee and was officially designated his father's successor. Since assuming power following his father's death in 1994, Kim Jong-Il has made virtually all his policy decisions outside the public eye, rarely communicating with foreign heads of state or their representatives.

Kim rules not through genius but by the omnipresent surveillance of his secret police and the Communist Party's bureaucratic control over virtually

---

* Previously North Koreans distinguished between "Great Leader" Kim Il-Sung and "Dear Leader" Kim Jong-Il, but both are now referred to as "Great Leader."

every aspect of daily life. No one in North Korea receives food or shelter without the approval of the party. The Great Leader's "star power" owes much to a considerable effort to deemphasize his modest stature. He is usually seen publicly in dark glasses, platform shoes, and a pompadour hairstyle designed to add four inches to his height. Only a leader confident that his people have virtually no contact with the outside world would ask them to accept hagiography as biography.

If some (too easily) dismiss Kim as a megalomaniacal clown, the methods of his government are no laughing matter. North Korea has granted asylum to Japanese terrorists.* It has allowed millions of North Koreans to starve, shot down a South Korean passenger plane, assassinated South Korean government officials, kidnapped South Korean and Japanese civilians, sold ballistic missiles to Syria, Libya, and Iran, sold heroin to western drug dealers, and worked for years to develop an arsenal of nuclear weapons. The world has responded by deepening North Korea's isolation.

Isolation and Secrecy

To protect the DPRK's isolation—and therefore its stability—the North Korean leadership has used tactics familiar in other closed authoritarian societies, but it has taken them to extremes rarely seen anywhere else. Few foreigners are allowed into the country. Those who are admitted are allowed virtually no meaningful contact with locals. They are shown "Potemkin villages," hastily built movie-set-style communities meant to persuade outsiders that the standard of living is substantially higher than it is. In general, aid workers are no more welcome in the DPRK than are international weapons inspectors. The leadership doesn't want foreigners to see North Koreans—or North Koreans to see foreigners. The country's J curve is already too low to allow such a threat.

One event in particular captures the absurd and tragic extremes of North Korea's isolation. On April 22, 2004, sparks from a railyard electrical cable reportedly ignited chemical fertilizer stored in train cars in the north-

---

* North Korea has given sanctuary to the surviving members of the Japanese Communist League—a Red Army Faction that hijacked a Japanese commercial jet in 1970 and landed it in North Korea. http://cfrterrorism.org/sponsors/northkorea2.html#Q12.

ern town of Ryongchon, close to the Chinese border. The resulting explosion killed nearly 200 people, injured over 1,000, and left more than 10,000 homeless. Some believe the explosion was actually an assassination attempt on Kim Jong-Il, who had passed through the town by train several hours earlier.

Pyongyang's first reaction was to try and hide the massive blast from the outside world. The DPRK's already limited international phone service was cut. The regime declined China's offer to accept the most badly wounded into Chinese hospitals and rebuffed South Korea's offer to truck in emergency supplies. Without official explanation, North Korea announced it would accept emergency supplies only by sea—which Pyongyang knew would take significantly longer—because the North Korean government didn't want its people to see modern South Korean trucks or the South Koreans who drove them. International aid organizations say a substantial number of North Koreans died during the delay.

In short, the DPRK's dangerously dilapidated infrastructure caused a massive accident, which, despite the regime's best efforts, was too large for even secretive North Korea to cover up. North Koreans who didn't live in the area or know anyone who did probably knew nothing of the accident other than what the Central News Agency reported: a terrible tragedy had occurred, but local residents had demonstrated heroic patriotism by running into burning buildings to save portraits of Kim Il-Sung and Kim Jong-Il.

For ordinary North Koreans, the country's isolation is doubly damaging: it both hides from them the depth of their country's failure and enables the continuation of that failure. Decades of catastrophic economic policies, natural disasters, and revenue funneled directly to the country's military-industrial machine have left the DPRK's economy dependent on foreign handouts for survival. Despite millions of tons of food from foreign donors and international organizations, as many North Koreans have died of starvation and starvation-related diseases since 1995—2 million—as North and South Koreans died in the war. According to international relief organizations, when the Soviet Union collapsed in 1992, 18 percent of North Koreans were malnourished. By 2005, the figure was 37 percent.

Despite this, the leadership of the DPRK trumpets two philosophical principles as the guardians of its people's welfare: self-reliance, or *juche,* to minimize the influence of outsiders within the DPRK, and a declared policy of "liberating" South Korea through war—the same policy that led Kim

Il-Sung to press Stalin for support of an invasion in 1950. *Juche* is the regime's attempt to guarantee no movement along the J curve will ever be needed. It is the Korean word best translated as "never having to open, never having to fear." The DPRK is no more likely to renounce the myth of self-reliance than it is to renounce its nuclear program. This refusal to accept reality as a touchstone for policymaking has, over the decades, bankrupted the country.

How poor is North Korea? Satellite photographs taken of Northeast Asia at night reveal the bright lights of modern capitalist Japan, the robust growth of twenty-first-century China, the relative prosperity of dynamic South Korea, and complete darkness from the northern half of the Korean peninsula. As the photo below shows, from space, South Korea looks like an island, floating in the Sea of Japan between China, Japan, and Russia. Even the capital city of Pyongyang goes dark once the sun sets. No photograph better tells the story of today's North Korea. The DPRK's government keeps its people in the dark: it is unable to provide them with electricity and unwilling to provide them with information.

A Satellite Photograph of North Korea at Night: North Korea's government cannot afford to provide its citizens with electricity after dark. The northern half of the Korean Peninsula is virtually as dark at night as it was a thousand years ago.

Yet, even a regime determined to fully isolate its people cannot succeed forever. The construction of cellular relay stations along the Chinese side of the North Korean border in 2004 has allowed some North Koreans living nearby to use Chinese cellular phones to call family members—even journalists—in South Korea. After DVD players became widely available in northern China in 2003, local merchants collected discarded videocassette recorders and sold them in North Korea. Videotapes of South Korean soap operas have since become so popular that North Korean state television has warned North Koreans not to adopt South Korean hairstyles. South Korean journalists report their North Korean contacts have asked for "cell phones with cameras attached."

In response, Kim reportedly ordered the creation of a special prosecutor's office in November 2004 to jail North Koreans who sell South Korean videotapes or use South Korean slang. Pyongyang has also reportedly begun border patrols using Japanese-made equipment capable of tracking cell-phone calls. While Chinese cell phones only work within a few miles of the Chinese border, videocassettes have reportedly spread into every area of North Korea in which there is even sporadic electricity. To crack down on the viewing of these videos, North Korean police have reportedly adopted the tactic of surrounding a neighborhood, cutting off electricity, and then inspecting video players to find tapes stuck inside. Recent defectors have also reported that police cars with loudspeakers circle North Korean neighborhoods, warning residents to maintain their "socialist lifestyle" and to shun South Korean pop culture.[3] North Korea's leaders can't hold off foreign influences forever. But they will continue to do their best.

The Arsenal

The DPRK has also used its international isolation to secretly develop its nuclear program. The country began work on a reprocessing facility in 1989. In 1992, Pyongyang informed the International Atomic Energy Agency that it had reprocessed plutonium. Negotiations with the DPRK produced an "Agreed Framework," signed in Geneva in October 1994, which required North Korea to freeze construction of its nuclear power plants and eventually to dismantle its nuclear programs in exchange for guarantees that an international consortium would provide the country with fuel and two light-water reactors to generate electric power. But in the summer of 2002, U.S. intelligence discovered that Pyongyang had violated the agreement by secretly producing highly enriched uranium suitable for the development of nuclear weapons. In December 2002, North Korea announced it was removing UN monitoring equipment from the sealed nuclear reactor at Yongbyon. A month later, North Korea announced it would withdraw its signature from the Nuclear Non-Proliferation Treaty. Thus began the current North Korean nuclear standoff.

The ultimate guarantor of *juche* in a security context is the DPRK's nuclear-weapons program. Yet, North Korea would enjoy a powerful military deterrent even if it had no nuclear weapons. North Korea's enormous army is poised just north of the demilitarized zone, a mere twenty-five miles from the South Korean capital. Seoul is easily reachable by North Korean artillery, and North Korean troop strength is more than double that of the South Korean army and the 37,000 Americans still in the south. But the Bush administration's "axis of evil" approach upped the stakes for the North Korean leadership. The invasion of Iraq convinced Pyongyang that no expense should be spared in bolstering the DPRK's capacity to deter a U.S. attack. Development of nuclear weapons began, of course, before the election of George W. Bush. But Bush's willingness to actually use the "doctrine of preemption" to head off a potential nuclear threat in Iraq pushed Pyongyang to accelerate its nuclear buildup and to resolve to see it through.

If North Korea had no weapons program, it would be of little interest to the United States beyond a humanitarian desire to help the country's starving people. It would occupy no more attention in Washington than do Belarus and Burma. But North Korea does have a nuclear-weapons program, and it's not going to give it up. Much discussion of the DPRK has been devoted to finding the right combination of inducements and threats to convince North Korea to voluntarily renounce its nuclear ambitions. Washington's stated goal is the Complete, Verifiable, Irreversible Dismantlement (CVID) of North Korea. But there are no carrots or sticks that will achieve North Korean denuclearization, verifiable or otherwise. North Korea is dependent on the outside world for fuel to power its economy and for food to feed its army and as many of its starving people as possible. The DPRK needs its weapons program because weapons and weapons technology are the only resources it has to leverage. To exchange its entire nuclear program for food and fuel today leaves it with nothing to trade for food and fuel tomorrow.

Another reason Pyongyang will never verifiably renounce its nuclear program is that the men who rule North Korea believe it is their only absolute guarantee against a U.S. invasion. No treaty was ever officially signed between the two Koreas ending the Korean War. For Americans, that's a footnote of history. For North Koreans, it's a central fact of life. Pyongyang was spooked when George W. Bush included North Korea as part of an "axis of evil" in his 2002 State of the Union address. And when bombs began falling on Baghdad the following year, the regime saw its worst nightmare in living color. The DPRK will never voluntarily renounce its nuclear weapons program because it fears the Bush administration intends to topple statues of the Great Leader in Pyongyang.

The third reason North Korea will not give up its nuclear program is that, to maintain control over his country, Kim Jong-Il must keep his people completely isolated. Allowing international inspectors to verify suspected nuclear sites is to give foreigners free access to the North Korean people. Kim Jong-Il cannot allow that and hope to remain securely in power. This is a key difference between North Korea and Libya or Iran. Libya and Iran go to some lengths to resist foreign influence. The Kims, on the other hand, have tried to create a hermetically sealed state.

To preserve its hopes of maintaining a stable, closed North Korea for the indefinite future, the DPRK's leadership will push its country as far up the left side of the J curve as it can. Any deliberate move down the curve—toward a reformed economic system plugged into the forces of globalization—would start an avalanche that Kim Jong-Il and those who serve him would not survive. That is North Korea's catch-22: it cannot sustain itself indefinitely without substantial foreign economic help. But economic aid opens the country to influences that will one day break Kim's grip on his people.

North Korea is today the most dangerous country in the world. It has nuclear weapons capable of striking South Korea and Japan. It may soon have a missile capable of carrying a nuclear warhead to the west coast of the United States. Yet, the danger is not that Kim Jong-Il will wake up in a bad mood one day and launch missiles on Seoul, Tokyo, or Seattle. North Korea has no intention of committing suicide—which is what such an attack would amount to. And nuclear missiles aren't reusable. Pyongyang is highly unlikely to cash in any of its very, very few chips. North Korea is the world's most dangerous country because it will always be tempted to sell the world's most dangerous weapons to the world's most dangerous people.

North Korea has good reason to believe it can sell nuclear technology without being caught: it has already done so on more than one occasion. We now know that in 2001 Libya bought two tons of enriched uranium stocks, not, as previously thought, from the A. Q. Khan network in Pakistan, but from North Korea.* By secretly selling arms and weapons technology, North Korea can earn cash, destabilize its enemies, and avoid blame and retaliation for doing so. North Korea is also involved in drug and counterfeit-currency trafficking, and the sale of ballistic-missile technology. But it is nuclear technology that could bring in the biggest money for Kim's depleted treasury.

Policy

So if North Korea can't be bribed or blackmailed into relinquishing its weapons program, what is to be done? The right U.S. policy toward the DPRK can be expressed in two words: regime change. Clearly, Kim Jong-Il's continued rule is not in the interest of international stability. But regime change, in this case, does *not* mean a shock-and-awe military campaign—although it's important that Kim, and even some of his neighbors whose support Washington needs for a tough policy, believe that possibility remains on the table. Regime change in North Korea means finding ways to gradually expose the North Korean people to outside influence in order to create demand for change from within the DPRK.

The immediate objective of such a policy is not to quickly make the government of North Korea look like the government of Sweden, or even to try to force the DPRK to hold elections. But if Pyongyang governed its people a little more like China does today—granting them some meaningful economic and social freedoms even as it restricts political liberties—this would

---

* Pakistani scientist Abdul Qadeer Khan is the architect of Pakistan's nuclear program. In 2004, a network he established to sell nuclear technology abroad was publicly exposed. Stephen Fidler, "North Korea 'gave Libya material for nuclear arms'," *Financial Times*, May 26, 2004.

be a solid start toward the opening up of North Korea and its managed transition toward the right side of the J curve. In the long run, it will enable the North Korean people to change their own regime. Kim Jong-Il and the elite that supports him have done everything possible to avoid the need for even these modest reforms. But North Korea needs cash. If the United States and North Korea's neighbors can prevent North Korea from selling weapons and weapons technology, Pyongyang will have little choice but to look elsewhere for revenue.

In the meantime, Washington must recognize that Kim Jong-Il and his dependents will do everything they can to keep the DPRK completely sealed off from the rest of the world. The United States must not continue to pursue policies that help North Korea achieve that objective. Imposing punitive sanctions and cutting off opportunities for North Korea's people to interact with outsiders is self-defeating. Contact between North Korea's citizens and the outside world is essential if the lights are to be turned on in North Korea and the energy of the North Korean people is to be let loose on the world's most oppressive police state.

The best tool for opening up North Korea is the insertion into the DPRK of a Trojan horse. North Korea is well aware of the potential traps that contact with outsiders can bring. The regime can't easily be fooled. But the North Korean leadership knows it needs help to survive—help that must come from beyond the DPRK's borders.

Washington *has* contributed to the flow of information penetrating North Korea. In 2004, Congress unanimously passed the North Korean Human Rights Act, which provides for increased Korean-language radio broadcasting into the DPRK and for aid to North Korean refugees in China. The measure is among Washington's most promising initiatives on North Korea.

But ultimately, the Trojan horse cannot be American. Kim Jong-Il is not about to let the Peace Corps go wandering around his countryside talking to farmers and handing out leaflets. It probably won't be South Korean. In 2003, a group of human-rights organizations launched a series of balloons into North Korea with small solar-powered AM-frequency radios attached. The South Korean government, fearing Pyongyang's reaction, stopped the program. It's too bad, because it's an example of one low-cost, effective way of undermining Kim's ability to isolate his people. The Trojan horse certainly won't be Japanese. Relations between North Korea and Japan will suffer for the foreseeable future from the same historical tensions that have alienated Tokyo from many of the states it colonized before and during the Second World War.

If North Korea is to swing open its heavily fortified gates to gifts from outsiders, the horse that's wheeled in must be Chinese. It is China on which North Korea depends for food, energy, and diplomatic breathing room. It is China that Kim Jong-Il is sometimes willing to trust—of necessity, if for no other reason. It is with China's permission that Kim has considered creating a "special economic zone" along their shared border. And it is China that provides a realistic model for a North Korea that the world can live with in the middle term. China knows its long-term stability depends on its people's prosperity and recognizes the compromises with openness that must be made to achieve and sustain that prosperity in today's world. China's reluctance to destabilize the North Korean regime comes from its fear of millions of North Korean refugees pouring across the Chinese border. But North Korea will collapse one day, no matter what policies foreign governments pursue. It will be better for China to be inside the DPRK when that happens and to help manage the DPRK's descent down the J curve toward chaos.

If North Korea is willing to open its economy to trade, development, and investment projects with China, almost everybody wins. China is able to minimize the possibility that an unstable North Korea might create a health and humanitarian disaster by sending millions of refugees across the border. North Koreans will no longer starve, and the DPRK will become less dependent on South Korea and the West for food aid. South Korea, Japan, Russia, and the United States benefit because the Korean peninsula will become more stable, and because outside influences will help end North Korea's isolation. The only long-term loser in this scenario is the ruling elite of the DPRK, which will have unleashed a hunger for change among its people the regime won't be able to satisfy.

That said, the J curve also demonstrates the dangers for the region once North Korea begins to be exposed to Chinese and, therefore, other outside influences. The slide toward instability may come fast as large numbers of North Koreans, suddenly aware of the lies and lethal mismanagement to which they've been subject for decades, begin to assert themselves at the expense of their leaders. Once the prisoners get a good look at their jailers, the results are hard to predict.

How might the slide begin? North Koreans will find out Chinese workers sometimes go on strike and win concessions from the government. Used cell phones and text-messaging equipment bought from Chinese vendors then allow North Korean workers to discuss the idea of strikes and other coordinated demonstrations. Talk of protests leads to the formation of informal organizations. These gatherings are banned, and many of their organizers are jailed or executed. But once a line has been crossed and the ban is resisted, people who never before discussed politics with one another will begin to communicate. North Koreans who haven't yet seen bootleg videos of South Korean soap operas discover through books and photographs, Internet access, and cell-phone contact with the outside that life in South Korea is nothing like they've been told. The government loses credibility and the people lose some of their awe of the Great Leader. Once the awe is gone, fear is lost as well. The resulting unrest will lead to serious volatility and divisions within the ruling regime over how to respond. How fast could this happen? Ask Nicolae Ceauşescu. The revolutions of 1989 proved that the slide down the left side of the curve can take a matter of days.

This brings us to another important aspect of regime-change strategy: managing the transitional volatility. Just as no outside power is as great a long-term threat to a closed regime as its own people, no outside power can guarantee that another country's transition through the dip in the J curve won't produce catastrophic violence. But the United States *can* work with others in the region to help ensure that nuclear weapons play no role in North Korea's transition. Without question, North Korea has become the world's biggest proliferation threat. Chaos in the DPRK could produce a nuclear-technology fire sale, with scientists and the military cutting private deals with all interested parties.

Simply waiting for North Korea to fall and doing nothing to limit its weapons proliferation is a dangerous option. Washington could instead craft an interim strategy to limit North Korean proliferation; U.S. allies in East Asia could help. The ideas that Beijing and Seoul currently have in mind for North Korea's nuclear program are exactly like Washington's policy of Complete, Verifiable, Irreversible Dismantlement—except that any agreement they might independently strike with Kim Jong-Il won't be complete, verifiable, irreversible, or require Kim to dismantle his nuclear arsenal. If China and South Korea cut their own deal with Kim's regime, North Korea will be allowed to keep its existing weapons, inspections will be both limited and controlled by North Korea's government, and the nuclear infrastructure will be frozen rather than destroyed. China and South Korea want to avoid crisis at all costs—they have to live next door to the North Koreans. And a sudden crisis inside the DPRK impacts them far more directly than it does Washington.

Yet, Washington does have a mechanism for enforcing nonproliferation, if it can build a meaningful consensus around the policy. The Proliferation Security Initiative (PSI), a multinational effort that presently includes fifteen states, provides the international legal framework for snap inspections of every plane, train, and boat arriving in, or departing from, North Korea. The current problem with PSI is that China and South Korea do not support it. To combat the danger of North Korean proliferation, the United States needs to convince China and South Korea that full implementation of the PSI is very much in their national interests.

The United States has very little leverage with North Korea. But it does have leverage with China and South Korea, which, in turn, have leverage with the DPRK. Washington could persuade Beijing and Seoul to support PSI by promising to deliver comprehensive aid to the North Koreans, including emergency food, medical supplies, and energy. Together with other PSI participants, the offer could include the creation of meaningful, nonnuclear energy infrastructure. North Korea will claim it has concessions from the superpower and offered nothing in return. Washington will counter that it isn't negotiating with North Korea. It is working with its allies to produce the outcome everyone wants: a stable North Korea that can't sell dangerous weaponry to the highest bidder.

The United States need not publicly renounce CVID. Washington could provide North Korea with short-term humanitarian assistance and nothing more. Provision of a nonnuclear energy-production capacity—teaching the North Koreans to fish for themselves—could still be linked to clear, definable steps by Pyongyang toward verifiable denuclearization. Over time, a "normalized" policy environment in North Korea might even make such an option possible, though that's unlikely. A policy of humanitarian assistance coupled with vigorous enforcement of PSI would recognize that it is not possible to conclude an acceptable agreement with Kim Jong-Il and that no unilateral policy on North Korea can achieve Washington's hoped-for outcome. It would amount to nothing less than a fundamental shift in America's North Korea strategy.

North Korea won't like PSI, because it limits the DPRK's sovereignty and prevents the regime from selling its only valuable export. In fact, Kim Jong-Il has said publicly the imposition of quarantine would be an "act of war." So be it. Kim Jong-Il has said a lot of things. He wants to remain in power and is extremely unlikely to start a war he cannot win. A strategy that opens North Korea to foreign influence while containing Pyongyang's weapons proliferation doesn't require North Korea's approval. And it serves the long-term interests of peace and stability in East Asia and beyond. As North Korea slides down the J curve into instability, the international community can help manage the consequences.

"SOCIALISM OF THE TROPICS": CASTRO'S CUBA

In the spring of 2003, just as the Bush administration was pulling down statues of Saddam Hussein and pushing Iraq down the left side of the J curve, Fidel Castro was throwing large numbers of Cuban dissidents in jail. The timing was probably not coincidental. Authoritarians rarely welcome world attention when they are putting political prisoners behind bars, and America's shock-and-awe campaign in Baghdad provided an excellent international diversion for Castro's crackdown on domestic dissent.

While the world watched Iraq, a Cuban court sentenced seventy-eight Cuban citizens to an average of nearly twenty years in prison following secret, one-day trials. Almost two-thirds of the accused had circulated a petition calling for broader political freedoms. Because the United States had encouraged the petition drive, prosecutors added "conspiracy with a foreign power to overthrow the Cuban government" to their list of crimes. Around the same time, three more Cubans were sentenced to death and quickly executed after trying to hijack a ferry to Florida.

As the Bush administration worked to demonstrate in Iraq that the United States had the will to destroy dangerous "rogue states," Castro was hoping for his own demonstration effect—to deter further calls from within Cuba for democratization. Since 2003, Castro has moved to tighten central planning of the Cuban economy, to limit Cuban access to the Internet, and to outlaw the use of U.S. dollars by Cubans. In short, Castro has further closed his country.

Only during the Cuban missile crisis has Cuba occupied a position near the top of America's foreign-policy priorities. Cuba's foreign policy, even when its troops helped advance Communist Cold War goals in Africa, has never had the geopolitical consequence that North Korea and Iran have now and that Saddam's Iraq had during the 1980s and '90s. Castro's regime is included in this book to illustrate revealing variations in how closed, consolidated regimes stay that way and to articulate how U.S. policy toward these regimes can produce the opposite of its intended consequences when the lessons of the J curve are ignored.

Cuba has been an isolated state for decades, but never as closed as Kim Il-Sung and Kim Jong-Il's North Korea; Cuba lies ninety miles off the Florida coast and is today the only Communist regime in the western hemisphere. It was easier for Castro to isolate Cuba when he could rely on the Soviet Union as protector and benefactor. But since the Soviet collapse, a lack of economic aid has forced Castro to experiment with limited local entrepreneurship. He has also eased his control of freedom of assembly and speech. In fact, it was exactly that kind of experimental indulgence and the use ordinary Cubans made of it that led to the 2003 crackdown—once Castro began to fear his small-scale market experiments and the relaxation of political restrictions might gain momentum and escape his control. Few outside the Soviet Union were more horrified than Castro when events unleashed by reform in Moscow overtook Mikhail Gorbachev.

Not that Castro began the new century with ideas of a Cuban *perestroika*. The Cuban leader agreed to experiment with market ideas only with considerable reluctance, and the pressure for a loosening of Castro's political grip came not from within his government but from Cuban dissidents. In 2002, one such dissident, a medical-equipment engineer named Oswaldo Paya, presented Cuba's National Assembly with a petition signed by more than 11,000 people. The petition called for a referendum on civil rights, an amnesty for some nonviolent political prisoners, electoral reform, and the introduction of limited free enterprise. The petition drive, known as the Varela Project, brought together dissidents and opposition figures from across the island. Castro's first response was to begin a petition of his own, on which he collected millions of signatures, to amend the Cuban constitution to declare Communism "irreversible."

But if Castro is to keep his country on the left side of the J curve—where he can control it—he must continually find new ways to stoke the Cuban economy with as little exposure as possible to world market forces, and with as few accommodations of his enemies in Washington and Europe as he can manage. Arresting Paya would make the dissident leader an international symbol of resistance to authoritarianism—a weapon Castro's enemies would be only too happy to use against him. So Castro decided to ignore him. Europeans, Americans, and a good number of Cubans only became more interested in Paya.

In 2002, Paya was allowed to travel to Europe, where he received the Sakharov Prize for human rights and received the blessing of Pope John Paul II, himself a former anti-Communist dissident. On the way home, he was warmly received in Washington by Secretary of State Colin Powell. None of this was reported in the Cuban media. With Paya's return to Cuba, and as his Christian Liberation Movement and the Varela Project gained strength, Castro decided Paya and his supporters had to be tamed. Of the seventy-eight arrested in the spring 2003 crackdown, forty-six were members of Paya's organization.

The Failure of Sanctions

There is an important area of disagreement between Cuban supporters of the Varela Project and Castro's more famous critics in the Cuban-American community: Paya and his allies oppose the four-decade-old U.S. embargo of Cuba. While most of the Cubans of South Florida support sanctions to signal their hatred of Castro and his regime, Oswaldo Paya looks to undermine Castro's rule directly by enabling ordinary Cubans to establish the financial independence needed to challenge the regime from within. This distinction goes directly to the heart of Castro's efforts to keep Cuba as far as he can up the left side of the J curve, and it helps explain why U.S. sanctions on Cuba amount to one of the most obvious U.S. foreign-policy failures of the last forty years.

Since 1960, the United States has sought to undermine Castro by closing Cuba to the outside world. When Castro took power, the United States hoped to destabilize his regime by squeezing the island economically and by encouraging the Cuban people to oust Castro in favor of the prosperity that might come from better relations with Washington. Yet, Castro has survived nine U.S. presidents, the collapse of his great benefactor the Soviet Union, and four decades of U.S. attempts to undermine his hold on the island. Castro's grip on power is as sure as ever. Yet, four decades later, Washington refuses to try a different approach.

It's not that most U.S. lawmakers don't recognize the uselessness of sanctions against Castro's government. But in countries on the right side of the J curve, like the United States, foreign policy is the product of the friction produced by many competing interests. Many Americans support a punitive policy against Castro, because they believe deeply that a government that denies its citizens the most basic rights and freedoms should be punished. Supporters of the trade embargo argue that it is immoral to do business with a dictator who imprisons dissidents and exercises authoritarian control of a country so close to American shores. In fact, there is no better example than the Cuban trade embargo of a policy based on the view that repressive foreign governments should be punished. But to punish Cuba is to help Castro realize his goal—the reinforcement of his police state.

There is another reason Washington remains determined to punish Castro's regime. In October of 1962, Castro played host to Soviet nuclear missiles aimed at the United States. While much attention is paid to the role Cuban-Americans play in shaping U.S. policy toward Cuba—and rightfully so—it's worth remembering that Fidel Castro helped bring America face-to-face with its nuclear nightmare. Few who experienced the Cuban Missile Crisis will ever forget it. It's true that Castro has a flair for anti-American rhetoric. Others with the same talent—Muammar Qaddafi, Hugo Chávez, and Manuel Noriega, for instance—have felt Washington's wrath at different times and in different ways. But Castro is more than an anti-American megaphone in the Caribbean: he's the man who played a crucial role in pushing America closer to the brink of nuclear war than it's ever been. The urge to punish such a regime is understandable.

There are also domestic political reasons why Washington continues to try to "punish" Castro. Cuban exiles play a famously disproportionate role in the formulation of U.S. policy toward Castro's Cuba, because they represent a sizable voting bloc inside a closely contested state that can single-handedly give a candidate—or prospective candidate—10 percent of the electoral votes he needs to be elected president. Virtually all of Florida's

Cuban exiles go to the polls, and many tend to base their votes on the candidates' willingness to maintain a policy of punitive sanctions against Fidel. In other words, most lawmakers don't maintain sanctions on Cuba because they believe sanctions are achieving their goals; they vote to maintain sanctions because they want to be reelected.

Cuban-Americans aside, Castro does have a special genius for irritating Americans. In one version of a famous story, when Castro visited New York City in 1960 for a meeting at the United Nations, President Dwight Eisenhower conspicuously failed to invite him to a luncheon at the Waldorf-Astoria. Castro checked into the Hotel Theresa on Manhattan's 125th Street, saying it would be his "honor to lunch with the poor and humble people of Harlem." He further angered the administration by receiving a special guest there: Soviet leader Nikita Khrushchev.

An Enemy of the People

Even without Washington's help in isolating Cuba, Castro uses all available tools to maintain his grip on power. At the center of Castro's strategy to unify his people behind the revolution is vilification of the great and fearsome enemy, the United States. Through monopoly control of Cuban media, Castro builds the image of a hostile, aggressive, immoral, and determined America that threatens Cuba's "independence," if not its survival. And because Washington is ever ready to play the role assigned to it—American sanctions help keep average Cubans relatively poor and under-employed—El Comandante (as Castro likes to be called) effortlessly pushes tensions up and down to suit the needs of the moment.

There have been U.S. presidents who sought to relax tensions with Cuba, but Castro has always known he needs his American enemy to ensure that the Cuban people will continue to defend the revolution. Castro has proven many times he can upend any U.S. attempt to warm relations with tactics designed to ratchet up bilateral hostility. As in North Korea, Iran, and other regimes that rely on anti-Americanism to rally the population, Castro's rhetoric is never more toxic than when he feels Washington is paying attention to his regime. In 1980, when President Jimmy Carter offered asylum to a few Cuban "boat people," refugees trying to flee Cuba by sea, Castro launched the Mariel Boatlift, sending more than 100,000 Cubans, many of them criminals and mental patients, out into the Florida Strait toward the U.S. coast. In 1996, when President Bill Clinton began to talk of a thaw in U.S.-Cuban relations, Cuban fighter jets shot down two private planes carrying Cuban-Americans, which had violated Cuban airspace to drop anti-Castro leaflets over Havana. As a consequence, Clinton signed the Helms-Burton Act, which tightened sanctions on Cuba. Castro then seized the self-created opportunity to accuse Cuban dissenters of complicity with U.S. aggression bent on destroying Cuba's revolution.

The Money

As in other stable and closed states, Castro maintains virtual monopoly control of wealth in his country. For many years, remittances from Cubans living abroad to their relatives on the island have sustained both a few fortunate Cubans and the regime itself. In 2003, remittances reached an estimated $900 million a year, nearly 3 percent of Cuba's GDP. Because Cubans can only spend their dollars in government-run stores, Castro's regime is the ultimate recipient of almost all those dollars, and Cuban-Americans directly undermine the economic sanctions they demand. As we'll see similarly in Saddam's Iraq, Castro uses the sanctions and the remittances to concentrate money in the hands of the very elite the policy intends to destabilize.

In advance of the 2004 U.S. elections, President George W. Bush sought to address the fact that remittances were enriching Castro's treasury by limiting the amount of money Cuban-Americans could send to the island. Before June 30, 2004, Cuban-Americans were allowed unrestricted annual visits to Cuba of any duration to visit anyone in the traveler's "extended family" and could take up to $3,000 with them. They were also allowed to send as much as $300 to anyone in Cuba. After June 30, 2004, Cuban-Americans were limited to one two-week visit every three years and only to members of the immediate family. Rather than $3,000, the traveler was allowed to carry only $300.

Castro, seeking an opportunity to rally his people against the actions of the United States, led demonstrations of more than a million people past the U.S. diplomatic mission in Havana. Not since the saga of Elián Gonzáles*—who, along with his father, joined in the protest against the tightening of sanctions—had Castro found such a ready-made opportunity to strike the pose of defender of the poor against the inhumanity of the rich and to deflect international criticism of his own refusal to allow political and economic freedoms in Cuba.

Protest was not Castro's only response to Bush's new restrictions. From November 8, 2004, Castro banned all use of U.S. dollars for commercial transactions. Cubans were still allowed to possess dollars and to convert them into Cuban pesos—for a 10 percent commission. The dollar had been legal tender in Cuba since 1993, when the need for hard currency made the regime's access to dollars a necessity. While Castro was prepared to live without dollar reserves for the time being, he knew he couldn't dispense with foreign currency altogether, and he encouraged Cubans to ask their relatives abroad to convert their dollars to other currencies before transferring the money. Meanwhile, all the dollars Cubans had been hoarding under their mattresses had to be passed on to the Cuban government in exchange for usable currency.

The decision allowed Castro to replenish the government's dollar reserves just at the moment the Bush administration sought to squeeze the regime; it also gave Castro more direct control of Cuba's financial system. Managing monetary policy in a system that uses two currencies is especially complicated when the issuer of one of the currencies, the U.S. Treasury, actively looks for ways to undermine the regime. Castro may eventually need the inflow of dollars from America again. But, for the moment, keeping out dollars helps him maintain control of his people's access to wealth and makes the island's monetary policy much simpler to manage.

Another means Castro has of controlling access to wealth—and the threat it might pose his regime—is through restrictions on the independence of Cuban business. With the tough times on the island that followed the Soviet collapse, Castro believed he had to allow some experiments with

---

* Between November 1999 and June 2000, six-year-old Elián Gonzáles was the object of a fierce custody and immigration battle between Cuban-Americans and the United States government after a vessel carrying him from Cuba toward Florida sank and he was rescued and brought to Miami. His mother drowned during the passage. In June 2000, Elián was returned to his father in Cuba, which angered Cuban-American relatives who had sought custody of the boy.

small-scale entrepreneurship. As we'll see in Chapter Six, China's tremendous economic growth began with the creation in the 1970s of "special economic zones" in which entrepreneurs were given limited freedom to create businesses. Aware of China's success and desperate to grow out of the economic hardship of what Cuban officials called the "special period," Castro decided in 1993 to allow limited freedom for Cubans to set up small businesses in 157 different categories.

While these experiments in free enterprise did reinvigorate the Cuban economy, Castro remained intent on limiting their power to generate income for those who might use the financial independence it provided to demand greater political freedoms. Indeed, many of the signatures on the Varela Project petition came from small-business owners with aspirations of joining a potential Cuban middle class. The threat of a Varela Project is a perfect illustration of why Castro keeps business owners on a tight rein. "Socialism of the tropics" does not allow for the creation of a middle class. Castro ensured that any merchant class that might emerge from his experimentation would be stillborn by regulating small businesses almost to death—and by taxing them heavily and in advance.

But it is not only Fidel Castro that undermines the ability of the Cuban people to establish economic freedom; U.S. sanctions accomplish the same thing. No one was hit harder by the new restrictions on remittances and visits than the owners of Cuba's fledgling family businesses. Those who operate bed-and-breakfast houses or small restaurants were hit directly by the tightening of money from America. Tourism is an important source of income for millions of Cubans who would be hard-pressed to survive without it.

A feature that distinguishes Castro's Cuba from other closed societies is that tourism provides a badly needed source of income for the island. North Korea doesn't find its way onto cruise-ship itineraries, and tourists weren't flocking to Saddam's Iraq. But Cuba can bring in revenue by opening itself, in a limited way, to tourism. Castro, like any dictator looking to keep his country as closed as possible, would prefer to live without foreign visitors to the island. In fact, he regularly disparages foreign tourists and complains of the disease, drugs, and other impurities he says they bring with them.

Yet, as much as Castro would prefer to live without tourists, Cuba needs the hard currency to pay for vital resources once provided by Moscow and to maintain its foreign reserves. Tourism brings Cuba about $3 billion a year, more than 40 percent of its hard currency. In fact, about 200,000 American tourists visited Cuba in 2001. Sixty percent of U.S. visitors were Cuban-Americans,* and an estimated 20,000 Americans entered Cuba through a third country, many in violation of U.S. law.†

U.S. sanctions have accomplished three things since they were first imposed more than forty years ago: they've strengthened Castro's ability to keep his country closed to the forces that might open it, they've punished the Cuban people, and they've alienated governments that are usually friendly to America but take exception when Washington sanctions one of their companies for doing business in Cuba.

Dreaming of Oil

Since President Hugo Chávez was elected in 1998, Venezuela has become Cuba's primary petroleum supplier. Under an agreement signed in 2000, Venezuela sends Cuba about 53,000 barrels a day of crude oil and refined products, including gasoline, and diesel and jet fuel, all at preferential prices. Chávez, who considers Castro a revolutionary role model, has survived considerable instability in his own country—much to Castro's relief.

Fidel Castro's dream has always been to build Cuba into an economically self-sufficient socialist state. He believed that, were he not dependent on the Soviet Union, China, or Venezuela for vital resources, he would be virtually invulnerable to political instability. The need to find a sympathetic oil-exporting state exposes his country to the political risks that come with vulnerability to foreign pressure. The discovery of oil might also help pay down the island's $12 billion foreign debt. In short, Castro dreams of Cuban oil.

Cuban oil may actually be discovered and brought to use in Cuba's economy in the next several years. The Spanish oil giant Repsol YPF signed a drilling contract with Castro in December 2000, authorizing the company to drill in Cuban territorial waters in the Gulf of Mexico. Later Repsol invested more than $50 million to drill an exploratory well in an area along Cuba's northern coast. A Repsol spokesman announced in July 2004 that,

---

* According to Cuba's Office of National Statistics.
† According to the U.S.-Cuba Trade and Economic Council.

although the quality and quantity of oil found beneath the first site was not "commercially viable," the drilling was "able to prove the presence of high-quality reservoirs." The company then promised to return to drilling in the area within a year. Repsol hasn't yet found what it's looking for, but the size of the company's initial investment and its readiness to continue the search suggest Repsol's optimism isn't just for show. On December 25, 2004, Castro announced that two Canadian energy companies had discovered estimated reserves of 100 million barrels of oil in an area of the Gulf of Mexico under Cuba's control. Castro told Cuba's state-controlled media that the deposits were lower in sulfur than those from Cuba's other oil fields. If true, the Canadians may have discovered lighter-grade, higher-quality oil than the limited quantities of heavy oil now produced in Cuba.[4]

The oil that foreign companies may find off Cuba won't have a dramatic impact on the global energy market, but it could be more than enough to restructure the Cuban economy and its relationship with the United States. First, if Cuba becomes a net exporter of oil, or at least energy self-sufficient, Castro will no longer need nearly as many of those foreign tourists—and the foreign influence they bring with them—to provide hard-currency reserves. Anything that allows Castro to deepen his people's isolation, while still having the cash to provide them with basic services and a strong social safety net, keeps Cuba on the left side of the stability curve and strengthens Castro's grip on power.

Second, the oil might help Castro keep his promises of prosperity to the Cuban people. Cuba has endured a decade of energy shortages and blackouts. In 2004, the country produced around 80,000 barrels a day of very heavy crude with a high sulphur content suitable only for limited generation of electricity. If expectations begin to rise that better times are on the way, the Cuban people's faith that the revolution can offer a better life might rise too.

Third, energy independence would provide Castro a buffer against the political troubles that befall his few loyal friends. Castro's principal ally in the region, Hugo Chávez, has survived coup attempts and a recall referendum. Reducing Cuba's energy dependence on politically volatile Venezuela will only make Castro's regime more stable. Fourth, paying off some of Cuba's debt and inviting foreign companies to help bring Cuban oil to market would give Havana access to foreign capital and credit.

Finally, if Cuba is suddenly awash with oil revenue, Washington's ability to maintain sanctions against the Cuban regime may collapse under the weight of pressure from abroad—and from home. Given the tightness of the world oil market, even America's most reliable allies won't hesitate before moving in to do oil business with Cuba. A number of energy multinationals have privately indicated interest in exploration projects if the results of Repsol's drilling are favorable. In the rush to sign contracts with Castro, only American companies will honor—and be limited by—sanctions against Cuba. U.S. oil companies, unwilling to stand by and watch everybody else cash in on the new find, will work to end the sanctions. They may prove a more powerful lobby in Washington than even South Florida's Castro-loathing Cuban exiles.

Four decades ago, the United States pinned Cuba's revolutionary regime into a corner. But Washington has never been willing to step into that corner and dismantle Castro's Caribbean revolution. Despite forty years of international isolation—or, more aptly, because of it—Castro is now the world's longest-serving head of state. And if someone really does find oil in Cuban waters, Castro's revolution may do more than survive him: it might finally step out of the corner.

In the longer term, however, the entrance of foreign oil companies into Cuba and the end of U.S. sanctions might ultimately accomplish what the sanctions could not: the undermining of Castro's control of Cuba. If Cubans go to work in the oil industry and living standards rise as a result, there may be more Oswaldo Payas demanding political reform. The introduction into Cuba of a large-scale oil industry could create a Cuban middle class that demands the right to organize and to strike. Castro's biggest fear—like Kim's and Saddam's—is the potential power of his own people to destabilize the police state from within.

Succession

After so many years of stability on the left side of the J curve, the ultimate threat to the Cuban revolution may come from Castro's advancing age and failing health. There are countries on the left side of the curve that survive leadership transitions without a crisis. Enver Hoxha's Albania was able to navigate political transitions. Power passed from Kim Il-Sung to Kim Jong-Il, from Hafez al-Assad to Bashar al-Assad, and from Mao Tse-tung to Deng

Xiaoping to Jiang Zemin to Hu Jintao without apparent strife. None of this guarantees that Fidel Castro can bequeath his revolution to someone else.

Now that El Comandante has reached his eightieth birthday (in August 2006), two principal figures seem likely to seek the Cuban presidency, if not exactly to replace Castro. The first is Carlos Lage, Cuba's vice president and the man thought to be the architect and chief defender of the modest economic reforms of the 1990s. Lage, twenty-five years younger than Castro, is barely old enough to remember prerevolutionary Cuba. The second possible successor is Fidel's younger brother Raúl. Already in his mid-seventies, Raul fought alongside his older brother in the revolution and is Cuba's defense minister. Raúl Castro is as responsible as anyone in the regime for the "anticorruption" crackdowns that led to the arrest and imprisonment of the seventy-eight dissidents in 2003. The choice between the two men seems clear. Lage represents generational change in the aging leadership. He has pursued policies that seem predicated on the idea that economic reform and incremental steps toward greater public participation in government are the future of Cuban socialism. Raúl Castro best represents the old revolutionary guard. His greatest skill is the protection of his brother's police state through tight control of dissent.

When Castro dies, Cuba will inevitably slide down the left side of the J curve toward instability. The Cuban people may then have an opportunity to choose between a candidate like Raúl Castro, who would almost certainly try to move the country back up the steep left side of the curve, or a man like Carlos Lage, who *might* take measured steps toward the right.

The potential discovery of oil might well play a role in the succession. The ability to earn revenue by exporting large amounts of oil raises the entire J curve and makes a power transition within a closed regime easier for its subjects to accept. We'll see that idea again when we turn to Iran, Russia, and Saudi Arabia in the next chapter. It's also easier for absolute dictators to trust their blood relatives—as we'll see in Saddam Hussein's Iraq. Substantial Cuban oil revenue will make it easier for Castro to pass control of the revolution to his brother. Lage has earned considerable political capital from the Cuban people by steering the island's economy through tough times with resourcefulness and discipline. But Lage is more a technocrat than an ideologue. Castro would probably prefer to keep the revolutionary succession in the family and to hand ultimate authority to a man who's made his reputation commanding the Cuban army. With the economy less reliant on Lage's ingenuity and Castro under less pressure for reform, the choice of Raúl Castro becomes easier.

Yet, Castro seems loath to relinquish an ounce of his control to anybody. Following a bad fall during a speech in October 2004 in which he reportedly broke his left knee into eight pieces and suffered a hairline fracture of his left arm, Castro quickly sought to address the fears—and perhaps hopes—of his people that the time had come for him to relinquish at least some of his authority. Castro let it be known through state-run media that he had refused general anesthesia during a three-hour, fifteen-minute operation in order to make cell-phone calls during the surgery on "numerous important issues." His chief of staff reportedly stood by in surgical scrubs. According to a letter read on Cuban state television, Castro permitted himself to be anesthetized only from the waist down during the procedure and never re-linquished executive decision-making.

Perhaps the story is false and was intended only to convince his subjects and potential rivals that El Comandante was fully in charge of himself and his country. Or maybe the story is true and reveals Castro's determination to hold off the inevitable handover of control of Cuba. Either way, Fidel Castro may not have confidence that his revolution will long survive him.

In the meantime, Washington should find ways to open Castro's Cuba to the influences of the outside world. U.S. lawmakers, if they are genuinely in-terested in undermining, rather than simply attempting to punish, Fidel Castro's government, should ease and then drop sanctions. In the process, the United States will be helping move Cuba from the left toward the right side of the J curve. The beneficiaries of this policy will be Cubans who be-lieve their future lies with men like Carlos Lage—or perhaps Oswaldo Paya—who are committed to ending Cuba's isolation and bringing lasting prosperity to the Cuban people.

IRAQ UNDER SADDAM

If Cuba faces threats to its political stability when leadership is passed from Castro to a successor, no country better illustrates the difficulty in peace-fully transferring political power than Iraq. Under Saddam Hussein, Iraq was, like North Korea and Cuba, a country whose stability largely depended on the health and physical safety of one man. In fact, there hasn't been a truly peaceful transfer of power in Iraq in nearly half a century.

Authoritarians like Kim Jong-Il, Fidel Castro, and Saddam Hussein do not allow for the creation of the independent institutions on which peaceful political transitions depend. A country that is stable only because it is closed will not remain stable for long if competing institutions create political rivalries. In a closed society, elites are not subject to laws that peacefully resolve the conflicts those rivalries create. In a consolidated authoritarian state, the law is whatever the leader says it is.

The leaders of all three countries have tried to cement their authority by persuading their people they were indispensable. Just as North Koreans are asked to believe that the Great Leader is a genius and Cubans are told that Castro is their last line of defense against American aggression, Saddam alternately portrayed himself as a champion of Iraqi, pan-Arab, or Muslim interests, depending on the needs of the moment, and as a strongman ever ready to face down the world's most powerful nation. Castro and Kim insist their legitimacy derives from Marxist historical inevitability. Saddam claimed to be the direct descendant of ancient Mesopotamian kings.

Like Castro, Kim Il-Sung, and Kim Jong-Il, Saddam Hussein often took measures to ensure that those who didn't love him had good reason to fear him. In fact, Saddam used violence as a political tool more often than Castro or the Kims, because Saddam's rule—and his country's stable position on the left side of the J curve—faced a fundamental challenge the leaders of Cuba and North Korea need not fear: religious, ethnic, and tribal fault lines within the country. Saddam was the representative of a minority population within Iraq. In that sense, the precariousness of Saddam's position had more in common with the white rulers of South Africa than with the Communist dictators of North Korea or Cuba. Saddam didn't even have Communist ideology to give his arbitrary rule a veneer of legitimacy.

There is, of course, one other important fact that separates Saddam from Castro and Kim: he's no longer in power. Saddam took few risks with his personal security, but in the end, he repeatedly gambled on foreign policy and ignited wars that produced the shocks that pushed Iraq down the curve toward instability. Saddam the gambler is in prison today because he violated the cardinal rule leaders must respect if they are to manage their country's position on the left side of the J curve: If your country is built on fault lines, don't produce your own earthquakes. Saddam Hussein and

Iraq's J curve are the subjects of this section. The country's current instability and the political controversy surrounding the 2003 war and subsequent occupation will be examined only as they relate to the period of Saddam's rule between 1990 and 2003.

Saddam is not an aberration in modern Iraqi history. He is the product of a particular political culture in which a minority elite relied for decades on conspiracy, tribal and family ties, and a monopoly on large-scale violence to maintain authoritarian control of an artificially created nation. To understand Saddam's methods and the relationship between stability and state control in a country that faces a very different set of challenges from those of North Korea or Cuba, it's necessary to look briefly at Iraq's past.

Some History

Iraq's fault lines are not new. Ottoman Turks consolidated their control of the territory of present-day Iraq during the sixteenth and seventeenth centuries. The land that is now Iraq was then divided into three provinces formed around the cities of Basra, Baghdad, and Mosul. Following the collapse of the Ottoman Empire during World War I, the provinces were combined into a British protectorate without regard for the fault lines that naturally divided them. After twelve years of British control, Iraq became a sovereign constitutional monarchy in 1932. Because the British cartographers who created modern Iraq knew they had simply papered over the area's tribal, ethnic, and religious divisions, the British decided so inherently unstable a place would not survive on the right side of the J curve, where conflicts produced by competing institutions are peacefully resolved by laws. Iraq, they believed, was not prepared for mature governance and would have to be assigned a place on the left side of the curve, where conflicts are resolved by absolute rule. So Britain established the Hashemite monarchy.

The Hashemite kings and the officials who served them developed and extended the politics of patronage created by the Ottomans. They knew which tribal leaders had the power to compromise any organized opposition, and spent freely to buy their favor and to create a network of dependency on the monarchy. These patronage networks formed the structure on which rule of Iraq has always been based. As we'll see in Saudi Arabia, Russia, and elsewhere, these networks are widely used tools for establishing and maintaining political control in a left-side-of-the-curve state.

Despite the outside imposition of territorial unity, Iraq remained a country profoundly divided along religious and ethnic lines. The center of Kurdish influence was in the north of the country. Sunni Arabs controlled the center. Shiite Arabs dominated the south.

While 90 percent of the world's Muslims are Sunni, Shia form a majority in Iraq: roughly 60 percent of Iraqis are Shia, Sunnis make up about 20 percent, and Kurds account for 15 to 20 percent. Although Sunnis have always been a minority population in Iraq, they have always held disproportionate political power there—at least until the 2003 overthrow of Saddam—by virtue of the prominence of their position within the Ottoman, and then British, establishments. Ottoman Turks were naturally more closely allied with Sunni Arabs than with Shia, and it was simply more efficient for the British to leave in power the same Iraqi elite the Turks had favored. As a result, Iraq's Sunni leadership has always looked on the disenfranchised majority Shia and the oft-rebellious Kurds with a mix of fear and contempt.

Since independence, the Iraqi state has been an instrument of domestic political power for those who governed it. He who controlled the state decided what sort of country Iraq would be and how Iraqi history should be interpreted. The ruler personally controlled the state's wealth, its army, and its security forces. In this sense, Iraq has for decades been the object of a "turf war" between competing tribes, clans, and cliques. In any state as tightly controlled as Saddam's Iraq, those in power do what they will; those without power suffer what they must.

In independent Iraq's first decades, other political patterns were established that would be repeated many times in later years. The military coups and power plays that have punctuated modern Iraqi history reinforced a culture of secrecy, conspiracy, and paranoia. Personal trust and loyalty, more than any respect for national institutions or law, became the political coin of the realm. The men who made Iraqi history, then and since, have treated political power as a weapon to be wielded against personal enemies and as a source of personal profit—rarely as a tool for serving the national interest.

Saddam's Rise

Saddam Hussein was, without question, one of the most destructive, dangerous, and vicious tyrants of the twentieth century. He was not, however, an accident of history. His rule was built on conspiracy, brutality, patronage, military rule, and the use of exemplary violence to maintain political control—his only means of dominating the vast majority of the population.

As the Baath Party seized Iraq's government in 1968, but before he reached absolute power in 1979, Saddam helped his kinsman Hassan al-Bakr consolidate Baathist rule. As head of internal security, Saddam used the party militia to intimidate, arrest, and torture Communists, Nasserists, dissident Baathists, and others who threatened al-Bakr's rule or his own plans for the future. If even the most remote threat to his route to power (real or imagined) could be eliminated, Saddam eliminated it.

There was never a fully articulated Baath Party ideology in Iraq. For Saddam and those around him, the Baath Party was an extension of their personal power, an organized-crime syndicate that divided Iraqis into members of the gang and everybody else. The gang had an interest in promoting the absolute authority of the leader, because the leader protected the interests of the gang—the only Iraqis he could trust. Over time, the size of the core group around Saddam dwindled further as the Iraqi dictator refused to allow access to real power to almost anyone who wasn't related to him by blood. As in North Korea and Cuba, a consolidated authoritarian state becomes identified thoroughly with one man: the Great Leader or El Comandante.

Years before he assumed the role of Iraq's absolute dictator, Saddam established himself as the provider of the resources needed to service the contacts, clients, protectors, and friends that extended an ever-wider web of patronage through Iraq. The clans of Tikrit, Saddam's birthplace, could be expected to serve their kinsman because they knew they would benefit from his rise to absolute power. Clan members could also rely on contacts in other Sunni regions to defend their interests against the demands of Shia, Kurds, and others.

Shia, in particular, threatened Saddam's rise to power by their very existence as a majority. In 1970, two years after the Baath Party rose to power and Saddam was named head of internal security, an exiled Iranian Shiite cleric,

Ayatollah Ruhollah Khomeini, gave a series of lectures in the Iraqi Shiite-dominated city of Najaf in which he called for the establishment of an Islamic theocracy in Iran. That the target of the message was the Shah of Iran (and not Saddam's kinsman al-Bakr) is the only reason the Baath Party allowed the lectures to take place. Yet, given that 60 percent of Iraqis are Shia, the message threatened Sunnis like Saddam. There were, at the time, a number of Shia active within the Baath Party, drawn in by its pan-Arab and socialist politics. But the Baath party Saddam intended to build would have no ideology beyond subservience to his authority, and Shia were ultimately not to be fully trusted.

Much as the Communist Chinese did following their 1949 revolution, the new Iraqi government sought to buy the goodwill of its peasants with land grants and subsidized food. The state had plenty of land to offer. In the mid-1970s, about one-third of Iraq's cultivable territory was owned by 3 percent of the landowners.[5] In fact, the state—and therefore the clan that controlled the state—remained Iraq's largest single landowner. As in any closed state, the nation's elite controls and distributes vital resources as it chooses, creating a culture of near-total dependence on the regime. The state confiscated land from those whose loyalty was not reliable and gave it to those who could be counted on for support.

In 1972, the regime nationalized the Iraq Petroleum Company, taking control of the one Iraqi resource that might generate significant wealth. The market price of oil and the revenue it provided to producer states like Iraq rose sharply in the mid-1970s. Between October 1973 and December 1975, Iraq's annual oil income rose 800 percent to nearly $8 billion. To establish its political legitimacy beyond areas controlled by loyal clans, the Baathists used some of that windfall to build hospitals, housing projects, and a modest system of social security. But 40 percent of the revenue was spent on arms. Around this time, Iraq stopped publishing data related to arms purchases, and the publication of such statistics became a crime.[6]

The oil revenue was also spent on the patronage networks, deepening the political and economic dependency of Iraqis on their government. By the late 1970s, Saddam's mastery of the state security apparatus and party organizations made him the de facto Iraqi ruler. In 1977, Saddam took control of every aspect of Iraqi oil policy. Saddam decided the level of output and controlled information about how much revenue it produced. He began to transfer millions of dollars of revenue to private accounts overseas, which he would later use to buy weaponry with which he believed he could repel any challenge to his authority, foreign or domestic.[7] All that stood between him and his ambition to rule Iraq was his kinsman and patron Hassan al-Bakr, a man Saddam knew he was well positioned to push aside.

The Leader Necessity

In his recent book *Saddam Hussein: The Politics of Revenge,*[8] Saïd Aburish describes a meeting in 1979—the year Saddam officially claimed absolute power—that the dictator held with a Kurdish politician, Mahmoud Othman. Saddam received Othman in a small office in one of his presidential palaces. Othman noticed a small cot in the corner of the room. The president welcomed him wearing a bathrobe, giving the impression he had slept in his office. Next to the bed, Othman remembered, were "more than twelve pairs of expensive shoes. And the rest of the office was nothing but a small library of books about one man, Stalin. One could say he went to bed with the Russian dictator."[9]

Stalin would have recognized Saddam as an apt pupil. In the summer of that same year, he announced that his security forces had uncovered a plot to overthrow Iraq's government, involving the Baath Party's own Revolutionary Command Council (RCC). At a special session of the Baath Party Congress, an RCC member was forced to publicly confess to involvement in the fictional plot, supposedly masterminded by Syria. Saddam, seated on a stage in front of the assembled Baathists, called out names chosen more or less at random and demanded those named to stand. As each man stood to hear his sentence, Saddam either denounced him as a traitor or thanked him for helping uncover the plot and praised his loyalty. The denounced were led forcibly from the hall and shot just beyond the doors of the auditorium—within earshot of the assembled party members. As the condemned were led away, Saddam smoked a cigar and brushed away tears.

Because the plot was entirely fabricated, no one knew as he rose from his seat if he were about to be praised or executed. The rising terror in the hall exploded into shouts of allegiance to Saddam Hussein. Just as no man wanted to be the first to stop clapping when Stalin finished a speech, no

Baathist wanted to be the last to stand to pledge undying loyalty to Iraq's absolute dictator. Dozens of members of the regime were arrested and shot that day. By the time a series of show trials and purges was complete, hundreds of Baathists had been executed.

The son of a peasant and without a military background, the dictator's resourcefulness was immediately tested. To establish a power base for himself independent of al-Bakr, Saddam used the security services to establish a network of personal obligation and domestic espionage. He had inherited a huge state bureaucracy that, as in any state that seeks absolute control of a divided country, placed emphasis on discipline, conformity, and surveillance.

To surround himself with only those Iraqis he believed he could trust, Saddam bestowed real power on a very small group. Most were blood relations. The rest were known as Ahl al-Thiqa, or "The Trustworthy," Sunnis unrelated to Saddam who had proven their loyalty during his rise to power. The Ahl al-Thiqa became so closely identified with Saddam and his clan that his power became both their cause and the source of their own safety and enrichment. Yet, like Stalin, Saddam was wary of anyone he considered a potential rival. He arrested and executed more than a few.

To cement his legitimacy in the eyes of ordinary Iraqis, state-controlled media established a "national myth." Saddam was its central figure. As Kim Jong-Il was born on a sacred North Korean mountaintop under a rainbow, Saddam cast himself as the direct lineal descendant of the pre-Islamic rulers of Mesopotamia. After he declared war on Shiite Iran in 1980, Saddam assumed a more Islamic identity to counter whatever appeal Iran's revolutionary army might have had for Iraq's Arab Shia. Propaganda campaigns now portrayed Saddam as a pan-Arab leader and the direct descendant of the Prophet. In 1982, Saddam bestowed on himself the title of Al-Qaid al-Durura, the "leader necessity," creator of the Party's "ideology." He told the mayors of Najaf, Karbala, and Misan in a 1987 speech that Baathist ideology was whatever he decided it was.[10]

To keep a country closed to outside influence, an authoritarian regime must control its intellectuals. Just as the Khmer Rouge imprisoned or killed Cambodians caught wearing eyeglasses, and as Stalin's security apparatus shipped thousands of artists and intellectuals to the gulag archipelago, Saddam forced hundreds of thousands of professionals, artists, and writers into exile between 1979 and 1985. As a result, one of Iraq's greatest challenges in the post-Saddam period of reconstruction will be to build a new society without some of Iraq's finest minds.

Many of those that Saddam did not kill or drive from Iraq became, over time, a client base with a direct stake in his survival. While Sunnis from the clans of the center and west of the country dominated the highest positions of government, military, and security police, Saddam ensured that representatives of Shiite and Kurdish communities held symbolically important positions within the government bureaucracy that allowed them access to the regime's patronage networks, if not to real political influence. Saddam understood he could not completely bankrupt any Iraqi group that might undermine the country's stability. But at the same time, he eliminated direct threats to his absolute control by exploiting Iraq's divisions. When Kurdish loyalties were divided in the early 1980s between attempts to court Iranian help against Saddam and loyalty to Baghdad, Saddam profited from the division by extending his patronage to some Kurdish leaders and not others. Pitted against one another, Kurdish leaders attacked each other instead of coordinating resistance to Saddam's influence in their tribal lands.

When Kurds rose against the regime in the late 1980s and tried, for instance, to seize oilfields in northern Iraq, Saddam ordered the use of exemplary violence against Kurdish civilians, just as the head of Syria's Baath Party, Hafez Assad, had flattened the Syrian city of Hama in 1982 to crush one rebellion and discourage others. In 1988, determined to assert absolute control over the Kurdish areas in the north, Saddam called on Ali Hassan al-Majid (better known in the West as "Chemical Ali") to begin a campaign of violence against Kurds. During Al Anfal, or the "Spoils of War," villages were razed; inhabitants slaughtered; men, women, and children gassed. On one March day in 1988, chemical weapons killed an estimated 4,000 people in the Kurdish town of Halabja.[11]

More dangerous for Saddam than Kurdish resistance in the north, Iran's new revolutionary government began in 1980 to encourage Iraq's Shia through Shiite Islamist groups within Iraq to rise against Saddam in the south and in the Shiite ghettos of Baghdad itself. Shiite insurrectionists responded to mass arrests and executions with an attempt on the life of Saddam's deputy prime minister and confidante, Tariq Aziz. Saddam retaliated by arresting Iraq's highest-ranking Shiite cleric and began exiling Iraqi Shia in large numbers. Shiite land was confiscated. The executions and exile of so many senior Shiite figures left an alternative, more servile Shiite hierarchy, whose loyalty would soon be put to the test when Iraq went to war with Iran.

The War with Iran

In 1980, fearing that Iran might persuade and help Iraq's majority Shia to destabilize Iraq, Saddam declared war on Iran. In doing so, he knew he enjoyed the support of the leaders of both the United States and the Soviet Union, who feared the spread of radical Islam more than they worried that Saddam might prove a brutal dictator. Saddam also knew his effort would have the approval of the Sunni-dominated Gulf States, threatened by Iran's stated intent to export a Shiite revolution to the Arab world.

Saddam's decision to go to war was a mistake. In 1980, Tehran appeared divided, isolated, and weak. Saddam believed the war would be glorious and brief, that a source of instability among Iraqi Shia would be eliminated, and that he could extract profitable concessions from his defeated enemy. He hoped Iraq's show of force would lift its prestige and its army to a position of leadership in the Arab world. Instead, the war revealed the incompetence of the Iraqi military and of Saddam as its commander. Just as Stalin's insistence on giving orders to capable Soviet military leaders nearly cost the Soviets the war with Hitler, so Saddam's failures as a battlefield strategist cost Iraq tens of thousands of lives. The war rallied Iranians to their revolution and forced Saddam to hide huge battlefield losses from the Iraqi people.

The Iran-Iraq war settled into a grim stalemate. To build Arab support for his government and to punish Iraqi Shia for perceived disloyalty, the Iraqi government paid non-Shiite Iraqi men to divorce their Shiite wives. The regime then brought the Iraqi Shiite hierarchy under even tighter control. It monitored sermons, took control of Shiite mosques, and made all Shiite *ulama*, or religious authorities, employees of the Iraqi state.[12]

In 1988, after eight years of war, Iraq and Iran were forced to recognize that the conflict could not continue. Both sides declared victory and signed an armistice. The human and economic costs of the war diminished Saddam's status as Iraq's "necessity," left 150,000 Iraqis dead, 70,000 in captivity in Iran, and Iraq $80 billion in debt. Iraq's creditors became more assertive in demanding repayment, and a steep drop in oil prices left Iraq's petroleum revenue at half its 1980 level.[13] If increased oil revenue raises the entire J curve to higher levels of stability, empty coffers lower the entire curve and make it necessary for a dictator to stamp out any threats to internal stability. (See figure below.)

Saddam was no ordinary dictator; he left nothing to chance when it came to domestic repression. But the disastrous war with Iran did nothing to diminish Saddam's compulsion to gamble on foreign policy. What does a risk-taking dictator do to pay off a huge war debt and to reassert himself as a necessary leader? If he's Saddam Hussein, he starts another war.

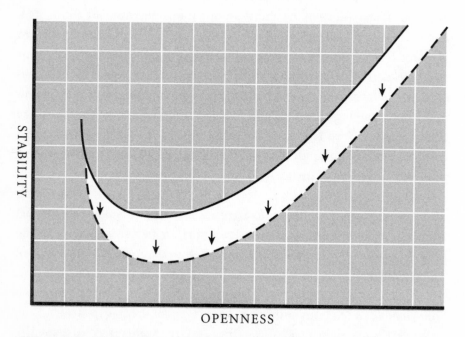

STABILITY

OPENNESS

Shifts of the Entire J Curve: If increased oil revenues raise the entire J curve to higher levels of stability, empty coffers lower the curve and make it necessary for an authoritarian government to quell threats to internal stability.

The Mother of All Miscalculations

Damage to Iraq's oil infrastructure left the regime with little revenue to pay its debt or to service the patronage networks fundamental to Iraqi stability. To reestablish his hold on Iraq's security and armed forces, Saddam attacked his military elite with the same basic strategy of "divide and conquer" with which he so often assaulted Iraq's Shia and Kurds. Some Iraqi officers were promoted; others were demoted. Still others were arrested. Several of the more popular met with unexplained accidents. In the process, Saddam destroyed enough of the officer corps' institutional memory to head off near-term challenges to his authority.

Just as financial hardship forced Castro to open his economy to limited reform, now Saddam relaxed price controls, encouraged limited entrepreneurial activity, and privatized state-owned factories. Saddam's intimates profited mightily from much of the new economic activity, but the inflation some of these measures produced forced the reimposition of state control and a concerted move further up the left side of the J curve. Austerity measures also backfired. The demobilization of thousands of Iraqi soldiers added to the unemployment problem, and the orders were rescinded.[14]

Even if the new market activity had produced sustained economic growth, it could not solve the underlying problems facing an unstable economy. It was the debt problem that led Saddam to call for help from two of his neighbors: Saudi Arabia and Kuwait. Saddam asked those countries to lead OPEC in cuts in oil output to raise global oil prices. He also asked them to write off the wartime financial support they had given him and to contribute more money to Iraqi reconstruction. The royal families of Saudi Arabia and Kuwait refused.

Saddam and his small core of advisors then developed a strategy essentially to take Kuwait hostage. A successful invasion of Kuwait would help Saddam regain the stature at home and abroad he had lost in the war with Iran. It would either force the payment of a ransom or would allow Saddam access to the Kuwaiti oil that would finance the Iraqi debt, revive the economy, and refill the coffers of his patronage network. It would demonstrate to other Gulf States that when Saddam asked for a change in OPEC policy, he should get it. It mattered little if Iraq eventually annexed Kuwait, set up a puppet government there, or sold it for ransom. Any of those scenarios would bail Saddam out and tighten his hold on a divided and stricken Iraq.

When the Gulf States made clear they would not bow to his threats, Saddam, on August 2, 1990, launched the mother of all miscalculations. A leader that spent so much time, energy, and resources pushing Iraq up the left side of the J curve decided to risk the stability he had created on another foreign-policy gambit. Again rolling the dice, he invaded a neighboring country. But while much of the outside world had supported his war on Iran, the Arab League and the United Nations condemned the invasion of Kuwait. Iraqi assets were frozen. Iraq's oil export pipelines through Turkey and Saudi Arabia were cut off, and the UN Security Council imposed an economic and trade embargo. Worse still, the United States quickly called for Iraq's unconditional withdrawal. After assembling a broad coalition of committed countries, President George H. W. Bush ordered an airlift that would put 500,000 troops on Saudi soil. The coalition of U.S. and allied forces quickly defeated Saddam's troops.[15]

Iraq Pays the Price

A nation's stability is based on two factors: the capacity of the state to withstand the effects of shocks, and the ability to avoid producing them. Saddam's Iraq was always less stable than Cuba and even North Korea, because its internal ethnic and religious divisions undermined the consolidation of federal authority in the country, and because Saddam created his own shocks. Iraq's dictator had misjudged the reaction of the international community. Castro in the 1970s dispatched Cuban troops to Cold War battlefields such as Angola. North Korea has saber-rattled nearly every day for half a century. Neither has ever taken the risks Saddam took in starting a war he could not win. Iraq's neighbors and all who value stability in the Persian Gulf region began to view Saddam's tendency to create instability as a risk they could no longer afford.

If the Iraqi dictator was ill prepared for the external political shock he provoked from the international community, he was well prepared as usual to withstand internal challenges. Relying on the cousins, half-brothers, and brothers-in-law that made up the oligarchy at the core of his leadership, Saddam began a defensive campaign of domestic repression.

In March 1991, thousands of Shia rose in revolt. Army deserters and others seized control of several southern towns, but the rebellion was as leaderless as it was spontaneous. Many Shiite leaders, still on the payrolls of Saddam's patronage network, waited to see who would win the struggle. Others collaborated with his security troops. Many of Saddam's elite Republican Guard divisions, held back from Kuwait to protect the regime from internal attack, routed Shiite rebels and sent tens of thousands of refugees flooding into Saudi Arabia and Iran. Thousands were killed. Thousands more were sent to Iraq's infamous prisons to languish for years.

Kurdish forces in the north rose up. Unlike those who benefited from Saddam's patronage in the Shiite areas, even the Kurds who were on his payroll joined the fight against Saddam's troops. Kurdish fighters seized the oil-rich town of Kirkuk, but once the Shia were defeated in the south, Republican Guard units turned their attention north. Fearing a repeat of the chemical attacks of Al Anfal, more than a million Kurds fled into Iran and Turkey.

The Shiite and Kurdish rebellions crushed, Saddam returned to the exploitation of Iraq's divisions. His task was made simpler by the U.S. imposition of "no-fly zones" in the northern and southern thirds of the country. Intended to protect Kurds and Shia from further attack, the move also served to protect Saddam from his most rebellious citizens. The no-fly zones allowed him to devote all his security forces to the control of Sunni central Iraq, the area already most sympathetic to his regime. This was only the first of many international attempts to weaken and isolate Saddam. Failure to understand Iraq's divisions instead enabled his survival.

Sanctions

After Iraq's retreat from Kuwait, a consensus developed on the UN Security Council that Saddam should never again be allowed to threaten his neighbors. Punitive sanctions, harsher and more widely supported than anything ever imposed on Iran or Cuba, were established. Sanctions were to be lifted only when any nuclear, chemical, and biological weapons or material and long-range surface-to-surface missiles were destroyed and all other requirements of UN resolutions were met. The first UNSCOM (United Nations Special Commission on Disarmament) inspection teams began work inside Iraq in May 1991, and quickly discovered that Iraq had successfully developed a considerable stockpile of chemical and biological weapons and was closer than most believed to the development of a nuclear device.

If the war with Iran left Iraq in dire straits, the invasion of Kuwait and the war that followed devastated the country. Six weeks of coalition bombing in 1991 had destroyed more of Iraq's infrastructure than eight years of war with Iran. Electricity and water-purification systems went unrepaired. Fertilizer supplies were exhausted. Worn-out agricultural machinery could not be replaced. The resulting shortages generated levels of malnutrition, disease, and infant mortality not seen in Iraq since the early 1950s.[16] Sanctions made the conditions worse.

Saddam skillfully portrayed the sanctions as a brutal American and UN assault on Iraqi dignity. In 1992, hoping to lighten the burden on Iraqi civilians, the UN offered to allow Iraq to sell $1.6 billion worth of oil to purchase food and medicine. Saddam refused because the offer included a proviso that the UN would administer the funds, and that 30 percent of the proceeds would go toward war reparations to Kuwait. He knew his control of the funds was critical to maintaining internal repression. Only in 1996 did the Iraqi regime agree to the so-called Oil-for-Food Program, an agreement that allowed Iraq to sell $2 billion in oil every six months for the purchase of supplies to alleviate the hardship to the Iraqi population. That amount was later increased to $5.52 billion in 1998 and to $8.3 billion in 1999.[17] Crucially, Saddam was given control of the resulting revenue.

Saddam used that opportunity to again become an oil producer and to use the proceeds to purchase consumer goods from supportive countries in order to divide international opinion on Iraq's treatment. He courted France and Russia, to whom his government still owed considerable sums, to push the Security Council to allow him to sell more and more oil. However, Saddam had good reason to avoid a rush toward a lifting of sanctions. As long as sanctions were in place, he controlled virtually all revenue coming into the country. None of that income was available to his domestic enemies.

Beating the System

At the end of the 2003 war, U.S. investigators found no weapons of mass destruction, the primary public justification for the invasion. They did find Iraqi government documents containing evidence of an elaborate scheme by which Saddam used the Oil-for-Food Program to earn illicit revenue.

According to a report published by the CIA's Iraq Survey Group, Saddam earned as much as $2 billion between 1996 and 2003 through kickbacks from the program and the sale of secret "oil vouchers" to reward foreign companies and individuals that helped Iraq undermine sanctions.[18]

The subversion of the Oil-for-Food Program illustrates how U.S. and UN policy helped Saddam to tighten his hold on power and keep Iraq high up the left side of the J curve. The no-fly zones created a buffer between the regime and the Shiite- and Kurdish-dominated areas of the country. Virtually all Iraq's oil fields are located in those regions. The sanctions ensured that Saddam received and controlled all the revenue produced in the Kurdish- and Shiite-dominated areas. The no-fly zones guaranteed that he faced none of the threats the Shia and Kurds posed for his regime.

Saddam also used the income he controlled to shield his loyal followers from the sanctions' worst effects and to deprive those whose loyalty remained open to question. In the process, he gave Iraqis good reason to support his rule and disincentives to challenge him. Those whom Saddam shielded from sanctions, the so-called Umana Saddam (Saddam's Faithful), were not always relatives of Saddam or even Sunnis. Some were Shiite or Kurdish tribal leaders strategically chosen to co-opt resistance to central authority. Sanctions also made Iraq the object of international sympathy as Saddam allowed children and the elderly to die of hunger and disease.

Saddam kept control of the security forces within his family—the group he mistrusted least. Yet, despite his precautions, Saddam narrowly avoided several attempts at assassination. While he usually considered it safer to rely on kinsmen and allies of long standing, Saddam often used competing clans within the security services to spy on his closest associates and to add layers of redundancy to the protection of his personal safety. A state whose survival depends on the health of one man is only as stable as its internal security arrangements. The last line of defense of Iraq's national security was thus provided by metal detectors, which ensured that when Saddam and his closest aides held a meeting, the Iraqi leader was the only man in the room with a weapon.[19]

Another necessary element in the stability of a regime dependent on the life of one person is the ruthless use of revenge. In 1995, family rivalries led Saddam's sons-in-law, Hussein Kamil and his brother Saddam Kamil, to flee with his daughters to Jordan. Safely beyond Saddam's reach, Hussein Kamil, a former minister of industry and military production during the

Iran-Iraq War, revealed details about the weapons programs Saddam had developed in the 1980s.

Discovering they were deeply unpopular with other Iraqi exiles and unhappy with their reception in Jordan, the brothers accepted Saddam's invitation to return to Iraq in exchange for a presidential pardon. Saddam promised the men's father he would not harm them, and the brothers arrived home in February 1996. On arrival, they, their father, and other close family members were executed.* The brothers were airbrushed out of official family photographs.

By 1999, recognizing that sanctions did not undercut Iraqi military strength enough to leave Saddam at the mercy of his enemies, the United States adopted a new strategy to bring Saddam into compliance with UN resolutions. On December 17, 1999, the Security Council adopted Resolution 1284, which replaced UNSCOM with UNMOVIC, the United Nations Monitoring, Verification, and Inspection Commission. The intent was to reestablish effective weapons inspections in Iraq by offering Saddam a way out of sanctions. But, because sanctions served Saddam's purposes, and because Russia, France, and China encouraged Iraqi intransigence by abstaining on the resolution, UNMOVIC was doomed to failure. Iraq rejected the resolution and refused to allow the return of international inspectors. Further demonstrating his determination that the sanctions regime be maintained, Saddam also ordered stepped-up Iraqi attacks on U.S. and British planes patrolling the no-fly zones.

Meanwhile, the 2000 U.S. presidential election campaign was in full swing. Republican candidate George W. Bush criticized the Clinton administration's ineffectiveness in bringing Saddam to heel. When Bush was elected in November 2000, he brought with him to power many veterans of his father's administration who had worked to evict Saddam from Kuwait in 1991, and some who regretted not toppling his regime at the time. Following the terrorist attacks of September 11, the White House concluded that Saddam's risk-taking foreign policy was too destabilizing for a critical oil-exporting region and for what Bush believed was a key battleground in the new War on Terror. In March 2003, Saddam's dictatorship was brought to a violent end.

---

* Saddam's daughters have remained loyal to their father.

Policy Failure

When the Gulf War came to an end in 1991, international inspectors had pronounced themselves shocked to discover that Saddam's regime had managed to build and maintain considerable stockpiles of chemical and biological weapons. They should not have been surprised. Saddam had used these weapons during the Iran-Iraq War and on Iraqi Kurds, and he clearly believed he had good reason to protect them. Inspectors also discovered that Iraq had made substantial progress toward the development of a nuclear-weapons program.

Former President George H. W. Bush has said several times over the years that he gave virtually no consideration in 1991 to toppling Saddam's government by force. He concluded that such a move would shatter the international coalition he had constructed, force a lengthy U.S. occupation of an Arab country, and produce unforeseen consequences in the region. He and most of his advisors believed that the imposition of harsh sanctions would fatally weaken Saddam's hold on power and accomplish the hoped-for regime change without further U.S. casualties or a costly occupation.

Yet, sanctions failed to destabilize Saddam's government, because they made it considerably easier for Saddam to control his country's resources and brought some patriotic unity to Iraq's beleaguered people. Like Stalin and Kim Jong-Il, Saddam cared nothing for human rights. His willingness to starve his own people provided him with political opportunities to exploit Iraq's suffering at the expense of his international enemies. The no-fly zones, which were intended to protect Iraq's Kurds and Shia from Saddam, also accomplished the reverse. In sum, Saddam survived as long as he did in large measure because U.S. and UN policy throughout the 1990s helped Saddam minimize the susceptibility of his regime to internal shocks by ignoring evidence of how stability and instability are actually created. Iraq is now at the bottom of the J curve because the United States ignored the danger that the artificially created country would fragment and descend into chaos.

It is now clear, in the war's aftermath, that Saddam no longer possessed an arsenal of weapons of mass destruction in 2003. Some credit the sanctions with depriving Saddam of the resources necessary to build and maintain a dangerous arsenal. Perhaps they're right. But by the time George W. Bush arrived in the White House in January 2001, Saddam's ability to subvert sanctions, his propensity for confrontation and risk, and a growing international consensus that sanctions were not working led the new president to feel that the United States could no longer accept what he believed was an eroding status quo.

The 2003 war in Iraq revealed, once again, the brittleness of Saddam's regime. If there were an external intervention into Cuba, Iran, or even Saudi Arabia, regime loyalists and ordinary citizens would almost certainly fight to defend their country. Not so in Iraq, where at the first opportunity, forces "loyal" to Saddam blended back into the population. The United States won a quick military victory, and Saddam's brutal regime passed into history.

Much of the international community believes there was little reason for the United States to go to war. Had international inspectors been given more time to work in Iraq—assuming Saddam's regime would have cooperated with them—the war might have proven unnecessary. Indeed, before the United States chose to push Iraq down the left side of the J curve by force, George W. Bush could have heeded the advice of those who warned that a lengthy U.S. occupation would produce unforeseen consequences, destabilize the region, and, in the post-9/11 world, create opportunities for Islamic radicals to attack U.S. troops at close range. Both the president's rationale for going to war and the planning for operations designed to stabilize and rebuild Iraq have justly been criticized. Better preparation for all these problems could and should have been made. Instead, the quick American-led military victory has come at considerable and far-reaching cost.

But these critiques miss the heart of the failed American policy on Iraq: U.S. policymakers should never have had to choose between the best of three bad options: counterproductive sanctions, capitulation, and a costly war that left U.S. troops to play a principal role in rebuilding Iraq's stability. The lesson of the J curve is that a process of creating opportunities for ordinary Iraqis to profit from access to the resources of the outside world would have destabilized Saddam at less cost to both the Iraqi people and to the United States. To be fair, it is not realistic to believe that George H. W. Bush or Bill Clinton could have made an effective political case for punishing Saddam by extending Iraq an invitation to join the World Trade Organization. Nonetheless, policies that provided resources and created opportunities for Iraqis to interact as fully as possible with the outside world and with one another might have forced Saddam to contend with pressures for change from within Iraq. U.S. policies designed to isolate North Korea and

Cuba have led inevitably to the same false choice: capitulation or costly confrontation.

After a dozen years of international sanctions and the war that brought Saddam's regime to a bitter close, Iraq is now at the bottom of the J curve—and will struggle to even survive as a unified entity. By misunderstanding the nature of Iraq's profound divisions, U.S. policy has compromised Iraq's ability to recover. If the country is to remain in one piece, it can only begin an ascent up the right side of the curve if and when the fledgling Iraqi government no longer needs foreign troops to protect its internal stability and can build an entirely new Iraqi identity. It is far from clear that the United States and the international community still have the political will to help the new Iraq reach that point. It may also be impossible for the country's bitterly divided factions to sufficiently reconcile their differences to construct a new Iraq.

But if the architects of U.S. and UN policy ignored the J curve's power to explain why sanctions helped him stabilize his dictatorship, the Iraqi dictator ignored the J curve's lessons as well. Saddam himself helped produce the external shocks that ultimately brought his regime to an end.

CHAPTER THREE

The Slide Toward Instability

It is dangerous to be right when the government is wrong.

—Voltaire

I ran, Saudi Arabia, and Russia are three of the most complex and potentially unstable countries in the world. Like North Korea, Cuba, and Iraq,
they can be found on the left side of the J curve. But Iran, Saudi Arabia, and
Russia are more open to the outside world than the states in the last chapter
and are, therefore, prone to frequent moves in both directions along
the curve—up the slope toward consolidated authoritarianism and down
toward potential chaos. This volatility and the enormous importance of
these states for global politics and markets make the stakes for the futures of
these countries particularly high.

Policies designed to help move these states through instability to the
right side of the curve, to produce greater political and economic openness,
and to bring these closed states into harmony with the crosscurrents of
globalization, should not be pursued with complacency. As an authoritarian regime slides toward the dip in the J curve and risks total collapse, the
international community can find ways to bolster its stability in the short
term, which is particularly important if there is no promising political alternative to the ruling elite ready to establish stable governance on a foundation of popular legitimacy. Closed regimes work hard to eliminate any
such political alternatives. To that end, elites in Russia and Iran have manip-

ulated national elections. Saudi Arabia doesn't need to. It has yet to hold national elections.

In Iran, there *are* well-organized reform forces more or less ready to inherit a failed state from the ruling conservatives. In Saudi Arabia, there are not yet any such viable alternatives to the kingdom's royal family. Openness and democratization are virtues in mature and stable societies. But the absence of an authority capable of ensuring baseline political and social stability requires that policies designed to open Saudi Arabia recognize the necessity for short-term compromises on political reform—even as international policymakers continue to develop ideas to encourage long-term democratization there.

In a state like Saudi Arabia, it need not be hypocritical to talk up democratization while working to manage the pace at which it occurs. A short-term strategy to protect stability in the world's largest oil-exporting state is preferable to slavish adherence to a principle that might unleash large-scale violence and chaos. That said, the need for caution doesn't justify the indefinite postponement of all meaningful reform. Policies intended to help shepherd the Saudis toward a more open society and a better-diversified, modern economy can help create the alternative to absolute monarchy on which Saudi Arabia's future openness and stability will depend.

It's fine to say that a nation more politically, economically, and socially open to foreign markets and ideas will be freer, more prosperous, and, in the long run, more stable than a closed nation. Yes, open is better than closed. But, if pressure for change is not released incrementally and with care—for instance, if free and fair national elections were held tomorrow in Pakistan, Egypt, or Uzbekistan—much of the rest of the world would not like the result.

The problem is not hypothetical. Consider the Algerian elections of 1991 and the Western response to the outcome. Believing that an Islamist party with a violent military wing, the Islamic Salvation Front, was about to win an overwhelming election victory, Algeria's army, with support from France and the United States, canceled the vote. Islamists then went to war with Algeria's government security forces, and 150,000 Algerians were killed in the ensuing near-decade-long conflict. The West has since become more guarded in its support for democratic elections in Algeria and a host of other states ill prepared for a mature renegotiation of power between the government and the governed.

Unfortunately, the rulers of most closed states have little incentive to begin preparing their societies for mature governance in the first place. Arab regimes, in particular, have made it difficult to establish a viable political alternative to the ruling elite. Often, only religious leaders are allowed to speak directly and without obstruction to the general public. Arab leaders have discovered they can quash opposition political movements far more easily than they can control the content of sermons.[1] In states like Egypt, Algeria, and Tunisia, religious authorities, many of them politically radical, offer the only outlets for antiestablishment anger these governments are prepared to tolerate. The case of the Muslim Brotherhood in Egypt makes the point: while the group itself is banned as a terrorist organization by the Egyptian government,* 88 of its members have used the vocal support of fundamentalist clerics to win seats in the 454-seat Egyptian parliament. Those 88 seats make the outlawed Muslim Brotherhood the largest unified opposition force in Egyptian politics. Were Egypt to hold truly free elections, only the Muslim Brotherhood would have the capacity to organize a viable electoral alternative to the government. They, and similar Islamist organizations in other Arab states, would surely win a fair vote, just as fundamentalist Wahhabis dominated Saudi Arabia's 2005 municipal elections, and just as the Islamic Salvation Front would have won the aborted election in Algeria.

Outside actors like the United States and the European Union don't have much influence inside Muslim states. But the United States, the European Union, and others can still help responsible agents for change in the Muslim world. The international community can materially and politically support a new generation of Arab leaders who want far-reaching reform of their societies, reform that won't create chaos before its energy can be harnessed for constructive purpose. U.S. policy toward Arab states has too often been predicated on a false choice: coercion or conversation, demands or diplomacy, all with only the existing authoritarian leadership in mind. Too little effort has been made to look beyond ruling elites toward others who seek peaceful change and greater openness.

Those who believe, for example, that only the threat (or the reality) of military action can create pressure for reform are dangerously shortsighted.

---

* The United States government does not classify the Muslim Brotherhood as a terrorist organization.

But those who believe that committed diplomats can always find the right combination of incentives to modify any tyrant's behavior are mistaken as well. Durable reform movements, like Solidarity in Poland* or Charter 77 in then Czechoslovakia,† were homegrown. Soviet-era governments were not open to meaningful negotiation with the West. But support for Solidarity and Charter 77 made a lasting difference in undermining Warsaw Pact governments.

Providing independent groups within closed states with the resources they need to speak directly to potential supporters—to offer their citizens an alternative to both the authoritarian regime and to dangerous radicals—is a wise investment in the stable and progressive futures of these countries. Just as U.S. policymakers have usually been too preoccupied with punishing Fidel Castro to help empower Cuban dissidents, Washington has virtually ignored would-be Arab reformers in favor of cajoling their rulers to undertake reforms they know will undermine their regimes.

In the Muslim world in particular, there is, of course, the problem of the "poisoned messenger." Direct American or European public support for an opposition movement within a Muslim state may discredit that group in the eyes of a public suspicious of foreign intentions. But the support need not be public or direct. U.S. and European aid for nascent reform movements can be woven into policies toward the states in which these groups operate. Greater U.S. support for Iranian exile groups that mobilize and coordinate internal resistance to clerical rule is one example.‡ International support for free and fair regional elections in Saudi Arabia is another.

In fact, there are many different kinds of outside influence—not all of them the result of government policy—that undermine a closed regime's ability to control and isolate its people, particularly in left-side-of-the-

---

* The Soviet bloc's first independent trade union.

† Charter 77 was a petition calling on Czechoslovakia's Communist authorities to respect the international human rights agreements they had signed. It was drafted in secret in the fall of 1976, initially signed in Prague by 243 Czechoslovak citizens, mainly dissidents, and released to foreign journalists in January 1977. http://plato.acadiau.ca/courses/pols/grieve/3593/Czech/Charter77.html.

‡ In 2006, the U.S. government announced plans to spend $75 million to promote democracy in Iran by supporting nongovernmental organizations and expanding broadcasting of Voice of America into the country twenty-four hours a day. Congress later cut $19 million.

curve states that are partially open to such influences. Foreign direct invest-ment gives foreign firms and governments a stake in the direction of the closed state's development and local actors a stake in deepening commer-cial relationships. That's why the Russian government is wary of foreign in-vestment in the nation's oil industry and why Iran restricts the access of foreign companies to the country's telecom market. A people's access to in-ternational media, particularly when that media airs criticism of the ruling elite the citizenry might not otherwise hear, diminishes a closed regime's domestic legitimacy. That's why the Saudi government publicly reaffirmed in September 2004 that state employees who spoke to foreign media would be prosecuted. An active diaspora population can help change an oppressed people's notions of what they have a right to expect from their rulers. That's why National Iranian Television, produced by Iranian expatriates in Los Angeles, broadcasts antigovernment messages toward Tehran.

Iran, Saudi Arabia, and Russia are far more open to the forces of global change than are North Korea, Cuba, or Saddam's Iraq. But each of these states has a complicated relationship with those forces and has resolutely resisted movement toward the right side of the J curve. The rulers of Iran and Saudi Arabia have good reason to suspect they would no longer hold sway in a country that freely chose its own leaders, and Russia's ruling elite knows its members are only as popular as Vladimir Putin.

It's not just states that move; the J curve itself shifts up and down as cir-cumstances within a particular state change. A regime headed toward col-lapse may benefit when an infusion of revenue lifts the entire curve. Because the added inflow of cash makes every point on the curve more sta-ble than it was before the money streamed in, energy-rich states like Nige-ria, Kazakhstan, and Venezuela can use the added revenue from high oil prices to move in either direction along the curve—either to implement painful reforms or to further consolidate control. The added revenue can be invested in new schools or health-care clinics in areas where education and medicine are scarce; it can subsidize short-term make-work projects to ap-pease the angry unemployed or patronage networks that control dissent at the local level; it can finance the construction of better roads and bridges to open internal trade; it can bankroll the imposition of martial law.

Unfortunately, many closed regimes "blessed" with substantial oil re-serves use the extra cash from high energy prices to keep their countries closed. That's why some refer to oil not as a blessing but as a curse for the citizens of these states. There are now thirty-four developing nations that earn at least 30 percent of their total export revenue from oil and/or natural gas. Yet, twelve of these countries' annual per capita income remains below $1,500, and two-thirds of the thirty-four countries are not democratic.[2]

Of course, oil and gas prices don't always rise, and other shocks do occur. A sudden drop in revenue—when those same energy prices dip, a war is lost, a financial crisis or natural disaster erupts—can force a potentially unstable regime to take actions that further undermine the government's legitimacy. The devaluation of the Egyptian pound in 2003 created high inflation and provoked demands for subsidies that drove up Egypt's unemployment. Striking oil workers in Venezuela sparked rioting and government reprisals in 2004 and forced a referendum on the president's legitimacy. After foreign investment in the Kyrgyz Republic's fragile economy failed to materialize during the 1990s, then Kyrgyz President Askar Akaev gave his prosecutor-general free rein to intimidate, disqualify, and imprison opposition politicians who called for change. For every such action, there is the reaction of resistance. In Akaev's case, the reaction eventually pushed his government off a cliff.

International isolation cannot be maintained forever, although some leaders, as we saw in the last chapter, seem determined to give it a shot. The first problem facing leaders who open (slightly) their closed regimes is that the processes of globalization are accelerating. Any autocrat that plugs into these processes opens his country to forces he can't control. Membership in the World Trade Organization, for example, has its privileges, but it also comes at a price—compliance with WTO rules can be enforced. Even investment in improved communications, development of air, rail, and road infrastructure, and other technological advances empower individual citizens and would-be entrepreneurs to establish a certain amount of independence from their rulers. The simple act of connecting two villages by telephone can threaten a ruling elite's ability to control its people's access to information. Once a farmer discovers that a fertilizer shortage is not limited to his village but shared with others across the country, he is less likely to fault bad luck and more likely to blame his government. Once contact between farmers is established, they may demand freedom of association.

As noted, if isolation is to be maintained, it isn't only an authoritarian state's literal borders that must be sealed against foreign influence; such regimes must seal figurative borders as well. Arab governments have largely succeeded in doing so for decades. According to the 2002 United Nations Arab Human Development Report, the first of three studies authored by Arab political scientists with UN backing, "The whole Arab world translates about 300 books annually, one fifth the number that Greece translates. The cumulative total of translated books since the Caliph Mamoun [more than 1,000 years ago] is about 100,000, just about the number that Spain translates in one year."[3]

But there are widening and deepening cracks in this wall as cable television and the Internet give ordinary citizens a glimpse of the other side. Al Jazeera and Al Arabiya are only the best known of several Arabic-language cable news channels beaming information into the region about life outside the Arab world. And because Arabs have been isolated for so long, the news beamed in from outside finds a fascinated audience. Arab citizens are now more aware than ever how badly governed they are, how much less free and less prosperous they are than the citizens of Europe, North America, and East Asia. They now have an opportunity to see their regimes as others see them.

Another problem with an authoritarian regime's self-imposed isolation in the twenty-first century: it's increasingly expensive. The creation of jobs that keep a potentially restive population nourished and occupied demands a robust economy that grows steadily over time. A growing economy in today's global marketplace requires openness to the outside world. The catch-22 can be avoided for many years, as it has been in several Muslim countries and as it was in the Soviet bloc. But it can't be avoided forever. That's why left-side states like Iran, Saudi Arabia, and Russia have all made efforts to join the WTO.

In addition, as we saw in the last chapter, leadership transitions offer special challenges in left-side states, even in states that aren't as isolated as North Korea. A new ruler must reconsolidate his regime's control over society and earn the loyalty of an elite support structure dedicated to the preservation of a status quo that may have died with the former leader. Syria's ruling Baath Party chose to preserve predictability following Hafez Assad's death by elevating the son to replace the father. The same occurred in Azerbaijan. Egypt's Hosni Mubarak may soon follow suit. New leaders in closed states must take the necessary measures to maintain the old regime's grip on the throat of the societies they rule. The moment when the hold on power is transferred from one hand to another is a time of potential instability. Any relaxation of that grip might allow a competing voice to speak.

Some states on the left side of the curve, many of them friends of the United States, recognize the futility of trying to maintain stability by indefinitely maintaining isolation. These governments hope to introduce reform, but at a pace they can manage. Pakistan and Egypt provide ready examples. Yet, even these governments are prone to deliberate moves back up the left side of the curve whenever they feel threatened.

The ruling elites of these countries understand there is dissatisfaction just on the other side of another kind of wall—the one they build between themselves and their citizens. Their hope, knowing the wall won't hold indefinitely, is to let off pressure in increments, to manage the transition, to avoid a catastrophic explosion. China's leaders saw in the progression of Gorbachev's *perestroika* what might happen when reform of a centrally planned system takes on a momentum of its own. In the weeks immediately following the June 1989 massacre in Tiananmen Square, China's ruling elite saw the fates of Poland's Wojciech Jaruzelski, East Germany's Erich Honecker and, especially, Romania's Nicolae Ceauşescu. Arab authoritarians are haunted by the fate of Iran's monarch, Reza Pahlavi.

A regime's slide toward the dip in the J curve—the point of greatest instability and uncertainty—is dangerous for an entire region and beyond, particularly when that country is an important regional actor, like Iran or Egypt; a vitally important global economic player, like Saudi Arabia or China; or has nuclear weapons, like Russia or Pakistan. Of the countries that have a transition to make from closed to open societies, few are more complex or offer greater hope for success than Iran. Because it provides rich examples of movements up and down the left side of the J curve and is a country that wields considerable geopolitical influence, Iran deserves a closer look.

IRAN AND WHY IT MATTERS

Among the most populous countries in the Middle East and one of the world's leading energy producers, Iran is too big and too influential for the rest of the world to ignore. Consider the country's position in a vitally important region. To the east is Afghanistan, a country caught between modernizing forces intent on opening the country to the world, tribal warlords fighting for power and cash, and Islamists intent on returning the country to the Taliban. To the northwest is Turkey, a member of NATO, a potential future member of the European Union, and a Muslim democracy. To the southeast is Pakistan, the only nuclear-armed Muslim country in the world (so far) and a potential source of ethnoreligious civil war. To the south and southeast are the Gulf sheikhdoms, the Persian Gulf itself (through which flows 40 percent of the world's oil), and Iran's chief regional rival, Saudi Arabia. To the west is Iraq, with whom Iran fought an eight-year war of attrition in the 1980s and which is currently home to more than 100,000 U.S. troops. It's a rough neighborhood, a crucially important region for the war on terror, and a principal source of the world's energy.

Iran is itself an important energy producer. It holds about 11 percent of global oil reserves and the world's second-largest deposits of natural gas. Home to the only religious revolution in modern history, Iran's is a vitally important voice, which influences theological debate throughout the Islamic world. At the same time, Iran has a history—albeit a limited one—of representative government and constitutionalism. And it is one of the only nations in which a president can be considered an opposition figure.* If it so chooses, Iran could serve as a key player in any regional transition toward greater openness and political reform. It could also export substantial instability.

One way to measure the gulf of misunderstanding between Americans and Iranians is to ask a citizen of either country when the U.S.-Iranian relationship began. Most Americans believe the trouble started on November 4, 1979, when Iranian students took fifty-two Americans hostage in Tehran. Over the next 444 days, Americans were startled to learn that Iranians considered America the "Great Satan" and blamed the U.S. government for a quarter century of domestic misery. Iranians point to an earlier date for the

---

* There are certainly other examples of states with a ceremonial presidency and a powerful prime ministership. But Iran may be the only mature country in modern history in which the country's most powerful elected official must answer to an unelected "supreme leader."

beginning of the animosity: August 19, 1953, when a CIA-engineered coup overthrew the elected government of Iranian Prime Minister Mohammed Mossadegh and restored near-absolute power to Reza Pahlavi, Shah of Iran. Iranians and Americans have very different narratives in mind when they tell the story of the twentieth century.

Yet in Iran, there is both an attraction to American culture and contempt for its influence. On the positive side, while there were no candlelight vigils in sympathy for the victims of 9/11 in Egypt or Saudi Arabia, there were in Iran. In Egypt and Saudi Arabia, many blame their American-backed governments for the iniquities of their domestic leadership. Because Iranians believe they took control of their country's destiny and cast out foreign powers and their puppets in 1979, fewer Iranians blame America for their country's political and social malaise. Many reform-minded Iranians welcome any opportunity for better relations with the outside world in general and the West in particular.

Despite this, for Iran's most dogged conservatives, "Death to America" remains a standard refrain. For them, America continues to represent every humiliation and affront modern Iran has endured at the hands of outsiders. This is a minority view, but it is held by the men who maintain a near-monopoly on the country's levers of domestic coercion. It is these men who want to keep Iran on the left side of the stability curve—and to use George W. Bush's "axis of evil" speech and America's "cultural decadence" to persuade their countrymen that Western values are toxic.

To understand modern Iran's relationship with the West, it's useful to briefly step back even further. From the beginning of the twentieth century, the Anglo-Iranian Oil Company (AIOC), owned mainly by the British government, held a monopoly on the production and sale of Iran's oil. While the oil itself and the profits from its sale helped maintain the British Empire, most Iranians, including the workers that manned the pumping stations, lived in the cold shadow of pampered British expatriates. Iranian resentment of London's domination grew over the first half of the century and found its voice in the person of Mohammed Mossadegh, a fiery and eccentric legislator best known for his charismatic fulminations against the British and the dramatic fainting spells with which he punctuated them. Mossadegh's nationalist condemnation of the AIOC brought him to power in 1951, as Iran's young Shah was forced to appoint him prime minister or risk popular fury that might have spelled the end of the Pahlavi dynasty. Once in place, Mossadegh quickly nationalized the British oil company, which had, up to that point, provided Europe with 90 percent of its petroleum.

The crisis that followed made Mossadegh an international star, but brought the Iranian economy to the point of collapse, as London deprived Iran of the British tankers necessary to move its oil to international markets. British Prime Minister Winston Churchill pressed President Harry Truman to support a British coup to topple Mossadegh's government and to return Iran's oil fields to AIOC-controlled production. Truman, suspicious of Churchill's imperial motives, refused.

With the election of Dwight Eisenhower in November 1952, however, the dynamic changed. In Eisenhower's secretary of state, John Foster Dulles, and his CIA director, Allen Dulles, Churchill's pleas found a more sympathetic audience. Convinced that Mossadegh might move Iran into the Soviet orbit, the Dulles brothers set to work on a CIA operation, captained by Theodore Roosevelt's grandson Kermit, which ousted Mossadegh and placed Reza Pahlavi in a position of unrivaled power.[4] Iranians consider the coup America's "original sin" in Iran; the Shah never overcame the perception that he was a Washington-installed puppet.

Over the next quarter-century, the Shah solidified a system of power based on patronage, paranoia, dependence on the United States, and brutal autocratic rule. He wasted oil money by the billions to realize his grandiose vision of an opulently rich, secular Iran, and profits from the sale of Iranian oil were reserved for the Shah's closest, most trusted allies and clients. Iran's religious conservatives were angered by their exclusion from the oil revenue, by the Shah and his family's "Western habits," and especially by his attempts to secularize Iranian society. Thousands of mosques across Iran became meeting places for planning and protest.

By the end of his reign, it was clear to Iranians the Shah only remained in power because successive U.S. administrations kept him there as a bulwark against Soviet Communism and Arab nationalism.* The consequence of

---

* Pahlavi's dynastic claim was hardly ancient—his father became the first of the Pahlavi line in 1926. Even the family name provoked Islamists: "Pahlavi" derives from a language Persians spoke before the advent of Islam in the seventh century.

the Shah's rising unpopularity was a classic slide down the left side of the J curve toward state failure in 1979.

Installing and propping up the Shah was intended to ensure Western access to Iran's oil and gas and to limit the influence of Communists in Iran—both Soviet and domestic. Public opinion was ignored. The Shah and his regime were deliberately installed on the left side of the J curve precisely because Washington feared that an open expression of Iranian public opinion might undermine the entire American Cold War strategy in the region. There were no alternatives to Pahlavi's rule, short of revolutionary ones. No structure existed for a peaceful transfer of power.

The events of 1979 illustrate something important about the power of outsiders to stop a country's slide down the curve toward instability: that power is limited. The United States played a key role in bringing the Shah to the pinnacle of absolute power and helped keep him there for twenty-five years. Washington had every incentive to protect the Shah from his opposition. Pahlavi was a key Cold War ally and a reliable supplier of oil. Never was the Shah's Cold War role more important than in the Arab-Israeli conflicts of 1956, 1967, and 1973. Iran provided a useful check on Moscow's attempts to expand its influence in the region. Never was the Shah's petroleum more welcome than in the oil shocks of the 1970s.* But Pahlavi's fall was steep and quick—and Washington was powerless to stop it.

Ayatollah Ruhollah Khomeini's return to Iran from exile in Paris capped the modern world's first religious revolution. Khomeini's call to the world's Muslims to rise against oppressive, secular governments found an audience in neighboring Iraq, a majority Shiite nation that had always been governed by Sunnis. Fearing Iraq's Shiites might threaten his rule, Saddam Hussein attacked the revolutionary movement at its source in Tehran. The result was a brutal eight-year war that killed an estimated 300,000 Iranians, wounded 600,000 to 700,000 more, and made refugees of 2 million. The war, fought mostly inside Iran, devastated the country's economic infrastructure.

While there is no evidence the United States played a role in Iraq's invasion of Iran—which happened at a moment when fifty-two American hostages were held in Tehran—Iranians have good reason to believe that Washington sided with Saddam. Fearful of the influence of revolutionary Islamic fundamentalism in a region on which America was increasingly de-

---

* Iran did not join its Arab neighbors in the OPEC oil embargo.

pendent for energy, the U.S. Navy protected U.S. oil tankers in the Persian Gulf by sinking several of Iran's ships.

Iran's revolutionary government was, from the beginning, founded on two principles: a political rejection of the Shah's oppression and an assertion of Iran's identity as the beating heart of an Islamic revolution. Once in power, Iran's clerics banned the formation of political parties. But even religious conservatives divided into rival camps: some advocated a pragmatic approach to the West and a kind of "Islamism in one country"; others sought a more ideologically rigid and confrontational foreign-policy approach. This division into pragmatic and dogmatic factions ultimately pushed Iranian civil society toward pluralist party politics.

Khomeini, hoping to purify Iran by isolating it, banned satellite dishes, Western music, and alcohol—a good example of a deliberate move up the left side of the J curve. He used the U.S. embassy siege and the Iran-Iraq War to marginalize and destroy rivals in the clergy, as well as the Communists and liberal revolutionaries. To prevent the revolution from further dividing on itself, it became necessary to find a unifying enemy. Saddam certainly did his part to bring together diverse groups of Iranians toward a single purpose. America provided another.

But another important effect of Iran's revolution was to mitigate the antagonism Iranians felt toward the West. With the expulsion of Western influence from the country, Iranians had a new authority to blame for their dissatisfaction: Iran's own revolutionary leadership. In order to deflect criticism and to maintain the tension with the West on which much of the revolution's moral authority was based, the conservative government improvised new ways to demonize the West in general and the United States in particular. In addition, Iran found itself weakened after its war with Iraq, and it needed to reestablish its place at the vanguard of the Islamist movement. Wahhabis from rival Saudi Arabia claimed victory for the expulsion of the Soviets from Afghanistan and had far more money to spend than devastated Iran on the construction of Islamic schools and hospitals throughout the Muslim world.

Khomeini's February 1989 *fatwa,* or religious decree, against the life of Salman Rushdie, author of *The Satanic Verses,* helped provide Iran with what it needed: a battle cry with which to reenergize support for the Islamic revolution. "I ask all Muslims of the world to rapidly execute the author and publishers of the book, anywhere in the world, so that no one will again dare to offend the sacred values of Muslims," Khomeini said, promising paradise for the executioner and a $2.5 million reward for his family.

On June 3, 1989, Khomeini died and Ali Khamenei replaced him as Iran's supreme leader. To protect the integrity of the revolution following Khomeini's death, Iran's senior clerics maintained tight control of Iran's political process, universities, and public gatherings. With the parliamentary elections of 1992, the split within Iran's ruling clerical class produced rival factions devoted to his successor, Khamenei, or to the more pragmatic Ali Akbar Hashemi Rafsanjani. Hard-liners, fearing they might be unable to establish their authority without Khomeini's mandate, used the Guardian Council, a constitutionally created body of unelected conservative officials, to disqualify candidates whose ideas were judged insufficiently Islamic.

Rafsanjani was first elected president in 1989, but enjoyed virtually none of the independent decision-making power reserved by the constitution for Iran's supreme spiritual leader and a group of religious scholars appointed by him. What success Rafsanjani did enjoy came from splits in the conservative leadership in the aftermath of Khomeini's death. These splits illustrate the difficulties of maintaining stability through isolation when there is a political transition. Leadership rivalries open doors that reveal aspects of the governing process that a unified leadership hides from the public. These rivalries undermine the illusion of leadership infallibility that one-party systems work hard to maintain. They reduce the public's confidence in those in whom they have tacitly invested their trust—or at least given their acquiescence.

Over time, however, as the social restrictions of Iran's conservatives became more and more unpopular, reformers began to gain public support and greater influence in the Majlis, Iran's parliament. In 1997, Mohammed Khatami won the presidency on a platform that emphasized rule of law (as opposed to clerics) and the restoration of civil society at the expense of religious conservatives. Many Iranian women responded to the new political climate by pushing their headscarves further back on their heads to reveal more of the hair Islamic authorities had been trying to keep covered for a decade and a half. Measures designed to promote a freer press were introduced.

But, over Khatami's eight years as president, the clerical establishment thwarted his most ambitious attempts to open Iran to global markets and the West and to relax religious control of the social and political life of the country. Conservatives have used the leverage given them by Iran's constitution to disqualify reformist candidates from election ballots, to close newspapers, to control judges, to declare reformist laws unconstitutional, and to arrest and otherwise intimidate would-be opposition figures. Iran's most conservative leaders see themselves as the defenders of a pure Islamic, antimodernist, anti-Western revolution. They see the presence of any Western influence in Iran as a corruption of the country's ancient culture and Islamic values. They will not compromise their vision, certainly not with Americans or Europeans—nor with Iranians who have a different vision of Iran's place in the twenty-first-century world.

The populist appeal of the country's newest president serves the conservatives' purposes. Mahmoud Ahmadinejad has been harshly critical of attempts to improve relations with the West and has expressed defiance toward U.S. and European attempts to negotiate away Iran's nuclear program. He is also likely to roll back many of his predecessor's social reforms. Most important, with his victory, the president of Iran can no longer be considered an opposition figure. Conservatives now control virtually every aspect of Iran's governance.

Iran Now

When the Shah left his country a quarter century ago, there were 30 million people in Iran. Today, there are around 70 million—nearly 70 percent of them under the age of twenty-four. As Iran's population has grown, its economy has been steadily shrinking. Iran's real per capita income is a third of what it was in 1978. Before the revolution, Iran pumped 6 million barrels of oil a day. In 2004, it pumped 4 million. The once-comfortable middle class is now trapped between high inflation and stagnant wage growth. To maintain current levels of employment, Iran needs to create 800,000 to 1 million jobs a year; it's not coming anywhere close. Four hundred thousand jobs were created in 2000, and that was a good year. With a poor regulatory environment for attracting foreign direct investment, a corrupt business climate, and a rusting manufacturing sector, it's hard to see how Iran will soon emerge from its economic lethargy.[5]

As a result, there is a hunger for change inside Iran. In a poll published in May 2002 in *Noruz,* then Iran's leading reformist daily newspaper, 6.2 percent declared themselves satisfied with the status quo in Iran, 49 percent opted for "reform," while 45 percent preferred "fundamental change." * The answer, of course, would be to pursue ambitious economic reform, but the current conservative government in Tehran—buoyed by revenue from oil exports—isn't interested. They hold onto effective political control the way conservative governments in the region have done it from time immemorial: political patronage. They use the levers of crony capitalism to steer money toward key constituents, the security services, and the opinion-makers in key conservative groups. They also fix elections. The Guardian Council banned hundreds of reformist candidates from running in the February 2004 election for the Majlis, ensuring a sweeping conservative victory.

Will the people of Iran accept or reject this state of affairs? Before the 2005 presidential election, they seemed more likely to ignore it. Voter turnout for the 2004 parliamentary elections was 51 percent, the lowest in any election since the revolution and down from 67 percent in 2000. In Tehran, less than a third of eligible voters cast ballots. Disillusioned with the failures of the Khatami government to bring real change and with Iran's isolation from the outside world, the country's sometimes restive youth seemed, for the moment, to have simply withdrawn from politics.

But the two rounds of the 2005 presidential election seemed to reenergize many voters. First-round turnout was a surprising 63 percent. Ahmadinejad won a landslide victory in second-round balloting with 60 percent turnout. While indifference remained strong on the cultural and international issues that dominated Khatami's failed reform efforts, Ahmadinejad's success can largely be attributed to rising anger over corruption and clerical mismanagement.

Still, the mullahs remain confident they can ride out any domestic storm caused by popular resentment of their actions. After all, they reason, the Islamic Republic survived a horrific war with Saddam Hussein, economic sanctions, the transition that followed the death of Ayatollah Khomeini,

---

* *Noruz* has since been closed by the government. Its publisher, Mohsen Mirdamadi, has been banned from publishing, jailed, and badly beaten by Islamic vigilantes following his release.

student unrest, international isolation, two American wars just across Iran's borders, and Mohammed Khatami. What's to prevent them from keeping Iran isolated and from ruling indefinitely? And even if Ahmadinejad won what was essentially a protest vote, Iran's new president has professed his loyalty to Iran's supreme leader.

Policy

Largely because of windfall revenues from 2005's historically high oil and gas prices, the hard-liners have room to operate. The added inflow of cash could allow Iran's leaders to pursue reform, if they were so inclined. In October 2004, the head of Iran's parliamentary committee on energy said he expected that Iran would earn $100 billion in oil revenue, money that could be spent, he said, to "improve infrastructure and social services significantly." The result, he continued, meant that "Iran could be turned into the paradise of the Middle East in view of the growing oil income."[6] They could use the extra money to invigorate Iranian entrepreneurship and to add social safety-net protections to absorb the shock of transition away from the crony capitalism that discourages investment from abroad toward a more open commercial climate. In other words, they could use the extra money to begin a deliberate move down the J curve from a protectionist economic system to one more open to global market forces with substantial foreign cash reserves to absorb the shock of social dislocation. They could afford the move down the left side, because oil revenues have lifted the entire curve. Therefore, even the depths of the J curve are more stable than they were before the high price of oil brought in all the extra money.

With its 70 million people, Iran enjoys an ample supply of both skilled and unskilled labor. The regime could profit from its generous cash reserves, proximity to the markets of Europe, South Asia, the Persian Gulf, and the emerging markets of Central Asia, potential investors among the wealthy Iranian diaspora, and a well-educated elite familiar with Western business practices to revitalize Iran.[7] The country is thus well positioned for a managed transition along the J curve from left to right, if that were the goal of Iran's conservative elite. Which it isn't.

Instead, Iran's ruling elite has used the added oil revenue to make its repressive governance more palatable to would-be reformers who might challenge its control of the country and to take a tougher line with the United States and Europe on the development of its nuclear program. Iran can afford to talk tough with the United States and European Union, because Iran's oil and gas are more valuable for the world than ever, and because Iran's government has money with which to prop up its economy in the short term and to minimize the effects of international sanctions on Iran's labor force without undertaking real reform.

In fact, Iran's theocrats have moved resolutely to reinforce their country's isolation. Foreign reserves estimated at $45 billion have convinced the conservative-dominated Majlis they can afford to overturn reformist laws—like the 2002 Foreign Investment Protection and Promotion Act—designed to bring foreign investment to Iran. In 2004, Revolutionary Guards shut down the newly opened Imam Khomeini International Airport and tore up the contract of the Turkish-led consortium that financed it. Why? Conservative politicians claimed it was "an affront to Iran's dignity" to accept foreign ownership of an Iranian airport. Some have suggested the Revolutionary Guards wanted the airport contract for one of their own companies and to embarrass the reformist transportation minister responsible for the deal.[8] In the end, the motives don't matter. The net effect is to discourage foreign investment—and therefore foreign influence—in Iran.

The determined move back up the left side of the curve by Iran's conservatives does not mean the country is reaching the same level of isolation as North Korea or Cuba. Civil society remains strong despite the government's attempt to intimidate it or to shut it down. Iranians still enjoy access to Western ideas and commerce that North Koreans and Cubans simply don't have. As mayor of Tehran, Ahmadinejad tore down billboards featuring British footballer David Beckham. As president, he has banned Western music from state-run television and radio and imposed fines on female pedestrians whose ankles are visible. But there's little he can do to undermine demand among Iranian youth for a more modern, outward-looking culture.

In the meantime, Washington's conflicts with Tehran continue to grow. There are profound differences between the two governments over Israel's right to exist. Iran has supplied money and weapons to the Lebanese Shiite militia Hezbollah, which has attacked Israeli military and civilian targets in southern Lebanon and northern Israel. Iran has given financial backing, political and, perhaps, military support to the Palestinian movements Hamas and Islamic Jihad.*

Iran's leaders promote unrest among the Shia of Iraq, maintain some cooperation with known Qaeda operatives,[9] and, most troublingly for the United States, seek more aggressively than ever a nuclear-weapons capability that is popular with all segments of Iranian society.

Since 1980, it has been U.S. policy to isolate Iran and to try to discredit its government in the eyes of the world and of its own people. This approach doesn't work for three reasons: the Europeans, Chinese, Japanese, and Russians don't support the isolation; Iran's rulers use sanctions as an opportunity to blame the United States for Iran's unemployment and social unrest; and, most important, the sanctions reinforce the isolation from the outside world on which the continued authority of Iran's conservatives depends. Millions of Iranians want U.S. investment and better relations with the United States. It is worth remembering that 70 percent of Iran's population was born after the revolution. The crimes against Iran committed by the American-backed Shah—to say nothing of the CIA-led ouster of Mossadegh—are, for most young Iranians, a subject taught in history classes by conservatives whose repressive attitudes they resent.

Here as elsewhere, American policy should be predicated on finding ways to open a closed society to the world. The power of Iran's conservatives depends on their ability to shut out the forces of globalization. That's why, a quarter-century later, Iran's revolutionary constitution still bans virtually all foreign investment. Iran's suspicion of outsiders is not an invention of the mullahs. Iran *was* manipulated and exploited by outsiders—particularly European and American governments—for much of the twentieth century. British Petroleum reportedly treated Iran as one big oil field whose workers deserved no better than to live in miserable conditions during the period of BP's domination of Iran's oil industry.[10] Washington treated Iran as a pawn on the Cold War chessboard, stage-managing the toppling of Mossadegh and supporting the Shah through twenty-five years of domestic repression. But Iran's young people want jobs and a vibrant

---

* Iran even refuses to allow its Olympic athletes to compete against Israelis. In 2006, Ahmadinejad argued publicly that the Holocaust was a "myth." Following the controversy over the publication in Denmark of cartoons depicting the prophet Mohammed, Iran's president launched a contest in Iran for cartoon images of the Holocaust.

economy. They want access to Western culture, even as they reinvent their own. U.S.-enforced isolation pushes this new generation of Iranians back into the corner in which the nation's conservatives would like to keep them. And the isolation reinforces the conservatives' xenophobic message: the West hates you and is working to undermine your dignity and your hopes for the future of Iran.

During the Clinton years, an important opportunity to remake the U.S.-Iranian relationship was lost. Following the election of the would-be reformer Khatami in 1997, President Clinton tried to capitalize on Iran's potential value as a source of modernity in the Middle East and as a possible strategic partner on the eastern flank of the Arab world. Clinton took some small steps toward a kind of rapprochement with Tehran, referring to Iran publicly as "a great civilization" and arguing that, under certain conditions, diplomatic relations could be restored. In 1999, Clinton acknowledged that the U.S.-Iranian relationship did not begin with the taking of American hostages in 1979 and that the West shared responsibility for the poisoned relationship. "Iran, because of its enormous geopolitical importance over time," he said, "has been the subject of quite a lot of abuse from various Western nations." The Clinton administration eased sanctions slightly, allowing Iran to import food and to export carpets, caviar, and pistachios.[11] But the opening ultimately failed to yield results.

Political rhetoric and symbolic gestures couldn't fill the gap between America and Iran reinforced by earlier Clinton administration failures. In 1995, one of Iran's most consistent and venerable pragmatists, then President Rafsanjani,* tried to open commerce between the United States and Iran. Believing the key to Iran's future prosperity lay in participation in the global economy, Rafsanjani nodded his approval of a multibillion-dollar deal with Conoco, an American oil company, to develop some of Iran's oil and gas fields. Warren Christopher, then U.S. secretary of state, found out about the pending deal and, reportedly angered that he had not been included in negotiations and embarrassed that his former law firm was representing Conoco, made known his opposition to the agreement. Clinton then scotched the deal, and an opportunity was missed to strengthen the arguments of Iran's pragmatists that the way forward for Iran was in better relations with the West. Rafsanjani later told ABC News

---

* It was Rafsanjani that Ahmadinejad soundly defeated in the 2005 presidential election.

that the deal should have been seen as "a message" that, whether or not they enjoyed normalized diplomatic relations, the two countries could and should engage in mutually profitable commerce. The message, he complained, "was not correctly understood." [12]

On the other hand, it's possible that America's political culture made it impossible to see past the desire to punish Iran for past wrongs against U.S. interests toward a policy that redressed those wrongs by changing the patterns that produced them. It is true that, to protest U.S. cooperation with the Shah, Iranian radicals took Americans hostage and humiliated the United States for more than a year. In Beirut in 1983, Shiite extremists with links to Iran killed more than 300 people, many of them Americans, in a pair of bombings. Iran was reportedly behind the hostage-taking of several Americans in Lebanon during the 1980s. Iran still supports militant groups that target Israel.

But the goal of American policy should be to drive a wedge between Iran's ruling conservatives and everyone else in Iran. Punishing the entire country is a poor way to achieve that goal; it drives average Iranians toward conservatives who insist the "Great Satan" America is the source of all Iran's problems. The mullahs hope to discredit Iran's reformers, to argue that they offer nothing but opportunities for outsiders to steal Iran's wealth and to undermine its dignity. President Clinton had real opportunities to strengthen reform in Iran—and he missed them.

George W. Bush continued the failed policy after some early attempts at reengagement. Before the September 11 terrorist attacks, prominent Bush administration officials argued that sanctions against Iran should be eased, or even removed. In August of 2001, then National Security Advisor Condoleezza Rice lobbied Congress (unsuccessfully) to reduce the Iran-Libya Sanctions Act, a 1996 law that required the United States to impose sanctions on foreign companies that invest more than $20 million a year in Iranian oil or gas development. As CEO of Halliburton, Dick Cheney lobbied then President Clinton to ease sanctions on Iran. An April 2001 report by an energy task force headed by Vice President Cheney noted that UN sanctions on Iraq and U.S. restrictions on energy investment in Iran and Libya "affect some of the most important existing and prospective petroleum producing countries in the world. . . . The [Bush] administration will initiate a comprehensive sanctions review and seek to engage the Congress in a partnership for sanctions reform." Whatever the task force's motives, investment in Iran might have politically strengthened Iran's reformers. But after September 11, 2001, Bush administration officials closed the door.

Just before Bush's 2002 State of the Union speech—in which the president first introduced the phrase "axis of evil" and included Iran in its ranks—a boatload of weapons intended for Palestinian militants with Iranian backing was seized by Israel. Fearing President Khatami's domestic standing might be strengthened at the expense of the mullahs, it's conceivable that conservative forces in Iran's security services deliberately dispatched the weapons knowing they would be seized, precisely in order to provoke the Bush administration. In any case, the event was a disaster for Iran's reformers. Bush responded by demonizing Iran, and Tehran's conservatives went on the attack, calling Iranian reformers dupes of the West who would naïvely open the country to foreign domination. Just as Castro scuttled attempts to warm U.S.-Cuban relations with a provocative act, Iran's theocrats demonstrated their determination to poison Iran's relations with Washington. Just as Clinton responded by reinforcing the Helms-Burton Act, Bush gave the mullahs precisely what they wanted: an opportunity to rally Iranians away from better relations with the West.

How should the United States craft policy toward Iran? U.S. policymakers should seek out opportunities for "selective engagement" with Iran and stronger ties with Iran's reformers. Washington should, of course, hold a firm line on Iran's nuclear program, working with Europeans, Arabs, Russia, and China to reduce incentives for Iranian proliferation. But the U.S. absence from European-led multilateral talks with Iran only provides conservatives more room to isolate themselves, and so is a mistake. Indeed, many conservatives in Iran strongly prefer a hard-line policy from Washington—and perhaps even a limited military strike against Iran's nuclear facilities—to any rapprochement with their useful enemy. The crisis a military strike would provoke would only help Iran's conservatives close down domestic institutions that remain relatively open to outside influence.

It is important to recognize that Iran is serious about obtaining nuclear weapons. Iranians believe that if they had possessed nuclear weapons in 1980, they would have been spared the horrific eight-year war with Saddam. In fact, it would be easier to destabilize Iran's conservative government than to persuade *any* Iranian government to renounce a nuclear-weapons capability.* U.S. policy on Iran is somewhat contradictory: a U.S.-led military strike is one of the few things that would increase the legitimacy of Iran's existing regime. A strike on Iran's nuclear facilities would rally the Iranian people around their government, however much many Iranians resent their leaders. Such a strike would therefore increase the existing regime's reserves of political capital. On the other hand, efforts to destabilize the conservatives are much more likely to be successful here than in a country perched higher on the left side of the J curve. The mullahs continue to face strong internal opposition. It's much easier to send and receive information into and out of Iran. Yet, even if ordinary Iranians rose up tomorrow and accomplished full regime change from within, and men like Rafsanjani or even Khatami were given full authority over Iran's foreign and domestic policy, the problem of persuading Iran to forego its nuclear-weapons program would continue.

The proliferation of nuclear weapons is one of the central drivers of instability in the twenty-first century. That is one important reason Iran is included in this book. Those states that remain on the left side of the J curve and have, or may soon have, nuclear weapons pose the gravest threat to successful navigation of the J curve's least stable segment. A nuclear state that descends into chaos may send nuclear equipment and technology in all directions. Because the world can't afford such a catastrophe, the United States and its allies can't simply accept another potentially unstable nuclearized state.

Yet, preventing Iran from enriching uranium and making bombs will not be as simple as Israel's destruction of the Iraqi plant at Osirak in 1981. Iran's nuclear facilities are spread widely across the country. Some of them are housed deep underground, possibly beyond the capacity of U.S. or Israeli warplanes to destroy. Any such attack might provoke military retaliation against Israel. That said, even if a strike can't destroy Iran's nuclear capability, it might well set it back four or five years. Such a strike—and the threat of future strikes—would empower Iran's conservatives in the short

---

* Even persuading a reformist Iranian government to improve relations with Israel and to stop funding groups like Hezbollah and Hamas wouldn't be easy. The religious conservatives now ruling the country are not the only Iranians contemptuous of Israel and of U.S. support for the Israeli government.

term. But they might ultimately persuade Iran's reformers that nuclear weapons, however popular, are not worth the costs. That change in the political dynamic could offer hope that Iran can make its transition through the J curve before its nuclear program reaches maturity.

The United States spent much of the two years after the September 11 terrorist attacks battling two of Iran's mortal enemies—Saddam Hussein's Iraq and the Taliban's Afghanistan—and yet the coordination with Iran over this period was virtually nil. Nor has there been enough meaningful U.S.-Iranian cooperation since. That needs to change, even if Iran develops nuclear weapons.

Despite their ideological differences and the often-hostile rhetoric between the two governments, Iran and the United States have a number of common interests. While Washington and Tehran envision different outcomes for the new Iraq, both have good reason to support the development of a stable Iraq capable of governing its own territory. Iran considers a functioning Shiite-dominated Iraq a potential ally in a Sunni-dominated region, and a stable democratic Iraq substantially frees the United States from responsibility for the new government's security. If Iraq and Afghanistan descend into chaos, these failed states might well incubate terrorist threats, refugee flows, organized crime, and drug trafficking that undermine both U.S. and Iranian interests.

In the long term, Washington and Tehran could also profit from the development of more durable bilateral trade ties. The United States could play a positive role in helping to develop the Iranian energy industry by seizing the opportunity that was missed with the aborted Conoco deal. Iran needs the investment, and when the United States and Iran are prepared to make deals, both Iranian reformers and American business will benefit.

There will one day be regime change in Iran, and the energy that produces it will come from within Iranian society. Unlike many states in the world (and almost all in the region), a regime change in Iran is likely to produce a government more in tune with the West in general and the United States in particular. Iranians may try to keep their nuclear weapons in any case, if only to defend themselves from future aggression from Iraq or Israel. But a new Iran might one day decide it's in its interest to have a more pragmatic relationship with all its neighbors.

Ultimately, the greatest threat to Iran's mullahs does not come from Washington. It comes from the millions of un- and underemployed Iranian young people. The conservative government is deeply unpopular in Iran, but it has succeeded in intimidating its opposition, stealing what it cannot earn democratically, and using Washington's shortsighted policy of isolation to further its own ends. Iran will one day begin another move down the left side of the J curve toward less stability in the short run and greater openness in the longer run. It may take a decade. It may take longer, but the slide is inevitable. American policy should be designed to take advantage of every opportunity to help Iranians to pry open their own society and to manage the difficult transition toward a future of Iranian participation in global politics and markets.

SAUDI ARABIA

If oil revenue allows the conservatives of Iran to postpone or ignore the inevitable opening of Iran's society and economy to the outside world, oil income serves the ruling elite of Saudi Arabia even more generously. As in Iran, Saudi oil income buys the services of security police, flows through patronage networks that ensure the loyalty and dependence of local leaders, creates temporary make-work projects to appease the angry unemployed, and buys off the regime's critics.

Countries *can* sometimes buy their way out of trouble, and high oil prices will allow the Saudis to spend away their problems a while longer. But Saudi royals, like the clerics of Iran, can't close out the modern world forever. Over the long term, the threat of Saudi instability makes the kingdom one of the world's greatest political risks—defined as the probability of eventual upheaval multiplied by the magnitude of its likely impact on international security and the global economy. For the moment, though, Saudi Arabia is more stable than is commonly understood. Headlines about attacks on Saudis, foreigners, and oil infrastructure, unrest among Saudi Shia, and dissension within the royal family are deceptive, because they tell us only about shocks to the system. But again, shocks alone do not cause instability. It's important to look closely at how well a closed system is equipped to withstand shocks. Up to now, violence in Saudi Arabia has damaged little more than the kingdom's reputation. But there are internal contradictions in Saudi politics and society that have virtually no chance of being resolved without fundamental change. One day, these shocks to the system will damage more than the Saudi façade: they will destabilize the kingdom's foundation.

The Saudi royal family has purchased protection for its anachronistic political system by ceding to radical Muslim clerics the chance to educate Saudi youth as they choose and to preach whatever they want in the kingdom's mosques. In return, the clerics are expected to accept the legitimacy of the monarchy. Yet, Saudi Arabia's evolving relationship with the outside world leads each side to take actions that threaten the other. The September 11 terrorist attacks, carried out largely by Saudi citizens and directed by the son of a well-connected Saudi family, Osama bin Laden, dramatically demonstrated the fault lines in Saudi society. The 9/11 attacks are only the most spectacular of a series of confrontations that have tested the two sides' willingness to honor the deal that binds Saudi society. When that deal is finally broken, the kingdom's slide into instability could be sharp, chaotic, and violent. If so, the earthquake will be felt all over the world.

Why Saudi Arabia Matters

Soaring petroleum prices underline the vital importance of Saudi oil for the global economy. It's not simply that the Saudis export more oil than any other producer; they also have more reserves. In fact, more than a quarter of the world's known oil reserves lies beneath Saudi Arabia.[13] That gives the Saudi royals important influence in world oil markets and, therefore, in the global economy.

Reserves, of course, have to be developed. More immediate help for world oil supply comes from Saudi spare capacity, the oil that the Saudis could begin selling on short notice. Today's global oil market is exceptionally tight. There is a serious danger that supply won't be able to keep pace with demand, particularly if terrorism disrupts oil supply in Saudi Arabia or Iraq; if political turmoil in Nigeria, Venezuela, or the Caucasus threatens production; if Iranian oil is pulled from global markets; and if demand in China and India continues to rise at its current pace. Saudi spare capacity provides the best hope that supply can keep pace with sharp rises in demand—and with enough breathing room that prices will remain low enough for continued global economic growth.

That spare global capacity, over which the Saudis now enjoy a near-monopoly, has become more precious over time. In 1985, the Organization of the Petroleum Exporting Countries (OPEC)—within which Saudi Arabia has, by far, the most oil—held about 15 million barrels a day of spare capacity, about 25 percent of world demand at the time. The cartel could quickly raise the level of output to absorb the shocks of several global political or economic disruptions at once. In 1990, OPEC still had about 5.5 million barrels a day of spare capacity, or about 8 percent of world demand. Today's spare capacity of about 2 million barrels a day equals less than 3 percent of global demand, almost all of it controlled by the Saudi royal family.[14]

Jihadis know this too. Hoping to discourage foreign influence and investment in the kingdom, Saudi terrorists have kidnapped and killed foreigners living and working there. Tens of thousands of Westerners work in Saudi Arabia, and analysts have warned that Saudi militants could compromise their government's ability to do business with the West.* Given the tightness of the world oil market and Saudi Arabia's position as the world's only viable swing producer, the recent flight of expatriate oil workers from the kingdom tells some observers that the coal mine canary has gone quiet. If the foreign technicians and engineers, on whom the Saudis depend for the operation and maintenance of foreign-made machinery, leave Saudi Arabia, for how long can the Saudis continue to produce oil at the needed rate? Without secure long-term operation of the oil industry, how will the Saudi royals continue to finance their rule? What happens if they can't?

A revolution in Saudi Arabia led by religious radicals would send political shockwaves across the Muslim world. While Iran's neighbors saw its 1979 Shiite revolution as a threat to Sunni dominance in the region, the citizens of states neighboring Saudi Arabia might sooner promote a Saudi

---

* In North Korea, it is the government that keeps foreigners out. Cuba must, to some limited extent, sell itself as a tourist destination to survive, but there too the government limits the presence of foreigners. In Saudi Arabia, the forces most hostile to the presence of foreigners are the religious conservatives with whom the government has its Faustian deal. The Saudi royals don't want an unlimited number of foreigners bringing Western ideas of governance and individual freedom into the country, but Saudi prosperity is dependent on the presence of foreigners to such an extent that the kingdom must welcome a significant number of them.

revolution than block it. Only 10 percent of the world's Muslims are Shiite; more than 85 percent are Sunni. The dearest dream of Al Qaeda and other jihadi groups is radical fundamentalist control of Saudi Arabia and the expulsion of all foreign influence from the land of Mecca and Medina, Islam's holiest cities. Islamist radicals could use Saudi oil, the revenue that comes with it, and the threat to withhold it to undermine the economic security of every country in the developed world.

Some History

Saudi Arabia is unusual among countries in the region—and among developing countries generally—in that it was never colonized. Prior to the discovery of oil in the 1930s, the peninsula was considered a desolate area of little interest for those who might have sought to control it. There were nineteenth-century military garrisons of the Ottoman Empire there, but no single authority dominated the area until the Saud family unified most of it in the early twentieth century.

Because Saudi Arabia was never the colonial possession of a foreign power, there are none of the usual patterns of development for a country under foreign domination: a colonial bureaucracy, a sophisticated system of education, or an educated class trained to staff the institutions of colonial rule. Nor was there an anticolonial nationalist movement organized around the principle of evicting an imperial overlord. Before the turn of the twentieth century, the peninsula was peopled by hundreds of tribes and clans with no loyalties beyond their small groups. Violent rivalries within and among tribes were the order of the day, and there was no central authority to arbitrate them.

But the partnership that would eventually unify the peninsula was formed long before the dawn of the twentieth century. The alliance in 1744 of Muhammad bin Saud, a local chieftain from the peninsula's interior, and Muhammad bin Abd al-Wahhab, an Islamic preacher, created a durable partnership that elevated each toward the dominant positions their descendants hold today. The two men laid the foundation for an Islamic kingdom inspired by an earlier golden age of Muslim greatness. The alliance provided an organizing principle for some of the peninsula's still endemic tribal conflict: some tribes and clans became part of the *ikhwan,* or brotherhood, and followed Abd al-Wahhab; others united against this movement. What had been chaotic conflicts of all against all became battles between the *ikhwan* and those who resisted its influence.

At the beginning of the twentieth century, Abd al-Aziz ibn Saud—also known as Ibn Saud—began his conquest of the land that is today Saudi Arabia. Saud sent out members of the *ikhwan* as his emissaries to the various tribal settlements to win their loyalty to him and to a Wahhabi interpretation of Islamic practice.* The combination of Saud's military skill and the brotherhood's single-mindedness of religious purpose established the Kingdom of Saudi Arabia in 1932. By naming the kingdom for his family, Saud established himself and his descendants as the focus of loyalty to the new state.† Wahhabi ideology provided the family its Islamic legitimacy and established religious conformity as the chief virtue for all those that came under the family's sway. In case local tribal leaders weren't impressed with the righteousness and fervor of the Wahhabis who supported his rule, Saud ensured their loyalty by marrying male members of his family to their daughters or by buying them off.

Some of the most ideologically rigid of the *ikhwan* refused allegiance to Saud because they were unhappy with the king's ties to Christian Europe—particularly Britain—and with the sudden introduction into the peninsula of automobiles, telephones, radios, and other challenges to Islamic purity. This tension within the kingdom between the political and religious establishments—the alliance on which the Saudi state was founded—was only the first manifestation of the conflict that has begun to push Saudi Arabia slowly down the left side of the J curve.

Oil was not discovered in large quantities beneath Saudi Arabia until just

---

* Followers of al-Wahhab believed that the practice of Islam must be based only on the first three centuries of Islamic tradition. Their "reform" was essentially an attempt to purge Sunni Islam of all modern influences.

† It is a common feature of societies on the left side of the stability curve that politics is highly personalized. The "cult of personality" is only the most extreme illustration of this idea. In North Korea, Cuba, Saddam's Iraq, and Stalin's Soviet Union, loyalty to the leader himself—rather than to his office or to the nation—becomes a central organizing principle. That Ibn Saud named the country for his family underscores his hopes for eternal control and suggests the danger for Saudi Arabia's future if the royals are delegitimized.

before the outbreak of the Second World War. Once the oil began to produce significant revenue, tension between the royal family's newly affordable taste for European-style modernity and the Wahhabi drive for ascetic purity became a fact of Saudi life. A paradox emerged: the same oil money that allowed the royal family to subjugate the peninsula's various tribes under the banner of Wahhabi principle, also bought the luxurious Western lifestyle to which many of the Saudi royals were increasingly becoming accustomed.

Oil money also helped establish a burgeoning state bureaucracy. Money was spent on education in areas where literacy was virtually nonexistent and on the development of industrial infrastructure. A small working class emerged in new Saudi cities and in oil-producing areas. But, however more aware average Saudis became of the world around them, conformity to Wahhabi principle ensured that royal legitimacy was not publicly questioned and that Islam remained the dominant force for national unity and identity.

From the founding of the kingdom, Islam became the basis of the state and the law. The Koran is the Saudi constitution. *Sharia,* Islamic law, is the kingdom's established code of personal and public behavior. The responsibility of Saudi Arabia's kings is to guarantee the observance of Islamic principles. There are no officially recognized political parties in Saudi Arabia; indeed, there is no officially sanctioned means of political expression outside the context of Islam. Clergy control key political and judicial institutions. The Commission for the Promotion of Virtue and the Prevention of Vice (CPVPV) polices public conduct and female modesty.

The Royal Family

Members of the Saud family played key roles in the tribal politics of the northern interior of the peninsula from the eighteenth century onward. Originally from a village north of Riyadh, the family slowly extended its control of territory across the Arabian peninsula. After thirty years of expansion and conquest in the first decades of the twentieth century, Ibn Saud took control of the area around Islam's two holiest cities, Mecca and Medina, in 1925. In 1932, he proclaimed himself king of Saudi Arabia. Since then, the Saudi royal family has institutionalized its control of Saudi foreign and domestic policy by keeping control of key ministries like defense, foreign affairs, and security within the family. Many of the Saudi royals who don't dominate important areas of the central government serve as regional governors, ambassadors, and high-ranking military and security officials.

Keeping every lever of political control in the family is not uncommon in the region, even in Arab states that are not monarchies. Saddam Hussein, as we've seen, relied on family members to staff key government positions. What is uncommon in the Saudi case is the sheer size of the royal family.

Ibn Saud had enough wives and descendants to produce thousands of male family members, all of whom receive government salaries or stipends.* The downside to maintaining such a large royal family is that much of the elite's time is taken up finding appropriate jobs for pushy relatives. The upside is that, because the Saudi royals are a family, they are usually able to keep their disputes within the group. However dysfunctional the family may be, they quickly become an efficient instrument of elite control whenever their rule is threatened. The family speaks with one voice on the subject of oil reserves—and on accusations they aren't honest about how deep they are. To manage the firestorm of criticism that followed the 9/11 attacks, the Saudi royals closed ranks, and, whatever their personal disagreements about what had happened and what should be done in response, divergent interpretations in the media never spilled over into public personality conflicts.†

Family government is hardly the best model for political openness. Consider the issue of royal land grants: Ibn Saud and his successors have granted Saudi land to family members for decades. This land became a source of tremendous wealth after the sharp spike in property prices that followed the economic boom of the mid-1970s. In essence, the royal family allocated itself more and more money, even as Saudi unemployment was rising. As the Saudi elite becomes wealthier, awareness of the enormous—and growing—gap between rich and poor has increased among ordinary Saudis.

---

* Islamic law permits men to have four wives at any one time and to divorce and remarry with few restrictions.

† Following the 9/11 attacks, Crown Prince Abdullah expressed sympathy for the United States and promised to work with President Bush to address the problems of international terrorism. His half-brother, Prince Naif, has publicly argued that, since Muslims would be made to suffer for the attacks, only Israeli intelligence could have masterminded them. But neither prince has publicly criticized the other. Naif speaks mainly in the Arab media, while Abdullah and Prince Bandar comment in the West.

In addition, with the explosion of oil wealth in the 1970s, the involvement of Saudi royals in influence peddling, and the awarding of state construction and weapons-procurement contracts frequently embarrassed senior family members. And while most of the population of Saudi Arabia benefited in one way or another from the oil boom, the spoils were not shared equitably. An infusion of cash into state coffers lifts the kingdom's entire J curve and makes the country more stable. But the inequities of how wealth is distributed in Saudi Arabia—and the royal family's efforts to hide this unfairness—undermine the legitimacy of the monarchy and the family's right to protect Islam's holiest sites.

Oil

In 1973 and 1974, Saudi oil income more than quadrupled. Since that windfall of wealth, oil has provided between 70 and 90 percent of government revenue. There are important structural consequences for a country that pulls such a high percentage of its income from one natural resource. Entrepreneurship remains underdeveloped in Saudi Arabia since few Saudis recognize the need to invent anything new. Wealth is simply pumped out of the ground, poured into barrels, put on ships, and payment is transferred to Saudi banks.

Because the Saudi government earns so much income from oil, it doesn't have to collect taxes from individual Saudis or Saudi businesses. In other words, the Saudi state doesn't depend on its citizens for revenue; the Saudi government is the *provider* of wealth—to some, of course, more than others. The state is the source of employment, health care, welfare, and education. It need not, therefore, respond to political demands from below.

How much wealth are we talking about? In 1965, Saudi Arabia earned about $655 million in oil revenue. By 1973, the number jumped to $4.3 billion. But it was the crisis of 1973–1974 that sent Saudi income through the roof. In 1974, spikes in oil prices brought $22.5 billion into Saudi Arabia. Following the chaos of the Iranian revolution in 1979 and the resulting jump in prices, Saudi oil income hit $70 billion.*

---

* In that sense, Iran's fall down the left side of the J curve made Saudi Arabia more stable— by sending oil prices up and providing the House of Saud with more money to buy off opposition, to create short-term jobs, and to provide ordinary Saudis with better services.

Ordinary Saudis have few means of protesting against the inequitable distribution of all that wealth. Most of the productive work in the kingdom is done by foreign migrant workers on short-term work contracts, who are dependent on private Saudi citizens for their residence permits.* Many high-end jobs are occupied by Americans and Europeans with specialized training in operating the technology in which the royal family invests. Even if the Saudi government were dependent for income on Saudi taxpayers and, therefore, more subject to public pressure, Wahhabi religious authorities would still consider democracy an insidious and unwelcome Western invention. Thus, no one in Saudi society has the political leverage to challenge the official prohibition against political parties, trade unions, and women's organizations that develop naturally in societies in which government depends on tax revenue from a prosperous merchant class.

As a result, Saudi stability is deeply dependent on oil markets. The steep drop in prices in the 1980s led to cuts in government spending and urgent pressure on the underdeveloped private sector to try and produce more jobs for university graduates. With the rebound in oil prices, the royals have been able to withstand most calls for social change. Oil revenue has, for example, made it possible for the state to observe strict Wahhabi prohibitions on basic freedoms for women.†

Purity and Backlash

While Saudi women are still denied important social and political freedoms, they have, over the last two decades, enjoyed an increase in educational opportunity. In 1969, only 12.5 percent of Saudi secondary-school students, 2,000 in total, were female. By 1986, at a time when the falling price of oil was nudging Saudi Arabia down the steep left side of the J curve,

---

* According to Human Rights Watch, "By the government's latest count, in May 2004, there are 8.8 million foreigners in Saudi Arabia—one foreigner for every two Saudi citizens. We know, again from statistics, that the government provided to us in 2003, that foreigners hold 90–95 percent of the jobs in the private sector and comprise 65 percent of the total labor force." http://www.hrw.org/english/docs/2004/07/19/saudia9137.htm.

† At the same time, restrictions on female participation create a challenge for Islamic purity: to fill the workplace vacuum created by restrictions on women, foreign ideas about women's rights enter the kingdom with the imported workers.

more than 42 percent of those students were girls—85,000 of nearly 200,000 students—and half the kingdom's 15,000 university graduates were women. Pressure on the Saudi establishment to enable an entrepreneurial class allowed women to enter the Saudi workforce for the first time. Once oil prices and government revenue again began to rise, however, the economic pressure to give women greater freedoms eased—even as the expectations for change were rising among newly educated Saudi women.[15]

The controversy surrounding the role of women in Saudi politics and the economy leapt onto the front pages of international newspapers in 1991 when forty-seven Saudi women climbed into the cars they weren't supposed to know how to operate and drove directly into the center of Riyadh. Wahhabi authorities condemned the women as "prostitutes." The Saudi government's first response was to placate religious conservatives by punishing the women for "insulting Islam": The state introduced restrictions on women's travel abroad. Those who were teachers were fired. But the government also recognized that the kingdom had taken a black eye in the Western media. It responded publicly by introducing an appointed Shura Council to consult on women's rights.

The Saudi royals have been confronted, of course, with political challenges far more dangerous than public demonstrations that women had secretly learned to drive. Protests from radical Wahhabis have ranged from the takeover of the Holy Mosque of Mecca in 1979 to fiery sermons condemning the presence of U.S. troops in Saudi Arabia in 1991, to domestic terror attacks linked to Al Qaeda. In short, Islam has provided legitimacy for the House of Saud, but it has also created the ideological foundation for opposition to their rule.

The Saudi royals have withstood many political shocks over the decades, some as violent as they were unexpected. The first dangerous confrontation between Wahhabis and the Saudi establishment occurred in November 1979,* when a Saudi student named Juhaiman Utaibi and 250 others seized control of the Mecca mosque, one of Islam's most sacred sites, and held it for two weeks. Juhaiman condemned the ruling family as apostate, claiming that it did not follow the Koran and the Sunna,† and accused the royals of forming an alliance with Western Christians. In the violence that followed,

---

* The same month Shiite radicals seized fifty-two American hostages in Tehran.

† The Sunna are the collected sayings of the prophet Mohammed.

102 militants and 127 Saudi troops were killed. Only with the help of French commandos were the Saudis able to evict the radical students. The royal family requested a special *fatwa* from the *ulama* in order to obtain permission for non-Muslim Special Forces to enter the mosque and to use force inside the Holy Site. It was after this incident that the Saud family began making major concessions to the clerics as a reward for their support during the crisis.

When the Iraqi army invaded and occupied Kuwait in 1990, Saudi Arabia was forced to choose between accepting American boots on sacred Saudi soil and taking its chances that Saddam Hussein wouldn't round off his conquest of Kuwait with the seizure of oil-rich areas of eastern Saudi Arabia. The House of Saud chose to welcome the U.S. military, hoping their protectors would capture Saddam's attention, but maintain as low a profile as possible within the kingdom. Wahhabi clerics responded with vitriolic anti-American and anti-Western sermons distributed from local mosques on audiocassettes. The fault line between royals and radical Wahhabis widened further.

Wahhabis have used the Koran itself to challenge the royal family. Chapter 27, verse 43, of the sacred text calls for the just overthrow of all corrupt monarchs. Citing moral and financial corruption within the ruling family, radical clerics have demanded that those who gain wealth illegally, regardless of rank, be punished. Because the royals understand they can't rule Islam's holiest ground without Islamic legitimacy, they have quietly tried to purge those religious authorities who publicly call for their ouster. But they also know the danger of repeating the Shah of Iran's mistake and antagonizing the entire religious establishment. As a practical matter, the royals recognize that charitable fund-raising provides income for some religious authorities. But the money they collect allows these clerics to stay outside the patronage network that creates dependency on the royal family. The royals have created restrictions on charities within the kingdom, but they have been weakly enforced, because religious authorities have influence within the bureaucracy and because many within the royal family itself are sympathetic to the Wahhabis' anti-Western ideology. The restrictions have proven impossible to enforce on Wahhabi charities outside the country.

Over the decades, the U.S.-Saudi relationship has been a focal point of Islamist opposition. The royal family's long-standing informal alliance with Washington manifests itself in Saudi foreign policy and in its oil-supply decisions and pricing policies. U.S. military-industrial companies have sold the Saudis their most advanced weaponry. Inevitably, American military personnel have accompanied the arms into the kingdom as advisors and technicians and brought American culture with them. The most radical of the Wahhabis are deeply offended by the presence of these troops and the Western influence they might have on ordinary Saudis.

The Cold War made Saudi-U.S. cooperation somewhat easier for religious conservatives to accept, since the official atheism of the Soviet Union and the Soviet occupation of Afghanistan were even more offensive to Wahhabi radicals than the influence of Christian America. But Washington's support for the Saudi monarchy has always been part of a trade-off for the royals: America protected the Saudis from Arab nationalists, Iranian revolutionaries, and Saddam Hussein in exchange for reasonably priced oil, the maintenance of a bulwark against Soviet expansion into the Persian Gulf, and moderation in Arab opposition to the existence of Israel.

Beginning in 1980, Saudi youth took up arms provided by Washington to help the Afghan *mujahedeen* fight a decade-long guerilla war that forced the defeated Soviets to retreat in 1990. But in the process, the conflict radicalized thousands of Saudi young men, trained them to fight, encouraged them that religious faith could conquer superpowers, and set them against both Americans and the Saudi royals who consorted with them. Osama bin Laden was a highly successful recruiter of Saudis in support of Afghan resistance. From their numbers, he built Al Qaeda, radicalized its adherents against Jews and Christians, and trained them for terrorism.

The investigations that followed the September 11 terrorist attacks in New York and Washington make clear that much of the funding that has fueled the growth of Al Qaeda came from Saudi charities. In response to pressure from Washington, the Saudi government has further tightened its regulation of Islamic charities operating in the kingdom. Fundamentalist Wahhabis argue these restrictions prove the Saudi royals take orders from the White House.

The House of Saud finds itself in an increasingly precarious position: they hope to placate antimodernist religious conservatives devoted to a version of Islam rooted in the fourteenth century while bringing Saudi society more into harmony with the globalizing movement of the twenty-first century. In that respect, Saudi royals are caught in a dilemma similar to the one Soviet leader Mikhail Gorbachev faced in the late 1980s: how do you keep your balance with one foot in each of two boats headed in opposite directions? Before the decisive moment when the boats have moved too far apart for the regime to maintain its balance, the leadership must choose between the two sides or lose influence over both. In the meantime, Saudi Arabia is slowly sliding down the left side of the J curve.

Saudi Arabia Now

In the short term, a takeover of the country by Wahhabi radicals is highly unlikely, and a near-term terrorist attack on the Saudi oil industry large enough to seriously undermine the government's ability to function is unrealistic. There have been attacks on foreigners in the kingdom, attacks that have pushed some companies to pull out significant numbers of their workers. But the concern that Saudi oil production is vulnerable to attacks on infrastructure is exaggerated.

A number of expatriates have left Saudi Arabia, but Saudi Aramco—the national oil company—doesn't need them in order to maintain current levels of production. Plenty of Arab workers with world-class engineering skills already fill Aramco's technical staff. Even if the outflow of foreigners intensifies, it is unlikely to affect short-term output. Just as there are enough technically qualified personnel to ensure steady Saudi oil production, there are redundancies in the country's oil transport infrastructure. There is plenty of spare pipeline capacity to allow Saudi engineers to bypass damage to one pipeline or pipeline group without missing a beat in output. Terrorists are left instead to try to attack extremely well-guarded bottlenecks. According to one advisor to the Saudi royals, "At any one time, there are up to 30,000 guards protecting the Kingdom's oil infrastructure, while high-technology surveillance and aircraft patrols are common at the most important facilities and anti-aircraft installations defend key locations." [16] Further, to do lasting, large-scale damage to Saudi Arabia's refinery capacity, terrorists would have to hit Abqaiq, the world's largest oil-processing complex. But Abqaiq is simply too large a target to damage with anything short of a hijacked 747 or a missile, an extremely difficult logistical challenge for any terrorist group. Two would-be suicide bombers discovered as much during an attempted assault on Abqaiq in February 2006.

Might the Saudi regime collapse from within? No one recognized the scale of the Iranian crisis of 1978–79 until it was too late. Might Saudi Arabia produce the next Islamic revolution? Not this year. A look at the differences between Iran in 1979 and Saudi Arabia today is instructive. The intelligence services permeate Saudi society more broadly and deeply than the Shah's Savak penetrated Iran in the late 1970s. And, unlike the Shah, the Saudi royal family has largely co-opted the radicals. There is still too much money flowing through traditional tribal patronage networks, buying loyalty where it isn't compelled, to quickly dislodge the monarchy. More to the point, the Saudi royals have given control of education and cultural policy to Wahhabi clerics. This "arrangement" frustrates the United States, and may ultimately destabilize the Saudi regime, but it should be noted that, so far, this scheme has worked to reinforce Saudi stability. In Tehran in the 1970s, the Shah actively alienated Iran's mullahs with modernist social and political policies and a determined secularism. The Saudis recognize the Shah's mistake. The freedom and influence Saudi royals give Saudi clerics continue to keep challenges to the monarchy at bay.

If oil is only becoming more precious and the royal deal with Wahhabi clerics is still holding, why is the descent toward instability in the kingdom virtually inevitable? Because the population of young people in the country is growing, there are no jobs for them, and their only opportunities to find a place for themselves in today's Saudi Arabia are in schools and mosques run by men well armed with money and influence who are at war with the modern world.

The Longer-Term Threat

There is a demographic disaster coming. With a rising birthrate and virtually no family planning, Saudi Arabia's population has jumped from 7 million in 1980 to more than 27 million in 2006. Because the Saudi economy has never adequately diversified beyond the energy industry, per capita income has fallen and unemployment has risen sharply. At the height of the oil boom in 1980, the kingdom's per capita income was around $21,000. By 2001, this figure had dropped to around $12,200, further widening the gap between the richest and poorest Saudis.[17] Corrected for inflation and exchange-rate changes, the fall is even sharper. Worse still, according to the

U.S. Energy Information Administration, "In 2004, Saudi Arabia earned around $4,564 per person [in oil-export revenues], versus $22,589 in 1980. This 80 percent decline in real per capita oil-export revenues is due in large part to the fact that Saudi Arabia's youth population has nearly tripled since 1980, while oil-export revenues in real terms have fallen by over 40 percent (despite recent increases)."[18] Following a decade of zero growth, GDP grew by only 1.6 percent between 1990 and 2000, while the country's population grew at an annual rate of 2.7 percent.[19] The kingdom now has fewer available resources for many more people.

Today, real unemployment hovers above 20 percent.* An even larger percentage lives below the poverty line. The worsening economic situation is manifesting itself in new and troubling ways. The country's deeply conservative society is facing a rapid and unprecedented rise in crime. Because nearly 60 percent of the Saudi population is under twenty years old, the most severe stresses on the economy have yet to hit the labor market.

As in too many other Muslim states, most young Saudis can only afford the education provided by Wahhabi schools. These schools teach students a fundamentalist view of Islam, but do not prepare them to compete in the global economy or to even begin to understand the world beyond the kingdom's borders. Few Saudi graduates find work to support their families and, given the religious nature of their schooling, they are an easy mark for Islamic radicals who preach hatred of Jews, Christians, and even Shiite Muslims, and urge them to join the armed struggle to return Islam to an imagined golden age of world dominance. Even a nonstate actor like Al Qaeda understands the importance of education. Its version of Islam demands tight control of the education of young people in any state it hopes to influence or dominate. Modern education promotes openness to all the world's civilizing influences and feeds curiosity. That model of intellectual development is anathema to Al Qaeda and its sympathizers, who can only construct the societies they want if strict control of information and ideas is maintained.

---

* The Saudi government claims an unemployment rate of 10 percent. A study published in 2000 by King Abdulaziz University in Jeddah estimated the Saudi unemployment rate at 27 percent. "Saudi Workers in Private Sector Fall Short," *Gulf News,* July 9, 2000. Cited from http://www.cfr.org/publication/5291/more_than_targets_or_markets.html.

The recent exodus of foreign workers from the kingdom exacerbates a serious problem for the Saudi economy: the lack of skill diversification. While there are highly capable Arab engineers to man the oil industry, Saudis are not properly trained to manage the high-skill sectors outside the energy sector. In addition, unskilled workers have long been imported to do the manual labor so many Saudis consider beneath them. Speaking at an energy conference in Washington in December 2003, Saudi Minister of Petroleum and Mineral Resources Ali al-Naimi outlined reform plans for the kingdom's economy and pledged that the government had committed itself "to expand and diversify the Saudi economy and to create new jobs for a growing population." But Saudi ministers have been saying that for years, and progress toward real diversification of the economy and job creation isn't happening nearly quickly enough to create new jobs in new economic sectors. Recent high oil prices and the wealth they produce relieve some of the short-term pressure for labor-market reform. But when prices fall, demand for real solutions will rise again.

As more Saudi young people grow disillusioned with a system they know is rigged in favor of the few, religious radicals are able to leverage youth anger against modern society. The Saudi royals, anxious to quell the frustration that they fear might be aimed at their rule, allow Wahhabis to try to control personal behavior. The religious police—the Commission for the Promotion of Virtue and the Prevention of Vice—exercise extraordinary power.* The most egregious example of their protection of virtue at the expense of civil rights: in March 2002, the religious police blocked schoolgirls fleeing a fire that erupted inside their school. According to eyewitnesses, the religious police forced the girls back into the fire because, in their haste to leave the burning building, many of the girls were not properly dressed to be seen by Muslim men. Fifteen of the girls died inside the school.

In such a society, it's natural to fear that change will not be peaceful.

---

* In fact, Prince Naif, a man not known for rigorous personal piety, is the Wahhabis' most reliable ally within the royal family. Through his control of the religious police, Naif enjoys a political base with the radicals that other members of the family can only envy. Naif's ties to the Wahhabis also illustrate why Saudi Arabia is still stable and not in the danger the Shah of Iran faced in 1979: the ties that bind royals and Wahhabis form some complicated knots.

What's Next?

One of the greatest challenges to the hope that Saudi Arabia can move toward openness without collapsing is the fragmented nature of the Saudi royal family itself. Since King Fahd's death in 2005, the question of how power may eventually be passed to a younger generation of Saudi royals has hung over the royal family.

After King Abdullah, the (arguably) most influential man in Saudi Arabia today is his half-brother, Interior Minister Prince Naif. These two men represent the rivalry within the family, between those who support modernization, reform, and membership in the World Trade Organization and those who would maintain the kingdom's international isolation for the sake of Islamic purity. Abdullah is the face of Saudi Arabia in the West. Naif controls the security police and is an ally of the kingdom's most radical Wahhabis. Abdullah and Naif represent the ideological schizophrenia that obstructs the coherent formulation of policy in Saudi Arabia—and the divide within Saudi society.

The two sides diverge over a vitally important question: should the royal family move to limit the power and influence of Wahhabi clerks? Those who say no believe America, Europe, Israel, and, especially, Shiite Muslims threaten Saudi Islamic purity. They want to permanently close the kingdom to all foreign influence and to push Saudi Arabia to the top of the left side of the J curve.

Prince Naif himself is a firm supporter of jihad against the West. He also controls Saudi funding for the Palestinian *intifada,* which Saudi conservatives consider justified resistance to the encroachment of infidels into Muslim holy land. Through Naif, Wahhabi clerics have access to the levers of law enforcement as a weapon against challenges to their beliefs and privileges. On their behalf, Naif uses his considerable influence to reinforce the siege mentality of conservative principle. It is Naif who publicly absolved the fifteen Saudi hijackers of any responsibility for 9/11 and argued that Israel must have carried out the attacks—since the attacks provoked so much hostility toward Muslims.[20]

Abdullah remains an adherent of the doctrine of *taqarub,* or peaceful coexistence with non-Muslims. He has supported more open public debate, political reforms, and a reduction in the power of Wahhabi clerics. In 2003, Abdullah presided over an unprecedented "national dialogue" with

well-known Saudi liberal reformers. In the process, he accepted two important proreform petitions: the "National Reform Document," which called
for direct elections, an independent judiciary, and more social freedom for
women, and "Partners in the Homeland," a call for greater political freedom
for Saudi Shia. The first document offended religious conservatives; the
second enraged them. Although Shia make up 12 to 15 percent of the Saudi
population and occupy the kingdom's most oil-rich provinces, they have
virtually no religious freedom and are considered by many conservatives to
be heretics at best and "Jewish converts to Islam" at worst.[21]

This divide within the kingdom's elite reveals the extent to which terrorist bombings within Saudi Arabia are directed less at the foreigners who
might be killed than at reformers within the royal family. With each bombing, the Saudi government pleads for help from the public in apprehending
the accused. Those opposed to reform then accuse the government of following American orders to round up pious Muslims.

Reform

If the eventual fall down the left side of the J curve is to occur without catastrophic consequences, Saudi Arabia must further open itself to the globalizing world. King Abdullah has laid out an ambitious reform agenda that
includes privatization of key industries, political liberalization, and diversification of the economy. The centerpiece of economic reform is known as
"Saudization"—a development strategy by which Saudis replace foreign
workers in the economy. The plan's guidelines mandate that by 2007, 70
percent of the workforce must be Saudi. There are several challenges that
must be overcome if Abdullah is to achieve these goals.

The most conservative members of the royal family resolutely oppose
most of the proposed reforms. Naif and others will work hard to scuttle
them. In addition, these reforms will be expensive. By some estimates, the
financial cost of state-led economic diversification may exceed $100 billion
over the next generation, while the country's national debt remains nearly
two-thirds of GDP. Even with increased oil revenues, the Saudi government
may simply not be able to finance the diversification of the economy without the extensive private-sector participation that many conservatives are

determined to avoid, since that development hinges on contacts between Saudis and Westerners.

Further, many Saudis still refuse to accept what they consider to be menial jobs. As for the more appealing jobs, very few graduates of Saudi universities and technical schools are yet qualified to perform them. And immigrants from South Asia and other parts of the Middle East keep coming. The idea of Saudization isn't new. The sixth in a series of five-year development plans (1995–2000) was intended to create nearly 320,000 jobs for Saudis through the replacement of foreign workers. But instead of a reduction in the foreign workforce, the number of expatriates over the relevant period swelled by nearly 60,000 with the steady inflow of Arab and Asian low-skilled laborers hoping to earn more money in Saudi Arabia than they could at home.*

In addition, many Saudi firms in the service sectors fear Saudization will undermine their competitiveness by saddling them with underqualified Saudi workers. As a result, some firms have left the kingdom for what they consider more business-friendly environments. The loss of business to other regional banking centers undermines efforts to put more young Saudis to work and pushes many of the best-qualified Saudi workers out of the kingdom in search of better jobs.

Finally, Saudization threatens badly needed foreign direct investment in the kingdom. Some foreign firms complain the Saudization program is unpredictable; its rules and quotas for the hiring of local workers change without warning. The government is aware of these issues and has reduced the tax burden on foreign investors to encourage investment and prevent capital flight. But quotas for hiring Saudi workers are no substitute for a determined effort to overhaul the Saudi education system and its ability to produce workers ready to add value to private-sector enterprises.[22]

To complicate reform further, the government's repeated failures reinforce the nation's "expectations gap"—the differences between younger and older Saudis in how Saudi wealth is perceived. The older generation of

---

* The Saudi government is undermining its own reforms. In 2005, they enacted a new citizenship law that allows expatriates who have been residing in the kingdom for at least ten years to apply for Saudi citizenship. This enabled expatriates who possess the necessary skills to make a claim for naturalization and therefore maintain their positions within the Saudi economy.

Saudis knew grinding poverty, mass illiteracy, high infant mortality, and low life expectancy. They grew up without hospitals, schools, and telephones. The oil boom years of the 1970s and '80s produced an explosion of wealth so vast and so sudden that the generation that experienced it can only think of Saudi Arabia as a remarkable success story. Today's Saudi youth—the clear majority of the population—take Saudi oil wealth as a given. They see the enormous gap between the opulence of the Saudi royals and the declining living standards of nearly everyone else and know only that they don't own a share of Saudi prosperity, and that there are no jobs for them.

At the heart of the problem is an education system that fails to train young Saudis to meet modern challenges.* Saudi universities remain significantly overcrowded and continue to turn out waves of students with degrees in "Islamic Studies"—not the best preparation to diversify the Saudi economy away from dependence on the oil industry or the Saudi political system away from the cynical alliance of convenience between royals and radicals. Only the most ambitious reform of Saudi education can move society off the dangerous path it's now on.

Because Saudi Arabia is not yet in crisis, Washington may choose the path of least resistance in U.S.-Saudi relations, limiting the agenda to American rhetoric about "the need for reform" and empty promises of change from the Saudis. It will be easy for a U.S. president to avoid the tough questions that face the U.S.-Saudi relationship.

That would be a grave mistake.

Education First—Then Democratization

So how might Saudi reformers begin to prepare for the kingdom's inevitable move down the left side of the J curve? What role might outsiders play? The immediate focus of the Saudi reform effort should be education,

---

* Largely because the Saudi system of education continues to be based on rote learning of patriotic and religious texts, university students are ill prepared to study subjects that demand technical competence. Of the 120,000 graduates that Saudi universities graduated between 1995 and 1999, only 8 percent studied technical subjects such as architecture or engineering, and these students accounted for only 2 percent of the total number of Saudis entering the job market. "People Pressure," *The Economist,* March 21, 2002. http://www.economist.com/printedition/PrinterFriendly.cfm?Story_ID=1033986

not democratization. It's not that democracy is less important in the long term. It isn't. It's that, because Saudis are still so poorly prepared for the economic and governance challenges of the twenty-first century, fast democratization would likely drive them to retreat from the world rather than to engage it. Many Americans now urge Washington to use whatever leverage it has with the Saudi royals to push them toward sweeping democratic reform; such urging should be resisted until radicals are much less able to use Islamist populism to produce dangerously destabilizing results.

A growing and secure middle class with a stake in economic development and political stability protects any society transitioning toward modern governance and economics. As Saudi political scientist Turki Hamad has said: "The problem in Saudi Arabia is that the middle class is shrinking . . . and the more poverty you have, the more fundamentalism you have." [23] Until a modern system of education prepares young Saudis to revitalize the country's economy, antimodern voices will dominate the political and social debate.

A transitional period of limited political reform and social change are necessary before Saudi reformers can build a more open and democratic Saudi Arabia. The international stakes are too high to let change follow a course dictated by either the most ambitious, charismatic, and radical demagogue or by the vagaries of public opinion in a society with so little available information about the outside world. But to suggest that Saudi Arabia is not ready for full-speed democratization is not to imply that all steps toward the expanded participation of the Saudi people in their government can be indefinitely postponed. Abdullah has already announced modest democratic reforms. Following through could empower Saudi reformers at all levels of society. In fact, the kingdom held three rounds of long-overdue municipal elections in 2005. Over time, this electoral process could incrementally extend to the national level. Genuine efforts to tackle corruption in the judiciary, tolerance of local civil-society organizations and human-rights groups, more open media, and the holding of multiparty elections on the local level already have a track record elsewhere in the Arab world. Saudi Arabia would benefit from all of them.

Economic reforms, especially those that were required for accession to the World Trade Organization, have already begun.* But if the Saudi gov-

---

* Saudi Arabia joined the World Trade Organization in December 2005.

ernment doesn't reduce existing subsidies—except for social safety-net payments—development of the private sector will remain stunted. A significant part of future growth in Saudi Arabia will come from small- and medium-sized businesses that are still constrained by the government's overmanagement of the economy. If the government incentivizes, or at least stops creating obstacles to, entrepreneurship, the Saudi economy might begin to build its own momentum. If, on the other hand, the royals continue to buy political loyalty by pumping millions into patronage systems, Saudi entrepreneurship won't have a chance. In addition, if the privatization of state-owned sectors of the economy slows, the already considerable disparities in Saudi wealth and access to capital will get worse.

Political and economic reforms reinforce one another. Only an elected council will give ordinary Saudis the necessary leverage to even attempt to trump the influence of entrenched business and social elites. The major economic reforms the kingdom enacted in order to qualify for membership in the World Trade Organization and to address the goals laid out in the UN's Arab Human Development Report require some degree of public support; they cannot simply be imposed from above. Election of local and, later, national representatives creates the popular basis for sustainable economic, political, and social reform.

The long-term success of political and economic reform in the kingdom depends on the emergence of a citizenry capable of playing an informed role in Saudi society. Much public debate within the kingdom has focused on the need to eliminate those aspects of the Saudi curriculum that promote intolerance, extremism, and violence. Obviously, an internal debate is more likely to produce welcome results than finger-wagging by foreigners. But foreigners can influence the debate, because Saudi airwaves are increasingly open to the outside world.

Even in the Saudi media, social reform (including of the roles of religion, women, and education in society) is more and more the object of public and private debate. Saudis have come a long way in the quality of this public discourse since September 11, and particularly since the beginning of Al Qaeda attacks in Saudi Arabia in May 2003. For English speakers, *Arab News* and *Saudi Gazette* are certainly worth an online read to get the flavor of the current debate. Increasingly, these papers are a fair reflection of what can be found in the Arabic-language press. A great deal of what Saudis now write and say publicly about themselves and their society would have been dismissed by most of the population as "Zionist propaganda" as recently as two years ago. That's real progress.

Any thoughtful strategy for addressing Saudi Arabia's problems and internal contradictions offers difficult, expensive, long-term fixes, with little or no short-term benefit. Because the Saudi system remains so opaque, progress will be tough to gauge. But if the need for reform—particularly of education—is ignored, the Saudis won't be the only ones who pay.

Saudi Arabia, like its regional rival Iran, is a stable society today only because it is a closed society. In the short term, those who would formulate and implement political, economic, and educational reforms will produce instability. The Saudi royal family, with support from the United States and others, must set in motion a process that offers few near-term rewards and threatens to open the flood gates of Saudi frustration and fear. But the beginnings of a transition toward a more transparent and competitive Saudi Arabia can no longer be avoided.

Some ask, "Will the Saudi kingdom as it is governed today fall apart if it reforms or if it doesn't reform?" The answer to both questions is yes. The current Saudi system is headed down the left side of the J curve whether it begins to reform or not. But if reform that gives the Saudi people a stake in a more promising future is not undertaken, a more radical Saudi regime, exposed to the world against its will, may well lash out and produce a political and economic shock from which the world will not soon recover. The risk is the same if the walls are pulled down too quickly. A managed move toward a Saudi Arabia in greater political, economic, and social harmony with the rest of the twenty-first-century world offers no guarantees. A refusal to try virtually guarantees catastrophe.

RUSSIA

When a closed country falls down the left side of the J curve toward instability, there is no guarantee the country will reemerge (on either side of the curve) as a coherent nation-state. South Africa survived the passage from left to right. Yugoslavia did not. From the wreckage of the Soviet system came the Russian Federation, a new state that inherited much of the Soviet Union's assets* and its liabilities.†

Russia provides an interesting case because, at its birth, it also inherited the chaos of Soviet collapse. The new state's first government made a determined move toward the right side of the J curve, but headed resolutely back to the left once fears for stability overwhelmed early hopes for a successful transition toward more open governance—and authoritarian habits reasserted themselves.

For Boris Yeltsin, the Russian Federation's first president, the key to the country's future as a "normal nation" lay in leading Russia through the transition from a command to a market economy, from authoritarian police state to pluralist democracy, and from empire to modern nation-state. Most of the Russian people hoped simply for an end to the exhausting chaos of the last half-decade of the USSR and for a stable and prosperous future. Yeltsin's plans and his people's hopes were not immediately compatible.

. The only roadmaps for a transition from a Communist command economy to a free-market system available in 1992 were provided by the beginnings of similar transformations in the former Warsaw Pact states of Eastern Europe. For a variety of reasons, the model was not ideal for Russia. In Poland and then-Czechoslovakia, for example, Communists had been cast out of government in favor of former dissidents who needed no political reeducation. The Russian government, on the other hand, was filled with former Communists—including Yeltsin—who had to look for ideas to a younger generation of economic theorists with little policy experience. "Shock therapy," the early abandonment of state protections in the economy in favor of market-mechanism-based adaptation, produced early success in Poland. In the far more complicated situation in Russia, the result of early reform was, as Clinton administration official Strobe Talbott once remarked, a need for "less shock and more therapy." [24]

Price ceilings were lifted. The result was spiraling inflation that shook the lives of millions of Russians who lived on fixed incomes and created a new class of impoverished people not seen in the Soviet Union in decades. The

---

* Like its nuclear weapons and its seat on the UN Security Council.
† Much of the Soviet debt and the mistrust of most of its fourteen new former-Soviet neighbors.

black-market economy and the payment of bribes that played a large role in the underground commerce of the Soviet days emerged aboveground, as people stepped outside the law in order to survive. The collapse of the police state following the end of Communist rule left law-enforcement poorly equipped to keep streets safe, and many of its officials took bribes to make ends meet. Crime statistics had never been reported honestly in Soviet times. With the first free Russian media, the feeling of insecurity was multiplied, as society's ills were aired with a frankness for which few were prepared.

The deepest fear of many Russians became the disintegration of the new state. Having experienced the collapse of the Soviet Union, fears for Russia's survival were hardly abstract. Soviet schoolchildren had been taught that the tsarist Russian Empire had been a "prison of nations," and that only Lenin's principle of "self-determination for all peoples" had liberated them. But Russia, which still covers 13 percent of the world's land surface, includes a wide range of distinct ethnic, religious, and linguistic groups. Some 20 percent of the population is not ethnically Russian. Many non-Russians are concentrated in ethnic enclaves with varying degrees of political autonomy, and therefore have an interest in protecting that autonomy from any encroachment from Moscow. Yeltsin himself encouraged their drive for greater levels of political freedom, encouraging them in the final days of the Soviet Union to "take all the sovereignty you can swallow." In doing so, he hoped to help pull the Soviet Union down the left side of the J curve. Once he became the man in the Kremlin, he regretted the comment, particularly when Chechen leaders took him at his word and threatened Russia's own place on the curve. The fear of a chain reaction of breakaway movements within Russia was immediate—even before Chechen separatists gave the fear a focal point.

Nor was it hard to imagine the violence and bloodshed that Russian disintegration might provoke. The Soviet breakup quickly produced armed conflict in the former Soviet republics of Tajikistan, Moldova, Azerbaijan, and Georgia. The nearly 2 million ethnic Russians living in the Baltic States were made to feel distinctly unwelcome. And the horrific violence of full-scale civil war in the former Yugoslavia hinted at what a similar conflict might look like in the nuclear-armed territories of the former Soviet Union.

The Russian people wanted peace, security, and a promise that Russia could again become the force on the international stage it had been in better times. What they got was the booze-sodden, chaotic, roller-coaster ride of the Yeltsin presidency. As a result, Russians began to see "democracy" and "free markets" not as the antidote to moribund Communism, but as the source of the new Russia's injustice, immorality, insecurity, poverty, crime, disease, and humiliation. Chechnya's refusal to sign a union treaty to remain part of the Russian Federation led in 1994 to a savage and unpopular war. Yeltsin's approval ratings plummeted to less than 10 percent.

Not everyone hated the new Russia. A small class of businessmen profited from Yeltsin's market reforms and the near-complete absence of rules of the game to become fabulously wealthy through the rigged privatization of lucrative sectors of the economy. Because so many of them then used their wealth to gain access to political power and influence, these men came to be known as the "oligarchs." For them, Boris Yeltsin's government was the source of virtually everything they wanted. The oligarchs knew whom to cultivate.

They also knew whom to fear. Yeltsin's most powerful opposition at the time came from Gennady Zyuganov's Communist Party. Although Russia's Communists were more a motley assortment of nationalists, fascists, and militarists than Marxist-Leninists, they were certainly not going to privatize Russia's richest state-owned properties for the benefit of the new capitalist elite. So as Yeltsin's popularity plummeted and reelection loomed, the oligarchs calculated that Boris Yeltsin's presidency had to be rescued. The deals they made with the Kremlin helped Yeltsin cling to power—and made the oligarchs the wealthiest and most powerful men in Russia.

Essentially, Yeltsin sold the oligarchs control of Russia's media. The robber barons used that media to promote Yeltsin's candidacy and to distort the news and the messages of his rivals. Control of the media enriched the oligarchs further, since they also used their newly acquired television networks to promote their business interests. Once Yeltsin was safely reelected in 1996, the oligarchs used their new platforms to promote themselves and to influence, as directly as possible, the creation of public policy.

The deal between Yeltsin and the oligarchs has something important in common with the similarly Faustian bargain between the Saudi royal family and the Wahhabis. Just as the Saudi royals cede real power and influence to radical clerics in exchange for vitally needed ideological and political support, Yeltsin sold the oligarchs the keys to the kingdom for the cash he needed to survive the electoral process. Both Saudi Arabia and Russia can rely on oil revenue to help keep their countries stable. In Saudi Arabia, Wahhabi approval—or at least acceptance—helps hold chaos at bay. In Russia, the cash flow and media control of the oligarchs helped achieve much the same for Yeltsin. And just as the Saudi royals fear the Wahhabis will one day use their power at the expense of the system, so Russia's reformers and reactionaries alike began to fear the oligarchs held too much wealth and influence.

A key difference in the Russian and Saudi cases: the stroke that debilitated King Fahd did not incapacitate the Saudi government. Power simply passed to then Crown Prince Abdullah, who minded the store for the benefit of the royal family. That's part of why Saudi Arabia today remains more stable—and higher up the left side of the curve therefore—than Russia, where the oligarchs usurped much of the absentee president's authority and used it mainly to enrich themselves further.

At the same time, Yeltsin's administration sheltered the oligarchs from the hostile forces of Communist opposition, from political liberals fighting to force business leaders to submit to the rule of law, and from a public suspicious of the oligarchs' unchecked wealth and power. Yeltsin's various illnesses, his drinking, and the oligarchs' political intrigues created a culture of official secrecy that pulled Russia away from the transparency necessary for a successful transition to the right side of the curve and yanked Russian society back to the left. That dynamic defined most of Yeltsin's presidency.

As the oligarchs made fortunes, they also made enemies. Stripping the assets of state-owned companies and shifting profits to overseas bank accounts, they helped leave most ordinary Russians considerably worse off than they had been in the final decades of Soviet rule. Over the course of Yeltsin's second term (1996–1999), the nation fragmented as Yeltsin's poor health and his drinking binges pushed him further and further from day-to-day operation of the Russian government. Central authority slackened, oligarchs elbowed for position in Yeltsin's entourage—which became known, archly, as "the family"—and provincial leaders filled the power vacuum in the vast Russian expanse. Boris Berezovsky, the most notorious and powerful of the oligarchs, bragged in 1996 that seven men owned half of Russia's GDP.[25] Although Berezovsky's penchant for bravado is well documented, his claim was probably not far from the truth. Together, the oligarchs and Russia's regional governors formulated economic policies that helped enrich a tiny percentage of the population and did little for the impoverished majority.

Despite Yeltsin's abdication of direct leadership and the halting progress of economic reform, by the second half of the 1990s, Russia seemed on a road that might eventually lead to pluralist democracy and free markets. The political crisis of 1993, which climaxed when Yeltsin shelled the Russian parliament to put down a Communist-nationalist insurrection, produced a new constitution that substantially increased the power of the president, but did not substantially alter Russia's course away from Soviet Communism and the Soviet Union's place on the left side of the J curve. Peaceful parliamentary and presidential elections were held on time and were largely free and fair. Russian and Chechen leaders reached a cease-fire agreement in time for Yeltsin's 1996 reelection. Yeltsin's personal relationship with President Bill Clinton helped head off potential international crises over NATO expansion and conflict in the former Yugoslavia. Investor confidence rose to new heights as the Cold War receded and as Russia seemed to make progress on economic reform.

But in August of 1998, with little warning, an inexperienced prime minister, Sergei Kiriyenko, simultaneously devalued the ruble and announced that Russia would not meet its obligations to foreign bondholders.* A new Russian financial crisis materialized that pushed foreign investment out of Russia and financial markets into a downward spiral. Russia had fallen back into the depths of the curve. Only slowly did the Kremlin begin to recover from this self-inflicted wound, and, as new national elections approached, Yeltsin's search for a successor who would protect his legacy from his rivals—and his "family" from formal corruption charges—intensified.

Yeltsin orchestrated a surprisingly smooth transition in 2000 to a relative unknown, Vladimir Putin, the first truly consensual transfer of power from one living man to another in 1,000 years of Russian history. As in any unconsolidated, unstable state, succession is a dangerous process. Yeltsin helped the process along with a surprise early resignation on New Year's Eve 1999 that allowed Putin to seek the presidency three months later as an incumbent. Russia's oligarchs, sensing that Yeltsin had handpicked a succes-

---

* Kiriyenko proved to be the second in a series of four prime ministers fired by the increasingly erratic Yeltsin over a period of seventeen months.

sor who would defend their interests, used their wealth, influence, and media holdings to drive off potential competitors and to smooth Putin's electoral ascendance.

Putin promised predictability. Ordinary Russians, robber barons, and potential foreign investors in the country all approved. The devaluation of the ruble and high oil and other commodity prices led an impressive economic rebound. Following a string of apartment bombings in Moscow and elsewhere in 1999 that were blamed on Chechen separatists, a new war in Chechnya rallied Russians to their government in a way the first conflict had not. The new president's popularity soared on the strength of his hard line toward the Chechen rebels.* Putin gave Russians what they wanted: a young, sober, dynamic leader who projected strength and resolve. Once president, it became clear that Putin's most dangerous potential enemies were not Chechens, but the oligarchs who felt they owned Yeltsin's presidency—and who had done much to lift Vladimir Putin from obscurity to the Kremlin.

President Putin and Lessons Learned

Since Putin's first term began in 2000, foreign investors have recovered much of the confidence in the Russian government they had lost following the 1998 default, and Russian bond and equity markets have performed consistently well. In October 2003, Moody's Investors Service acknowledged the turnaround by giving Russia an investment-grade rating, allowing it to attract an entirely new class of portfolio investors. Foreign direct investment returned to the country, as international bankers once again filled business-class seats on flights to Moscow and financial institutions began hunting for class A office space. With his steady leadership, a percolating economy, and the near-universal relief that he wasn't Yeltsin, Putin's domestic approval ratings consistently topped 70 percent.

What the investment bankers and investors who lauded Putin's steadiness and growing reputation as a "Westernizer" missed, however, was that to consolidate power in a country with virtually no experience of nonauto-

---

* As prime minister, Putin promised in October 1999 to "flush the Chechen bandits down the toilet." The comment was very well received at home, less so abroad.

cratic government, Putin was in no hurry to pursue political reform—at least not the kind that might cost him real political capital. In essence, Putin decided that the left side of the J curve was the safest place to consolidate power. A move toward the right would invite other actors to have their say in Russian reform and to create friction that would make his enormously difficult task of economic stabilization even more daunting.

Democracy is now on hold in Russia. Former Soviet leader Yuri Andropov once said, "First we'll make enough sausages and then we won't have any dissidents."[26] In the early 1980s, Andropov ordered his then-protégé Mikhail Gorbachev to conduct a study of the Soviet economy so secret that few in the Soviet high command even knew it existed. The findings of that study led Gorbachev, once he became general secretary, to pursue the radical reform needed to revitalize the Soviet economy, a program of sweeping change Andropov would never have approved—or even imagined.

Andropov was also Putin's former boss in the KGB.* Putin knows as well as anyone that Andropov would never have launched *glasnost* or *perestroika*. There was no room in Andropov's worldview for dissidents to unleash the hidden creative potential of the Soviet system. The cure for dissidents was sausage in sufficient quantities—or prison. Political reform that actually encouraged dissent, Andropov believed, was a recipe for chaos.

As chair of Saint Petersburg's committee on external relations with responsibility for economic development and investment, Putin witnessed both the chaos of early Russian capitalism and the weakness of the Russian economy. In his first month as president, Putin restored a memorial plaque in Andropov's honor at the KGB's Lubyanka headquarters that had been removed during the Gorbachev era. Since then, Putin has adhered far more closely to Andropov's idea of central control of the state than to Gorbachev's belief that society should be free to participate in the process of change.

---

* Putin was never more than a junior officer in the KGB and had no direct access to Andropov.

Putin versus the Oligarchs

Putin's conviction that a greater centralization of power could support reform was not entirely mistaken. Many financial analysts and investors wrongly believed at the time that a lack of political reform provoked the 1998 financial crisis. But it was a lack of central authority—not a lack of democracy—that produced the upheaval. When Putin became president in 2000, economic policy was still effectively created and implemented by ad hoc coalitions of regional governors and businessmen—a law unto themselves. Putin decided that rebuilding strong central authority and consolidating the Russian state had to be his priorities. And that meant, above all, finding some workable accommodation with the oligarchs.

When Putin took office, he reportedly called together the new business leaders and forged an unwritten but plainly understood pact with them: the oligarchs could keep the cash and property they had amassed in the rigged privatization deals of the Yeltsin years without fear of prosecution, as long as they paid their taxes and steered clear of political conflict with the president. The latter condition precluded use of the oligarchs' media holdings to criticize Putin or his administration.

The warning to stay out of politics was clear enough, but it was not rigorously policed until two of the original oligarchs, Berezovsky and Vladimir Gusinsky, used their television stations to broadcast blunt criticism of the Kremlin. In an early taste of how Putin meant to enforce the unwritten contract, security guards brandishing automatic weapons and legal documents raided the Ostankino Tower offices of Gusinsky's NTV television network in the middle of the night on Easter Sunday 2001.[27] By sunrise, NTV was a new television network with an editorial philosophy more in harmony with the Kremlin's worldview. Berezovsky and Gusinsky soon found themselves under criminal prosecution for money-laundering and other charges. Both eventually fled the country, and their media outlets were purged of all journalists willing to directly criticize presidential policy. The move up the left side of the J curve had begun in earnest.

Other channels of political influence remained open to oligarchs more willing to observe the rules of the road. Putin retained Alexander Voloshin, Yeltsin's capable and savvy chief of staff, who helped push through Putin's early economic reforms and was the point man for dealing with the new

Bush administration. Voloshin was also the intermediary within the Kremlin between Putin and the holdovers from the Yeltsin era who had maintained close ties with the business elite. With Voloshin as Putin's right hand, the oligarchs had a man to protect their interests within the new administration.

The oligarchs continued to exercise considerable influence, including, allegedly, over tax legislation. Putin may not have been content with their continuing sway over economic policy, but he was more immediately concerned with political challenges to his authority. After Berezovsky and Gusinsky fled into exile, there was one remaining billionaire who, in Putin's view, refused to honor the rules Putin believed he had established. This was Mikhail Khodorkovsky, the CEO of the oil giant Yukos and Russia's wealthiest man, worth an estimated $8 billion.

The Khodorkovsky Affair

Khodorkovsky was enthusiastically feted in the West as a man of taste and sophistication—and because he was the first of the Russian oligarchs to practice open, Western-style accounting standards. The West treated Khodorkovsky as the man they needed in Russia's business world—the Michael Corleone who really *had* taken his business legitimate and who, in the process, helped his rivals accept that Russia's violent era of lawless business practices was coming to an end.*

But like most beneficiaries of the Yeltsin-era "time of troubles," Khodorkovsky remained deeply unpopular with the Russian people. The memory of how he, and the rest of the oligarchs, had acquired wealth—using his po-

---

* Yukos trumpeted the following favorable review from the *Wall Street Journal* on its Web site: "The 2001 World Economic Forum came to a close in Davos, Switzerland, on 30 January 2001. This year good corporate governance and business practices have been a focal point in the Forum's discussions and was one of the key criteria for attendance. According to the *Wall Street Journal*, ' . . . Only one prominent Russian tycoon has survived the forum's reassessment: Mikhail Khodorkovsky, chairman of oil company YUKOS, will be on hand. A WEF official said that YUKOS has become more transparent and improved its corporate governance in recent years.' "

litical connections to purchase some of Russia's choicest oil assets at fire-sale prices—lingered in the public consciousness.

At first, Khodorkovsky managed to cultivate cordial relations with Russia's new president and was a frequent visitor to the Kremlin. Some spoke of Khodorkovsky as a potential future prime minister (although this story may have been concocted by Khodorkovsky's media machine). But over time, and particularly as the Russian political class began to focus on the December 2003 Duma elections, Khodorkovsky began to provide substantial funding—directly and indirectly—for many of the parties likely to win seats. In particular, he gave generously to the two best-known liberal-reformist, promarket parties, Yabloko and the Union of Right Forces.

In Putin's estimation, Khodorkovsky's political activities now extended beyond normal business lobbying. To many observers, including the Russian president, it seemed clear that Khodorkovsky hoped for a future in politics. Rumors began to circulate that Khodorkovsky was even positioning himself to run for president in 2008, when, under the term limits established by Russia's constitution, Putin would have to leave office.

For Putin, this amounted to a clear challenge to his authority, despite the weakness of the liberal parties and Khodorkovsky's slim electoral chances. While Castro has (so far) chosen not to arrest the popular dissident Oswaldo Paya, Vladimir Putin had no such hesitation in going after the resented Khodorkovsky. The controversial businessman further angered Putin when he took a number of initiatives that encroached on Kremlin control of domestic and foreign policy. Khodorkovsky effectively blocked passage of several of the government's economic proposals in the Duma. He campaigned publicly for the privatization of Russia's external pipeline system. He was reportedly on the point of selling his company to ExxonMobil, passing ownership of a Russian oil company into foreign hands. Finally, Khodorkovsky signed an agreement with the Chinese government in May 2003 to build a private pipeline linking Russia and China.

Two months later, the Kremlin sent a none-too-subtle warning with the arrest of Khodorkovsky's business partner, Platon Lebedev, on charges of fraud and tax evasion. Khodorkovsky himself was brought in for questioning. Perhaps persuaded that his position as CEO of Yukos and the strong international support he enjoyed offered him special protection, Khodorkovsky stepped up his political activities. Putin, determined that

Russia's oligarchs must no longer be permitted to conduct their own foreign policy or to establish a rival center of influence, moved against him. On October 25, 2003, armed agents stormed his private plane during a refueling stop, arrested him, and returned him to Moscow in handcuffs. Khodorkovsky is now serving an eight-year prison sentence in a Siberian penal colony.

The story of Mikhail Khodorkovsky reveals much about Vladimir Putin's view of stability in Russia. Putin's chief ambition as Russian president has been to build Russia into an economic powerhouse. He has argued that developing Russia's economic muscle will allow Moscow to reassert itself politically—in its traditional sphere of influence and beyond. Putin's choices suggest he believes both that Gorbachev's improvised attempts at political reform ran the Soviet Union aground and that the diffusion of national authority during the Yeltsin years led the few to exploit Russia at the expense of the many. He has a point. But Putin has chosen to right this perceived wrong by breaking any organized opposition—an efficient means of keeping his country on the left side of the J curve where he has the best opportunity to control it.

Khodorkovsky represented a risk to Putin's plans to consolidate the power necessary to focus Russian resources for the construction of a powerful, self-confident, and influential state. As we'll see in other areas of Putin's record as president, no risk to the project is too small to try to eliminate. Deng Xiaoping once defended his reform program against charges he was betraying Communist principle with the words "It doesn't matter what color the cat is—as long as it catches mice." Putin might say the same for rule of law in Russia. There is no tradition in Russia's political life that establishes law as a safeguard for the individual against the state. In fact, the law that Putin studied at Leningrad State University taught him that law was society's best defense against the greed of the individual. If, on behalf of the exploited Russian people, Putin might ask, the government can't use the law to create a just and prosperous future for all, what purpose does it serve? In this case, the law was used to destroy the agenda of a man bent on undermining the construction of a unified and self-confident Russia—or so Putin's argument goes.

Khodorkovsky, like all the oligarchs, *was* guilty of some of the crimes with which he was charged. But he committed his crimes with the complicity of Boris Yeltsin's government. Berezovsky and Gusinsky ruthlessly stripped Russia of billions of dollars in national treasure. They also used some of their wealth to ensure Yeltsin was not defeated at the polls by unreconstructed Communists and xenophobic thugs. All three oligarchs helped elevate Vladimir Putin. The Russian president genuinely seems to want to use his power to build an economically stable and prosperous Russia. At what point, however, do Putin's moves to consolidate state control reflect a desire to amass power for its own sake and to hold personal rivals at bay? Once power is amassed, will Putin and the men he's brought to the pinnacle of power in Russia willingly give it up? That question will probably be answered in 2008, when the next presidential election takes place.

A stability built on obsessive risk-aversion drives a nation up the left side of the J curve, because openness involves obvious risks. If the process of opening never comes, the society in question becomes incapable of reinventing itself and begins an inexorable process of decay. Whether or not Putin's consolidation of power is the means to help Russia navigate the bottom of the curve and ultimately to make the transition from closed to open, left to right, remains to be seen.

Meanwhile, Putin knew that Khodorkovsky's arrest on fraud, tax-evasion, and other charges, and its aftermath—the freezing of Khodorkovsky's equity stake in Yukos and the subsequent resignation of his chief of staff, Alexander Voloshin—would shake international investor confidence and threaten Russia's four-year economic boom. The Kremlin immediately sought to limit the damage. Publicly and privately in his meetings with foreign and Russian bankers, Putin emphasized that the arrest was a unique case for a unique individual and not the start of a crusade against Russia's business elite. Russia, like Saudi Arabia, has resources to sell and commerce to establish. As long as foreign influence doesn't undermine the right of the rulers to rule, the presence of foreigners and their cash provides an opportunity to earn the revenue that builds prosperity and protects political stability. Reassuring foreigners that Russia remains open for business is a vital part of Putin's plan to build his nation's economic power.

The Putin School of Risk Management

Putin's efforts to minimize political risk and to consolidate power began very early in his presidency.* Aside from the deal he struck to sideline the oligarchs, Putin sought to constrain the abundant power of regional governors by organizing Russia's eighty-nine provinces into seven federal districts to be presided over by supergovernors appointed directly by the president. Putin removed powerful regional leaders from the upper house of the Russian parliament, the Federation Council, depriving them of their votes on federal legislation. Reining in the oligarchs meant bringing broadcast media under direct Kremlin supervision. In short, as the former Communists of Putin's presidential administration sought to bring stability and predictability to Russian politics, they recreated what they knew: a left-side-of-the-J-curve system of vertical power and central control.

Following a horrific Chechen terrorist attack on a school in the southern Russian town of Beslan in September 2004, Putin seized the opportunity presented by his nation's shock to put forward some unexpected ideas on further centralizing national political power. He proposed an end to popular election of governors. According to the plan, the president, subject to ratification by the local legislatures, gained the right to handpick the leaders of Russia's regions. Why risk political challenges from unruly regional leaders if you don't have to?

There is also a bit of tactical cleverness in these proposals. Might the regional governors be reluctant to support a move to directly control their political futures? Putin also proposed an end to gubernatorial term limits. Sitting governors can now hold their posts indefinitely; all they need is the favor of the Kremlin. And were the Russian president to do away with his own term limits, the governors could be seeking his favor for many years to come.

---

* It remains an open question to what extent moves up the J curve come from Putin himself or from the former security officers, the so-called *siloviki,* whom he's brought into the Kremlin in significant numbers. Given the opacity of the Russian government, it's difficult to know how such decisions are made. Over time, this question may be answered. For the purposes of this book, I argue that Putin is the ultimate arbiter of behind-the-scenes Kremlin policy formulation.

Putin also proposed that all parliamentary seats be filled from national party lists, a move that effectively relieved elected officials of political dependence on any particular local constituency. Members of Russia's lower house now depend for their seats not on local voters but on party leaders, an effective way for Putin to reduce the number of variables he faces as he pushes reform (or refuses to push reform) through parliament. Why accept the political risk involved in the disorder of grassroots politics if you aren't forced to?

It's not just regional governors who find themselves serving at the pleasure of Russia's president. On October 1, 2004, by a vote of 175 to 2, Russia's upper house of parliament passed a measure to give Putin effective control over the body that approves would-be judges for the country's highest courts. It also gives the president the power to discipline and dismiss senior judges if, once chosen, they demonstrate qualities the Kremlin wants to discourage. Why risk an independent judiciary if it isn't necessary?

In 2004, Putin feared that insufficient voter turnout might nullify his easy reelection. Two weeks before the election, Putin unexpectedly sacked his prime minister, Mikhail Kasyanov. According to Kasyanov, Putin was concerned that, if low turnout prevented timely certification of his reelection, Russian law might allow Kasyanov to become acting president. Others said Putin could not tolerate Kasyanov's open criticism of the Yukos affair. Although Kasyanov had served Putin for four years, the Russian president saw another risk he chose not to accept.*

In fact, Putin's low tolerance for pointed political criticism—particularly in the Russian media—will only reinforce his authoritarian approach to the reform process. The Russian broadcast media has been under the Kremlin's vigilant control since Putin's first raid on Ostankino. The print media—less influential, in the Kremlin's estimation—has been allowed noticeably more freedom. But the editor of the respected daily newspaper *Izvestia* was forced from his job in the fall of 2004 after publishing a critical account of the government's mishandling of the hostage crisis at Beslan, complete with a half-page photo spread of the horror of the attack. Why

---

* Kasyanov may not be the most reliable witness. On the other hand, in June 2005, less than a month after he announced that he might seek to establish a coalition of opposition parties and run for president in 2008, prosecutors began investigating Kasyanov on corruption charges. To date, he has not been convicted of any crime.

allow the public to see, hear, or read media criticism of your government if you don't have to?

The president maintains a heavy influence in the Russian parliament, firm control of the security forces, increasing power within the judiciary, and the loyalty—or at least the obedience—of the remaining oligarchs. And speculation continues that Putin may try and enjoy these powers beyond their original 2008 expiration date. Article 81, section 3, of the Russian constitution stipulates that "no one person may hold the office of President of the Russian Federation for more than two terms in succession." Some suggest Putin may use the "in succession" loophole and find a loyalist to keep his Kremlin seat warm for four years before engineering a triumphant electoral return in 2012,* though he is unlikely to take such a bold step, Putin could also decide it's easier to simply change the constitution. He may provide himself a seven-year term or simply do away with term limits altogether. In the name of national security and reform, Putin could wave off the inevitable domestic and international condemnation of such a move. Why risk the instability that might come with a transfer of executive power if you don't have to?

The Real Challenges to Russian Stability

Not all threats to Russian cohesion are the invention of a risk-averse authoritarian in the Kremlin. The ongoing conflict with Chechen separatists and the terrorist threats it poses create the single most dangerous challenge to Russian stability. Beginning in 1994, Russia's military efforts to prevent the breakaway province from establishing sovereignty have been a brutal affair. Tens of thousands of civilians have been killed, and the war has produced terrorist activity in the North Caucasus and elsewhere in Russia. There are still no prospects of substantive negotiations between Moscow and representatives of Chechen fighters. The most obvious possible Chechen negotiating partner, Aslan Maskhadov, was killed in March 2005 by Russian security forces.

Chechen alienation from the Russian government is near total, and the

---

* Putin himself hinted he might consider a third term in 2012 in a meeting with media executives in Hanover, Germany, on April 11, 2005.

rebels' capacity to disrupt the Russian state is increasing. The 2002 siege at Moscow's Dubrovka Theater, in which Chechen rebels held more than 800 Russian hostages—150 of whom were killed when Russian security troops stormed the building—demonstrated that Chechen fighters could strike virtually anywhere in Russia. The September 2004 terrorist assault in Beslan—which killed more than 350, most of them schoolchildren—showed there were no limits on what they were willing to do.

Chechen militants are responsible for the only known incident of radiological terror against a civilian population, having buried high-isotope cesium in Moscow's Ismailovsky Park in November 1995. With the help of Arab jihadis, Chechen fighters are becoming more and more technologically sophisticated in the use of such weapons. A "dirty bomb" attack in a Russian city is an increasingly credible threat, and while it might not produce large-scale casualties, the psychological and economic consequences would be immediate and devastating.

Indeed, Russia is the only country in the world with the combination of substantial amounts of unaccounted-for radiological material, large numbers of highly trained and specialized scientists who are significantly underpaid, and well-organized indigenous terrorist groups. Russia is, therefore, at greater risk of a large-scale terrorist attack with radiological weapons than any other country in the world. In the event of such an attack, Putin's government would be hard-pressed to find an internationally acceptable and proportionate response. Putin knows that, if the Russian people lose faith that his government can protect their physical security, his ability to accomplish anything else will be fatally compromised. A slide toward instability would quickly follow. In the past, the Russian people have rallied to their president in the aftermath of an attack, no matter how far up the left side of the J curve he pushed the nation. If the attacks continue to escalate in scale and frequency, however, Russians may turn to nationalist politicians who see the left side of the curve as Russia's natural place.*

The second challenge to Russia's stability and internal cohesion is the nascent rivalry between China and Russia over influence in Siberia. Russia

---

* Putin has made substantial efforts to shore up Russia's place on the left side of the J curve. It remains unclear, however, whether he believes Russia must always be governed as a left-side state. Many Russian nationalists believe it must and criticize Putin's free-market, open-society rhetoric.

maintains complete political control over the resource-rich, India-sized expanse of its Far East and Siberia, but the economic and demographic balance is increasingly, and rapidly, tilting toward China. Local Russian leaders estimate that ethnic Chinese already control nearly half the Siberian economy. The demographic trends are striking: there are about 18 million Russians in Siberia; there are more than 250 million Chinese just over the border in China's northern provinces. And the internal balance is shifting as Russians leave the already sparsely populated region, and as legions of (mostly illegal) Chinese migrants arrive in droves. The potential for interethnic violence is bound to grow. Local Russo-Chinese relations now dominate Siberia's elections and are likely to develop into problems the Kremlin must manage directly. If those problems are not well managed, blame is likely to fall squarely on the man who has amassed so much power and who, in the eyes of his people, must accept the responsibility that comes with it.[28]

The third issue Putin faces is political pressure for democratic reform. What happens when Putin has consolidated power and carried out the many components of his economic reform package, when the controversial dislocations from energy reform are at an end and Russia is a full member of the World Trade Organization? Will he then be willing to start spending some of his political capital in order to create a truly representative political system with legitimacy invested in durable democratic institutions rather than in the person of the president? The further up the left side of the curve a state moves, the more difficult it becomes for a regime to let go of the power and control that have been established.

Policy

American policymakers are divided over how best to manage Washington's relations with Putin. As the Russian president pushes his country further up the left side of the curve, the Bush administration has taken a tougher approach. Secretaries of State Colin Powell and Condoleezza Rice have diplomatically taken Putin to task over the heavy-handedness with which he has concentrated political authority in the Kremlin. The White House vigorously supported a fair presidential election in Ukraine (a former Soviet republic) while Putin actively aided the men who sought to steal it. In her

Senate confirmation hearings, Rice identified Belarus (another former Soviet republic which enjoys a political union with Russia) as an "outpost of tyranny." On the other hand, the United States needs Russian support on critical issues—like thwarting Iran's nuclear ambitions.

Putin can't easily deflect the pressure by playing the United States and Europe off one another. With the accession in May 2004 of ten new states into the European Union (several of which are former Soviet satellites and three of which are former Soviet republics), the Kremlin discovered that "Europe" has tilted toward a stance more suspicious of Russian intentions.

There is another challenge to stability facing the Russian economy, one that makes the United States especially uneasy. Putin's relative popularity and the stability he's built in Russia have risen—and may fall—with oil prices. Despite the revenue that oil brings to the Russian economy, Putin faces limited, but growing, dissent as reforms begin to again hit Russians in the pocketbook. If there is significant social dissent when oil is fetching more than $60 per barrel, there is going to be an enormous problem for the country when oil prices drop substantially toward a more stable equilibrium price. The price drop will come, since oil markets are cyclical. What will happen to Putin's popularity and Russia's stability when the entire J curve shifts downward?

It is a fine line for Washington to draw. The Bush administration talks increasingly of supporting democratic values around the world, even in the former Soviet states of Ukraine, Georgia, and Belarus. The Bush team knows it can't promote democracy in Russia's traditional sphere of influence while ignoring Vladimir Putin's authoritarian tendencies. On the other hand, the White House wants to be supportive (even strongly supportive) of a more sustainable economic plan for Russia, with greater private-sector involvement in key economic areas and hopes for continued Russian help on proliferation and War-on-Terror-related issues. If Washington pushes too hard, it risks driving Russia into closer strategic alignment with China, an outcome the White House very much hopes to avoid.

Putin's Future

What of Putin's personal plans? An important feature of governments on the left side of the curve is that leaders become more important than the of-

fices they hold. Saddam portrayed himself as the direct descendant of ancient kings. The Saudi royals claim to rule by divine right. Kim Jong-Il
works hard at self-deification. Putin has repeatedly and publicly claimed he
has no intention of amending the Russian constitution to stand for a third
time. But in 2008, the Russian president will only be fifty-six years old.
Members of Putin's cabinet and the governors whose careers he controls
will no doubt push him to stay on—in many cases for selfish reasons. Large
segments of the public may want that too.

Succession produces uncertainty. The higher a country moves up the
left side of the J curve, the greater that uncertainty. It isn't surprising then
that Kim Il-Sung, Hafez Assad, and the Saudi royals would turn to family
members to ensure an easy transfer of power and legitimacy. After all, that's
how executive power was transferred for much of human history in much
of the world. Yeltsin looked within his metaphorical "family" for a successor
he could trust. Putin will likely do the same—unless he decides to hold onto
power beyond his original mandate.

Were Putin to subvert the constitution in an attempt to stay in power
past 2008, it would be a disaster for Russia's hopes of transitioning to the
right side of the J curve. If Russia can maintain its economic growth in
coming years, and if President Putin has ended the threats to central state
control from Russia's oligarchs and regional bosses, there will be no reason
for him to deny Russians the chance to make their own political and economic choices and to allow the country to move toward a pluralist society
whose stability comes from the openness of its political and economic life.
A reinvigorated Russia might move successfully through a period of uncertainty and begin to climb the right side of the J curve toward political maturity. Such a transition would require one thing Vladimir Putin may not have
in sufficient quantities: tolerance for political risk.

Geopolitically important states that move up and down the J curve, like
Iran, Saudi Arabia, and Russia, pose the greatest challenges for global political and economic stability. If the political development of these states is ignored by the outside world, they may descend fully into chaos or take
actions intended to avert catastrophe that are even more dangerous for the
world. If any of these states becomes unstable, nations that depend on oil
for their economic well-being—in other words, most of the world—will

suffer serious consequences. Russian and Iranian instability could send nuclear technology and the scientists trained to develop it into the hands of terrorists and profiteers.

Neither the United States nor any other nation (or group of nations) can shepherd these countries through the dangerous transition from the left to the right side of the curve. But they can craft a strategy designed to strengthen forces within those countries to manage their own revolutions. How that works is the subject of the next chapter.

CHAPTER FOUR

The Depths of the J Curve

And on the pedestal these words appear:
"My name is Ozymandias, King of Kings:
Look on my works, ye mighty, and despair!"
Nothing beside remains. Round the decay
Of that colossal wreck, boundless and bare,
The lone and level sands stretch far away.

—FROM "OZYMANDIAS,"
BY PERCY BYSSHE SHELLEY

There was a time when the world's most stable governments administered empires. The British, Ottoman, and Russian empires, among
many others, endured for centuries. But over time, as thought and values
evolved, even the works of Ozymandias came to sand.

All states on the left side of the J curve are eventually headed for instability and fundamental change, because repression and isolation from the outside world cannot be maintained forever. Every wall erodes. Over time, for
every repressive action, there is an equal and opposite reaction of resistance.
The most fully consolidated authoritarian regimes of history have all evolved
toward some degree of convergence with the broader currents of civilization
or collapsed under the weight of internal contradictions, largely because
they had no organic means of adapting to the evolution of human values.

It's true that "globalization" is a centuries-old process and not simply a
late-twentieth-century phenomenon. But the speed at which ideas, infor-

mation, values, goods, services, and people cross borders today is *qualitatively* different from the forces set in motion by Marco Polo or the Hanseatic League. The pace of institutional change (and history) is quickening. Men dreamed of flying for centuries. Human beings went from gliding across the countryside for a few seconds to bouncing across the surface of the moon in a matter of sixty-six years, a blink of an eye in human history. As the process of global change accelerates, today's authoritarian states have little chance of enduring as long as did the empires of the Bourbons or the Romanovs.

The central question of this book is not "will tyrannies collapse?" As noted in the foreword, the book is an attempt to address the following questions: How can we better understand the processes that destroy tyrannies and nourish open governance? In an age when instability can produce nuclear terrorism, severe international economic disruption, and the transnational movement of crime, refugees, drugs, and disease, how do we prepare for the time when closed states go under? What role can the international community play in helping these states manage their transitions toward greater harmony with everything around them?

When a state hits the bottom of the J curve, it must quickly move in one direction or the other or it will drop off the curve and cease to exist. That's because that country faces pulls in both directions. One side or the other must win the tug of war or the rope will snap.

When Mikhail Gorbachev opened the Soviet Union via *perestroika,* he created two opposing camps that pulled the Soviet state in opposite directions. By loosening state control on information and permitting limited dissent, *perestroika* unleashed calls for sweeping change from the Soviet republics and from within Russia itself. But he also unified conservative opposition within the Communist Party and provoked calls to roll back reform and to push the Soviet Union back up the left side of the curve.*

By 1991, only Gorbachev and his most loyal supporters believed the Soviet Union could become a right-side state. Once the conservatives launched a coup in August and sidelined the Soviet president, the battle for

---

* To obstruct the efforts of Communist Party conservatives to oust him, Gorbachev arranged for the Supreme Soviet to elect him president of the USSR in 1990. The move was intended to give the Soviet leader a power base outside the Party. Previously, the presidency had been a ceremonial position.

the USSR's future became a fight between those who wanted to reconsolidate authoritarian power and those who wanted to pull the empire apart. After the coup failed, Gorbachev tried unsuccessfully to keep the nation intact. But with no move possible up either side of the curve, the centrifugal forces of change pulled the country in a dozen different directions, and the Soviet Union dropped off the J curve altogether.

To better understand how, when, and under what circumstances states drop into the least stable sections of the J curve, we turn to two other states that have been there: South Africa and Yugoslavia. The former Yugoslavia could not sustain the stresses of the descent down the left side of the curve and came apart. South Africa survived the transition and emerged on the right side of the curve.

SOUTH AFRICA

The passage from the left side of the J curve through the dip to the right need not destroy a state as it destroyed Yugoslavia and the Soviet Union. The end of apartheid South Africa and the emergence of stable, open governance in its place demonstrate that, under favorable domestic and geopolitical circumstances and with the right leadership, a new and open state can emerge from the old, closed one without new boundaries, civil war, or chaos.

Some History

War gave birth to the Union of South Africa in 1910. Following the final British defeat in 1902 of small bands of fierce but overmatched Afrikaners (Dutch colonists who settled in the region in the late eighteenth century), South Africa was formed from the unification of Cape Colony, Natal Colony, the Orange Free State, and the Transvaal. To reconcile the two warring sides, Britain gave the Afrikaners two things they wanted: relief from war debt and a promise that black Africans would only be allowed to vote in the British-dominated Cape Colony.

Institutionalized racism began in the new country with the 1913 Native

Lands Act, which limited the land available for black ownership to areas totaling 7 percent of the new nation's territory. But the system that came to be known as "apartheid" was formally introduced only in the early 1950s by the National Party government, which held power from 1948 until the end of white rule in 1994. The National Party began to establish South Africa's place in the whites-only section of the J curve in 1950 with the imposition of the Group Areas Act, which formally divided regions of the country by race. That same year, the Population Registration Act officially inaugurated the racial classification of South African citizens. European slave-owners had restricted the movement of blacks by forcing them to carry passes as early as the 1760s. But the Pass Laws Act of 1952 forced all nonwhites over the age of sixteen to carry a passbook that contained several pages of personal information.* Similar internal passports have been used in the former Yugoslavia and Soviet Union, China, and several other left-side-of-the-J-curve countries. But in South Africa, only nonwhites were required to carry the passes. The Separate Amenities Act of 1953 segregated most public places.

Organized opposition to white rule is virtually as old as the nation. Black South African activists formed the African National Congress (ANC) in 1912, and alongside dozens of other opposition groups, launched public demonstrations, strikes, and other acts of resistance throughout the period of whites-only government. In response to the introduction of modern apartheid in the early 1950s, a number of these groups drafted and signed the Freedom Charter in 1955, demanding respect for universal human rights and an end to racial inequality. The state responded a few months later by jailing 156 leaders and supporters of the ANC on charges of high treason.†

---

* Passbooks contained an ID photo, fingerprints, employment history, government permission to travel in particular areas of the country, work qualifications, and reports from past employers on the bearer's personal conduct and work performance. If an employer was dissatisfied with a worker's behavior, he could refuse to "endorse" his right to remain in the area, in effect forcing the eviction of the worker and his family. Each year, tens of thousands of blacks were arrested for crimes related to the Pass Laws. http://david.snu.edu/~dwilliam/f97projects/apartheid/Laws.htm, among others.

† Even under apartheid, the South African judiciary maintained considerable independence from the National Party government. All 156 activists were eventually acquitted of all charges, but only after they had served five years in prison.

Following the Sharpeville Massacre in March 1960, in which government troops killed 69 reportedly unarmed blacks protesting the Pass Laws, the National Party government granted itself emergency powers, including the right to hold citizens without trial, and formally banned the ANC and many other opposition organizations. In response, the ANC moved underground and formed a militant wing, Umkhonto we Sizwe (Spear of the Nation). The radical group, of which Nelson Mandela was a founding member, committed a number of acts which antiapartheid activists called "sabotage" and the white government called "terrorism." *

In response to fierce resistance to race-based law, the National Party government pushed South Africa further up the left side of the curve in the 1960s by intensifying the enforcement of apartheid. In addition, the state tried to frustrate challenges to its rule through a program of "separate development," which divided black South Africans into "nations" (Bantustans), which were organized around set-aside "homelands." The state tried to pacify black resistance to the program with promises that the homelands would eventually gain independence from white rule.

The international isolation of South Africa began in earnest in May 1961 when, faced with condemnation from fellow members of the British Commonwealth, South Africa formally withdrew and proclaimed itself a republic. The following year, the United Nations General Assembly approved Resolution 1761, which called on UN member states to break diplomatic and trade relations with South Africa in order to end apartheid. In 1964, South Africa was forced out of the International Labour Organization. In 1968, the General Assembly asked all member states and organizations "to suspend cultural, educational, sporting and other exchanges" with South Africa and with "organizations or institutions within the country that practice apartheid." In 1974, South Africa was stripped of its seat in the UN General Assembly. In 1977, the UN Security Council unanimously adopted Resolution 418, which imposed a mandatory arms embargo on the country.

At a critical moment in 1985, it appeared that South Africa might publicly renounce apartheid. In what was billed as a "Rubicon speech," members of President P. W. Botha's government told international journalists in

---

* Mandela was arrested in 1962. A year later, following the capture of other senior ANC leaders—including Walter Sisulu—Mandela and Sisulu were sentenced to life in prison and dispatched to Robben Island.

advance of his appearance before a provincial National Party congress that the president was prepared to announce irreversible changes to South Africa's governance—changes that reflected a fundamental renegotiation of power between blacks and the white minority government that would begin the process of dismantling apartheid. But between the press leaks and the actual speech, some of Botha's senior political advisors warned him that such an announcement would drive white conservative voters into the arms of rival white nationalist parties. As a result, Botha stunned the journalists gathered to hear his historic speech with a finger-wagging declaration of defiance, in which the South African president reaffirmed the government's commitment to apartheid and warned the international community not to "push us too far."

In essence, the government had been prepared to move South Africa down the left side of the J curve. But the fear such a move would end the National Party government led Botha to abandon the plan and to try and cement the country's place on the left. The immediate result was international condemnation of the speech and a currency crisis, as a number of banks, led by Chase Manhattan, refused to roll over some $14 billion in loans to the government.*

The End of Apartheid

In the mid-1980s, the National Party's battle with domestic antiapartheid resistance came to a head. There were 469 strikes in South Africa in 1984. By 1987, the number had climbed to 1,148—an average of more than 3 a day.[1] While reliable figures are hard to come by, a number of credible press reports suggest that thousands were arrested and held without charges between 1984 and 1988; thousands more were killed in political violence.

During the 1980s, the South African government's struggle with external opposition also reached a critical moment, as the sanctions movement gathered momentum. While the United States was slow to join the interna-

---

* It's worth mentioning that representatives of Chase Manhattan and other banks have acknowledged their decision was primarily a business, and not a political, decision. After 1985, South Africa looked increasingly like a bad risk, and commercial pressure on international banks from shareholders opposed to apartheid reached critical mass.

tional isolation of South Africa, the Treasury Department issued South African Transactions Regulations in 1985, which prohibited loans to South Africa by U.S. financial institutions. A year later, the Comprehensive Anti-Apartheid Act ended trade in agricultural products and banned U.S. loans to, and investments in, South Africa's private sector.

African states added to the pressure. Liberation movements in Mozambique, Zimbabwe, and Namibia became what they called "frontline states" against apartheid South Africa. Tanzania, Algeria, Ghana, Zambia, and Botswana provided material and financial support to the ANC and other black South African political organizations.

By 1989, the leadership of the minority white government began to recognize that the costs of international isolation, protection from black anger at home, and the stability of South Africa's place on the left side of the J curve could not be sustained. Even as Mikhail Gorbachev was leading the Soviet Union into the most ambitious *perestroika*-inspired reforms, South African President P. W. Botha entered into secret talks with the only man in the country considered a legitimate representative of the black South African majority, Nelson Mandela.

In September 1989, as left-side-of-the-curve states like Poland, East Germany, and Czechoslovakia tottered on the edge of collapse and Yugoslavia faced civil war, F. W. de Klerk—who had become president after Botha suffered a stroke—released opposition leader Walter Sisulu and several other antiapartheid fighters from prison.

On February 2, 1990, de Klerk lifted the ban on the ANC and several other black African parties. Nine days later, exactly thirty days before the Soviet Congress of People's Deputies abolished the Communist Party's constitutional monopoly on power, Nelson Mandela emerged from his prison cell.

On March 18, 1992, less than three months after the collapse of the Soviet Union, a referendum was held in which white South Africans were asked to decide the country's future. Nearly 70 percent of them voted to end apartheid and for the construction of a power-sharing multiracial government. In 1993, a government of national unity was formed that combined members of the old regime and representatives of the African National Congress. Twenty-one political parties approved an interim constitution.

South Africa held its first democratic elections in 1994. Nelson Mandela was elected president. De Klerk and the ANC's Thabo Mbeki were chosen deputy presidents.

The Closed Politics and Economics of Apartheid

Any political system in which 80 percent of citizens cannot vote is, by definition, a closed, left-side-of-the-J-curve government. In order to maintain that system and to protect itself against the black majority, the white South African government often resorted to brutality and violence. Political prisoners were held indefinitely without charges and, over the apartheid period, 169 of them were hanged. Police death squads secretly tortured and murdered many more.*

As in other countries that are stable only because they are closed and repressive, National Party leaders went to extraordinary lengths to control national and local media and South Africans' access to information. The South African Press Council had the power to fine newspaper editors who violated the regulations of emergency rule. The state arrested and held dozens of reporters and editors, often without charges, and shut down newspapers that published politically embarrassing stories. It regularly expelled or denied entry visas to uncooperative foreign journalists and banned all non-state-controlled coverage of illegal political organizations and their leaders. Government-run media rarely acknowledged demonstrations, protests, and strikes. All political news came from the state-controlled Bureau of Information. Following the Publications Act of 1974, a Publications Control Board censored books and movies that contained unacceptable political content. According to "Jacobsen's Index of Objectionable Literature," apartheid regulations banned everything from T-shirts to leaflets to cigarette lighters with political inscriptions—dangerous threats all to South Africa's national security.

In addition, South Africa had an extensive security apparatus made up of both legally established and secret elements. The government had various legal means and clandestine resources for spying on civilians; organizing vigilante attacks on opposition groups; intimidating, torturing, and even killing black South Africans; and legally carrying out violent attacks by police on demonstrations and other unauthorized public gatherings. Government attempts to protect the apartheid system were not limited to do-

---

* A significant amount of the violence of the period was black-on-black, although some of it was induced by the apartheid government. Divisions among blacks made it more difficult for the ANC to rally the entire black population against apartheid.

mestic policy. South Africa occupied what is now Namibia and sought to destabilize unfriendly governments in Zimbabwe and Mozambique that supported antiapartheid groups.

International political and economic isolation forced the South African government to become as self-reliant as possible. As we'll see, South Africa's efforts at self-sufficiency paid some dividends in the development of particular economic sectors, but overall, the progressive effects of sanctions and the costs of enforcing apartheid became as prohibitively expensive for South Africa as extreme economic inefficiency was for Yugoslavia and the Soviet Union.

As dozens of foreign governments and nongovernmental organizations imposed sanctions, South African economic growth began to stagnate. By the mid-1970s, the cost of imported oil was skyrocketing and the price of gold—of which South Africa provided almost 60 percent of the world's supply—was falling. Gold prices rebounded to help South Africa out of a recession in 1976, but a series of droughts in the early 1980s pushed agricultural output lower. Over the course of the 1980s, GDP grew at an annual rate of just 1.5 percent, and living standards dropped by 10 percent. The economy actually contracted in 1991 and 1992. The combination of increased violence within the country, the high cost of repression, and the impossibility of economic self-sufficiency convinced President F. W. de Klerk that fundamental change was required if South Africa was to avoid chaos and possibly civil war.

How Did South Africa Survive the Transition?

Just as Mikhail Gorbachev came to see that the two extremes of the new Soviet politics were headed in opposite directions at high speed, de Klerk and Mandela understood that black and white South Africans needed one another and that they had to manage South Africa's transition in concert if disaster for both sides, and for the country, was to be averted.

In the Soviet Union in 1990, neither the Communist conservatives nor the democratic reformers needed Gorbachev. Conservatives knew they could never again trust him to protect party interests, and they feared that every day of his reforms deepened the Union's crisis. Liberal reformers no longer needed Gorbachev because he had freed them to act on their own.

The interests of Soviet conservatives and democratic reformers were diametrically opposed.

In South Africa, on the other hand, blacks and whites each had much to gain from a successful transition from minority to majority rule. Black South Africans finally had the opportunity to claim ownership of their country. From whatever tribe, "nation," political party, or region, blacks had been laboring for decades to assert themselves in the country's political life. The opportunity to negotiate their way toward a new South Africa, one governed by a black president and served by black ministers, encouraged them to accept substantial sacrifice and compromise as they established the new nation and sought recognition and support from the international community.

Black leaders also knew they needed the political cooperation and economic contribution of white South Africans. They understood that the apartheid system of Bantu education, which provided virtually no instruction in mathematics or science, had ill prepared blacks for the work that twenty-first-century economic challenges would demand. And they understood that, if white South Africans emigrated in droves, they would take their wealth with them. Keeping that wealth in the country and winning new foreign investment through sound fiscal and monetary management meant keeping white bureaucrats and financial managers in South Africa, since black South Africans had been excluded from jobs that would have given them the experience necessary to run the government and economy on their own.

The white minority government was willing to negotiate its way out of power for several reasons. First, they recognized that the change to majority rule was inevitable. Whether through violence or negotiation, the remaking of South Africa was coming. Better, they reasoned, to strike a favorable deal than to be shoved aside and left with nothing.

Second, de Klerk's government finally accepted that neither partition of the country nor the creation of independent homelands would ever satisfy black South Africans. The former South African president has since defended the idea of partition by noting that "this is what happened in India/Pakistan; in Malaysia/Singapore; in Czechoslovakia. It is what would happen with the disintegration of the Soviet Union and Yugoslavia; and it became the universally recommended solution for Israel/Palestine."[2] Leaving aside the wars fought between India and Pakistan, the Yugoslav blood-bath, and the inability of Israelis and Palestinians to reach a "two-state solu-tion," black, Asian, and mixed-race South Africans firmly and consistently rejected these proposals, not least because the black majority (78 percent in the early 1980s) had only been allocated 13 percent of South Africa's land.

Third, the apartheid elite was fiercely anti-Communist. But the fear that a black South African government would allow the Soviet Union to estab-lish a dangerous influence in the country died with the end of Communism in Eastern Europe and Russia. The end of the Cold War and the discrediting of socialism encouraged whites to believe that, if a new black government opened the country to unprecedented levels of foreign investment and trade, and allowed the white business community to keep its assets, the white elite could keep their wealth and earn a lot more following the lifting of sanctions. In negotiations over South Africa's transition to majority rule, Mandela assured de Klerk he accepted the need for responsible fiscal and monetary policies and openness to foreign direct investment.

Fourth, the promise of a Truth and Reconciliation Commission with the authority to amnesty virtually anyone accused of apartheid-era crimes meant that wholesale, and possibly violent, black retribution for the sins of the past could be avoided, since amnesty required those who committed such crimes to freely confess and to accept moral responsibility for them.* Further, most white South Africans had no obvious place to go. They were of European descent—mainly Dutch and British—but considered them-selves thoroughly African. The families of most white South Africans had lived in Africa for many generations and were no more "European" than are Americans or Australians whose ancestors arrived from the Old World in the eighteenth or nineteenth centuries.

In short, the white elite had a choice: continue to try to hold on to mi-nority control of a government it knew it would eventually lose, possibly in a bloodbath, or accept the status of privileged and wealthy minority in a so-ciety that might soon become more prosperous than ever, thanks to the end of international isolation. White minority rule thus became black majority

---

* For more on the Truth and Reconciliation Commission, here is its official Web site: http://www.doj.gov.za/trc.

rule in South Africa in 1994, and the new government quickly charted a course for the right side of the J curve.

Why did Nelson Mandela choose stability based on openness over a stability based on tight control of the population and its environment? Why did he choose to move South Africa from the bottom of the J curve toward the right? Because domestic and international circumstances reinforced South Africa's stability, because the historical moment that immediately followed the collapse of the Warsaw Pact and Soviet Union favored the choice of democracy and market economics, and because Mandela was a visionary leader.

First, when revolutionary change occurs, the new government's chances of survival are enhanced if the rest of the world welcomes the change. The 1917 Bolshevik Revolution, like the French Revolution, produced a new regime whose very existence threatened the international status quo and the world's other great powers. The Soviet Union survived early attacks by hostile countries mainly because the great powers were otherwise engaged in the end of, then recovery from, the First World War. The black government of South Africa, on the other hand, was warmly welcomed by nearly every government in the world, many of whom were anxious to demonstrate that the age of colonialism was truly dead and that they were committed to the promotion of democratic change in Africa.

Second, the received wisdom in 1994 was that socialism had died with the Soviet Union and that an embrace of liberal economics was the key to future prosperity. Communist governments in Eastern Europe and the former Soviet Union had collapsed. Socialism's record in Africa was abysmal. The so-called Washington Consensus represented an intellectual convergence around a particular set of economic principles: fiscal discipline; investment in physical and educational infrastructure; tax reform; liberalization of trade, interest rates, and rules concerning inflows of foreign investment; a competitive exchange rate; privatization; lifting of barriers to market entry and exit; and secure property rights.[3] The accepted means by which a developing country made progress toward the Washington Consensus goals was "shock therapy." Even in Russia, many were willing to endure shock therapy as the best means to reach Washington Consensus–based policies, because the Asian financial crisis, still three years away, had not yet called the consensus into question.

Third, Nelson Mandela had enormous reserves of political capital with

which to ask South Africans for the sacrifices implicit in these reforms.*
Twenty-seven years as a political prisoner, his refusal to accept early release
in exchange for political half-measures, his charisma and personal warmth,
his reputation for integrity, and the optimism of his political vision for
South Africa enabled him to ask the electorate for sustained sacrifices impossible in virtually any other multiparty system. And South Africans were
ready to accept hardship, in order to demonstrate their black government
could survive, prosper, and win international respect.

The Asian financial crises, and the fallout they produced all over the
world, shook the faith of many in developing nations in the wisdom of
globalized liberal economics. The lessons these financial disasters taught
the South African government, however, were the opposite. The ANC government saw capital flight from Thailand, Russia, Argentina, and elsewhere.
Determined to avoid this fate, the South African government maintained a
disciplined fiscal and monetary policy to an extent possible only in a state
whose rulers enjoy enormous political capital. During the financial crisis,
South Africa never imposed capital controls, despite sharp drops in the
rand, the nation's currency.

How Stable Is South Africa's Place on the Right Side of the J Curve?

From the beginning of democracy in South Africa, Nelson Mandela persuaded the left wing of his ruling coalition—the Congress of South African
Trade Unions (COSATU), Communists, and leftists within the African National Congress—that conservative fiscal and monetary policies were
needed to attract foreign investment and to create stability and prosperity.
South Africa, Mandela argued, must build a stability based on openness to
the prevailing economic trends in the outside world.

One result of that choice—and of the lifting of sanctions—is that South
Africa's gross domestic product has grown from an average of 0.9 percent
per year over the last decade of apartheid to 3.2 percent over the first decade

---

* How much political capital did Mandela have in 1994? Virtually no one, either in South
Africa or anywhere else, had political incentive to criticize his presidency. Of how many
twentieth-century leaders can that be said?

of democracy. Between 1993 and 2003, GDP grew from \$130 billion to over \$200 billion. South Africa's budget deficit remains a responsible 1.5 percent in 2005—better than in the United States and every country in the European Union. The feared massive capital flight following the end of white rule never materialized. By not abandoning the country en masse, the white corporations that stayed behind gave the Mandela government a vote of political and economic confidence.

But current President Thabo Mbeki has less political capital to spend than Mandela did. The winner of the 2008 presidential election will, in turn, have less political capital than Mbeki. Black South Africans were asked to be patient with economic reform and to make an investment in their country's future through short-term sacrifice. More than a decade after the fall of apartheid, most black South Africans are still waiting for their reward. If they don't get it, and if the continuing economic divisions between blacks and whites are not narrowed, South Africa's stability will likely be compromised. The government-managed redistribution of land from whites to blacks—which has done enormous damage to the stability of Zimbabwe—could become a central issue in future South African elections.

In addition, Mandela's disciplined fiscal and monetary policy and his refusal to sharply increase social spending helped reinforce the division of the South African economy into a white-dominated "first-world economy" and a black "third-world economy." Ongoing austerity measures have had opposite effects on the two internal markets. The wealthy, educated, and mostly white "first-world economy" has rebounded from apartheid-era isolation, while most of the black, less-educated, and poor "third-world economy" has sunk further into poverty and frustration.

In part, Mandela accepted "shock therapy" because it seemed to be paying dividends among the former Communist states of Eastern Europe. But wealth gaps in the former Warsaw Pact countries were, to some extent, based on a divide between urban and rural populations. Poorer citizens in those countries could hope to find relief from economic misery by simply moving to the nearest city. In South Africa, the division was not between city and country but between white and black. Largely because of the differences in their respective levels of education, even when the South African economy turned the corner, GDP growth reached 3.5 percent, and white unemployment dropped to 5 percent, black unemployment remained around 40 percent.

The shift from labor-intensive productivity, for which black South Africans were trained during apartheid, toward growth in the service sectors further widened the income and employment-rate gaps between whites and blacks. The apartheid-era closed economy ensured that every asset, including the black labor force, had to be utilized. But since the end of apartheid in 1994 and the increased trade liberalization of the economy, mining and agriculture—industries in which most blacks were employed—have declined as a percentage of GDP. The service sector's share of total output jumped from 51 percent in 1983 to 65 percent in 2003. The structural shift from manufacturing to services has therefore threatened to create a permanently unemployable class of blacks, who remain of little use to the banking, telecommunications, and other service sectors. Ten years after the end of apartheid, blacks still make up less than 5 percent of all qualified engineers in the country. Despite modest improvements in public housing, apartheid shantytowns like Alexandra in Johannesburg, Langa in Cape Town, and Soweto outside Johannesburg, continue to exist, and conditions in a number of them seem actually to have worsened.

In March 2003, President Mbeki unveiled a plan to address the continuing disparity. A program called "black economic empowerment" awarded grants to help black South Africans build new businesses and created a set of "scorecards" to measure black ownership and management of businesses across different economic sectors. The project has created a few black millionaires. But it has not been as popular among blacks as some might have expected, because most of the beneficiaries are believed to be ANC officials and their well-connected friends.

Today, the constituencies most supportive of economic openness—President Mbeki, moderates within the ANC, the corporate community, and the new black elite—continue to back trade liberalization, economic austerity, and tight fiscal and monetary policy. Their opponents include leftists within the ANC, labor unions, and the majority black rural, and increasingly urban, populace. More and more, Afrikaners (and white small-business owners in particular) whose profit margins have come under considerable pressure from Chinese imports, are also aligning against economic openness.

As long as the ruling ANC is able to provide poor black and Afrikaner communities with needed social services and hope for better economic opportunities, it can continue to pursue openness. But Mbeki's economic policies are losing popular support. The 2008 presidential election, in which Mbeki will not be eligible to seek reelection, may well turn on these economic issues. If the ANC nominates another centrist, the Congress of South African Trade Unions, currently part of the ANC's ruling tripartite alliance with South Africa's Communists, may well end the traditional strategic partnership and form a leftist black opposition movement intent on pursuing more protectionist, and less fiscally conservative, economic strategies. A dozen years after the end of apartheid, it appears the centrists have nearly exhausted their political capital. Recent strikes, rising urban crime, and a few cases in which blacks have seized white-owned land make clear that patience with calls for sacrifice is running out. It also demonstrates that, just because a country has begun a climb up the right side of the J curve, there is no guarantee it won't slide back toward instability.

Policy

What role did the international community play in South Africa's shift from the left to the right side of the J curve? Some argue that multilateral international sanctions brought down the apartheid government. Others suggest sanctions were incidental to National Party decision-making and that South Africa's internal pressure for change should receive full credit for the end of whites-only rule. Still others have devised complicated formulas for dividing credit between these and other historical factors.

These debates miss the point. International sanctions and the pressure for change from within South Africa worked together to move the nation toward democratic reform. They had a cumulative effect that eventually brought the country into the dip in the J curve. From there, the international community and the new ANC government worked together to build a new South Africa whose stability was based on openness to the political and economic influences of the outside world.

Multilateral sanctions played a critically important role. They didn't single-handedly bring the National Party to the negotiating table with the African National Congress—much less end apartheid. But without them,

South Africa's white leadership might have fended off pressure for change indefinitely, and opposition leaders would have been deprived of useful negotiating leverage. Sanctions legitimized resistance groups within the country and forced the National Party to pour increasingly precious resources into apartheid's enforcement. In the end, sanctions did not bankrupt the country, but they did make the maintenance of a closed, repressive system more expensive than the privileged status that minority whites discovered they could enjoy in the new South Africa. Sanctions tightly restricted the country's access to export markets, foreign capital, and, crucially, to the new technologies on which information-age economic growth is based. Sanctions lowered South Africa's entire J curve. But because Nelson Mandela and the African National Congress stood ready to inherit the South African government and had the popular legitimacy to do so without social upheaval during the transition, the country survived the depths of the curve in one piece.

The ANC and other antiapartheid groups used the sanctions to force the South African government to lift its ban on nonwhite political parties. Then they used them to free Nelson Mandela, Walter Sisulu, and others from prison. Once these concessions began to produce momentum for further change through greater domestic and international pressure, the ANC used the leverage that came with sanctions to negotiate a new constitution and a power-sharing government.

By 1992, white South Africans were overwhelmingly ready for change. When white voters went to the polls on March 17, it was to answer the following question: "Do you support continuation of the reform process which the State President began on February 2, 1990 [when the government lifted the ban on the ANC and other groups], and which is aimed at a new constitution through negotiation?" A number of white owners of large South African businesses, exhausted by sanctions, spent considerable sums on an advertising campaign urging a yes vote. Amid very high voter turnout, 68.6 percent voted yes. Following two more years of negotiations between the National Party leadership and the ANC, apartheid died. The international community was quick to embrace the new South Africa. De Klerk and Mandela were each awarded the Nobel Peace Prize. South Africa was readmitted to the British Commonwealth and regained its seat in the UN General Assembly after a twenty-year exile.

It is a central thesis of this book that sanctions often produce the opposite of their intended effect, and that closed states should be opened as far as possible to the integrationist, dynamizing effects of globalization. But South Africa is an exceptional case. Kim, Castro, and Saddam have welcomed sanctions, because they wanted their states isolated. They *needed* isolation to maintain virtual monopoly control of wealth, information, and coercive power within their countries. South Africa, on the other hand, never wanted isolation. In the 1950s, the National Party leadership hoped the international community would accept or simply ignore apartheid. As political violence in the country intensified in the early 1960s, and as it became clear the international community would not accept institutionalized racism in the postcolonial world, South Africa's leaders began a three-decade search for some separatist arrangement—through partition or the establishment of independent black "homelands"—to regain international acceptance and to escape sanctions. In the end, neither the black opposition nor the international community accepted those solutions either.

Sanctions, even in South Africa, were never as effective as those who imposed them intended. Through a variety of means, South Africa found ways to diminish some of the sanctions' worst effects. Through the National Party's resourcefulness, the apartheid regime resisted the most destabilizing effects of globalization's pull for more than four decades. In response to OPEC's 1970 oil sanctions, the government invested large amounts of its resources in Sasol, the national coal company. As a result, Sasol became a world leader in extracting oil from coal and the center of a robust petrochemical industry. The South African government further offset the oil embargo's worst effects by continuing to buy oil from Iran, at least until the Islamic revolution in 1979. The UN arms embargo forced South Africa to develop a world-class weapons-production capacity. By the 1980s, South Africa had one of the world's largest armaments industries and earned substantial revenue through arms exports.

Further, U.S. sanctions were never as effective as American anti-apartheid activists hoped, because the legislation that created them was vaguely worded, and because the Reagan and Bush administrations were never fully committed to vigorous enforcement of them.

Yet, even F. W. de Klerk, who rejects the argument that sanctions forced the end of apartheid, has acknowledged that sanctions had a significant impact on South Africa's apartheid leadership. "There is . . . no doubt that sanctions seriously harmed and distorted the South African economy," he wrote in 2004.[4] South Africa's real GDP grew by only 4.7 percent during the period from 1981 to 1987; the population grew by 2.5 percent a year during that six-year period. The result was a 10 percent fall in per capita income—and therefore living standards.[5]

South Africa's economy sustained its worst damage from the decision by several international banks to call in their loans in 1985. In addition, nongovernmental antiapartheid organizations raised the costs and risks of business relations with South Africa by forcing corporations to factor politics into their economic calculations and by challenging corporations who still did business with the apartheid regime with "boycotts, stock divestments, shareholder activism, and through persuading state and local governments to link municipal contracts to withdrawal from South Africa."[6]

Why did sanctions help move South Africa toward openness when they have done the opposite in so many other countries? Apartheid-era South Africa was hardly a liberal democracy, but unlike North Korea, Cuba, or Saddam's Iraq, it did have a functioning multiparty electoral system (though it only included whites) and a leadership willing to negotiate in good faith with foreign governments. South Africa's apartheid leaders never sufficiently consolidated the state's authoritarian character to push the country all the way up the left side of the J curve. And much of South Africa's white elite accepted the idea that a peaceful transfer of power was possible. Just as Gorbachev was unprepared to use all necessary violence to preserve the Soviet Union, the National Party leadership was not willing to fight to the death to preserve the whites-only government. Further, white South Africans were the descendants of Europeans. While Kim, Castro, and Saddam have worked overtime to antagonize Western leaders, few South Africans took pride in their country's image in the West as a social and cultural pariah. In other words, apartheid-era South Africa remained open enough that multilateral international sanctions could influence national political policy.

In the end, the National Party was willing to negotiate itself out of power precisely because its leaders and most influential constituents knew that acceptance of a black government and reengagement with the outside world would be less risky and more profitable than further attempts to sustain the unsustainable. And South Africa reemerged intact because the African National Congress was well prepared to form a stable government.

There is no guarantee that stable governance will continue as South Africa develops. Divisions within the ruling elite ahead of the 2008 presidential election threaten to deepen as progress lags toward a postapartheid reapportionment of South Africa's wealth. The United States has an opportunity to demonstrate that it recognizes the importance of South African stability for the entire region. The implementation of economic policy, in particular, can be based on an acknowledgment that South Africa's political stability depends on the ANC government's efforts to address the gap between rich and poor. Support for the country's economic stability *is* support for its political stability.

Nelson Mandela's place in South African history is well established. But it should also be noted that Mandela's role in South Africa's survival demonstrates that individual leaders—those who are remarkable for their ability to unite or to divide a nation—make choices with enormous implications for a state's direction on the J curve. Mandela's courage, integrity, and wisdom are deservedly well documented. But it is the legitimacy he provided the new South Africa that made an enormous difference in the country's ability to survive the transition from the left to the right side of the curve. He was a unifying figure. Arguably, he was the *only* unifying figure in South Africa.

Perhaps his survival and the popularity he enjoyed when he eventually emerged from prison are an accident of history. But as a symbol of resistance and then as president, his career perfectly illustrates how one man can play an enormous role in shaping his country's future. We now move to Yugoslavia and see how two citizens of that country played disproportionate roles in defining a quite different future: Josip Broz Tito and Slobodan Milosevic.

YUGOSLAVIA

Following South Africa's safe passage through the depths of the J curve and its emergence as a right-side-of-the-curve state, thousands of South African citizens faced a day of reckoning before the Truth and Reconciliation Commission in Cape Town. Nearly 1,200 received amnesty for apartheid-era crimes. More than a hundred citizens of the former Yugoslavia have had their day in court as well. But those ongoing trials take place before a war-crimes tribunal in The Hague.* South Africa has successfully established political, economic, and social stability based on engagement with the international community and openness within its borders. Yugoslavia no longer exists. Why do some states fail once their closed societies are opened? Why did Yugoslavia explode into war and fall completely off the J curve?

The conventional view is that Yugoslavia, like Iraq and many other states founded in the early twentieth century, was a poorly conceived creation that forced peoples who hated one another to live together in imposed harmony. According to this interpretation, the southern Slavs have been warring since the Middle Ages, and only the authoritarian rule of Josip Broz Tito restrained the region's warring ethnic and religious groups and enforced order. When Tito died in 1980, so the argument goes, it was inevitable that the state would quickly fall into violent chaos. A Google search combining "Yugoslavia" and "ancient hatreds" produces thousands of hits.

Like most conventional interpretations, this one is based on elements of truth but is ultimately a vastly oversimplified view of a region with a complicated history.

The First Yugoslavia

Before the collapse and the beginnings of war in 1991, Yugoslavia was essentially a federation of six republics (Serbia, Croatia, Bosnia-Herzegovina, Slovenia, Macedonia, and Montenegro) and two autonomous provinces (Vojvodina and Kosovo). Each of these regions was, to one degree or another, a complicated melting pot of national and ethnic minorities. (See map of Yugoslavia 1990 on page 168.) Contrary to much of the nationalist mythmaking of the 1980s from within all these ministates, the various peoples of Yugoslavia are not natural enemies. Serbs and Muslims lived together for more than four centuries as subjects of the Ottoman Empire. Croats were subject to rule by the Habsburgs for nearly as long. Thus, for half a millennium, the peoples of the future Yugoslavia were pitted not

---

* Former Serb leader Slobodan Milosevic died in The Hague in March 2006.

against one another, but against their respective imperial overlords. It's true there are important religious and ethnic differences among the peoples of the former Yugoslavia. Most Serbs, Macedonians, and Montenegrins are Orthodox Christians. Croats and Slovenes are historically Catholic. Most Bosnians and the vast majority of Kosovo's ethnic Albanians are Muslims. But the Slav identity of most of Yugoslavia's peoples united many of their most influential thinkers against domination by outsiders from the early nineteenth century. The natural rivalry among Yugoslavia's ethnic and religious groups actually dates from the period between the two world wars, following the creation of Yugoslavia as a unified state.

Map of Yugoslavia (1990): The six republics and two autonomous provinces of Yugoslavia in 1990, just before the country descended into the dip in the J curve.

The "first Yugoslavia" was formally established on December 1, 1918, as "The Kingdom of Serbs, Croats, and Slovenes" and encompassed virtually the same lands and peoples that made up Yugoslavia through the 1980s. The enmity that would later divide Yugoslavia's peoples grew from the fact that the kingdom's creation was essentially a forced marriage of Serbs and others who had fought on the winning side of World War I with the Croats, Slovenes, and other groups who had been subjects of the defeated Habsburg Empire. When the kingdom was formally established, Serbia's incapacitated King Peter became the titular head of the new state. His son Alexander ruled as his regent.

From the beginning, the victorious Serbs dominated the kingdom. Serbia's governing institutions became the new kingdom's political structure. The Habsburg bureaucracy that governed Croatia and Slovenia was dismantled. Although Serbs did not and have never formed a majority of Yugoslavia's population, the provisional cabinet created to govern the kingdom in advance of a new constitution was made up of thirteen Serbs, four Croats, two Slovenes, and one Muslim.[7] A number of Serb leaders, including those who lived among the Serb minority populations within Croat, Slovene, and other territories, used their influence in the newly unified kingdom to push for a centralized state that would promote the concept of a "Greater Serbia." Serbs dominated the national police and security forces, even in non-Serb provinces. In the name of monetary union, the four separate currencies that had been in circulation before 1918 were replaced with a single currency: Serbia's. Habsburg crowns were shipped in large quantities to Belgrade, Serbia's capital, and were used to pay much of Serbia's war debt. In essence, much of Croatia and Slovenia's wealth was transferred to Serbia as a kind of "war reparation."[8] To the First World War's victors went the spoils.

At the same time, if Serbs dominated political and economic decision-making in the kingdom, Croats must accept part of the blame. Of the kingdom's non-Serb peoples, only Croats might have had the influence within the state's young parliament to bring balance to policymaking. But Croat leaders boycotted much of the process by which the kingdom's first constitution was written. Once that constitution was ratified in 1921, Croat members of parliament were left to obstruct any meaningful legislation that might have brought balance and coherence to the kingdom's political and economic affairs.* As a result, the marriage of the war's winners and losers produced a Balkan state divided against itself.

In December 1928, frustrated by the parliament's inability to give the kingdom a sense of political direction, King Alexander (crowned in 1921 following the death of his father) decided that a push up the left side of the J curve could bring stability to his troubled kingdom. He dissolved the parliament, established himself as a virtual dictator, and renamed his country "Yugoslavia." In 1931, he introduced a new constitution that centralized power in the monarch's hands.

In the process, Alexander alienated all of the country's groups. Serbs feared their influence would be diminished as Croats and other non-Serbs were appeased in the name of unity. Non-Serbs suspected that Alexander (a Serb himself) would attempt to accomplish by force what he could not by parliament—a Greater Serbia.

Croat resistance to Serb domination grew over the kingdom's first decade, and, soon after the imposition of dictatorship, the most extreme of Croatia's nationalists formed the Ustasa-Croat Revolutionary Organization, essentially a fascist terrorist group.† Alexander forced the Ustasa to flee to Italy, where it was welcomed by Benito Mussolini. In 1934, a Ustasa member assassinated King Alexander during a visit to France and plunged the kingdom into instability.

Alexander's son was not yet a teenager, so Alexander's cousin Paul assumed the throne. The new king recognized that, if Yugoslavia were to rebuild its stability, Croats had to be granted meaningful political concessions. In 1939, he granted Croatia status as an autonomous province within the kingdom. The move further heightened tensions between Croats and Serbs (who saw their hopes dashed of a Serb-dominated state) and other territorial groups who resented Croatia's special status.

The arrangement was short-lived. Knowing Britain and France had no interest in protecting the Balkans from a newly aggressive Germany, Paul

---

* That same scenario may be playing out again in post-Saddam Iraq. Despite their higher-than-expected turnout for December 2005 elections, the chances that Sunnis will adopt the same strategies of boycott and obstruction in the new Iraq's governance process are increasing.

† *Ustasa* is the Serbo-Croat word for insurgent.

reluctantly agreed to limited accommodation of Adolf Hitler. Belgrade and Berlin signed trade deals, and limited military cooperation followed. A group of disgruntled Yugoslav military officers then launched a successful coup against Paul. Britain and France applauded. Hitler invaded. Serbia would never again enjoy the dominance over the other peoples of Yugoslavia provided them by victory in the First World War.

World War II

By the time Serb nationalism became a potent force in the 1980s, a simplistic portrait of Yugoslavia's World War II experience had gained currency. Unaware of the history, many in the West have accepted the view that the war years can be reduced to a battle between Nazis with their Croat allies and antifascist Serbs fighting alongside the Allies. In reality, the conflict in the Balkans during the early 1940s was one in which the most virulent nationalists among Serbs, Croats, Muslims, and many other groups fought out the political battles of the early twentieth century by other, far more violent, means.

There was very little Nazi military presence in the Balkans after 1941. Not wanting to waste troops and resources that were needed inside the Soviet Union, Hitler left the administration of Yugoslavia's various provinces to others. He established a puppet government in Serbia and gave control of most of the rest of the country to his Hungarian, Italian, and Bulgarian allies. Crucially, Hitler set up members of the Ustasa in power in the Croatian capital of Zagreb. Most Croats believed Hitler would lose the war and therefore had refused to back him. But by establishing Ustasa's terrorists in power, Hitler inadvertently unleashed a series of battles within Yugoslavia and undermined stability in the Balkans.

The Ustasas initially enjoyed limited popularity in Croatia.* Many of the Ustasa leaders came from areas of Croatia and Herzegovina most disadvantaged by Serb dominance of the kingdom, and sought to boost their legitimacy among Croat nationalists by beginning a bloody assault on the nearly

---

* The autonomous province of Croatia contained much of the land that is today within the borders of Bosnia-Herzegovina.

2 million Serbs and hundreds of thousands of other non-Croats living within Croatia's borders. The Ustasa plan was simple: kill as many Serbs as possible, drive more of them from Croatia, and convert the rest to Catholicism.* In the summer of 1941, concentration camps were established and entire Serb villages were massacred. As Christopher Bennett noted in his book *Yugoslavia's Bloody Collapse,* inside the concentration camps, "there were no gas chambers, nor were the *Ustasas* willing to waste bullets on their victims. Instead, death was by beating, starvation, and knives."[9] Hundreds of thousands died in the Ustasa camps, most of them Serbs. The mass killings provoked violent reprisals against Croats, particularly by Serbs and Muslims.

During the war, two important military figures emerged as threats to fascist control in the region: Draza Mihailovic (a dedicated royalist and Serb nationalist) and Communist insurgent Josip Broz Tito. Mihailovic and his guerilla fighters, known as Cetniks, enjoyed support among many Serbs, especially those who favored a postwar restoration of the monarchy. Tito's Communist Partisans, on the other hand, drew support from among all the region's religious and ethnic groups. When Italy surrendered in 1943 and it began to appear that Germany would lose the war, Mihailovic and Tito's forces increasingly targeted one another. In the end, Tito proved the better political and military tactician, and the appeal of a transnational Communist ideology trumped the narrow nationalisms of Mihailovic and others who resisted the coming imposition of Communism as long as they could.

As early as November 1943, a meeting of antifascist insurgents established that, once Yugoslavia had expelled the Nazis and their sympathizers, a new Yugoslavia would establish a Communist state made up of the six republics and the autonomous region of Kosovo and autonomous province of Vojvodina. As World War II ground to a halt, Tito's forces, made up mainly of peasants from across the former kingdom, drove most of their enemies (foreign and domestic) from the region and established this new Communist state by force. In November 1945, the Yugoslav Constituent Assembly formally created the Federal People's Republic of Yugoslavia and abolished the monarchy.

---

* Despite the Ustasa's pride in its nationalist Catholic ideology, the Vatican refused to recognize the Ustasa government.

Tito

Josip Broz Tito was the son of a Croat father and a Slovene mother, who joined the Habsburg army in Vienna in 1911 and fell prisoner to tsarist Russia during the First World War. The 1917 Bolshevik Revolution instilled in the then twenty-five-year-old Tito a deep devotion to Communism. When he returned to the Balkans after the war, it was to bring Marxist-Leninist thought to the Kingdom of Serbs, Croats, and Slovenes. Tito was jailed for his activism in 1928 and spent five years in a Yugoslav prison refining his understanding of the scientific principles on which Communist political, economic, and social thought are based. Once released, he became an active member of the newly formed Communist Party of Yugoslavia (CPY) and traveled to Moscow, birthplace of the revolution, to learn from the Soviet Communist Party. Recognizing Tito's talent and ideological fervor, Stalin enlisted Tito to purge the CPY. Tito vigorously carried out his orders.

As a dedicated Communist, Tito's first post–World War II priority for the country he had come to dominate was to construct a new Yugoslav republic on a Marxist-Leninist foundation. Nationalism was the first enemy to be conquered. The new state's Communists feared that the nationalist animosity that had divided the first Yugoslavia's peoples would sabotage Communist plans. To create a new universalist ideology that would bind all Yugoslavia's people together in a common project, Tito turned again for ideas to the Soviet Union, where, he believed, nationalism had already been defeated.

Stalin's early influence on Tito was everywhere apparent. Like the Soviet dictator, Tito created an official interpretation of World War II. In it, Yugoslavia's peoples had fought as one to repel fascists from the Balkans. Tito then organized show trials of hundreds of Yugoslavs accused of collaboration with the Nazis. Among the victims of these trials: Draza Mihailovic, who was found guilty of treason and executed.

To disseminate the Marxist message, promote the heroic version of Yugoslavia's role in World War II, and establish the new state's place high up the left side of the J curve, Yugoslavia's dictator brought the media under direct state control. Because the CPY reduced the history of the war to an all-Yugoslav antifascist struggle, there was never official recognition of the sectarian conflicts that had plagued Yugoslavia during the war. No blame was assigned for the nationalist hatreds that had provoked massacres between Croats, Serbs, Muslims, and others. There was no truth and reconciliation commission to heal past wounds, and nationalism itself was not addressed. Tito considered it unnecessary, since the achievement of the new republic's Marxist goals would naturally erode and eventually eliminate nationalism as a force in Yugoslav life. Yet, despite Tito's best efforts to control the flow of information within Yugoslavia, oral histories of wartime atrocities lived on and reemerged with a vengeance following his death.

This problem demonstrates a weakness inherent in a left-side-of-the-curve state's ability to control information. In a state where the ruling elite dominates the mass-media distribution channels, rumor and misinformation become more potent. When the national media are forbidden to even acknowledge the existence of dangerous rumors, these (often false) stories spread without any check on their veracity. To debunk an ugly rumor is to publicly acknowledge its existence. And in Yugoslavia, some of these stories and rumors were at least loosely based on ugly truths.

On January 31, 1946, the CPY completed the new republic's first constitution. As called for by the wartime Communist councils, the Federal People's Republic of Yugoslavia was established with six republics and two autonomous areas. Tito knew that Serb dominance of the Yugoslav kingdom had deepened fault lines across the region and that his fragile new state could not afford such stresses. He sought to create a balance of power within the new Yugoslavia based on an equilibrium that protected every group from every other group. The constitution thus gave the six republics the right to secede and to negotiate the borders between them, subject to the approval of all. Tito believed the mythology created around the victory over fascism would swell national pride and help create a new Yugoslav identity that would make secession unthinkable.*

As in other left-side-of-the-J-curve states, the revolutionary leader's personality became an integral part of this new national awareness and pride. Tito—like Stalin, Kim Il-Sung, Fidel Castro, Ayatollah Khomeini, Saparmurat Niyazov, Ho Chi Minh, and others—cultivated the image of

---

* According to census data, only 1.7 percent of Yugoslavia's citizens identified themselves as "Yugoslav," as opposed to Serb or Croat, etc., in 1961. By 1981, the number jumped to 5.4 percent. Other data reveal that "Yugoslavs" were more likely to be young, urban, and well educated than those who choose other designations. Eric Gordy, *The Culture of Power in Serbia* (University Park: Pennsylvania State University Press, 1999), pp. 4–5.

national "father figure," the ultimate arbiter of all disputes, a figure above pettiness and parochial concerns who dedicated his spirit and his labor to the well-being of his people. No left-side state can survive without an ultimate authority, a person or institution whose legitimacy cannot be publicly questioned and whose wisdom exceeds the challenges facing the people.*

On the Stalinist model, Tito nationalized Yugoslav industries and collectivized the country's agricultural production. But Tito's ambitions for the spread of Communist principles extended well beyond the borders of Yugoslavia. He financed Communist insurgents during the Greek Civil War and sought the establishment of a Communist Federation that would extend across Eastern Europe. He also founded the Cominform (Communist Information Bureau), an internationalist organization meant to increase cooperation among the Communist parties of France, Italy, Poland, Czechoslovakia, Hungary, Bulgaria, Romania, and the Soviet Union. Cominform meetings were first held in Belgrade. But Tito's activism soon cost him the relationship with his own father figure—Joseph Stalin.

It later became part of Titoist mythology—and conventional wisdom in the West—that the Yugoslav dictator had broken with Stalin over principle. In fact, it was Stalin who jettisoned Tito. The move had little to do with differences over ideology. As Stalin purged all potential challengers to his place in the Communist pantheon, the Soviet leader asserted Moscow's leadership of the Yugoslav-created organization, ejected Yugoslavia from its membership, and cast Tito as a counterrevolutionary. Tito tried for several years to reingratiate himself with his inspiration in the Kremlin, but following Stalin's death in 1953, Tito never again sought close relations with the Soviet leadership, and he purged thousands of Stalinists from the CPY.

As the waste and inefficiency inherent in the Soviet economic model pushed Yugoslavia toward crisis, and after the nation lost favor in the Kremlin, Tito sought to unify his people by invoking the threat to the nation from a dangerous enemy. Just as Fidel Castro and Venezuela's Hugo Chávez rally popular support for their governments by conjuring threats of an impend-

---

* As we'll see in the next chapter, the creation of a national "father figure" is a tool used by some who intend to establish a right-side-of-the-curve state as well. Men like Atatürk and Nehru have used it. American schoolchildren are taught to remember George Washington as the father of their country, and other American figures of the period are routinely referred to as the "founding fathers."

ing American invasion, Tito warned his people to expect an attack from the Soviet Union and its Eastern European allies. At first, the threat was credible; in fact, the Soviet bloc began an economic blockade of the country. But then the West, hoping to win a tactical geopolitical victory over Moscow, decided to try and drive a wedge between Belgrade and Moscow by sending large amounts of aid to Yugoslavia. That aid would support Yugoslav Communism for decades, but would ultimately help undo the country when the Soviet bloc collapsed and Yugoslavia became less important for Western leaders. How much aid did the West offer Communist Yugoslavia? By the early 1970s, Yugoslavia was nearly $2 billion in debt.[10]

Following the Soviet-Yugoslav divorce, Tito sought to establish Yugoslavia as the true capital of Marxist-Leninist principle. A core group of Tito's advisors constructed a new socialist philosophy, Titoism, which sought to prove that Stalin had strayed from the true path toward Communism. The Yugoslav dictator argued that Stalin had consolidated too much power in the hands of the central government. In Yugoslavia, he argued, the central government would slowly give way over time to a new system that increased local power at the central government's expense. It was a philosophy of convenience, since Tito had already decided that decentralization, the transfer of political and economic power from the center to Yugoslavia's constituent republics, would encourage all Yugoslavia's peoples to invest in the Yugoslav idea.

In essence, Tito believed Yugoslavia could become a Communist right-side-of-the-J-curve state: a command economy open to foreign investment with decentralized control of government decision-making. In the future, Tito's benign presence and the creation myth of Yugoslavia's founding as an antifascist workers' paradise uniting the diverse peoples of the Balkans would be enough to guarantee state stability. That was the theory. It did not take long for theory to rush headlong into reality.

In 1953, Tito announced the formulation of a new plan: Socialist Worker Self-Management. Agriculture was decollectivized, and the party approved a new constitution that created workers' councils for grassroots management of the Yugoslav economy. To highlight the reforms, the Communist Party of Yugoslavia changed its name to the League of Communists of Yugoslavia (LCY).

But as Mikhail Gorbachev discovered some thirty-five years later, an entrenched bureaucracy is the chief beneficiary of the system it was originally designed to administer—and it has a vested interest in preserving it. The Yugoslav bureaucracy thus obstructed nearly all genuine efforts at reform. Tito himself remained ambivalent about giving up central control in the short term and did little to push the changes through. When halfhearted reforms failed to open Yugoslavia's economy and to reduce dependence on Western aid, Tito purged the new program's principal architects from within the government. Further attempts to meaningfully liberalize the economy were effectively aborted.

While the economy remained closed, Tito certainly opened his country politically to the outside world. In 1961, he helped found the Non-Aligned Movement, a collection of states whose leaders believed stability depended on Cold War neutrality. Tito used the platform to trumpet Yugoslavia's socialist achievements.

Tito's country had genuine accomplishments to display. Financial support from the West lifted Yugoslavia's entire J curve by allowing Tito to invest in health care and education. Early industrialization, the country's increasing openness to foreign tourists, cash from the West, and Tito's magnanimous presence helped quell the cycle of sectarian violence that plagued the region during World War II. A secular society even produced marriages across religious and ethnic lines.* In 1965, Yugoslavia's citizens were free to travel and to work abroad virtually without restriction. Many of these workers provided a further boost for the economy through remittances sent to family members at home. Yugoslav artists, writers, and athletes earned international renown. Tito was feted in the West as an ally against the Soviet Union and in nonaligned countries as a champion of the rights of developing states.

To some extent, Tito also opened Yugoslavia internally. Schoolchildren were taught to love Tito and Yugoslavia. But they also learned the cultural traditions and (officially sanitized) histories of Yugoslavia's other republics and regions. The Yugoslav government, through both education and official propaganda, were told that they could and should celebrate both their ethnic identities and the accomplishments of their Yugoslav homeland.

---

* "Ethnically 'mixed' marriages increased from 8 to 9 percent of all marriages in the period from 1950 to 1957 to 13 percent of all marriages in the period from 1977 to 1981." See Gordy, p. 4.

Tito's approach to Yugoslavia's "nationalities problem" differed from the solutions found in the Communist behemoths, the Soviet Union and China. Russians dominated most aspects of Soviet political life, just as Han Chinese play the principal role in Chinese governance. But Yugoslavia had no single ethnic group whose influence could be extended over the rest of the country within a Communist framework. There were more Serbs in Yugoslavia in the late 1980s than any other ethnic group, yet they represented only about 36 percent of the population. Stalin tried at various times to force cultural assimilation among the Soviet Union's minority populations. He also moved ethnic Russians (and other Slavs) into lands overwhelmingly dominated by non-Russians.* Even today, the Chinese Communist Party encourages Han Chinese to migrate into China's predominantly Muslim Xinjiang Province to alter the ethnic balance in the area.

But Tito ruled a country with a much more delicate balance to protect. Far from trying to repress minority ethnic groups or to erase their collective cultural memories, by the 1960s Tito encouraged Muslims, Macedonians, and other minorities to self-confidently promote and celebrate their individual histories and national identities. It was only in Tito's Yugoslavia that Macedonians and Montenegrins won recognition as distinct nationalities and the country's Muslims won the right to openly celebrate their cultural and religious identity. Tito protected the minority Hungarian population of Vojvodina and, eventually, the ethnic-Albanian Muslims of Kosovo.

In addition, the urbanization that grew out of postwar industrial expansion mitigated the risks that nationalism posed for Yugoslav cohesion. As workers became more mobile and crossed republican boundaries to work in the country's growing cities, ethnic and religious bonds loosened, and Yugoslavs developed deeper ties to the places they lived than to the regions of their birth.

---

* Chechnya offers a prime example. In 1943, Stalin ordered the entire Chechen population exiled from the Caucasus to Kazakhstan by train. Ethnic Russians moved into the area to replace them. In the late 1950s, Khrushchev allowed the Chechens to return, but the Russians remained in Chechnya, even after the outbreak of war there in 1994.

The Seeds of Destruction

Yet, as long as Tito lived, Yugoslavia remained a dictatorship dependent on Communist Party officials for political, economic, and social stability. The J curve demonstrates that any partial opening of a closed society will produce substantial turmoil before it creates meaningful stability. And without Tito, there was no single political figure with the power and authority to build Yugoslavia's stability with either a concerted move up the left side of the curve or a determined reform effort to open the political process. In fact, Tito arranged for the establishment of a rotating presidency following his death, in the name of Yugoslav unity. Such an arrangement could never have filled the void left by a national father figure. The death of Tito substantially lowered Yugoslavia's J curve.

Another important contributing factor to the environment that eventually led to war: a worsening economy. Tito, like all dictators, feared the potential for domestic unrest. As a result, whenever economic liberalization (what the LCY called "market socialism") began to produce unemployment and protests, Tito fell back on the Western aid that financed Yugoslavia's illusion of economic stability and allowed the Communist leadership to continually postpone reform.

Tito had one important advantage over the other Communist states of Eastern Europe: Having established independence from the Soviet bloc, he felt he could allow Yugoslav workers to travel and work in the West. Remittances from Yugoslav workers in Germany and elsewhere in Europe helped stave off economic crisis for many years. But when the oil shock of 1973 took its toll on the economies of Western Europe, foreigners were the first to be laid off. Returning Yugoslavs only added to the unemployment burden on their own government.[11]

Tito tried to borrow his way out of debt.* In 1973, Yugoslavia's total foreign debt had been $3.5 billion. By 1981, a year after Tito's death, that figure hit $20.5 billion.[12] The wealth gap widened within Yugoslavia between the relatively prosperous republics in the north of the country (Slovenia and Croatia) and the poorer areas of the south (Serbia, Montenegro, Macedonia, and Bosnia). Between 1982 and 1987, Yugoslavia's standard of living fell by nearly 40 percent. In December 1989, inflation reached 2,000 percent.[13]

---

* The Yugoslav media were strictly forbidden to report on foreign debt.

Over the years, Tito had tried to head off social unrest by giving the republics the power to make some of their own economic decisions. As the economy declined further following Tito's death, each individual republic (and the autonomous provinces) began protecting its own interests at the expense of the whole. Each republic believed it needed its own steelworks, its own oil refineries, its own port. These projects served the immediate needs of the individual republics but created enormous inefficiencies in the Yugoslav economy as a whole.[14] As Europe made progress toward a common market and monetary union, Yugoslavia was steadily breaking down into ministates, each prepared to use protectionist policies to serve local interests against the Yugoslav republic across its border.

Political factors too helped bring Yugoslavia to the brink. The LCY's attempts at political openness virtually always produced instability. In the late 1960s, Tito sought to appease the ethnic Albanians of Kosovo, a predominantly Muslim autonomous territory within Serbia, by allowing them greater freedom to air their many grievances. Once the muzzle was off, street demonstrations in 1968 were punctuated with demands that Kosovo be made a full republic. Prior to the mid-1960s, Yugoslavia had earned a reputation for treating Kosovar Albanians, and any signs of dissent from them, ruthlessly. Tito, anxious to protect his country's reputation on the world stage, decided to give Kosovo greater autonomy, a sharp increase in financial subsidy, and a number of cultural freedoms.

Kosovo was not made a republic. Such a move would have deeply alienated Serbs and Macedonians, and Tito's aim was to quell unrest, not to provoke it. But Kosovo joined Vojvodina as an "autonomous province." The Albanian language gained official status. Much to the chagrin of Kosovo's Serb minority, Kosovar Albanians were encouraged to join the local League of Communists in ever-increasing numbers. All of this was codified in the 1974 constitution—Yugoslavia's sixth and last. Serbs had long dominated the political and economic life of the majority Muslim territory. The shift in the balance of power that followed Tito's decision pitted Serbs and Kosovars against one another, and acts of violence followed from both sides. While the Kosovo question was not central to the political life of the country in the 1970s, it would become an important trigger for the conflicts of the 1990s.

Tito was also forced to stem a rising tide of nationalist unrest in Croatia in 1971. He purged a number of senior Communist officials from the Croat League of Communists and banned a number of media outlets that had stoked the separatist fervor. To give the move a reformist veneer, he also purged technocrats in Slovenia and liberals in Serbia.[15] But Tito, as he did so often, combined this move up the left side of the J curve with more plans to appease local populations by granting their local governments greater independence from the center. Part of Tito's motivation for the devolution of power to the republics was a genuine desire to release nationalist pressure for the good of the whole. But many who knew him say he was also driven by a strong need to be remembered by all Yugoslavia's peoples as a champion of tolerance.

By the late 1970s, there were three forces holding Yugoslavia together: the League of Communists of Yugoslavia, the Yugoslav People's Army, and Josip Broz Tito. The LCY, like the country, became more and more decentralized in the 1970s and 1980s. As local leaders faced rising pressure to protect local interests, the eight Communist leagues began to pull the national Communist party in eight different directions. Tito, like the leaders of other left-side states, feared potential rivals and purged a number of the most talented and resourceful officials from the national government. The remainder, many of whom distinguished themselves only by their loyalty to Titoism, were out of their depth as economic and political challenges mounted.

The JNA, the Yugoslav People's Army, was always limited in size and resources by the standards of other East European Communist states. When the Soviets invaded Czechoslovakia in 1968, Tito raised the level of alert across the country. He recognized that the Soviets had quickly immobilized Czech resistance by concentrating its forces in Prague, the nation's political and military center of gravity. To counter the threat of a Soviet or Warsaw Pact invasion of Yugoslavia, the JNA implemented "General People's Defense," a plan that decentralized military command and control—and Yugoslavia's arsenal. The state's various administrative territories financed their own defense. Local commanders were given charge of their own troops. Stockpiles of weapons were moved to strategic locations around the country. In the event of a Soviet invasion, the enemy would have faced resistance from all over Yugoslavia.[16] But when Yugoslavs discovered in later years that the true enemy was coming not from abroad but from the neighboring province, they were also forced to recognize that the groundwork had been laid inadvertently for civil war.

The third pillar of Yugoslav unity, Josip Broz Tito, died on May 4, 1980. He left behind a country with a profoundly weak center of gravity, a floundering economy, and a growing number of local officials looking for the right political formula with which to create a following.

Milosevic

Serb nationalism, more than any other force, led to the breakup of Yugoslavia. There is no question that virulent, xenophobic movements appeared during the 1980s in much of the country. Many Serbs living in other Yugoslav republics were harassed, brutalized, even killed. But, in the context of Yugoslavia's J curve, Serb nationalism differed from other such Yugoslav nationalist movements in one important respect: most of its proponents wanted to preserve the Yugoslav federation. Croat nationalism was ugly and dangerous for minority populations within Croatia. Slovene, Croat, and Bosnian nationalists initially argued for a new Yugoslav structure with looser bonds: less a federation than a confederation. But Serb nationalists, who controlled the resources of much of the Yugoslav People's Army, were able to push tanks across borders and unleash the forces that provoked Yugoslavia's disintegration.

While Tito was alive, criticism of the dictatorship and Titoism was limited in public to vague and indirect complaints from within the republics about a particular policy or local official. Following Tito's death, and as the sputtering economy and social conflicts produced unrest in the early and mid-1980s, however, overt criticisms of Tito and Titoism began to appear. In particular, Serb nationalists aggressively attacked the 1974 constitution and the powers it granted majority Albanians within Kosovo. At first, Serb anger was limited to a few lone voices among Serb intellectuals, particularly those Tito had purged for nationalist agitation. But by 1986, increasing numbers of influential Serbs were accusing Tito of pulling Kosovo from its rightful Serb owners. In Croatia, resentment against Tito ran high since he had purged a number of Croat leaders in the early 1970s and, in order to water down Croat nationalism, replaced them with Serbs.

Following Tito's death, the republic-level politicians left to preside over the economic ruin of the decentralized state needed an issue, a cause on which to build durable popularity. In several of the republics, nationalist anger at the Yugoslav government's expense offered local politicians an opportunity.

There are several reasons why Serb nationalism was especially potent. First, Serbia (along with Slovenia) enjoyed the freest media in the country in the early 1980s. The Serbian press already aired a (relatively) broad range of opinions that created opportunities for exploitation by those with a strong point of view and a grievance. Again, small openings in an otherwise closed society invariably produce some degree of slide down the left side of the curve toward instability. Serbia in the 1980s illustrates the point.

There were certainly ugly manifestations of militant nationalism and xenophobia in other republics. Franjo Tudjman, widely credited as the founder of independent Croatia, did much to drive many of Croatia's minority Serbs from the republic and inspired acts of violence against them. A number of Bosnian chauvinists stoked much the same sentiment in Bosnia-Herzegovina. But non-Serbian nationalists hoped mainly to win greater autonomy within a new Yugoslavia or to secede and establish independence. While repressive within their own borders, few harbored illusions of forcibly remaking the political structures in other republics. Serb hard-liners in Belgrade, who hoped to create a new Serb-dominated Yugoslavia, were able to leverage their nationalist appeal into the use of JNA tanks and planes outside Serbia and to try and defend Yugoslavia's territorial integrity by force.

Second, the most influential Serb nationalists were able to construct an entire mythology to give their grievances a compelling context. In the last years of Ottoman domination, Serb nationalists were motivated by a well-articulated goal: to cast off the Muslim yoke and to create a Greater Serbia throughout the Balkans. On the winning side of World War I, Serb nationalists were able to realize much of their dream through domination of the Yugoslav monarchy that ended with the onset of World War II. According to the nationalist narrative, Tito then declared war on all Serbs by forcing them to relinquish control of Yugoslavia in the name of Communist equality among Yugoslavia's peoples. Economic hardship and the fact that nearly 40 percent of Yugoslavia's Serbs lived outside Serbia added to the sense of vulnerability, even among Serbs who preferred Tito's Yugoslav model to the nationalist dream of Greater Serbia.

But, in the late 1980s, no issue united Serbia's most determined nationalists more than did the conflict over control of Kosovo. Historically, Kosovo was the spiritual heart of the Serbian Orthodox Church. The village of Kosovo Polje was the site of a crucial battle in 1389 during which advancing Ottomans toppled what was then a Serbian empire in the region. Though Muslims have far outnumbered Serbs in Kosovo for four centuries, Kosovo Polje remained at the center of Serb nationalist consciousness.

In the early twentieth century, Serbia essentially colonized Kosovo, and the Serb minority there dominated the ethnic-Albanian Muslim majority. Until Tito's reforms in the 1960s, Kosovar Albanians were the object of not-so-benign neglect from Belgrade, and Kosovo remains today the poorest region of the former Yugoslavia. Tito's 1974 constitution freed the majority Albanians to assert themselves politically within the province and to openly celebrate their language and culture. But it did little to improve economic conditions, as the province's tepid economic growth could not keep pace with the rapid Muslim population expansion. In a sense, Kosovar Albanians, before 1974, found themselves in a predicament similar to that of black South Africans—a poverty-stricken and disenfranchised majority whose protests were regularly smashed by brute force.

By 1981, a year after Tito's death, Albanians outnumbered Serbs within Kosovo by nearly six to one. In March of that year, a student demonstration against economic misery spiraled out of control as outnumbered police unable to stop the protests responded with a brutality not seen since the 1974 constitution was established. The violence continued and, two months later, the Yugoslav government declared martial law. A media blackout makes reliable casualty figures hard to establish, but hundreds of Kosovar Albanians were arrested. Over the next half-decade, tensions increased between Kosovo's Albanians and Serbs, and there were a number of Muslim attacks on Serb citizens. Hundreds, possibly thousands, of fearful Serbs decided to retreat to Serbia.

If any Yugoslav citizen best illustrates the J curve principle that small openings in closed societies unleash instability, it is Ivan Stambolic. In 1986, Stambolic left his position as head of the League of Communists of Serbia to become Serbia's president. Like many of the presidents of Yugoslavia's republics, Stambolic had an ambitious agenda for his republic's renewal that was continually obstructed by the central government. Unlike most others, however, the new Serbian president adopted a dangerous strategy.

Stambolic understood well that nothing intimidated non-Serb Yugoslavs more than the specter of renewed Serb nationalism. So he publicly adopted a strong nationalist stance and gave prominent Serb chauvinists influential positions within his government and in the Serbian media. Stambolic believed he could control the nationalist forces within his government as he used them to intimidate representatives of the other republics into acquiescence to a number of Serbia's demands. But the nationalists began to seize on the issue of Kosovo and demanded that the 1974 constitution be amended to return control of the autonomous province to the Serbs who lived within it. They used the Serbian media to build on the already potent Serb fear of Kosovar Albanians and a sense of grievance over their actions—both real and imagined. In early 1987, tens of thousands of Serbs living in Kosovo signed a petition that claimed that the Albanian Muslim majority had begun a "genocide" against them and demanded that Yugoslav officials reimpose martial law. While Stambolic was willing to use Serb nationalists for his political purposes, he never lent official Communist credence to the dubious claims of genocide.

To address the demands of Kosovo's Serbs, and to appease those within Serbia who demanded forceful action on their behalf, Stambolic dispatched his little-known protégé, Slobodan Milosevic, to travel to Kosovo, to meet with Serb leaders there, and to allay their fears of Albanian violence. On April 27, Milosevic gave his boss a surprise and changed Yugoslav history. In a televised speech at Kosovo Polje, Slobodan Milosevic confirmed the charge that "genocide" was taking place and promised Kosovo's Serbs (and, by extension, Serbs watching television all over Yugoslavia), "No one will ever beat you again."

Within a year, Milosevic was the most popular and powerful political figure in Serbia, and Tito's idea of unity and equality among Yugoslavs was badly damaged. Milosevic won the internal battle with Titoists within Serbia's Communist League and brought official Communist legitimacy to Serbia's most extreme nationalists. Stambolic resigned, a figure without influence, in September 1987.

Slobodan Milosevic did not create Serb nationalism. Serb nationalism created Milosevic. In a relatively closed society plagued with a moribund economy, social unrest, and a vacuum of power at the center, local politicians look for ways to build political capital. Milosevic was not naturally

a Serb nationalist. He was a career Communist apparatchik, a clever political tactician who found a winning issue. Much as U.S. Senator Joseph
McCarthy harnessed anti-Communist hysteria in Washington in the 1950s
and used it to make a name for himself, Milosevic found Serb anger, fear,
and frustration and rode the crest of the nationalist wave to a position of
unrivaled power and influence within Serbia.

To maintain his newly acquired political capital, Milosevic purged
most of the remaining voices of reason from within the still relatively free
Serbian media and replaced them with xenophobes, conspiracy theorists,
and militarists. In a left-side-of-the-J-curve state, the ruling elite must
control its citizens' access to information. The cacophony of media voices
within a right-side state creates confusion and skepticism—even cynicism.
But many people who live within left-side states often have greater faith in
the media, because it speaks with a single clear voice whatever the effect of
rumors on others. There are no reliable opinion polls to tell us what most
Serbs thought of the nationalist message before Milosevic gave it saturation
coverage on Serbia's airwaves. Certainly, liberal reformers were among the
prominent public figures in Serbia immediately following Tito's death.
Many influential Serb voices warned that Milosevic would destroy Yugoslavia and Serbia. But following the flood of propaganda and misinformation of the late 1980s, and the mass rallies involving thousands of people
he staged in Belgrade to further accuse Kosovo's Albanians of the mass
murder of Serbs, Milosevic was sufficiently popular to threaten Kosovar Albanians with virtually anything.

Between 1988 and the outbreak of civil war in 1991, Serb fear and anger,
stoked by the media and the Communist leadership, turned from Kosovo's
Albanians to Yugoslavia's other peoples. The media blitz convinced even
skeptical Serbs that they were in danger, surrounded by foreigners who had
secretly hated them for centuries. The war crimes of World War II, particularly those committed by the Croat Ustasa, were resurrected. Muslim
"plots" were exposed. The siege mentality reached a fever pitch.

In October 1988, Vojvodina's government resigned under Serbian pressure. Milosevic supporters assumed power there. Much the same occurred
in Montenegro in January 1989. A thorough purge of society and the media
followed in both. When the already weak federal Yugoslav government tried
to interfere, hundreds of thousands of Serbs rallied in Belgrade to demand

an end to Yugoslav interference in Serbia's business.* In November 1988, the leadership of the League of Communists of Yugoslavia decided it was necessary to appease Milosevic by giving him Kosovo. On March 23, 1989, JNA troops forced Kosovo's parliament to ratify a new constitution that returned control of Kosovo to Serbia. Slobodan Milosevic now controlled four of Yugoslavia's eight territories, and the federal government had proven completely unable to stop him.

Yugoslavia reached the bottom of the J curve. When Slovenia proposed a new arrangement to keep the country intact, the nation that Tito built had one last opportunity to remain a state.

At the Bottom of the J Curve

The first real challenge to Milosevic's advance came from an unlikely source—Slovenia. For many reasons, the two republics had long enjoyed amicable relations. First, they did not share a border that might have been the scene of competition and tension. Second, there were relatively few Serbs living in Slovenia to create friction in the relationship from either side.

Certainly, Slovenia had its own nationalists. But Slovene chauvinists largely reserved their ire for the Communists of the central government. The republic had long been Yugoslavia's wealthiest. Thus, Tito's redistribution of assets to the less developed republics was a source of grievance. As economic conditions lowered Yugoslavia's J curve in the 1980s and Tito was no longer alive to grant Slovenia concessions, Slovene resentment of the LCY deepened. As JNA tanks descended on Kosovo, dispatched by the federal government to appease Milosevic, Slovenes began to wonder if they might not be vulnerable to Serb aggression as well. When influential Slovenes signed petitions and raised money for Kosovo's Albanians, the Slovene government's sense of vulnerability grew.

In addition, Slovenia's own Communist leadership was deeply unpopular with a population infected with the same anti-Communist zeal that was

---

* Just as the Russian Soviet Socialist Republic and the Soviet Union shared a capital, Serb nationalists didn't have to travel far to protest the actions of Yugoslavia's Communist Party.

sweeping much of the rest of Eastern Europe in the late 1980s. Like Milosevic, Slovenia's Communist elite needed an issue that would boost their political popularity. And they came to the same conclusion Milosevic had: they embraced nationalism. But in Slovenia's case, following the events in Kosovo, nationalism meant defense of the republic against Serbs.

Within Serbia, economic conditions were worsening. Following international complaints over the coercion in Kosovo, foreign credit evaporated. A desperate Milosevic turned to the Serb diaspora for help. He asked Serbs living abroad to raise $1 billion to resurrect Serbia's economy. He received only $25 million. As Kosovar Albanians launched a guerilla war against Kosovo's Serbs, the cost to Serbia for security in the province reached the equivalent of half of Yugoslavia's entire defense budget.[17] To protect his popularity and keep his movement intact, Milosevic responded to Slovene support for Kosovo with an intense anti-Slovene propaganda campaign. The fear and suspicion that had brought Yugoslavia to the bottom of the J curve was spinning out of control.

On September 27, 1989, less than seven weeks before the fall of the Berlin Wall, the ruling Communists of Slovenia renounced their monopoly on power, announced that open elections would be held, and reasserted the right to secede from Yugoslavia granted them by Tito. The move was not final. Slovene Communists were reluctant to challenge Milosevic and the LCY directly. The move was a bargaining tactic to increase their leverage as they offered one final solution to save the Yugoslav state. Slovenia proposed, in essence, that Yugoslavia should remain in one piece. But they asserted that the Yugoslav government should allow each republic to decide whether to maintain Communism or to embrace multiparty democracy.

Milosevic rejected the plan. Still, the leaderships of the various territories of Yugoslavia gathered in January 1990 for the 14th Congress of the League of Communists of Yugoslavia. The Slovene delegation tried to pitch its plan. Milosevic supporters shouted them off the stage. The Slovenes then walked out of the congress. The Croat delegation followed. Yugoslavia effectively ceased to exist.[18]

The horrific war that followed, the worst in Europe since World War II, is not a subject for this book. Nor is the assignment of blame for the start of the war or the crimes committed during the fighting. Yugoslavia is examined here in detail because it illustrates that a state may fall into the depths of the J curve and fail to reemerge on either side. It may simply fail. The Soviet Union and Yugoslavia are the world's most recent examples of how such a total state failure can occur.

SOUTH AFRICA VERSUS YUGOSLAVIA

South Africa (1994) and Yugoslavia (1989) entered the dip in the J curve during the same half-decade. There are several reasons why South Africa survived and emerged on the right side of the J curve while Yugoslavia erupted into war.

There are obvious differences in how the citizens of each state perceived the changes taking place in their country. Millions of Yugoslavs were more interested in establishing (or reestablishing) national identities within their respective nations and cultures than in remaining within an increasingly Serb-dominated union. They thus had an interest in diminishing the influence of the center. The overwhelming majority of South Africans felt they were finally taking title to their country and believed they shared an interest in strengthening it. Nearly 70 percent of white South Africans voted confidence in an end to apartheid and peaceful change.

The international community turned its back on Yugoslavia following the People's Army's actions in Kosovo. Western investment slowed to a trickle and instead flowed into Eastern Europe (and later the former Soviet Union) following the collapse of the Communist bloc. Western media attention turned toward the war that followed Saddam's invasion of Kuwait. In South Africa, western powers were eager to demonstrate that the age of colonialism in Africa had ended. Nelson Mandela was able to earn broad international political support quickly and to attract substantial foreign direct investment for South Africa's reconstruction.

In Yugoslavia in 1990, there was no second Tito, a single figure whose resolve or ruthlessness could restore stability to a still-coherent Yugoslav state. F. W. de Klerk, on the other hand, had the opportunity to pass South Africa intact to Mandela, who was prepared to govern with broadly recognized legitimacy.

Finally, Milosevic's aggressive militarism set in motion the centrifugal forces that pulled Yugoslavia apart. Mandela's political and moral authority was such that members of different racial, tribal, and ethnic groups joined together in a common project to show the world how progressive and strong a black African government could be.

Yugoslavia and South Africa are only two examples of the many states formed in the recent past that unite historically hostile groups in an artificial construction. As post-Saddam Iraq tries to construct a stable system of governance, Shia, Sunni, and Kurds will each assert their interests at the expense of central authority. As the international community watches anxiously from the sidelines, the J curve lessons of South Africa and Yugoslavia should not be far from our minds.

CHAPTER FIVE

The Right Side of the J Curve

Men may die, but the fabric of free institutions remains unshaken.

—CHESTER A. ARTHUR

A right-side-of-the-J-curve state is one that is stable precisely because it is open to the political, economic, social, and cultural influences of the outside world. This openness is reflected in its domestic political and economic life. It is a state that legally enshrines protections for the civil and human rights of at least the clear majority of its citizens. The institutions of government, independent of one another, reinforce state stability. Leaders govern with the consent of (at least most of) the governed. Barriers to participation in the economic life of the nation are relatively low. The movement of people, ideas, information, goods, and services across internal and external borders is free. The most stable of these states thrive on change.

At the same time, the shape of the J curve demonstrates that levels of stability vary much more widely on the right side than on the left. Some states on the right have such high stability that only a shock of unprecedented scope and severity could destabilize them. The 9/11 attacks didn't destabilize the American system of government. The 2004 terrorist bombings in Madrid did not prevent Spain from holding elections three days later or from peacefully transferring power once the results were tallied. The 1986 assassination of the prime minister did not undermine Sweden's system of government. The risk is slim that the Québécois separatist movement will produce profound social upheaval in Canada.

Think again of the U.S. presidential election in 2000. In a less stable country, such a crisis might have produced market chaos, government paralysis, even civil war. Yet, on a relative scale, public faith in the independence of the judiciary and a belief that the American political system could absorb any shock associated with a contested election eased anxiety over the outcome and reinforced confidence in U.S. stability.

In fact, the stability of a state near the top of the right side of the J curve has a special advantage over that of other states: Its stability is self-perpetuating. It is constantly revitalized by the forces for change to which it is open. It's often said during the rituals that accompany transfers of power in Washington that they are celebrations of the strength and durability of the nation's political institutions. That stable predictability exists in all nations that have a fully consolidated and open political and economic system. But not all states on the right side of the J curve are as self-assured. A similar crisis in South Korea or Argentina, for example, might well provoke widespread social unrest and a substantial loss of faith in market stability.

To understand the dynamism that comes with openness to change in a different context, consider the evolution of the English language. A primary source of the power and influence of English is that it absorbs and is enriched by so many non-English influences. This effect illustrates a right-side-of-the-curve culture in microcosm. The more open a culture, the more it develops and matures in organic ways toward a richer, truer expression of those who contribute to it. A number of legislative initiatives have arisen over the years in France—certainly a country at the top of the right side of the J curve—to protect the French language from the influences of other languages, particularly English. Laws restricting the use of English on billboards and in other forms of advertising are meant to protect the French language's purity. But, in the long run, cultural protectionism undermines cultural vitality as surely as economic protectionism limits economic growth.

For a state hoping to build its stability on participation in global change, all forms of protectionism—political, economic, and cultural—are ultimately self-defeating. Protectionist economic policies may serve the legitimate needs of select individuals, but, in the larger sense, they are barriers to the kind of adaptation on which right-side states thrive. Political protectionism—the formulation of policies that isolate a state from other states—serves only an elite. Individual leaders may not mind. They may calculate that their personal interests need not coincide with what most believe is the national interest. That's another reason that right-side-of-the-J-curve states depend for their stability not on individuals but on institutions and why British taxpayers, not the prime minister, hold the deed to 10 Downing Street.

For a country already on the right side of the curve hoping to climb toward greater stability, the ascent is not as steep—but it is a longer, slower journey. That's because it is much easier to guarantee stability by closing a nation than by opening it. A crackdown on public protests shows more immediate results than a pledge to build open and independent institutions of governance and a political system based on checks and balances. But the potential for greater stability in any left-side state is far more limited than that of a state on the right.

In this chapter, we'll look at three states on the right side of the J curve: Turkey, Israel, and India. All fit the above definition of stability based on openness. All have faced and, to some extent, continue to face challenges to their place on the curve. They are considered together because their domestic political circumstances, cultural histories, and religious identities are markedly different from one another's. Yet they have something very basic in common: they are dynamic, modern societies that have embraced market economics, multiparty democracy, and change.

TURKEY

Secular, democratic Turkey is a predominantly Muslim country on the right side of the J curve. That alone makes it an interesting case. But Turkey is also a state at a vitally important crossroads: Ankara and the European Union have begun talks that could eventually lead to Turkey's membership in the EU. The country's government has enacted substantive reforms to bring it into line with European norms. Yet, Turkey's admission is far from a done deal. For Turkey and for the world, the EU's decision is an important one. It may determine whether the state remains on the right side of the curve.

Dreams of Modernity

"Think of two men facing you: one is rich and has every means at his disposal, the second is poor and has nothing. Apart from the absence of means, the spirit of the second man is in no way different from or inferior to that of the first. This is precisely the position of Turkey as it faces Europe." This is how Turkey's founding father, Mustafa Kemal Atatürk, explained his country's relationship with Europe to an Austrian journalist in 1923.[1] The current Turkish prime minister, Recep Tayyip Erdogan, recently described his country's prospective entry into the EU as "the movement of Turkey toward the modern world." Throughout the history of the Turkish Republic, the nation's guiding principle has been the pursuit of modernization on a secular, democratic, and Western model. Yet, Turkey is still much poorer than its European neighbors.

Poverty isn't the only reason Turkey's membership in the Union is problematic. Although the Turkish government has enacted many of the ambitious reforms called for by the EU, others remain undone. And there are forces within the country—as there have been in most of the states that have considered entry into the EU—that fear the nation will surrender too much sovereignty if it joins the European club. There is anxiety in Europe over Turkish membership as well. Many there believe that, in an age of Islamism and the global war on terror, the admission to the EU of 70 million Muslims is not a good idea.* Many European countries are struggling to assimilate the Muslims already living within their borders.

Turkey is currently located toward the middle of the right side of the J curve. Because EU accession requires reforms that further open the country to the outside world and bind it to multinational institutions, entry into the EU is the best way to pull Turkey further up the curve toward greater stability and openness. Why did the Muslims of the Turkish republic move one way on the J curve while the entire Arab world moved another? How did the country arrive on the right side of the J curve? The answers are as old as Turkey's identity as a nation-state.

The 2002 Arab Human Development Report referred to in Chapter

---

* Turkey's current population is 70 million. By the time it is fully eligible to join, Turkey might have 100 million people, exceeding Germany, currently the EU's most populous country.

Three identified three broad reasons why political and economic development in the Arab world is so badly stunted. Some call them the "three absences": absence of political freedom, absence of knowledge, and absence of rights for women. Addressing these three deficits is a good way for a country on the left side of the J curve to move through instability to the right. That's precisely what Turkey did, beginning in the 1920s.*

In the Arab world generally, citizens lack basic freedoms of speech and association, as well as other fundamental civil-rights protections. Constitutions in Arab countries have historically been written more as concessions to political pressure than as genuine attempts to modernize the state. In Turkey, on the other hand, Mustafa Kemal (who ruled Turkey from its founding in 1923 until his death in 1938) used authoritarian means to put in place the legal protections necessary for what would eventually become a multiparty democracy, precisely because it was his ambition to bring his country into the modern mainstream of twentieth-century society.

In the Arab world, religious conservatives who hope to impose Islamic dogma on the region's youth have hijacked education in several Arab states. In Turkey, Kemal abolished the office of caliph, put religion directly under the control of the state, and denied imams any say whatsoever in education. In addition, Kemal stressed the importance of education for the Turkish people in a way no Arab leader ever has. According to UNESCO, 28.3 percent of Arab men and 52.2 percent of Arab women were illiterate in 2003. That same project reported that only 6 percent of Turkish men and 21.5 percent of Turkish women were unable to read or write.

Most Arab states still deny basic rights to women to an extent that deprives these states of a vital portion of the creative energy, intellect, and entrepreneurial talent they need to successfully compete in the twenty-first-century global marketplace. In Turkey, women were granted equal rights in the 1920s. Kemal discouraged the veiling of women and encouraged them to go to school.

In the last thousand years, said the authors of the UN Development Report, the twenty-two nations of the Arab world combined have translated fewer books than Spain translates in one year. In Turkey, Kemal's successor as president, Ismet Inonu, established a government office in the 1940s that

---

* In fact, the Ottoman Empire was, relative to the rest of the Muslim world, tolerant of diverse cultural and social practices.

published translated classics of world literature. He also set up "Village In-stitutes" in rural areas to teach peasants how to read them.[2]

In essence, Turkey and the Arab states each reached a crossroads with the collapse of the Ottoman Empire and the beginning of the end of Euro-pean colonialism in the Arab world. Arab states have yet to produce the durable institutions on which they can depend for stability as they slowly open their societies to the outside. Turkey's founding father, on the other hand, believed greatness for his country meant modernization and entry into the club of developed nations. He worked to achieve both.

Some History

In the nineteenth century, Christian subjects of the multinational Ottoman Empire developed extensive trade ties with their European coreligionists. These Ottoman Christians imported a European conception of national-ism that threatened the empire from within, even as the great European powers and Russia pressed from without. These two threats forced reform within the empire, and the first generation of young Muslims trained in Western ways, inspired by republican ideas from France, began to push for reform based on the ideal of a single nation-state bound together by com-mon language and culture. The first organized and active conspirators, the so-called Young Ottomans, maneuvered to introduce constitutionalism as early as the 1880s. The Young Ottomans were replaced around the turn of the century by the Young Turks, who launched an unsuccessful military coup in 1908 in the name of Turkish nationalism. When the First World War erupted in 1914, the Ottoman imperial leadership, hoping to win back the European territories they had lost in the Balkan Wars of 1912–1913, sided with Germany and Austria-Hungary and entered the war.*[3]

Mustafa Kemal, who admired the Young Turks, distinguished himself as a military leader with a victory over the Allies at Gallipoli in 1915 and, in the process, won the confidence and admiration of many within the army. Once the war was lost, Kemal's criticism of other reformers who had

---

* During the Balkan Wars, the Ottomans lost control of Macedonia and parts of what are today Bulgaria, Greece, and Turkey to the so-called Balkan League (Bulgaria, Greece, Serbia, and Montenegro).

pushed for entry into the war on Germany's side scored him points with the new sultan, Mehmet VI Vahdettin.

With the end of the First World War, a war for Turkish independence began. In an early display of diplomatic and military skill, Kemal organized resistance to an Allied advance into Turkish territory, appealed to Muslim solidarity to rally the local population to support him, played one European power off another and Bolshevik Russia off all of them, and limited his military goals to the defeat of the Greeks and Armenians. Turkey's War of Independence won, Kemal confined his territorial demands to the land that Ottoman forces held at the *end* of the First World War and disavowed the grand territorial ambitions of Ottoman emperors. He promised the British, French, and Italians he had no designs on any part of their empires. He persuaded the Bolsheviks he would never act to incite Russia's Muslims to rise against their new government in Moscow. He signed—and adhered to—treaties of nonaggression with Turkey's neighbors. In doing all this, he sharply reduced the number of potential shocks that might rattle the fragile new Turkish state and allowed himself breathing space to enact the modernization reforms he was ambitious to establish.[4] As we'll see later in this chapter when we look at Israel's David Ben-Gurion, the pragmatism necessary to limit a nation's aspirations to attainable goals is an important element of stability. Limiting the number of potential shocks matters—as we saw with Saddam Hussein, it's never a good idea to start a war you can't win.

On October 29, 1923, Kemal formally established the Republic of Turkey, with Ankara as its capital, atop the remnants of the Ottoman Empire. He assumed the name Atatürk—"the father of all Turks." But he was no "Turkmenbashi." His ambitious reform program was not intended for personal glorification or the establishment of a cult of personality—although no one who ever met Kemal failed to notice his considerable ego. Mustafa Kemal Atatürk worked until his death in 1938 to pull his Muslim people into the modern world and onto the stage of world politics alongside Christian countries. He replaced his people's traditional pan-Islamic aspirations with a national Turkish identity. He abolished the caliphate. Turkey's first constitution committed the nation to the path of secularism and republicanism.[5]

Kemal disbanded religious courts and Europeanized the legal system. He banned the wearing of the fez—the hat worn by Muslim gentlemen for more than a century—encouraged universal education, aligned the new nation with the Christian Common Era, established Sunday as a day of rest, and replaced Arabic script with the Latin alphabet. He exiled the Ottoman dynasty in 1924. Atatürk described the goal of all his policies as "peace at home and peace in the world."[6]

Like Boris Yeltsin seven decades later, Kemal inherited the institutional memory and administrative structure of a crumbled empire. But, as was the case for Yeltsin, this institutional memory was of limited value, since the institutions in which that experience was gained were relics of an old system. The collapse of law and order that followed foreign invasion and civil war also complicated his first tasks. Poverty was widespread, civil servants were demoralized, and crime and violence were endemic. The Ottoman Empire had plummeted down the left side of the J curve into instability and, like the Soviet Union, did not survive the fall. Atatürk's Turkish nation-state, like Yeltsin's Russia, was forced to make a choice. Atatürk opted to lead his country toward a stability based on modernity, openness, education, secularism, and democracy, even if he used distinctly undemocratic means to do it.

Kemal's first challenge was to extend the rule of his government and its laws across the new nation's territory. In that considerable task, he succeeded, but Kemal was not able to realize his most ambitious modernization goals before his death in 1938. He established a stable state with a liberal republican constitution, but he did it largely by decree. He alone formulated policies, dismissed dozens of those who disagreed with him, and ignored his own constitution when it suited him. He allowed his rivals to form a parliamentary opposition and then dissolved it when it became popular. In place of an organized opposition, Kemal allowed "independents" to question government policy in parliament, but actively undermined those whose independence was excessively genuine.[7]

Turks were considered equal before the law, but were seldom treated equally in practice. In the style of revolutionary France, Kemal addressed his subjects as "citizens." Yet, fifteen years was hardly enough time—even for a man of Kemal's Napoleonic talent, ambition, and energy—to redress the inequalities of wealth, status, political access, and education in the first days of the Turkish republic. Kemal believed that universal education was the best way to bring Turkish life into line with that of European countries. But when he died, two-thirds of Turkey's people were still illiterate.[8] Some have even accused Kemal of using the courts to execute former allies. In *Atatürk,* his biography of Kemal, Andrew Mango says of Turkey's founding father, "He was a man of the Enlightenment, and the Enlightenment was not made by saints." There is evidence, in fact, that in the early 1920s, Kemal led military campaigns against Russian Armenians living within the borders of what would become the Turkish Republic. These Armenians had returned to their homes following the killings and mass deportations that Ottoman authorities began in 1915. A number of credible historians thus accuse Kemal of extending the Armenian genocide.*

Certainly, Mustafa Kemal Atatürk is directly responsible for Turkey's place on the right side of the J curve. His greatest legacy, in fact, is "Kemalism," strict adherence to the secularism of the republic and the protection of Turkey's territorial integrity that the majority of Turkey's people have always considered the founder's gift to the nation. Kemalism is a kind of civic religion in Turkey, enshrined in all of the modern republic's constitutions, many of its laws, and in the oaths of allegiance sworn by Turkey's presidents, lawmakers, and other officers of state. Kemal did proclaim himself "father of the Turks," but it was only in death, as his successors developed the idea of Kemalism as their continuing mandate, that Mustafa Kemal was proclaimed *Ebedi Sef,* "the Eternal Leader."[9]

In reality, Kemalism, as it is most often interpreted, produces policies that help move Turkey more resolutely up the right side of the J curve than anything Kemal himself ever accomplished. He created a political system based on one powerful party. Yet, Kemalism is regularly invoked to celebrate Turkey's genuine and dynamic multiparty system. Kemal's statist economy has been replaced, under the banner of Kemalism, with a vibrant market-driven economy.

---

* Acts of mass violence by Turks against Armenians, and Kemal's role in them, remains a hotly debated topic. Armenia claims that between 1915 and 1917, the government of the Young Turks systematically murdered more than a million ethnic Armenians and exiled many more. The Turkish government claims that there were no more than 200,000 to 300,000 deaths, and that they were not the product of an organized genocide but died instead in battles between Turkish troops and Russian-backed Armenian militias. Most well-respected scholars in the West accept the Armenian account, and the Turkish government has faced international pressure to recognize that the massacre was indeed a genocide.

The Curious Role of the Turkish Military

The greatest irony of Kemalism is that Kemal himself argued passionately that the armed forces should never involve themselves in politics. Yet, while it is within the Turkish military that Kemalism is treated as a system of sacred guiding principles for the nation, the military has violated Kemal's principle of noninvolvement in politics for forty years. The Turkish armed forces have, in fact, appointed themselves guardians of Kemal's legacy and enforcer of their own interpretation of his beliefs.

In particular, the military elite believes it must protect Turkey against any threat from separatists, terrorists, and religious fundamentalists. The 1982 constitution, written essentially by the military, required the cabinet to give "priority consideration to the decisions" of the National Security Council (NSC), an advisory body of senior military and cabinet members the council considers "necessary for the preservation of the State."[10] Although the constitution suggested that the NSC was subordinate to the civilian government, it required that half its members be army officers.* In reality, the NSC remains Turkey's final arbiter of power. Simply stated, the Turkish General Staff (TGS) considers itself better placed than any civilian government to determine Turkey's national interest and to formulate the policies designed to pursue it. The military view is that civilian governments come and go; the Turkish military is the keeper of Kemalism's eternal flame.

Four times since Turkey's founding, the military has dismissed civilian politicians who challenged its authority or strayed from its interpretation of Kemalist ideology. It has pushed aside three prime ministers since 1960 and, as recently as 1997, engineered a bloodless coup to get rid of the Islamic Welfare Party (REFAH) and its unsteady coalition government.[11]

On the other hand, it would be a mistake to oversimplify the role of the armed forces in Turkish national life. None of Turkey's military leaders has ever attempted to hold absolute power following a coup, because, even with its sometimes self-serving interpretation of Kemalism, the Turkish military believes it is the country's guardian, not its dictator. It has always returned power to civilian control once order was reestablished.

---

* Recent changes reduced the number of military officials and enable the general secretariat to be held by a civilian.

Since 1990, anxiety has grown within the armed forces that Islamic radicalism threatens the Kemalist ideal of secular modernity. In 1992, the NSC drafted a National Security Policy report that identified "political Islam as a threat to the country's security." The army has dismissed officers for public demonstrations of excessive piety. In 2004, Ankara's central military academy declared a "war of liberation" against Islamic fundamentalism.[12]

In 1997, the NSC presented then Prime Minister Necmettin Erbakan with eighteen anti-Islamist measures, which he accepted but dragged his feet on implementing. Despite Erbakan's hesitation, laws were imposed restricting Islamist media; and an investigation began into contributions REFAH received from abroad. In 1997, the constitutional court banned the Islamic party. The bloodless coup came to a climax when Erbakan resigned soon after.[13] Turkey's armed forces prevent the nation from sliding down the right side of the curve into instability, but its leaders are also an important obstacle to Turkey's ability to consolidate democratic institutions and to move further up the right side.

Despite the fact that few in Turkey's military are unhappy with Turkey's membership in NATO, which it joined in 1952, there are nationalists within the armed forces who would like to keep the country out of the European Union. But much of the military leadership, most of the political leadership, and the majority of the Turkish people await the EU's invitation as the fulfillment of Atatürk's founding vision for modern Turkey.

The Road to the EU

Turkey's path toward membership in the European Union has been a circuitous one. Turkey and the European Community signed an Association Agreement in 1963, Turkey applied for EU membership in 1987, and became a formal candidate in 1999. Since then, it has made only incremental progress toward accession, and a number of European political leaders have campaigned aggressively against Turkey's bid.

In 2002, the EU set out all the conditions that Turkey needed to meet before membership talks could begin, including rules that required the country establish stable institutions that guarantee democracy, rule of law, human rights, and a viable market economy.

Turkey's leaders have enacted a number of these reforms. Ankara has implemented legislative and constitutional changes that relax restrictions on freedom of the press. In 2004, Turkey ratified Protocol 13, which abolished the death penalty. It adopted measures to ensure the independence of the judiciary. In response to criticism of its antiterrorism laws, the government eliminated statutes within them that restrict political expression.

Lawmakers have created new protections for the rights of the country's Kurdish minority, which makes up about 20 percent of Turkey's population. New laws guarantee the right of Kurds to education in their own language. The rights of Kurdish media have been codified and expanded, and a limited amnesty has been introduced for Kurdish separatists.[14]

Turkey has also enacted a broad range of economic reforms. The government has reduced inflation, interest rates, and delinquent loans. Thanks to the sure-handed fiscal and economic policies of the popular finance minister Kemal Dervis, Turkey earned a nearly $20 billion rescue package and loan agreement in 2002 that helped the government reduce the size of the pension system and reform bankruptcy law. Inflation fell to its lowest level since the mid-1970s. Economic growth came in at an impressive 8.9 percent in 2004 and 6 percent in 2005.

There have even been reforms that limit the power of the military over civilian government. In 2004, the European Parliament warned Ankara that the military still exercised too much influence in Turkish governance. Within two months, Turkey responded with a constitutional amendment that limits the military's power.

But what happens to all these reforms if Turkey is not invited to join the European Union?

Turkey Is Not Germany

The Justice and Development Party (known by its Turkish acronym AKP), won a landslide victory in parliamentary elections in November 2003. Led by Prime Minister Recep Tayyip Erdogan, the AKP has embraced a moderate, democratic political agenda.

But Erdogan has never fully escaped suspicion that his public adherence to Kemalist secularism is a strategic disguise that will eventually allow him to introduce Islamic principle into Turkish governance. Critics empha-size Erdogan's fundamentalist background and recent AKP positions on women's rights and education to argue that Turkey and Europe have not yet met the real Erdogan, and that they are likely to be disappointed when they do.

Recep Tayyip Erdogan was educated in religious schools as a devout Muslim. As a teenager, he was forced off a soccer team for refusing to shave the beard he considered it his religious duty to grow. His wife wears the tra-ditional headscarf. Elected mayor of Istanbul in 1994, Erdogan declared himself the city's "imam" and opened his first city council meeting by chanting from the Koran. As mayor, he banned the public consumption of alcohol, and criticized the use of contraception. After reading an Islamist poem at a 1998 rally,* Erdogan was convicted of using religion to provoke disorder and sent to jail for four months.[15]

An aside: This episode beautifully expresses the tensions that keep Turkey from moving resolutely in either direction on the right side of the J curve. The guardians of Turkish secularism believe that radical Islam is the most likely source of potential instability in the country—and of a slide down the curve toward chaos. They have often acted quickly to head off such a move. Yet, jailing a politician for publicly reading a poem is hardly the way a state moves further up the right side of the curve toward a more open society. It is a paradox that Turkey—and many other states—has yet to resolve.

Those most suspicious of Erdogan's intentions point out that it was four months in prison that reportedly converted the former "imam" of Istanbul to Kemal's vision of a secular, democratic Turkey. His considerable current popularity is based on a mix of populist appeal—some of it from religious Muslims—and his embrace of Kemalism. Erdogan now says he considers religion a private matter and that, though Islam guides his personal actions, Turkey's secular constitution inspires his political choices.[16]

---

* The poem read in part, "The mosques are our barracks, the domes our helmets/The minarets our bayonets, and the faithful our soldiers."

European Turkey

There is no step Turkey can take that better reinforces its long-term stability than joining the European Union. Erdogan has promised that winning the invitation is his most important task. EU membership could make Turkey a model of liberal democracy for the Muslim world, bind Turkey to Western institutions, and reinforce its position as a bulwark against Islamist extremism. An EU rejection of Turkey's application, on the other hand, could anger Turkey's citizens, reverse domestic reforms, embolden religious extremists, and provoke more military interference in politics. The result would be a clear slide into dangerous political and social instability and toward the left side of the J curve.

Joining the EU remains popular with most Turks. Political liberals and business leaders hope EU membership would bring new political and economic reforms. For the urban and rural poor, it promises a higher standard of living. For Turkey's secular elite, it points toward continuing movement in a modern and democratic direction. Many in the military believe it would guarantee Turkey's security; Islamists believe it would reduce the influence of the Turkish military in their affairs. Minorities, especially the Kurds, see it as a means of guaranteeing respect for their rights.[17]

Yet, many Turks fear the EU is forcing Turkey to reform for nothing, and that no EU invitation to a Muslim candidate will ever arrive. European governments, already struggling to assimilate Muslim minorities into their own countries, argue that pulling Turkey into the union would force them to accept responsibility for stability in the volatile Middle East. As a compromise—or perhaps as an escape mechanism—some EU leaders have proposed a new idea, one that promises more than partnership but less than full admission. France has suggested giving Turkey "special status"; German Chancellor Angela Merkel has called for a "privileged partnership." But Erdogan has ruled out Turkey's interest in anything short of full EU membership. He and other senior Turkish politicians complain that these formulations provide almost nothing that Turkey doesn't already enjoy as a member of other European institutions.[18] Perhaps Turkish skepticism of Europe's willingness to admit the country to the Union is well founded. In fact, there's good reason to believe Turkey will be left in the waiting room. Across Europe, anti-Muslim anxiety is giving Europeans pause as they consider the possible admission into Europe of a large, predominantly Muslim country. Their fear, and the ease with which applicants for membership can be turned away, may well create insurmountable obstacles to Turkey's accession.

Indeed, Europeans are becoming increasingly anxious about the growing Muslim populations in their midst. There are already 15 to 20 million Muslims living inside the EU, and their presence has provoked a backlash in areas where unemployment is high and where Muslims are seen to resist assimilation. The March 2004 bombings in Madrid and the July 2005 London public-transport attacks, both carried out by groups that claim affiliation with Al Qaeda, have convinced many in Europe that a large-scale 9/11-style terrorist attack there is increasingly likely. The November 2004 murder by Islamic militants of Dutch filmmaker Theo van Gogh—who had recently released a film about the ill treatment of women in Muslim society— unleashed a series of attacks and reprisals in the Netherlands. A string of tit-for-tat arson attacks there on mosques and churches had local police on a state of high alert for weeks. Anti-Muslim assaults have increased in several EU countries. Rioting in Muslim communities across France grabbed headlines in the fall of 2005. Violence across the Islamic world following the publication in Denmark of cartoon images of the prophet Mohammad produced further European anxiety in 2006.

European critics of Turkey's admission insist the EU is not ready for a Union that borders Iran, Iraq, and Syria. Following the war in Iraq and the back-and-forth on Middle East peace, these critics are ever more confident that the majority across the continent will agree with them. Opinion polls appear to support that view and reinforce the suspicion in Turkey that much of the public opposition is based on social and cultural fears. According to Eurobarometer, a public opinion survey requested by the European Commission and conducted in May and June of 2005, 52 percent of the citizens of the twenty-five-member European Union oppose Turkey's membership. Only 35 percent are in favor. More than half (54 percent) said, "Cultural differences between Turkey and the EU member states are too significant to allow [Turkey's] accession." In nine of the twenty-five EU states, the number was higher than 60 percent. A full 63 percent agreed that "Turkey's joining could risk favoring immigration to more developed countries in the EU." The number was higher than 70 percent in eight EU states. Only 29 percent agreed that "Turkey's accession would favor the rejuvenation of an ageing European population." More than 50 percent disagreed.[19]

Anger against Muslims in Europe has made its way into European politics. Anti-immigrant, far-right parties have appeared in recent years in several European countries: Austria's Freedom Party, Italy's Northern League, Switzerland's People's Party, and Norway's Progress Party work with like-minded groups in France, Germany, and other European countries. Even mainstream parties have responded to anti-Muslim popular sentiment.[20] Then French Prime Minister Jean-Pierre Raffarin captured the attitude in France toward Turkey's possible admission to the EU when he publicly asked in September 2004, "Do we want the river of Islam to enter the riverbed of secularism?" France's President Jacques Chirac, publicly in favor of Turkey's entry, then announced that France would hold a referendum on any further enlargement of the Union. Opinion polls in 2004 suggested that 56 percent of French citizens opposed Turkey's bid.* In effect, Chirac gave the French people a veto over Turkey's admission. The French president has assured his people their government will abide by the outcome of the referendum—and, crucially, a "no" vote from any single EU member-state would prevent Turkey from joining the EU.

That veto could come from any of a number of EU members. In Germany, the local government of Bavaria followed France's lead in 2004 in banning the wearing of Muslim headscarves in local schools. Denmark restricted the Muslim practice of arranged marriages. Britain now requires all would-be British citizens to take an oath of allegiance. In fact, it appears more and more likely that an ultranationalist, xenophobic party will eventually come to power in an EU member state—either alone, or as the lead party in a coalition. In France's 2002 presidential election, arch-xenophobe Jean-Marie Le Pen edged out the Socialist candidate, then Prime Minister Lionel Jospin, for a place on the second-round ballot opposite Chirac. Far-right parties have made important gains in regional elections in Germany and Denmark. But whether the veto comes from France, Austria, Germany, the Netherlands, Belgium, Denmark, or somewhere else, it is increasingly likely. Turkey's membership could be delayed for decades. Or it could be put off forever.

The loser in that event would be everyone who finds advantage in Turkey's presence on the right side of the J curve. If Turkey's substantive

---

* The 2005 rejection by voters in France and the Netherlands of a new EU constitution was, to some extent, a protest vote against Turkish membership.

and far-reaching reforms do not allow steady progress toward its entry into the union, there will surely be a backlash within the country. Religious Turks like Erdogan will no longer rein in their inclination to introduce and enforce Islamic restrictions on personal conduct—particularly for women. There is then no reason to believe Turkey's Kemalist army officers won't intervene in Turkey's democracy. The progress toward greater levels of freedom, openness, and the construction of stable independent institutions will be reversed in favor of a conflict between Turkey's most extreme powerbrokers. Conflict with Kurds within Turkey, in Iraq, in Syria, and in Iran may boil over.

For the United States, this means the possible loss of a reliable NATO ally that borders Iran, Iraq, and Syria. Israel, with whom Turkey is virtually the only Muslim country to enjoy good relations, may likewise lose a friendly nation in a geopolitically crucial location. EU-Turkey relations might not recover.

None of these worst-case scenarios is likely in the near term. But unless the current dynamic changes in favor of an EU embrace of Turkey's entry into Europe, it's hard to see how a slide down the right side of the curve toward instability can be avoided. As accession negotiations continue, the United States can and should do everything possible to encourage the European Union to welcome Turkey's bid and to urge the Turkish government to continue to meet EU requirements for membership. U.S. leverage with both sides is, of course, limited. Public statements on the issue may not be helpful. But Washington's behind-the-scenes influence still matters and can be put to use. Should Turkey's bid ultimately fail, Washington should vigorously reinforce America's political and economic ties with Ankara to help ensure that the end of Turkey's EU candidacy does not mean the end of Atatürk's dream of modernity.

ISRAEL

In creating the state of Israel, the nation's founders hoped to accomplish three things: they wanted to found a Jewish state, they wanted the new state to be a democracy, and they wanted to build this new homeland on the entirety of the biblical land of Israel—a territory stretching from the Mediterranean to the Jordan River and even into areas of present-day Jordan. But like so many states in the Middle East, the boundaries of the new state were drawn by European policymakers. In 1947, the United Nations offered the Jewish people about half the land they hoped for and set aside the other half for Palestinian Arabs. The leader of the Zionist movement of the time, David Ben-Gurion, argued that the presence of so many Arabs ensured Israel could only fully achieve two of the three goals. The choice of which two goals to pursue would define the identity of the new state.

The presence of a million Palestinians meant that a democracy covering all the historical land of Israel could not be a Jewish state, and that a Jewish state spanning all the biblical land could not remain a democracy. So Ben-Gurion built a constituency around the idea of a Jewish democracy that governed about half the hoped-for territory—that offered by the UN. The nation was established in 1948 as a democracy open to the outside world positioned firmly on the right side of the J curve. This status quo formulation remained in place for nearly two decades.

In June 1967, the Six-Day War erupted as Israel launched strikes against Egypt, Jordan, Syria, and Iraq to head off an expected attack. Israel won a quick victory and occupied the West Bank (of the Jordan river) and the Gaza Strip, extending Israeli rule over virtually all the land the Zionists sought. Yet, these territorial spoils of war substantially diluted Israel's overwhelming Jewish majority by bringing large numbers of Palestinians under direct Israeli occupation. Again the fundamental questions of boundaries and identity required a political answer.

Were Israel to keep the land and remain a democracy, Israelis would have to allow more than a million Palestinian Arabs in the occupied territories to vote in Israeli elections alongside the half-million Israeli Arabs already living inside Israel. Thus, were Israel to remain a Jewish democracy with control of the West Bank and Gaza, the nation's leaders had three choices. They could cede to the Arabs who wanted to destroy them most or all of the newly acquired, long-sought-after land considered sacred by many Israelis. They could evict the Palestinians living there. Or they could indefinitely postpone resolution of the dilemma, occupy the land, and deny Palestinians outside Israel's original borders basic political rights. Israeli leaders knew the international community would never support the forced expulsion of Palestinians from the West Bank and Gaza. And they believed a return to the pre-1967 status quo threatened to reignite the war and to undermine Israel's security. In the end, Israeli politicians discovered what leaders all over the world have found: it's easier to postpone a tough choice than to make a decision and to live with the consequences.

From the end of the Six-Day War, Israelis have faced the same choices the founders struggled over in 1948: Israel could be a Jewish police state that spans all the biblical land of Israel, a democracy covering all the land of Israel that renounces its Jewish character, or a Jewish democracy that rules only part of the historical land and cedes the rest to Palestinians.[21] Decades later, Israeli leaders have yet to implement an answer to this question. While Israel remains firmly on the right side of the J curve, this unresolved fundamental problem has undermined Israeli democracy, poisoned Israel's relations with much of the outside world, and initiated a slow Israeli retreat down the curve toward instability.

Israelis, of course, have their reasons for refusing to abandon the territories gained in war. First, they fear that Palestinians, many of whom have publicly dedicated themselves to pushing Israel into the Mediterranean, would use the recovered land as a staging area for attacks against Israel. Second, no Arab leader has ever been willing and able to guarantee Israelis that quitting the occupied territories would lead to sustainable peace agreements that all would honor. Immediately after the Six-Day War, Arab leaders—including those of the Palestine Liberation Organization—agreed in Khartoum they would not make peace with Israel, would not negotiate with Israel, would not even recognize Israel's right to exist.

It was not until Egypt broke ranks with its Arab brothers in 1978 and signed a peace deal with Israel in exchange for return of the then Israeli-occupied Sinai Desert that Israel enjoyed diplomatic relations with any of its immediate neighbors.* But on the more fundamental question of trading biblical land for peace, even Ben-Gurion, the pragmatist who first argued that the Jewish and democratic nature of the state was more important than any immediate question of borders, created obstacles for those who now seek to resolve the issues of Israel's identity. Speaking to the 20th Zionist Congress in Zurich in 1937, Ben-Gurion declared: ". . . it is better to have immediately a Jewish state, even if it would only be in a part of the western land of Israel. . . . [But in the long term] no Jew has the right

---

* Israel signed a peace deal with Jordan in 1994.

to relinquish the right of the Jewish people over the whole land of Israel. It is beyond the powers of any Jewish body. It is even beyond the powers of the whole of the Jewish people living today to give up any part of the land of Israel." [22]

As we've seen with Turkey's Atatürk and will see with India's Nehru, creating policy that contradicts the moral and political philosophy of a democracy's founding father can be a tall order.

Israeli Openness

At this point, Israel remains the only true democracy in the Middle East.* That Israel has maintained open governance despite the high level of outside pressure on the country is remarkable. Israel may be criticized strongly for foreign policies that have destabilized other states, particularly Lebanon. But the United States, France, and Britain, to name just three, are nations well entrenched on the right side of the J curve whose foreign policies are themselves hardly above reproach on that score.† However destabilizing for other states, a nation's foreign policy only alters its position on the J curve to the extent those policies reflect or alter internal policy.

Israel remains on the right side of the J curve because its citizens can change their government democratically. Regularly held elections have led to several peaceful transfers of power between political parties with divergent political philosophies since 1948. There are civil-rights protections for minorities. Israeli Arabs have the right to vote. Arab residents living within

---

* As of this writing, Palestinians, Lebanese, and Iraqis have taken first steps toward joining them. In January 1996, Palestinians elected Yasir Arafat president of the Palestinian National Authority. New elections have since been held in the West Bank and Gaza. In January 2006, the militant group Hamas won a landslide victory in parliamentary elections. In January 2005, Iraqis voted in the first multiparty elections in more than fifty years for members of a provincial council and a 275-member National Assembly. In June 2005, an anti–Syrian alliance won majority control of Lebanon's parliament. But Palestinians, Lebanese, and Iraqis have a long way to go to establish the legitimacy of democratic norms, the viability of local political institutions, or legal protections that ensure respect for civil rights.

† This is not to say Israeli foreign policies are identical with those of other Western democracies. After all, Israeli Jews have mandatory armed service in annexed territories directly on Israel's border, and Palestinians are forced to pass through security checkpoints to come into and out of Israel for work.

Israel's borders who are not citizens have all the same rights Israeli citizens do, except the right to vote in national elections.* Although Israel has no formal constitution, a series of basic laws has the force of constitutional principles.[23] Israel has maintained independent, functioning institutions that give the political system meaningful checks and balances. An example: Israel's highest court ruled in July 2004 that Prime Minister Ariel Sharon had violated the human rights of Palestinians when he ordered the construction of a security wall extending through sections of the occupied West Bank. While Sharon insisted his decision had been based on the highest imperatives of national security, the court ruled that twenty miles of the wall had to be torn down and rerouted. The prime minister submitted to the court's authority.

Israel has a vibrant free press. Newspapers are privately owned and are free to criticize the government. Print articles on security issues are subject to a military censor, as they are in many countries, though the scope of permissible reporting is wide, and editors can appeal a censorship decision to a three-member tribunal that includes two civilians.[24] While apartheid-era South African journalists could be—and often were—jailed for publishing criticism of the white government's treatment of blacks, Israeli media are largely free to criticize official Israeli policy on the treatment of Palestinian Arabs. And while apartheid South Africa banned nongovernmental organizations that campaigned for the rights of blacks, no such prohibition exists in Israel on groups that promote the interests of Palestinians.

Israelis (Jews and non-Jews) enjoy broad religious freedoms. Although Israel is officially a Jewish state, the government often acts in the interests of its secular community over the objections of the Orthodox establishment. In March 2003, for example, the Israeli government ordered the indefinite suspension of the enforcement of the no-work law during the Jewish Sabbath despite the activism of the Orthodox community. Israeli law also protects the religious freedoms of Christians, Muslims, Bahais, and other religious minority groups.[25]

Academic freedom in Israel is legally protected. Freedoms of assembly and association are respected. Demonstrations, including outside govern-

---

* Arab residents have the right to vote in municipal elections and are eligible to apply for citizenship. Although Israeli Arabs are not subject to mandatory military service, some have volunteered, and several have been decorated for their service.

ment buildings, are allowed. Israel features a vibrant civil society. Workers are free to join unions and have legally protected rights to strike and to pursue collective bargaining. Foreign workers who enter the country legally enjoy wage protections, medical insurance, and safeguards against employer exploitation.[26]

Israel is open to the outside world. More than a million foreigners visited Israel in 2003. In that same year 3.3 million Israelis traveled abroad.[27] Israelis are connected with the outside world and with one another. A study in 2002 reported that more than 80 percent of Israelis own cell phones, placing it sixth in the world on a percentage basis. A 2000 survey found that 54 percent of Israelis own personal computers, compared to only 42 percent of Americans.* More than 95 percent of Israelis can read and write.[28]

Women have achieved relative parity at almost all levels of Israeli society, although they are somewhat underrepresented in government: as of February 2005, 18 women sat in the 120-seat Knesset (though that figure compares favorably with the 14 women serving at the same time in the United States Senate). In May 1999, an Arab woman was elected to the Knesset for the first time. According to a 2005 report in the *Jerusalem Post*, "Women hold 61 percent of management posts in municipalities and 51 percent of the top academic, engineering, and technical positions."[29]

Israel has a dynamic market economy with substantial private investment in research and technology. Israel's high-tech sector, second only to California's Silicon Valley in concentration of firms, attracted $4.4 billion in foreign direct investment in 2000.[30]

In some ways, the government suffers from a surfeit of parliamentary democracy. In 2000, at a time when then Prime Minister Ehud Barak was involved in negotiations at Camp David with Yasir Arafat over the shape of a possible "two-state solution" to the Israeli-Palestinian conflict, no fewer than nineteen different political parties were represented in the Knesset.[31] The process of cobbling together coalitions of strange bedfellows undermines the effectiveness of any Israeli government, particularly those most ambitious to resolve the Israeli-Palestinian conflict and to address the question of Israel's borders and identity. Governments often don't last very long,

---

* The survey on computer statistics was conducted by the Global TGI market research company in New York and was reported in Hani Barbash, "Israel outranks U.S. in home computers and cellular phones," *Haaretz,* January 24, 2000.

budgetary processes get caught up in endless wrangling, and pork-barrel politics overwhelms the prime minister's agenda. While the presence of so many parties in parliament enhances stability in everyday governance, it undermines a state's ability to address the most intractable political problems—including those that threaten state stability.

Certainly, there are sharp divisions among Israeli Jews on the role of politics in the Jewish state. The 2005 withdrawal from Gaza highlighted conflicts between those who believe the government should be the ultimate political authority in Israeli life and those who believe that elected lawmakers have no right to violate what they consider to be God's laws. In general, these arguments are played out in the Knesset, where political parties that cover virtually the entire political and religious spectrum debate Israel's most controversial questions.

The Politics of Demographics

For decades, the United States has been the "guarantor of last resort" for Israel's security. There are many reasons for this. There is a political and economic affinity based on the fact that Israel is the only democracy and the only right-side-of-the-J-curve state in the region. It is surrounded by Arab states that are traditionally hostile to Israel's existence. In addition, there is a cultural affinity because the United States has a substantial Jewish minority and because the evangelical Christian community celebrates a "Judeo-Christian" connection. Both groups are well represented among the most influential men and women in American governance. To protect Israel from those who wish it did not exist, the U.S. government has helped arm the Israeli army for decades.*

Israel's stability is especially vulnerable for many reasons. The Western world's imposition of an Israeli state into a land then dominated by Palestinian Arabs and the subsequent Arab-Israeli War that pushed millions of

---

* That said, it was the British and the French, allies of the Israelis during the 1956 war with Egypt, who built the foundation for the Israeli military. The United States was on the opposite side of that conflict. And while the United States ultimately did little to prevent Israel from developing the nuclear-weapons capability most believe it has, the John F. Kennedy administration attempted, through diplomatic channels, to halt the Israeli nuclear program.

Palestinians into exile have earned Israel the enmity of much of the Muslim world. The stateless plight of so many Palestinians and the perception that the United States has not acted as an honest broker between the two sides have produced six decades of unresolved conflict and threatened Israel's security.

But today, the greatest threat to Israeli security—and its place on the right side of the J curve—comes not from without but from within. The multiparty system has worked reasonably well for Israelis—as long as Jews held a strong majority. But as Jewish immigration into Israel slows and Arab demographic growth continues, the balance is shifting.

In general, states with a nontitular ethnic minority population that plays only a marginal role in politics and the economy—like Kurds in Turkey—benefit internationally and domestically from open governance. When the nontitular nationality is extremely influential—like Han Chinese in Indonesia—there is no choice but to include them in the processes of government and the economy. But when the degree of influence of the minority group is between these two extremes, as it is in Israel, there is a greater danger that exclusionary nationalism will cause conflict. In Kazakhstan in the early 1990s, for example, Kazakhs were forced to accept the political and economic influence of ethnic Russians who remained there following the breakup of the Soviet Union and made up about 40 percent of the population. But as more than a quarter of these Russians emigrated, ethnic Kazakhs intensified a process of "Kazakhification" of the country's politics and culture.

It's the relative demographic weight of the minority group that makes the difference. Excluding the West Bank, Jews make up about 80 percent of Israel's population. With the occupied territories of the West Bank, Jews make up less than 60 percent. Before the evacuation from Gaza, Professor Arnon Soffer of Haifa University estimated that by 2020 the population covering the area between the Jordan and the Mediterranean would comprise a population that is 42 percent Jewish and 58 percent Muslims and others.[32] Professor Sergio de la Pergula of the Hebrew University predicted that Arabs would outnumber Jews as soon as 2010. His study suggested the population of Israeli Jews would drop to 47 percent by 2020, and 37 percent by 2050. He also calculated that a division of Israelis and Palestinians into two states based on the 1967 borders would allow Israel to remain a predominantly Jewish state, with Jews accounting for 79 percent of the population by 2010, declining only to 74 percent by 2050.[33] All these statistical projections include the now-evacuated Gaza settlements. And they are subject to the passions of Israeli politics and remain under dispute.

Palestinians know the Israelis fear the effects of the demographic shift, and they use it to strengthen their negotiating position on a final settlement of the conflict. They remind Israelis that the Palestinian birthrate in the occupied territories is double that of Israeli Jews and that the pace of Jewish immigration to Israel has substantially slowed. Saeb Erekat, a Palestinian cabinet minister, told a conference held by the Peres Center for Peace in January 2005 that "every additional house you add in the settlements prevents a solution of two states for two peoples. And then there will be one state, but you will be a minority in it."[34]

Estimates at the time (before the Israeli withdrawal from Gaza in August 2005) suggested that between 3.4 and 3.9 million Palestinians lived under Israeli occupation in the West Bank and Gaza. Yet some dispute these figures. A controversial study published in 2005 by a group of U.S. and Israeli Zionists suggests there are actually only 2.4 million Palestinians in the territories and that "if 50,000 Jews immigrate to Israel every year it will be possible to preserve the 60:40 Jewish majority over time."[35] The study argues, therefore, that Israel need not be in a hurry to cede the occupied territories to Palestinians.

Yet, all of these demographic arguments miss the more immediate point. The critical issue is not whether Israeli Arabs will demographically overwhelm Israeli Jews and form a majority that gives them a dominant position in any democratic Israeli government. Such a dramatic population shift isn't necessary to create tensions in Israeli governance that push Israel down the right side of the J curve into substantial levels of instability. At some point in the relatively near future, Arabs may form a large enough segment of the population that a political party that represents their interests would become a swing party in the Knesset—where they would be critical to the sustainability of a coalition government. If that happens, no governing coalition would be able to take meaningful policy action without the approval of a small party dominated by Palestinian Arabs.

That demographic political shift would be unacceptable to large numbers of Israeli voters. Because Arabs would then hold a veto over Jewish policy on the governance of the Jewish state, the Israeli government might well seek undemocratic means of excluding them from Israeli politics. Were

Arabs to revolt against this more authoritarian system, Israeli Jews would be forced to protect their most basic interests. The result would likely be a vicious circle that goes beyond the civil unrest, terrorism, and reprisals of the *intifadas;* the conflict would undermine the very democratic character of the Israeli state.

With the death of Yasir Arafat in 2004 and the election of a new Palestinian leadership, there was greater optimism that Israel had a partner with whom it could make a viable peace deal. Israeli Prime Minister Ariel Sharon pulled Israeli settlers and soldiers out of Gaza in 2005. To pursue a policy of further withdrawals without obstruction from conservatives within his ruling Likud, Sharon broke with the party he helped found in 1973 and created Kadima in November 2005. The Israeli prime minister suffered a stroke in January 2006 and was replaced by Ehud Olmert, who promised to carry forward with the policy of unilateral withdrawals. Debate continues to rage over whether the so-called "security wall" will become a permanent boundary between Israelis and Palestinians. If Israel is to avoid admitting the demographic Trojan horse into Israeli governance and a slide down the right side of the J curve into instability, Israeli leaders will have to finally and definitively answer the question they have so long avoided: where are Israel's boundaries and what kind of state is it?

INDIA

Charles de Gaulle once wondered, "How can one govern a country with 246 varieties of cheese?" A better question: How can one govern a country in which 35 different languages are each spoken by at least 1 million people (with more than 22,000 distinct dialects) and dozens of national and local political parties compete for votes? How can one govern a country that Winston Churchill once called "merely a geographical expression . . . no more a single country than the equator"?

In short, how can one govern India? The nation's first prime minister, Jawaharlal Nehru, believed India should be governed as a democracy. Determined that no leader or elite should dominate India's thousands of individual factions, Nehru once wrote an anonymous article warning Indians never to trust him with dictatorial power. "He must be checked," the prime minister wrote of himself. "We want no Caesars." [36]

India established itself on the right side of the J curve at midnight on August 15, 1947. Since that moment, multiparty democratic politics have provided India its political stability—even as failed policies based on command economics reinforced the economic stagnation that has kept hundreds of millions of Indians in poverty through most of the nation's first six decades of independence.

Nehru

Recognized as Gandhi's protégé, Nehru became India's first prime minister following the country's independence in 1947 and served until his death in 1964. Like Atatürk, Nehru quickly became a living symbol of his country's independence, and the policy precedents he set became as much a part of India's political tradition as Atatürk's became in Turkey. As a result, Nehru's political philosophy and personal values play an unusually large role in modern India's political life. His legacy consists of four main elements: the construction of democratic institutions, secular governance, nonalignment, and adherence to socialist economic principles. [37]

Nehru did not invent Indian democracy. Local-level democratic governance on the subcontinent began to develop centuries ago. The British made a contribution too. While they ruled most of what is now India for two centuries and denied Indians basic political rights, the British created an efficient government bureaucracy that Indians played a large role in maintaining. Further, those Indians who remained outside the bureaucracy and began the struggle for independence gained valuable organizational experience in unifying the country's diverse political, social, religious, and linguistic groups in opposition to British colonial rule.

Nehru believed democracy offered India its best hope for political stability. While Atatürk tried to establish modern governance by decree, Nehru allowed the nation's ceremonial presidents pride of place in India's democratic rituals and submitted himself and his ministers to parliamentary debate and to the slings and arrows of a boisterous opposition. He allowed the judiciary to play its proper role in a nation governed by laws. He established the precedents that would guide India's governments through periods when democracy might not have otherwise carried the day.

Nor did Nehru invent Indian secularism; the separation of temple and state is as old as the caste system. Nehru saw in that model the only means by which an Indian government could avoid sectarian war and maintain the loyalty of all India's religious groups. Nehru's secularism did not imply that religion should play no role in India's political life. It meant simply that no single religious doctrine should dominate India's governance. Nehru himself was agnostic, and the Nehru-Gandhi family and their Indian National Congress (INC) allies, who would provide modern India its prime ministers for forty-four of its first fifty years, embodied this principle.* He considered Hindu revivalism, in particular, a threat to India's cohesion as a nation.

Nehru also believed that, to protect India's independence and self-sufficiency, India had to remain neutral in the Cold War struggle between the United States and the Soviet Union. His experience under British rule—and his eighteen years in British jails—taught him to mistrust all forms of Western involvement in India. Allying the nation with either Cold War superpower, he feared, would create dependence on a superpower patron.† Because the humiliation of British rule provided Nehru and his generation their formative political experience, he believed independence should be modern India's primary political value.[38]

Yet, Nehru remained convinced throughout his life that the Soviet model of economic development best suited India. He was impressed with the rapid economic growth that Communism brought to the underdeveloped and multinational Soviet Union. At the same time, his socialist principles were both influenced by, and a rejection of, his experience of Great Britain. He abhorred what he considered Britain's predatory capitalist im-

---

* The family itself married across the boundaries of religion, sect, and caste, and in the case of Italian-born Sonia Gandhi, across nationality.

† No issue has divided Indian and American leaders more over the years than U.S. support for Pakistan. Washington has long considered Pakistan an important strategic partner, first against the Soviet Union and then in the war on terror. The beginnings of a U.S. rapprochement with India's other regional rival, China, in the early 1970s further damaged relations. Why, Indians have long wondered, would the United States cultivate better relations with military rulers in Pakistan and Communists in China than with India's committed democrats? The answer, of course, has more to do with realpolitik than with ideology.

perialism, but the Fabian Society socialism he encountered at Cambridge deeply impressed him. India would survive, Nehru argued, only if it became economically self-sufficient. He believed central planning and state control of the economy were the most "rational" and "scientific" means of establishing that self-sufficiency and of equitably distributing India's future prosperity. If Western corporations were allowed to exploit India's resources, he feared, they would inevitably follow the model of the British East India Company, which "came to trade and stayed on to rule." [39]

When Nehru died in 1964, there was no obvious successor to continue his plan for India's political and economic development. The INC chose Lal Bahadur Shastri, essentially as a compromise candidate with too few enemies to derail his nomination. Nehru and the INC, symbolically linked to defeat of the British and the only party that had successfully developed a national presence and name recognition, triumphed easily in the elections of 1964. But when Shastri died less than two years later, the INC again faced the challenge of finding a unifying figure with Nehru's appeal.

As Shashi Tharoor has written, "In a country as vast, as multilingual, as illiterate, and as poorly served by communications as India, national name recognition is not easily achieved. Once attained, it is self-perpetuating. . . ." With that in mind, the INC party elite turned to Nehru's daughter Indira Gandhi in 1966. The Nehru-Gandhi name represented a national—not a sectarian—identity for millions of Indian voters. Indira seemed to offer the INC leaders two things they wanted: a winning surname and a compliant personality they believed they would dominate. They were half right.

Indira

Indira Gandhi, who would serve fifteen years as India's prime minister, was a college dropout. She left Oxford to marry an ambitious young Congress Party member, Feroze Gandhi, in 1942.* While the two remained married until his death in a car accident in 1960, Indira devoted most of her energy

---

* Feroze was not only unrelated to Mohandas (Mahatma) Gandhi, he was not even Hindu. But the marriage of the names Nehru and Gandhi became a powerful political asset.

and attention to work as her father's private secretary and official hostess. She served briefly, in 1959, as president of the INC.

From her father, Indira absorbed a pro-Soviet socialist economic philosophy. Once in power, she stunned the INC elite that had elevated her by purging the party of moderates and aligning herself with Indian socialists and ex-Communists. She nationalized banks, ended the government's subsidies to Indian princes in compensation for the land it had redistributed, and pledged to tackle poverty. Fearing the impact on India of America's strategic partnership with Pakistan and newly opened relations with China, Indira relied increasingly on Soviet military, political, and economic support.* Her landslide electoral victory in 1971 was followed quickly by a military victory over Pakistan in the war that brought independence to Bangladesh. The Nehru-Gandhi dynasty reached the crest of its popularity.

But runaway inflation, unemployment, and pervasive corruption undercut Indira's popularity. In 1975, when a court convicted her of charges of fixing the 1971 election, she invoked Article 352 of the constitution and pushed India down the right side of the J curve into a state of emergency. Indira essentially ruled India by decree for nineteen months, a period in which the government jailed thousands of Indira's political opponents, censored the press, and postponed elections. In 1977, India's Supreme Court overturned her conviction.[40]

Because Indira had suspended freedom of speech and of the press during the emergency, she had no way of gauging how unpopular she had become. The inefficiencies of Indian socialism, the corruption that comes with one-party domination, and the abuses of emergency rule conspired to badly damage her political reputation. Driving the INC and the Nehru-Gandhi family's popularity down further, Indira's son Sanjay, though he held no formal post, engineered a number of repressive policies, including slum demolitions, forced sterilizations, and police beatings of protesters.[41] Confident of victory, Indira called for elections in 1977. A coalition of opposition parties crushed the INC. After thirty years in power, the INC and the Nehru-Gandhi family found itself in opposition for the first time, in large part because Indira used the state of emergency to cover abuses of power most frequently found in left-side-of-the-J-curve states.

Indira's decision to call elections in 1977 marks a crucial moment in

---

* India's purchase of Soviet military equipment began under Nehru in 1959.

India's history. After nearly two years of autocratic rule and the country's only real flirtation with a move to the left side of the J curve, Nehru's democratic legacy prevailed. Indira decided the Indian government's legitimacy could only be established by popular vote. India's people then asserted their will by casting out the party of modern India's founding fathers. Following the end of emergency rule and the INC's 1977 defeat, democracy in India has never again been suspended.

Return of the Dynasty

India's first non-INC-led government was inept and short-lived. In 1980, Indira was reelected and returned to power at the head of a splinter party, "Congress-Indira." Yet, many of the problems that had plagued her first eleven years in power reasserted themselves. The corruption and arrogance of power that brought down her government in 1977 returned with the family. Soon after, Sanjay was killed in a plane crash. Having sidelined all qualified deputies as potential rivals within the party, Indira turned for a political heir to her elder son Rajiv.

In October 1984, at a time when public support for the Nehru-Gandhi dynasty was again on the wane, Indira was assassinated by two of her Sikh bodyguards. Seven years earlier, some in the INC had decided to aid and protect a local Sikh extremist, Jarnail Singh Bhindranwale, who was useful as a political check on local opposition to Indira's government. The radical Sikh fundamentalist, who some claim enjoyed financial support from the Congress Party, began murdering his local enemies and agitating for an independent Sikh homeland. Indira realized she would have to stop the forces her allies had set in motion. A government raid on a Sikh temple suppressed the independence movement, but it also killed several innocent worshipers and did permanent damage to the temple. Indira's assassination was thus a revenge killing.[42]

The assassination and the violence between Sikhs and Hindus that followed have created a number of political aftershocks over the years. But a state that can absorb social unrest and the assassination of the prime minister without producing a crisis that threatens national cohesion enjoys a stability more durable than that of any state on the left side of the J curve.

Indira's martyrdom shocked the nation and, given her declining popularity at the time, probably saved the dynasty's political life. Rajiv, a political novice deeply ambivalent about his place in the family business, won an overwhelming election victory in 1984 and became prime minister.

Rajiv represented generational change. Younger Indians with little experience of British rule, fewer illusions about the Soviet model of development, and an admiration for Western culture and technology overwhelmingly supported his candidacy. But despite his initial ambitions to reform the INC and the Indian government, the party's old guard reasserted itself and blocked most of Rajiv's political and economic reform initiatives. A scandal involving kickbacks paid to Indian politicians (allegedly including Rajiv) by a Swedish defense contractor helped bring down the Congress government. In 1989, Rajiv was defeated by an anti-Congress coalition led by the socialist Janata Dal (People's Party) in alliance with the Bharatiya Janata Party and India's Communists.

The lesson Rajiv took from his loss was that he had allowed increased security (following Indira's assassination) to separate him from direct contact with the public. Running for reelection two years later, he sidelined much of his security detail and waded into crowds at campaign stops. Rajiv was assassinated by a Tamil suicide bomber in May 1991. Again the assassination of a member of the family led to electoral victory as the Congress Party returned to power.

Following the INC victory, P. V. Narasimha Rao led the party and the government for five years (1991–1996), but lost enough of the Congress's parliamentary majority that calls began for Rajiv's widow, the Italian-born Sonia Gandhi, to accept leadership of the party. Having seen her mother-in-law and husband murdered, Sonia was understandably reluctant to play any role in the political life of her adopted country. But the power of her name created intense pressures on her to extend the life of the Nehru-Gandhi dynasty into the new century. In 1998, she accepted leadership of the INC.

Also in 1998, the Bharatiya Janata Party (BJP), a Hindu nationalist organization with Hindu chauvinist allies, formed a government led by the capable Atal Behari Vajpayee. The BJP was, in a sense, the realization of Nehru's worst nightmare. India's founding father believed Hindu nationalism threatened the cohesion of Indian society, and the BJP, formed in 1980,

elevated the concept of Hindutva (literally, Hinduness) to national prominence.

Hindutva has always been a difficult-to-define concept, primarily because the BJP has continually recontextualized it to suit its political needs of
the moment. If traditional BJP ideology has a geographical center of gravity, it is in the town of Ayodhya, site of the Babri Mosque destroyed by
Hindu fanatics in 1992. Throughout the 1980s, the BJP supported the claim
of Hindu chauvinists that the mosque had been built atop the birthplace of
the Hindu god Ram and should, therefore, be removed and replaced with a
Hindu temple. When a mob finally destroyed the mosque, several BJP officials were directly implicated in the resulting violence.

The BJP also built its political reputation on calls for the establishment
of a single civil code for all Indians, which would require the abolition of
Muslim Personal Law. Established under British rule and continued under
Nehru and his successors, Personal Law grants Muslims and other groups
the right to live by their own rules on marriage, divorce, and inheritance.*
Before coming to power, the BJP also supported a hard-line approach to
India's relations with Pakistan, an end to Indian-controlled Kashmir's special status (Kashmiris have their own constitution), and opposition to the
opening of India's economy.

That the BJP's record once in power is quite different than these policy
positions suggest demonstrates how India's diversity and political openness
support its stability. Management of a twenty-party coalition requires compromise. Despite years of tough rhetoric on relations with Pakistan, Vajpayee opened the negotiations that have now produced the best relations
between the two countries since partition. While in opposition, the BJP
usually favored maintaining a closed economy. In power, Vajpayee continued the INC's economic reforms and opened several economic sectors to
foreign investment. Vajpayee never made a serious attempt to do away with
Muslim Personal Law. When the BJP sought reelection in 2004, it promised
to continue the opening up of the economy and investment in cutting-edge

---

* "... religious communities continue to be governed by their own personal laws (apart
from Muslims, this applies to Christians, Zoroastrians, Jews and Hindus, as well as
Buddhists and Sikhs who, for legal purposes, are classified as Hindus)." http://www.law
.emory.edu/IFL/legal/india.htm.

technology. The party emphasized the relative peace between Hindus and Muslims in the states it governed. During the campaign, the six Muslim candidates on the Hindu nationalist party's list were on display throughout the country. The party members most closely associated with Hindu-Muslim confrontation were conspicuously absent. In essence, India's right-side-of-the-curve political structure forced the BJP to moderate its policies.

One notable campaign promise the BJP kept: the testing of nuclear weapons. For the first time in nearly a quarter-century, India conducted a series of underground nuclear tests in May 1998. Two weeks later, Pakistan responded with three tests of its own.* While the world reacted sharply to both sets of tests and the United States and others imposed sanctions on both countries, India's tests have done little in the long run to undermine political stability. Sanctions on both countries were lifted in 2001, and the tests have arguably stabilized relations between the two. In fact, in March 2006, President George W. Bush and Prime Minister Manmohan Singh signed a landmark agreement that guarantees the United States will provide India with nuclear fuel and technical expertise. And now that India's economy has begun to open to the outside world and to push India further up the right side of the J curve, the Indian government has new reasons to moderate its policy initiatives. The costs of any incendiary rhetoric have increased—for India's economy and for all who would invest in its growth.

Despite the BJP's reinvention, the INC returned to power in 2004. And just in case anyone wondered if the Nehru-Gandhi dynasty had run out of political steam, much of the credit for the Congress victory went to party leader Sonia Gandhi, whose son Rahul was also elected to parliament for the first time.

Indian Socialism

If India's commitment to pluralist democracy is Nehru's greatest contribution to his country's place on the right side of the J curve, his faith in command economics has limited India's exposure to the market dynamism of the outside world and its ability to advance further up the curve. And while

---

* Pakistan claims six tests.

fragile coalition politics have forced the compromises needed to stabilize India's political life, they have also watered down attempts at substantive economic reform. In multiparty coalition politics, nearly everyone has a say—and nearly everyone has a veto. The BJP was forced not only to limit its Hindu nationalism, but also to restrict its efforts on pension reform and the opening of key economic sectors to foreign investment.

Inspired by Soviet models of economic development, India's first prime minister enshrined socialism in the form of five-year plans.* State-owned companies were maintained, without regard for efficiency or productivity, for the "public good." The state created and maintained protectionist policies in the name of avoiding social costs—job loss, poverty, and political turmoil. Indira extended her father's philosophy to the nationalization of banks and insurance companies.

Nehru did initiate a political tradition of substantial investment in university and technical education. That practice is now paying big dividends for the educated elite, as big players in the information revolution have set up shop in Bangalore. But Nehru and his successors have largely ignored the importance of primary education, and illiteracy has been reduced at an unnecessarily slow pace. It doesn't matter how many foreign books are translated to the local language (or in India's case, languages) when so many of its citizens are illiterate. If few can read, the outside world's influence is necessarily limited.†

Adherence to command economics *has* offered Indian politicians two important tools that serve their personal interests: extensive public-sector investment (useful for fueling patronage networks) and the power to grant large-scale subsidies (useful for winning key constituencies at election time). When political survival depends on fragile alliances, it's difficult to give up the power to decide how to distribute taxpayers' money to best political advantage.

But decades of protectionism, the preservation of inefficient companies and industries, and an economy largely closed to foreign investment trapped hundreds of millions of Indians in abject poverty and provided the

---

* South Korean and Taiwanese governments of that generation, among others, relied on five-year plans for their development. But they opened their economies to foreign investment much more quickly than India did.
† India's literacy rate remains below 65 percent.

rest with badly made, often scarce, overly expensive products. That's the price of left-side-of-the-J-curve economics.

A labyrinth of rules and regulations determined how many workers an Indian firm could hire, whether and how much they could invest, what raw materials they could import, and how profits could be distributed. A wide array of licenses was required for virtually any entrepreneurial initiative and the firing of workers remained an extremely complex legal undertaking. A failed business with more than a few dozen workers could not be shuttered without (rarely granted) official permission. The result was enduring inefficiency: In 1986, the Steel Authority of India paid 247,000 people to produce 6 million tons of finished steel. That same year, South Korea's Pohang Steel paid 10,000 workers to produce 14 million tons.[43]

While other countries in the region enjoyed growth rates of 10 to 15 percent between 1950 and 1980, India remained mired in what economist Raj Krishna once called the "Hindu rate of growth"—around 3–5 percent.* As India's share of world trade fell by 80 percent over the first decades of independence, its public sector expanded to become the world's largest outside the Communist bloc.[44]

In addition, the government spent very little on infrastructure until the 1990s. Roads, bridges, ports, and electricity-generation facilities were neglected for decades. In 1996, two years after the Indian government opened the doors for private telephone companies, only 9 million Indians—less than 1 percent of the population—owned a telephone, one-tenth the world average.[45]

That is the economic legacy of Jawaharlal Nehru—and Indira Gandhi made matters worse. She simultaneously reinforced her political power and the command structure of India's economy by providing licenses to those in the business community willing to promote her candidacy—businessmen willing to support national protectionism in exchange for the permits that freed the politically connected from its constraints.

---

* The causes of India's anemic growth have been political, not cultural, as evidenced by the productivity of Indians living abroad. Indian-Americans have the highest per capita income of any immigrant group. There are hundreds of Indian millionaires in Britain. While expatriates of any nationality are generally more productive than the countrymen they leave behind, the differences between nonresident Indians and those who remain in India are too large to dismiss.

By 1977, the need for fundamental change in economic policy was clear, even to Nehru's heirs. A limited relaxation of government control of the economy began under the Janata government in 1977, continued under Indira, and accelerated under Rajiv. At the same time, however, the government went on a spending spree to protect its political popularity. The level of subsidies nearly doubled between 1977 and 1987. Fiscal deficits rose sharply. Foreign debt rose nearly 400 percent in the 1980s.[46]

Then, the Warsaw Pact governments and the Soviet Union collapsed. Socialism was widely discredited. The Indian treasury was empty. Necessity became the mother of liberalization. In early 1991, a large percentage of India's gold reserves had to be flown to London as collateral for a $2.2 billion emergency IMF loan to avoid default on the nation's debt. It was a turning point. That same year, Prime Minister Rao appointed economist Manmohan Singh to head the Finance Ministry. Reform began, and the Indian government moved to open its economy to foreign investment, powering India higher up the right side of the J curve than it had ever been. In his first speech as finance minister, Singh quoted Victor Hugo: "No power on earth can stop an idea whose time has come."

When Singh took up his new portfolio, India's fiscal deficit was a full 8.5 percent of GDP. It held around $1 billion in foreign-exchange reserves. The new minister simplified the tax system and cut liberally into the system of quotas and licenses to promote entrepreneurship and growth. Foreign investors became majority shareholders in a number of Indian companies. The government sold off shares in state-owned firms that failed to produce upgrades to infrastructure. The rupee was dramatically devalued; tariffs were drastically cut. Quotas were loosened or eliminated. During Singh's tenure as finance minister, the economy grew at 7 percent a year.[47]

The government ended the state telecom monopoly in 1992. Nine million Indians owned telephones in 1996. As of 2005, there are more than 100 million telephones in India with an additional 2 million added every month. The Indian government says it hopes there will be 250 million mobile-phone users by 2007.[48] Foreign direct investment flowed into areas of the economy previously off-limits to outsiders. Previous Indian governments had taken small steps toward reform, but, under Singh's management, economic reform charged forward. Between 1947 and 1991, FDI totaled $1.5 billion. In 1996 alone, the total reached $2 billion. By 2004, it had climbed to $5 billion.[49]

While liberalization has become India's new consensus, such fundamental reforms always bring pushback. When workers learn for the first time that they can be fired, they protest. When domestic industries discover they will no longer be sheltered from the rigors of foreign competition, they resist. When rural voters believe that reform will widen the gap between rich and poor, they look for new politicians to represent their interests. All of this has taken place in India and has slowed the process of reform in all but the newest investment sectors. In the long run, India's economic reforms will promote political stability. But the pace must be managed. Some resistance to reforms reinforces short-term political stability as it softens the blows of social dislocation.

Despite the resistance to economic change from those whose interests it threatens, when the Congress Party won a surprise victory in 2004, Manmohan Singh found himself (much to his surprise) elevated to the post of prime minister. His efforts to enact further reforms will be carefully weighed against the need to win political support for his government. Singh's current coalition depends on support from the Communist Party. While India's Communists are not unalterably opposed to all forms of economic liberalization, their influence will certainly slow the process of privatization of key sectors of the economy. That is the price of coalition politics.

Diversity and Stability

That culture of coalition governance is the direct product of India's diversity. Diversity is the primary source of India's stability. The fragile coalition politics it promotes breeds compromise. Compromise absorbs shocks. If twenty different groups have a say in the final form of a piece of legislation, it is less likely the new law will arouse anyone's outrage. And because India has remained a democracy since independence, all those groups will have their say. In fact, in India's first-past-the-post electoral system, small groups wield big influence. Think Cuban-Americans.

Diversity also reinforces stability because the different regions of India are so culturally, linguistically, and ethnically distinct, and their interests are defined so differently, that a shock in one area of the country has little impact on another—or on the nation as a whole. The idea that factionalism in a democracy can be a source of stability is neither Indian nor new. James

Madison wrote in the *Federalist Papers* in 1787, "The influence of factious leaders may kindle a flame within their particular States, but will be unable to spread a general conflagration through the other States. A religious sect may degenerate into a political faction in a part of the Confederacy; but the variety of sects dispersed over the entire face of it must secure the national councils against any danger from that source."[50] Those words and Nehru's deep belief in democracy, more than any other factors, explain India's place on the right side of the J curve.

Over the decades, a variety of Hindu chauvinist movements have tried to unify Hindus at the expense of others. More than 80 percent of Indians are Hindus. But they are as divided by language, custom, and culture as any other Indian group. There are so many other forms of self-identification within Indian society (language, caste, class, region of origin), that Hindus have never regarded themselves as a unified majority. Again, thirty-five different languages are spoken by at least 1 million Indians. Only half of Indians understand Hindi. Without the pervasive influence of Bollywood, India's film industry, the percentage would be smaller. Less than 5 percent of Indians speak English. But because so many professional schools teach English and it is widely used among the social and political elite and by the national media, English serves as a kind of substitute national language.[51]

Hindu nationalism is also limited by the prominent role Muslims play in India's political, economic, and cultural life. India has had three Muslim presidents: Fakhruddin Ali Ahmed, Zakir Hussain, and the current president A. P. J. Abdul Kalam, who is also the scientist who created India's missile program. The country's first female chief justice, Fatima Biwi, is Muslim. Several of Bollywood's biggest box-office draws, dozens of pop stars, and many celebrated athletes are Muslim. There are Muslims in prominent positions in every major Indian political party—including the BJP. They have served as regional governors, ambassadors, and cabinet ministers. India's wealthiest man, Azim Premji, is Muslim. And there is a prosperous and growing Muslim middle class. None of that diminishes the violence that has been visited on India's Muslim community—at Ayodhya, in Gujarat, or thousands of other places. Without question, many of India's nearly 150 million Muslims are victims of many forms of discrimination. But when they have a grievance, it is far easier to air and to address it in India than in many majority-Muslim countries that lack India's durable, multiparty democracy.

Second, the nature of the Hindu faith undermines attempts to use it as a tool of exclusion. It is a religion with "no organized church, no compulsory beliefs or rites of worship, no single sacred book. . . . There are no compulsory dogmas. . . . It embraces an eclectic range of doctrines and practices." [52] It is, in fact, the only major religion in the world with no scriptural claim to be the one true faith, and it is practiced in different ways in different regions of the country. As a result, it is very difficult to unite Hindus in defense of any single idea or ideology.

Hindutva activists have attempted to unite Hindus into a chauvinist cultural movement, partly in response to assertions of religious solidarity from other groups, particularly Muslims. But they have enjoyed only limited success. They may have hoped that the rise to power of the BJP would enhance their national standing. And local BJP officials have been implicated in deadly attacks on Muslims, the most virulent expression of a Hindu nationalist movement that is otherwise peaceful in its attempts to construct a national Hindu identity.* But from India's founding, religious division has been widely treated as something ugly, part of the British strategy of "divide and rule." And because modern India was founded alongside the violent partition from Muslim Pakistan, India's governments have, in general, heeded Nehru's calls for the maintenance of a wall between priests and politicians.

Once and Future Conflicts

Another source of India's stability is the marked improvement in relations with its neighbors. India has made substantial progress toward resolution of its long-standing border disputes with traditional rival China that date from their war in the early 1960s. Relations with Pakistan seriously deteriorated when both countries tested nuclear weapons in 1998 and when they threatened to use them in 2002. But, as noted, Vajpayee backed away from the BJP's traditional hard-line approach to relations with Pakistan and began a process of (relatively) amicable negotiations with Pakistani Presi-

---

* In 2002, for example, the region of Gujarat was shaken by religious violence. More than 1,000 people, most of them Muslims, were killed. More than 2,000 died following the 1992 destruction of the mosque at Ayodhya.

dent Pervez Musharraf. Manmohan Singh has built on that base, and Indian-Pakistani relations are more stable in 2006 than at any time since partition. India also enjoys warm relations and an expanding trade relationship with Japan.[53]

In addition, there is a fundamental shift occurring in the geopolitical balance of power. As China emerges as a political, military, and economic superpower, it will find itself increasingly at odds with the United States and with its major Asian competitor, Japan. For strategic reasons therefore, all three—and others—are likely to try and strengthen their relations with India and to invest in its relatively stable emerging-market environment. In other words, the rivalries all around it may well serve to further stabilize India.

If there is any force in Indian politics that poses a threat to the nation's long-term position on the right side of the J curve, it is the possible unrest produced by the widening gap between rich and poor that comes with economic growth in an emerging market. This agent of socioeconomic change could exacerbate divisions between Indians of different social stations. Although the concept of caste dates to ancient Hindu texts and has not always produced social strife, the British heightened awareness of caste differences as part of a divide-and-rule strategy.*

The original Hindu word for caste, *varna*, literally meant "color," and caste has functioned in India historically as a kind of "apartheid." Indians have been taught that only if they lived according to their *dharma* (code of proper conduct) and the other dictates of their station could they hope for reincarnation as a member of a more privileged caste. But centuries of intermarriage have combined "colors" into millions of combinations. Both Mahatma Gandhi and Nehru argued that caste was a tool of exploitation used by outsiders and should be abandoned. Further, the urbanization of modern India has eroded the power of caste identity. Nearly 30 percent of the country's 1.1 billion people now live in India's crowded cities. Since it is impossible to know the caste affiliations of the people sitting next to you on the bus, the idea has increasingly little meaning.[54]

---

* The difference between class and caste is one of mobility. Because class is largely determined by economic and cultural factors, a person can move from one class to another in this life. A person's caste can only be changed in the next life. See "Caste and Class," http://country studies.us/india/89.htm.

As the period of British rule and Nehru's admonitions against caste consciousness have receded in the nation's collective memory, the idea of dividing Indians by religion, caste, or any other means has become less politically taboo. Politicians, particularly in the last two decades, have used their caste, regional, or religious identities to gain votes from members of their groups. Prime Minister V. P. Singh, for example, relied for much of his political support on members of the so-called "backward castes."* In 1990, Singh's Janata Party government reinstitutionalized caste awareness by formally approving the recommendations of the Mandal Commission which, in the name of what would be called "affirmative action" in America, set quotas for the allotment of government jobs. Since so many Indians of the lower- and intermediate-level castes voted, why not promise them jobs in exchange for political popularity?

Thereafter, 27 percent of government jobs have been reserved for members of the so-called backward castes. Another 22.5 percent are set aside for the "scheduled castes and tribes."†[55] Outraged by the moves, the Hindu nationalist BJP withdrew from Singh's minority government and supported Hindutva agitation that led to, among other things, the 1992 destruction of the Babri Mosque in Ayodhya.

While the Mandal recommendations were limited to quotas for government jobs, caste quotas have been created for universities, professional schools, and other institutions. Thus, the idea of caste has returned to Indian politics. Historically, people's opportunities were determined by caste identity. Following independence, caste was treated as irrelevant by those— like Gandhi and Nehru—who considered it a tool of the British to divide Indians. In urban social interactions, caste differences are still virtually meaningless. But caste has again become relevant as a determinant of opportunity.

It is possible that India's economic expansion will create such obvious gaps between rich and poor that Indians, more keenly aware of differences in standing and privilege, will be pitted against one another. The greater

---

* An intermediate-level caste. "Backward" is a term invented by the British that has never been amended because India's first prime ministers believed such a change would acknowledge that the idea of caste might persist.

† "Scheduled castes and tribes" are those of such low standing they are listed in "schedules" attached to the Indian constitution.

likelihood, however, is that India's diversity will continue to protect its stability. Modern India's open and stable democracy has survived the trauma of partition (and the Hindu-Muslim violence it produced), emergency rule, military defeat, Maoist rebels, secessionists in Kashmir, Tamil Nadu, Punjab, and the northeast, and thousands of smaller-scale conflicts based on caste, region, and religion. As it opens itself further to the forces of global change and deepens its political and economic engagement with other nations, India's place on the right side of the J curve should only become more secure.

Policy

The George W. Bush administration has done a lot to build on Clinton-era efforts to improve the U.S.-Indian relationship. Strategic calculations of geopolitical advantage have for decades obstructed U.S. engagement with the world's largest democracy. When India officially joined the nuclear club in 1998, Washington imposed sanctions. The lifting of those sanctions has already paid great economic dividends for both sides, though it may ultimately complicate the administration's broader nonproliferation agenda. Domestic critics charge that the president's efforts to promote U.S.-Indian cooperation on civilian nuclear technology and to sell India high-tech weapons systems is improper, if not unlawful, given that India has never signed either the Nuclear Nonproliferation Treaty or the Comprehensive Test Ban Treaty. Yet International Atomic Energy Agency Director Mohamed El Baradei quickly lauded the agreement and called India "an important partner in the non-proliferation regime."[56]

Ironically, the Bush administration's motivations for warming the bilateral relationship may owe as much to realpolitik as did the diplomatic chill of the Cold War years. As China becomes more militarily assertive, weapons sales to India have strategic importance. But a warmer and more constructive relationship, once created, can create a momentum of its own and may be remembered as one of the most significant foreign-policy achievements of George W. Bush's presidency. That's all to the good, because U.S.-Indian ties can help reinforce India's economic liberalization and yield political, economic, and cultural dividends that benefit both sides for decades to come.

. . .

The elements that make up a stability based on openness are not bricks, and such a stability cannot be built like a wall. Representative government and all its moving parts form a living organism. The nourishment of that organism is the business of the nation's citizens—and, less directly, of all those outside with an interest in healthy and forward-looking relations with that nation.

In other words, the right side of the J curve is not a destination; it is a process. Turkey, Israel, and India have all survived threats to the viability of their open, representative systems of governance. All three may face those challenges in the future. None of them has yet achieved anything that can't be undone. If they are to avoid the slide back into instability, all must continue to renew the processes of political openness. And the international community has a role to play in helping right-side-of-the-J-curve states that have not yet fully consolidated their stability to overcome these and other obstacles.

The Marshall Plan played a crucial role in anchoring Western Europe in open governance. Following the collapse of the Soviet Union, Western Europe's institutional embrace of much of Eastern Europe gave the former Warsaw Pact nations the opportunity to build a new kind of open society. In that regard, memberships in NATO and the European Union have served as catalysts to promote political and economic reform in many countries that might otherwise have descended into dangerous instability. Turkey's inclusion in NATO in the early 1950s helped keep it open to the world beyond its borders. An invitation to join the European Union could provide open governance a gateway into the Muslim world.

It may not always be in the interests of the international community to push a relatively unstable left-side-of-the-curve state directly into the transitional dip in the curve. If free and fair national elections were held tomorrow in Pakistan, Egypt, and Saudi Arabia, the result might well be destabilizing for everyone. And, as the United States has discovered in post-Saddam Iraq, no state on the right side of the curve, and no international organization, has the capacity to guarantee the success of an artificially imposed transition from left to right. In such cases, the wisest policy is to support the construction within those states—before they have begun the transition—of the political, economic, and cultural institutions they will need when they inevitably slide on their own toward instability.

On the other hand, the international community's efforts to keep a right-side state on the right are always good policy. Consider the stakes for the world if the open societies of Turkey, Israel, or India should close. Turkey offers the West an enormous opportunity to demonstrate to the peoples of other Muslim states hungry for modernization, political change, and economic dynamism that adherence to the principles of openness can bring about all those, and more, positive results. If the invitation never comes, the message is the opposite: our model of development is not for you. If Israel closes, decades of efforts at Middle East peace will have come to nothing, and the United States will likely be drawn into conflicts that further compromise its message of democratic change to the Islamic world. If India, the world's largest democracy, were to close and to harden its attitude to the outside world, the threat of nuclear conflict in Asia would rise sharply, hundreds of millions of people would remain indefinitely mired in poverty, and opportunities for commerce that might ultimately benefit billions would be missed.

States that have already even partially opened are, by definition, more easily influenced than states that are sealed off from the outside. If the international community wastes an opportunity to bring these states into greater harmony with the crosscurrents of globalization, all will be the poorer for it.

CHAPTER SIX

China's Dilemma

A revolution is a struggle to the death between the future and the past.

—FIDEL CASTRO

Where does China fall on the J curve? Does the Communist Party's unwillingness to meaningfully reform the nation's authoritarian political system consign China to the left side of the curve? Or has China's growing economic openness to foreign influence and investment already pushed the People's Republic through instability to the right? Is China too economically open for the left side? Or is it too politically closed for the right?

It's a question worth asking, because the internal political and economic choices the Chinese leadership makes over the coming two decades will play an enormous role as a driver of global stability or instability. The direction of China's political development is crucial for the sustainability of China's economic expansion and for global security. The success or failure of China's economic development will, to a great degree, determine the near-term future of world economic growth. The leadership of the Chinese Communist Party (CCP) wants to use its open economic system to finance its closed politics. The party believes that, if it provides prosperity, the Chinese people will allow the ruling elite absolute control of China's political life. But political and economic development aren't so easily separated. Therein lies China's dilemma. And because China's influence on world politics and markets is great and growing, China's dilemma is a global dilemma.

CHINA ON THE J CURVE

China remains on the left side of the J curve. Before exploring why that is, it's worth considering the best counterarguments.

China's emergence as an international trading power and the changes this process has brought Chinese society are undeniable. "China now has a stake in the liberal, rules-based global economic system that the United States worked to establish over the past half-century," wrote George Gilboy in the July-August 2004 issue of *Foreign Affairs.*[*][1] The Chinese Communist Party has opened China's economy to foreign direct investment, and the country has joined the World Trade Organization. All these changes have brought liberalization and rising prosperity, both within China and across East Asia. China already has the third-largest GDP in the world, measured in purchasing-power parity, and as part of its "Go Out" policy of promoting investment by Chinese firms in foreign markets, it is opening new commercial contacts all over the world. China is open for business to an extent far beyond anything Iran, Saudi Arabia, or Russia—let alone North Korea or Cuba—can match.

A number of China-watchers share Beijing's willingness to try and separate economics from politics as they try to predict the nation's future. Wall Street analysts, in particular, remain bullish on China's continued growth prospects.[†] China has sustained annual growth rates of around 9 percent for the past twenty-five years. Neither economic trend lines nor history, these analysts argue, explain why strong growth cannot be sustained for yet another twenty-five years. Because such growth depends on trade and foreign investment—a dependence that opens China a little more fully to the

---

[*] It's important to note that Gilboy himself does not argue that China's economic growth will, of necessity, open the country politically. He's included here because he ably combines all the elements others use to argue that greater Chinese political openness is inevitable.

[†] For examples of bullish sentiment on China, see the following: http://www.moneyweb .co.za/education/investment_insights/724404.htm and http://www.briefing.com/schwab2/ ratings.htm.

outside world every year—China's openness to foreign influence and to the social and political influences of globalization should only increase over the coming generation.

In addition, the Chinese people have a degree of access to information from the outside world and opportunities to communicate with one another they didn't have even five years ago. According to *China Daily,* the Chinese government forecast that the country would have a total of 120 million Internet users by the end of 2005.[2] As mentioned in Chapter One, Chinese consumers rang in the Lunar New Year in February 2005 by sending more than 11 billion text messages in just twenty-four hours. They sent a total of 217.7 billion such messages in 2003 alone.[3] More than 350 million Chinese now own mobile phones.[4] How can a closed regime on the left side of the J curve afford such connectivity?

ECONOMIC REFORM

Without question, China has opened its economy to an extent far beyond those of any of the countries we've identified on the left side of the J curve. In the late 1970s, the Chinese Communist Party embarked on a program of determined economic reform. The central government decreed that Mao Tse-tung–era collective farms and communes should be abandoned in favor of a "responsibility system" that leased land to individual farmers, raised rural living standards, gave families and individuals control of their household incomes, and freed up millions of peasants to work in local industries. Restoring a profit motive to rural agriculture, permitting local farmers to make many production decisions, and allowing for greater labor mobility infused China's economy with an explosion of economic energy.[5]

Deng Xiaoping first told China's peasants that "to get rich is glorious" in the early 1980s. Since then, the party leadership has increasingly staked its survival on its ability to raise China's production capacity and standard of living by progressively opening China's economy to the outside world. To revitalize China's economic system and to encourage foreign investment, the party began in 1980 to create experimental enclaves of managed capitalism, called special economic zones (SEZs). The party created SEZs in the cities of Shenzhen, Zhuhai, and Shantou in Guangdong Province, and

Xiamen in Fujian Province. It established the island of Hainan a special economic zone.[6] (See map of China on page 241.) Foreign investors in the SEZs enjoy special tax incentives. The local leaders who administer the SEZs have greater independence than other local officials in the conduct of international trade and more freedom for managerial innovation and to craft legislation.

In 1984, the PRC opened another fourteen coastal cities to overseas investment.* Since 1992, the Chinese leadership has also opened inland provincial capitals. At first, only in the special economic zones set up in 1980, but in other parts of the country later that decade, companies were given the freedom to link pay to performance and to lay off staff.

China's admission to the World Trade Organization in December 2001 obliged Beijing to cut import tariffs and to give foreign businesses much greater access to potentially lucrative markets that had been highly protected. More to the point, WTO membership forced China to liberalize its rules on investment and foreign ownership, and to reduce other barriers to trade. WTO membership and China's initial steps to honor its resulting commitments have inspired confidence in foreign investors that the potential rewards in China outweigh the decreasing risk that Beijing will change the rules of the game to favor Chinese firms. As a result, investment and purchase orders have poured in.†

How much investment? In 2002, China became the world's largest recipient of foreign direct investment (FDI).[7] In 2003, total FDI rose to $53.5 billion. It jumped to $58 billion in 2005. Between 1978 and the end of 2004, China attracted $563.8 billion in foreign direct investment,[8] more than ten times the total FDI Japan amassed between 1945 and 2000. China has aggressively promoted regional trade, including a free-trade zone with the Association of Southeast Asian Nations (ASEAN) and a bilateral trade agreement with Australia.[9]

This economic openness promotes internal change in China. Durable foreign-trade ties force reform of Chinese commercial law and greater regulatory consultation with Chinese consumers. It trims China's notoriously

---

* They are Dalian, Qinhuangdao, Tianjin, Yantai, Qingdao, Lianyungang, Nantong, Shanghai, Ningbo, Wenzhou, Fuzhou, Guangzhou, Zhanjiang, and Beihai.

† WTO membership alone does not imply a place on the right side of the J curve—Cuba and Burma have been members since 1995. But China does not face economic sanctions.

CHINA'S FIRST SPECIAL ECONOMIC ZONES (SEZS)

China's First Special Economic Zones (SEZs): China's first experimental islands of managed capitalism in the early 1980s: the cities of Shenzhen, Zhuhai, and Shantou in Guangdong Province, Xiamen in Fujian Province, and the island of Hainan.

inefficient bureaucracies and gives the central government incentive to respect enhanced international safety and environmental standards. The Chinese people are now freer to debate economic and social issues in the financial media, although it is still sharply limited by the standards of politically mature countries.

China's dependence on foreign investment is almost certainly irreversible. First, China's industrial and high-tech exports, whose success is vitally important for sustainable growth, are dominated by foreign-funded firms. Foreign-funded enterprises (FFEs) produced 55 percent of China's exports in 2003, a level of foreign involvement in the economy strikingly high by the standards of other recent Asian success stories.* By any measure, foreign firms and governments have a higher stake in Chinese economic growth than they do in that anywhere else in the region. The Communist Party believes its political capital is replenished by rising Chinese living standards. Those standards depend on foreign investment. And the influence of foreign firms is increasing.[10]

There is another trend that deepens China's dependence on foreign investment. During the 1990s, Beijing facilitated a move away from joint ventures toward wholly owned foreign enterprises (WOFEs). Today, for-eign-*owned* firms account for nearly two-thirds of new FDI in China. These foreign-owned companies transfer proprietary technology to Chinese firms far less often than do traditional joint ventures. Foreign-funded firms are contractually obligated to share knowledge with their local Chinese partners. Foreign-owned firms are not. In other words, Chinese growth remains deeply dependent on designs, critical parts, and equipment imported from developed states.[11] That dependence requires that the Communist Party—if it is to nourish China's economic growth and create the higher standard of living on which, the party believes, China's stability depends—accept an extraordinary level of foreign influence in the establishment and enforcement of its economic rules of the road. The states we have noted that are clearly on the left side of the J curve have all worked hard to avoid anything close to that level of dependence on foreign firms.

Combine Chinese citizens' access to information from abroad, economic openness to foreign influence, the financial independence of growing numbers of Chinese, and Beijing's acceptance of Washington Consensus–based rules of the road, and you have a strong argument for China's place on the right side of the J curve.

---

* In his recent article for *Foreign Affairs,* George Gilboy cites the following figures by Huang Yasheng of the Massachusetts Institute of Technology: "FFEs accounted for only 20 percent of Taiwan's manufactured exports in the mid-1970s and only 25 percent of South Korea's manufactured exports between 1974 and 1978. In Thailand, the FFEs' share dropped from 18 percent in the 1970s to 6 percent by the mid-1980s."

BUT . . .

Walk into central Beijing and take Natan Sharansky's "town square test." Sharansky argues that if a citizen can walk into the middle of the town square and express his views without fear that police will arrest or assault him, he lives in a free society. In Beijing, the town square test still produces a Tiananmen Square result. By Sharansky's definition, China's is not a free society and has no place on the right side of the J curve.

We've said that countries on the right side of the curve derive their stability from institutions rather than from individual leaders. China's current president, Hu Jintao, is not Mao or Deng. He's in no danger of finding himself the object of a cult of personality. And China's stability *is* safeguarded by an institution: the Chinese Communist Party. But that institution is the only game in town. In a political context, nothing is independent of the party. China is a police state.

Though China has opened its markets to substantial foreign influence, the Communist Party refuses to tolerate political dissent and has resisted virtually any meaningful political reform. The party makes its political and economic decisions in secret. It views China's citizens—particularly its ethnic and religious minorities—as risks to be managed rather than as potential contributors to China's development. Here is the limit of China's openness. Remember that the "openness" expressed by the horizontal axis of the J curve is not simply a measure of a country's openness to the outside world. It is also a reflection of openness *within* a state's borders. It is a measure of a people's freedom to communicate with one another, of a people's access to information about its government and society. If China is becoming more open within its borders, it is in spite of its government.

The two Chinese characters that represent "revolution" translate literally as "withdrawal of the mandate." [12] When the Chinese Communist Party crushed pro-reform demonstrators in Tiananmen Square on June 4, 1989, the episode was merely the most dramatic of many examples of Beijing's adherence to the belief that only its "mandate" to hold a monopoly on power separates China from the chaos found in the J curve's most treacherous depths.

Even before the collapse of the Communist governments of Eastern Europe and the Soviet Union, the Chinese Communist Party set a course toward a model of development that privileged economic might as the engine for political strength and stability. It was in 1982 that Deng first gave the official seal of approval to the pursuit of wealth. The 1989 Tiananmen Square protests convinced authorities they were right to fear organized domestic dissent and the large-scale social unrest it might unleash. The collapse of the Warsaw Pact states later that year reinforced the party elite's belief that it must provide the citizenry what other Communist governments could not: a rising standard of living. Failure to satisfy public demand for a more modern and prosperous life, the party feared, would lead to more Tiananmens and ultimately cost the party its mandate.

How has the party protected its monopoly on power? Secrecy remains a key element of its strategy. Virtually all the party's most important decisions are made in secret. Even though hundreds of billions of dollars in trade and investment depend on decisions taken by the party leadership, reading the tea leaves of China's decision-making process rivals Kremlinology for the inexactitude of its methods. The party's Politburo and Central Committee represent a tiny elite within an elite in a nation where even some of the most senior politicians don't have direct influence over vitally important political decisions. Economic decisions too, including those made by China's Central Bank, are still cloaked in the kind of secrecy that would be impossible to maintain in a right-side-of-the-J-curve state.

For many years, the primary means by which the CCP guarded its mandate and controlled its citizens was the so-called iron triangle: the residence permit, which established where people were allowed to live; the secret personnel file, which recorded a citizen's political reliability and any ideological offenses; and the work unit, which managed many aspects of a citizen's life.[13] Because economic openness has profoundly changed the structure of Chinese society, none of the three are nearly as binding or as pervasive as they were ten years ago. But none have been totally abolished.

The residence permit, or *hukou,* is a booklet that lists the bearer's family members and establishes where he is allowed to live. Without a Shanghai *hukou,* it was, until recently, impossible to legally establish residence in Shanghai—unless you were willing and able to bribe the right official or to use your *guanxi,* friends or relatives in high places, to pull strings. It was extremely difficult for anyone without extra cash or well-connected family or friends to gain permission to move from one city or province to another. It was especially difficult for a rural resident to gain official permission to move into a city. Some braved the restrictions and relocated without the permit. Such "criminals" were arrested each month in large numbers. Others, called "floaters," continue to migrate around the country with no legal residence.* With the changes to labor laws that have come with greater economic openness, *hukou* restrictions have been substantially eased. But the document itself still exists and can still be used to restrict movement within China.

The *dangan,* or secret personnel file, has proven a particularly effective means of discouraging dissent. Every Chinese citizen has two *dangan*—one held by his work unit, the other by local police. He is never permitted to see either file. Any incidence of "trouble-making," no matter how innocuous, might end up in the secret file and frustrate its subject when he needs something from the government—a new residence permit, a new job, or permission to travel.

The third corner of the iron triangle is the *danwei,* or work unit. Traditionally, the *danwei* was the provider of health care, housing, and ideological education. Its approval was needed to marry, to have a child, to travel, or to move. Social and economic changes have eroded the effectiveness of all these tools of absolute authority and forced party officials to become more resourceful in discouraging unacceptable behavior. But, even today, large numbers of Chinese live with these and other constraints on their personal behavior.[14]

The Chinese Communist Party has now recognized that labor mobility is essential to economic growth and that the state can no longer exercise near-total control over the everyday lives of its citizens. The party has therefore sought new ways to protect its mandate. The iron triangle has largely been replaced with suppression of independent political, labor, and religious organizations and with control of the media and other forms of communication. In particular, the Communist Party has ordered the arrest of a number of journalists and private citizens on charges of revealing "state se-

---

* In 2004, there were reportedly an estimated 100 million to 150 million "floaters" in China. See http://www.ecoi.net/doc/en/CN/content/2/9590-9633.

crets." Because the party has left the definition of "state secret" deliberately vague, researchers investigate many aspects of Chinese society at their peril.

In what could charitably be considered a comprehensive number of areas, the Chinese government has provided limited definitions of forbidden subjects of inquiry. These include statistics on war dead and wounded since the revolution; official policy on land use and development; reports on the environment; information on public-health issues; reports on industrial accidents and illnesses; unemployment and poverty statistics; accusations of wrongdoing against national party officials; statistics on strikes, protests, and demonstrations; and "data and statistics about natural disasters, epidemics, and negative social phenomena that, once released, are not beneficial to the human mind or society."[15]

MINORITY RIGHTS AND RELIGIOUS FREEDOM

Countries on the right side of the J curve base much of their social stability on legal protections for minority groups. To promote its chances for EU membership, the Turkish government has enacted laws that codify the rights of Kurds. The rights of Israeli Arabs are legally established. Muslim politicians and voters figure prominently in India's political life. But Beijing's anxiety over the political loyalties of Muslims in its northwest Xinjiang Province has produced decades of sustained repression.

The Xinjiang Autonomous Region, the largest of China's thirty provinces, covers an area four times the size of California.[16] (See map on page 247.) While Han Chinese represent around 90 percent of China's total population, Muslim Uighurs account for 45 percent of Xinjiang's 20 million inhabitants, while only 40 percent are Han.* The natural tension between China's official atheism and the religious practices of Xinjiang's most devout Muslims boiled over in 1990, when loosely organized groups of ethnic Uighur separatists declared "holy war" against the government and took up arms. The rebellion was crushed, but not before more than twenty people were killed and hundreds—possibly thousands—were arrested.[17] In September 2005, Chinese officials told the state's official news agency that

---

* Virtually all Xinjiang's ethnic Uighurs are Muslims.

China's Xinjiang Province: The largest of China's thirty provinces, Xinjiang is the only area of China in which Muslims outnumber Han Chinese.

Xinjiang's separatists represent the primary terrorist threat to China and accused extremists there of attacks on "kindergartens, schools, government offices and the People's Liberation Army."[18] Human-rights organizations accuse China of using the war on terror as a cover for domestic repression.

Beijing has good reason to covet Xinjiang. According to the Chinese government, the region contains 30 percent of China's oil reserves, 34 percent of its natural-gas reserves, 40 percent of its coal reserves, and one-sixth of China's total land area.[19] Yet, much of the local population considers Han Chinese to be foreigners—and occupiers. Mosques dominate Uighur towns throughout the region, and imams are more widely respected than Communist Party officials in Uighur communities. Public and private conversations in Xinjiang are far more often conducted in Turkish dialects than in Chinese.[20]

Beijing's methods of silencing calls for Uighur independence have never been subtle. In a typical month, hundreds of Uighur separatists are arrested. A substantial number have reportedly been executed. But Beijing's primary strategy for managing its problems in Xinjiang amounts to forced cultural assimilation. Throughout the province, Beijing has created what Ross Terrill calls "apartheid with Chinese characteristics." Streets and towns have been given Chinese names. School textbooks are in Chinese. Mosques are tightly regulated. In order to dilute Uighur ethnicity, the central government pays Chinese women to marry Uighur men. Han Chinese are encouraged to migrate to Xinjiang. This strategy of ethnic dilution is having its intended effect: the Han population in Xinjiang has grown from 5 percent in 1940 to 40 percent today.[21] Yet, Uighur separatist groups continue to secretly organize resistance and to demand independence. Han Chinese culture and Communist Party ideology remain alien to the region's Muslims, and Beijing won't likely change that anytime soon.

Many of the Buddhists of the Tibet Autonomous Region don't appreciate Beijing's authority any more than Xinjiang's Muslims do. Tibetan Buddhism is the most influential non-Han Buddhist strain in China, and many Tibetans reject Beijing's insistence that the Communist Party alone may select Tibet's spiritual leaders. After the tenth Panchen Lama—the second-highest spiritual figure in Tibetan Buddhism—died in 1989, Hu Jintao, then the party's manager of Tibetan affairs and now China's president, chose a reliably loyal local leader to lead a search for the Lama's replacement over objections from Tibet's clergy, who insisted that only the Dalai Lama had that authority. The Dalai Lama and the Tibetan Buddhist leadership announced their own choice for the sacred role, a six-year-old boy quickly denounced by Beijing as a "killer of animals" and the child of "speculators." Communist officials warned local monks that anyone caught carrying the boy's photograph would be executed. Jiang Zemin personally supervised the search for Beijing's preferred candidate and settled on another six-year-old whose parents were devoted Communists. Beijing then announced: "Any legitimate religion invariably makes patriotism the primary requirement for believers." Beijing's carefully chosen Panchen Lama immediately declared his loyalty to the Party.[22] Such is the bureaucratic management of spiritual life in a police state.

The party's fear that religion breeds contempt for its authority is not limited to residents of outlying provinces. On April 25, 1999, more than 10,000 practitioners of Falun Dafa,* an eccentric spiritual movement best known for its regimen of breathing exercises, meditation, and faith healing silently stole past security officers into a tightly guarded area in the heart of central Beijing and took up positions outside the party leadership compound. Inside, their representatives were said to have called on the prime minister, Zhu Rongji, to officially recognize their movement. The meeting finished, the silent demonstrators dispersed into the night—on foot, by bicycle, and via dozens of buses hastily provided by the state to ease their exit. It was the largest spontaneous public demonstration since the Tiananmen Square massacre.[23]

Three months later, the party banned the group. China has detained thousands of its members—more than a dozen of whom have reportedly died in Chinese custody—and denounced its nominal leader, Li Hongzhi, who lives beyond Beijing's reach in the United States. The demonstrations that first brought Falun Dafa to Chinese attention didn't technically meet the Sharansky "town square test." The protests were silent; no political opinions were expressed. But for China's government, the mere presence of a large organized group in central Beijing was a political statement—and a challenge that rattled the Party leadership.

Falun Dafa's next major demonstration fit Sharansky's definition perfectly. Despite a heavy police presence intended to protect the fifty-first anniversary celebration of China's revolution from any hint of dissent, Falun Dafa members managed a large and reportedly well-coordinated series of protests in Tiananmen Square. Some of the protesters raised banners in support of the group; others shouted praise for Falun Dafa and its leaders, still others sat in the square and meditated. Armies of police flowed into the square. Demonstrators were beaten and arrested by the hundreds.†[24]

---

* Falun Dafa and Falun Gong are often used interchangeably. Technically, Falun Dafa is the movement, Falun Gong the physical exercises its followers perform.

† That same day, the Vatican made saints of 120 Catholics who it said had been martyred in China over the past four centuries. The Chinese government operates its own Catholic church and forbids its adherents to recognize the pope's authority.

ONE CHINA, ONE SYSTEM, ONE PARTY

It is not just minority religious and ethnic groups who are denied civil rights in China. The Chinese Communist Party doesn't trust any of China's citizens with legally protected freedoms. Nor does it trust the judges who might guarantee those rights. The nation's judges have virtually no independence from the central government's authority. Lower court judges often have little formal legal training.

The party manipulates the rulings of judges in a variety of ways. First, the party reserves the right to approve all judicial appointments. Once chosen, judges who hope to keep their jobs watch for changes in party policy as they review cases. Second, the party directly influences the outcomes of individual cases through its Political-Legal Committees (PLCs) at every level of government. PLCs are usually staffed by the heads of law-enforcement agencies and Justice Ministry officials.

Local governments interfere in judicial decisions as well, in order to protect the interests of local industries or officials and to protect them from liability. Local leaders control judges' salaries, court finances, and the process by which judges are appointed. People's congresses and the office of the prosecutor exercise another significant form of external control of the judiciary. Under the Chinese constitution and national law, both have the power to oversee the work of judges and the courts and to insist, when necessary, that verdicts be reconsidered—a formula familiar to those who lead other left-side-of-the J-curve states.[25]

Nor is there media freedom in China. In its first Worldwide Press Freedom Index in October 2002, Reporters Without Borders ranked China's press the least free of any country in the world, save North Korea.* The report calls China "the world's biggest prison for journalists." All media in China are either state-owned or state-controlled. The English-language state press is less tightly restricted, but its censorship is largely self-imposed. For international stories, editors tend to choose wire-service reports that

---

* In the 2005 Index, China edged past Eritrea, Turkmenistan, Iran, Burma, Libya, Cuba, and Nepal into 159th place. Other left-side-of the-curve states: Saudi Arabia was 154th and Russia 138th. http://www.rsf.org.rubrique.php3?id_rubrique=554.

support the Communist Party line, although, unlike their Chinese-language counterparts, they don't often publish false reports.

Domestic news coverage focuses on citizens who unconditionally venerate "Socialism with Chinese characteristics." State television typically features stories on travel, children, and the good news of socialism. Corruption scandals are covered only with government approval. Social unrest is hardly covered at all. Violent crime stories are permitted, but only if they end with deviants and bandits brought to justice by efficient police work and prosecutorial heroism. Government officials often use the press to promote their friends' business interests and to discredit their rivals. Beijing blocks BBC and Voice of America radio broadcasts, interferes directly in the work of foreign journalists, and tries to block the distribution of foreign newspapers.[26]

Traditional media are not the only targets of Chinese censorship. The party has created what has become known as "the Great Firewall" to isolate the Chinese people from the untamed frontier of cyberspace. From the beginning, China's Internet architecture was designed for ease of control. There are only five hubs through which all Chinese online traffic must pass. No matter which ISP Internet users choose, the e-mails and files they download and send must pass through one of these hubs. According to a study by the Berkman Center for Internet & Society, "China blocks access to hundreds of thousands of sites. Some are blocked by their IP addresses, others by domain name."[27] But Chinese authorities have also cultivated more subtle methods of censorship, such as "DNS hijacking," by which someone searching for a particular site is automatically rerouted to another site or to an invalid address. Reporters Without Borders calls China the country in which e-mail interception and Internet censorship technologies are most fully developed. To foil government censors who search Chinese sites for politically provocative words, Internet dissidents use code words. Protests, for example, are sometimes referred to as "spring outings." There are reportedly as many as 50,000 Chinese security officials whose sole charge is to monitor chat rooms and to police the Internet.[28] They will be very busy. There are 100,000 new Internet users in China every day.[29]

The state also directly targets search engines. In their rush to tap into Chinese demand, some U.S. companies have accepted the party's censorship as the price of admission to China's lucrative Internet market. A search for "Taiwan independence" in China's version of the Yahoo! search engine yields no results. Yahoo, Microsoft, and Google have each faced sharp criticism in the West for submitting to Chinese restrictions.

Beyond its sophisticated censorship techniques, Chinese authorities held sixty-one Internet users in prison at the start of May 2004. In addition, 12,575 Chinese Internet cafés—already tightly regulated—were closed in the last three months of 2004 alone.[30]

At the same time, Chinese Web surfers have quickly become sophisticated in developing new ways of evading censorship. A technology race is under way between China's government and its most determined Internet users, each hoping to remain one technological step ahead in the race to use the Internet for its own purposes. The Chinese Communist Party knows that it cannot simply shut down the Internet during a period of social unrest. Even if it were technically possible, a widespread Internet shutdown would badly damage the Chinese economy. But in the end, the party's instinct to control access to information makes any argument that the People's Republic belongs on the right side of the J curve problematic.

WARNING SIGNS

Will China's economic growth sate its citizens' appetite for a better life and help maintain order? The Chinese Communist Party is counting on it. It's not hard to understand why earlier generations of China's authoritarian leaders feared that relaxation of the party's hold on social and political control would unleash chaos. Deng Xiaoping, who gave the final orders to crush the Tiananmen Square demonstrations, knew firsthand that disorder often led to violence over the course of China's twentieth-century history. Some historians say Deng's father was beheaded by bandits during the chaotic years of the Second World War. The Red Guards of China's Cultural Revolution attacked Deng's family, crippled his son, drove his brother to suicide, and imprisoned Deng himself.[31] For Deng, Jiang Zemin, and other older-generation Chinese leaders, many of whom remain influential, every social or political protest carries the threat of disorder and bloodshed.

But China's younger leaders, including President Hu Jintao and Prime

Minister Wen Jiabao, both in their early sixties, have come to political maturity in the most stable period of China's modern history. It's possible that, as Jiang Zemin and the rest of the "third generation" of China's revolutionary leadership leave the stage, their heirs will recognize that economic reform is unsustainable without political reform, and that a basic renegotiation of power relations between the state and society is overdue.

They'd better, because public protest in China has been growing—and becoming better organized—for several years. According to Murray Scot Tanner of the RAND Corporation, Chinese police admit to a nationwide increase of 268 percent in what the party calls "mass group incidents" between 1993 and 1999. According to Tanner, "In not a single year during this period did unrest increase by less than 9 percent." Official nationwide figures haven't been available since 2000, but a recent report from the public security chief of Liaoning Province revealed 9,559 protests, each involving at least fifty people, between January 2000 and September 2002 in that midsized province alone. That's an average of nearly 10 large-scale protests a day for three years in just one of China's thirty provinces.[32] These numbers continue to rise.

The *Washington Post* reported on November 4, 2004, that the official estimate of protests in 2003 rose some 15 percent over the previous year to more than 58,000 incidents. In August 2005, Reuters reported Chinese Security Minister Zhou Yongkang as saying that "some 74,000 protests and riots broke out across China [in 2004] involving more than 3.7 million people."[33] That number jumped to 87,000 in 2005.[34] Some excerpts from the *Washington Post* report, which quotes Chinese journalists and eyewitnesses:

As police battled to suppress deadly ethnic clashes last week in central China, tens of thousands of rice farmers fighting a dam project staged a huge protest in the western part of the country. The same day, authorities crushed a strike involving 7,000 textile workers.

A week earlier . . . nearly a thousand workers demonstrated outside a newly privatized department store in the northeast; and police used rubber bullets and tear gas to quell a giant mob of anti-government rioters in a western city.

Word of a traffic dispute between Han and Hui villagers in central Henan province spread so quickly last week that thousands rioted before police could respond. More worrisome for the authorities, residents reported that hundreds if not thousands of Hui from other parts of China learned of the clashes by telephone and rushed to the region.

Similarly, an altercation a week earlier in the western city of Chongqing between a deliveryman and a fruit market worker attracted a crowd of thousands within hours . . . The incident sparked a riot in which residents set fire to police cars and looted government offices. Local authorities attempted to impose a news blackout, but photos and accounts of the riot quickly appeared on the Internet.[35]

Many of these organized protests in China today are provoked by state seizures of land for development projects and the fallout from environmental damage. But the four paragraphs above underscore the variety of sparks that can ignite spontaneous, large-scale violence in China: a protest over government plans to build a dam, a strike, a privatized business, a traffic accident, or a simple argument. They also demonstrate that police are prepared to use force to stop the protests—unless they are overwhelmed by its size or the speed at which it builds. And as the final sentence suggests, the Internet can inspire outrage and spur large numbers to destructive action. Because the official Chinese news agencies are not allowed to report on the events, they are powerless to counter rumors and exaggerations that provoke spontaneous violence. The Internet also aids the coordination of demonstrations. Via the proliferation of text messaging, e-mail, and cellphone technologies, protesters can be quickly assembled, alerted when and where police are moving, and just as quickly dispersed.

Most of these protests are aimed at local, not national, leaders. One of the lessons that protest organizers learned from the Tiananmen Square crackdown is that central government officials will tolerate criticism of local officials—as long as the party's mandate to rule China is not called into question. But organizers also know the People's Liberation Army can't be quickly mobilized to put down every peaceful protest, every sit-in, or every strike. Without the intervention of the army and as these protests grow in size, frequency, and intensity, they will be harder for local officials, and even protest organizers themselves, to control. There have already been incidents of serious violence during these demonstrations. The threat of larger-scale violence is growing with each passing month. Official Chinese media announced in August 2005 that special police units had been set up in thirty-six cities, ostensibly to counter terrorist threats. The real threat they're meant to contain is that posed by China's growing social unrest.

Where do these protests come from? Even Chinese officials have set aside charges that these demonstrations are the product of foreign conspiracies and have begun to look inward for root causes. A quarter-century of reform of state-owned enterprises has produced profound social dislocation. Layoffs, unemployment, the withholding of wages, pensions, health-care benefits, and housing allowances have produced deep ill will among affected workers. And there are a lot of these workers: according to Tanner, police experts concede that 50 to 80 percent of all medium- and large-sized state-owned enterprises now face serious financial trouble, "a problem that by 2001 had affected the livelihoods of more than 27 million workers."[36]

China also faces enormous demographic challenges that will tax government revenue and imagination and threaten the nation's social cohesion. In 2001, 10 percent of China's population was sixty-five or older. Studies warn that number is likely to swell to 25 percent by 2030. When 300 million Chinese demand pensions and subsidized medical care, the state budget will be squeezed hard.[37]

Another source of social frustration: the state has been slow to react to public health crises, like the 2003 outbreak of severe acute respiratory syndrome (SARS), which killed hundreds and infected thousands. The party has hardly addressed China's AIDS epidemic at all. A million Chinese are reportedly infected with HIV. According to the United Nations, that number could rise tenfold by 2010, and the government is only now devoting resources to devising a strategy to cope with the impact. The party has also intimidated or arrested Chinese scientists who research disease outbreaks without government approval. In July 2005, for example, the state accused respected scientist Guan Yi of "leaking state secrets" after he and his colleagues published a report on an avian flu outbreak among migratory birds in northwest Qinghai Province. Guan Yi denies the allegations.

The party has also done little to protect China's environment from the worst effects of explosive industrial growth. Nine of the world's ten most polluted cities are in China. Half of China's rivers are polluted—perhaps irreversibly. Acid rain falls on one-third of China's agricultural land. A quarter of the country is already desert. This desert is advancing at a rate of 1,300 square miles per year. More than 60 million people struggle to find enough water to meet their daily needs. More than 600 million Chinese drink contaminated water every day.[38] More than 75 percent of river water in urban areas is "unfit for human contact." More than 1,000 new cars, and the exhaust they produce, hit the streets of Beijing every twenty-four hours.

China has no viable banking system. Major banks are insolvent. Borrowers default on anywhere from 35 percent to 50 percent of all bank loans.[39] In a right-side-of-the-J-curve state, a free press could report these problems to the public, and voters would hold elected officials accountable. But China has no free press.

Then there's corruption. If the Chinese Communist Party elite commits itself to political reform without first establishing a durable rule of law, the already widespread problem of corruption will deepen. At the grassroots level, local officials scramble to earn the cash they'll need to bribe their way through China's corrupt bureaucracy. The result is a wide—and widening—wealth gap. According to Chinese state media, the wealthiest 20 percent of Chinese earn half the country's total income. The poorest 20 percent earn just 4.7 percent.[40]

Chinese entrepreneurs live with this corruption. In fact, most Chinese companies keep three sets of books: one for the bank, another for the tax police, and an honest accounting for themselves.[41] The party loses its ability to hide the contradictions between its liberal economic agenda and its Leninist political rhetoric a little more every day.

Beyond the issue of corruption, Chinese officials are increasingly concerned about the wealth gap itself—and the public anger it could unleash. According to a report from the income research institute of China's Ministry of Labor and Social Security, urban incomes are growing nearly twice as fast as rural ones. There is a widening wealth gap between the prosperous cities of the coast and poorer inland cities. There is also a large and growing wealth disparity between the richest and poorest of China's rural farmers. The institute has developed a color-coded system that warns of the wealth gap's threat to social stability. According to the institute's director, China is now at "code yellow," the second-most-dangerous stage. He's warned that the country could reach "code red" by 2010 if the problem is not effectively addressed.[42]

There have been modest steps toward incremental local-level democratization. As in Saudi Arabia, China's ruling elite has allowed a few genuinely contested village elections in some areas. In almost all cases, however, all the candidates have been Communist Party members competing in an indirect "electoral college" system. In a very few townships, voters have chosen their local leaders through a direct vote. None of the candidates has called for reform of the central government, much less the separation of party and state.

In recent years, the party has widened its membership to include businessmen and entrepreneurs. But there is no indication that the party hopes to learn from China's latest wave of capitalists. It seems intent instead on giving those with access to capital an investment in the party's survival.

Finally, while China's leaders never face election, there *is* nationwide balloting taking place in China. In 2005, a satellite television station in Hunan Province aired a contest called *The Mongolian Cow Sour Yogurt Super Girl Contest*, and viewers were invited to text-message in their votes for a winner. During the final episode of the show, an imitation of the popular American television show *American Idol*, an estimated 400 million Chinese watched as more than 8 million people paid a fee to select a winner. Li Yuchun was crowned "Super Girl," despite concerns that some viewers may have exceeded the 15-vote limit and that the winner's musical performance was not in keeping with traditional Chinese culture. Communist Party officials have threatened to cancel the show before the contest begins again next year, perhaps because they fear that even an imitation of democracy will create demand for more meaningful elections.[43]

SIGNPOSTS

It is important to recognize that China belongs on the left side of the J curve. It's more important to identify the direction on the curve in which China may be moving. Is China cautiously reforming its way toward the right side of the curve? Or will the Communist Party tighten its grip when instability again directly threatens single-party rule?

There are a number of signposts to watch for an answer to that question. Will China expand multicandidate elections beyond the village level? Will China allow nonparty members to compete for elected office? Will government decision-making become more transparent? Will the party be more forthcoming about environmental and public-health crises? Can the economy avoid a "hard landing" that creates severe hardship for China's labor force? Will China establish an independent judiciary and the beginnings of a free press?

The answers to these questions are unlikely to point in the same direction, but most will likely signal a tightening of party control at the first signs of widespread unrest directed at the central government. Historically, the Chinese Communist Party has loosened its grip and allowed genuine reform only at times it believed it could do so without danger of sustained instability. But if a future Tiananmen Square–style mass protest succeeds in forcing concessions, it will probably only be because the party can no longer rely on the army for protection.

That day is not yet on the horizon, but the inherent contradictions of Communist Party rule over a capitalist juggernaut make that day all but inevitable. As noted, there are already tens of thousands of public demonstrations in China every year. We can expect that number to continue to grow—and for the protesters to become more determined and better organized—as the gap widens between rich and poor and as communications technology allows the boldest of the demonstration organizers to circumvent the government's ability to break up their protests.

The J curve demonstrates nothing so clearly as that reform of an authoritarian central government forces a left-side-of-the-J-curve state toward instability on the way to greater openness. There is nothing the party fears more than instability. That's why the government continues to hide information about the extent of political protests and domestic crises. Just as Gorbachev's Communist Party made a concerted effort to hide the true devastation of the disaster at Chernobyl, the Chinese Communist Party hides information on the level of danger posed by SARS, HIV, and avian flu.

Beijing has tried to avoid the worst effects of public unrest by channeling public anger toward other targets: local-level corruption, Taiwan, Japan, or America. When the party can no longer redirect its citizens' anger and frustration, it will try to do what it has always done: quash the protests and jail the protesters. That option becomes less viable every year, as protests grow in scale and frequency and as China slides down the left side of the J curve.

INDIA VERSUS CHINA, ECONOMIC VERSUS POLITICAL OPENNESS

India and China offer intriguing mirror images. Modern India has long been open politically and, until recently, closed economically. Modern China has opened economically, but remains politically closed. The comparison reveals that, *while politics and economics can never be fully separated, political openness is a better guarantor of long-term stability than economic openness.* Political openness prevents large-scale social and political shocks by allowing people to release their anger and frustration in legitimized ways. Economic openness within an authoritarian political system usually benefits only a small minority before wealth is more widely generated, producing social frustrations that have no politically acceptable outlet.

Both China and India suffer from widespread corruption at all levels of society. But Indians have a recognized right to take to the streets and vent their fury about it. They also have the opportunity to turn out corrupt politicians via the voting booth. Even when corrupt officials win reelection, most Indians don't feel the powerlessness to bring about social and political change so common in Chinese protests. Indian demonstrations do sometimes run out of control, particularly when they're rooted in ethnic or religious difference. But in China, the threat of violence is much more present during demonstrations because Chinese protesters can only hope to bring about change by frightening local officials into addressing their demands.

Further, Indians have the opportunity to pressure their leaders into addressing social inequities, public-health crises, environmental damage, and a thousand other problems by airing information and anger via a relatively free press. The people of China don't have that option. The state tries to impose its will on the Chinese people through control over the most basic aspects of their lives. There are a growing number of nongovernmental organizations contributing to China's development. But only with official approval can their work continue.

China desperately needs some release valve for public anger because, as in India, the distribution of China's new wealth has been so uneven. The relative prosperity of China's booming gold coast has only begun to trickle west, and hundreds of millions of Chinese don't enjoy any of the benefits of

China's economic opening. In Arab countries dominated by a single political party or a monolithic elite, the rise of religious fundamentalism flows naturally from the problem that only in the mosque can grievances be publicly aired. Only the mosque offers institutional support for public protest and a vehicle for public frustration for those excluded from a share in the nation's wealth. In India, dozens of political parties collectively represent the interests of virtually all Indians, of whatever station. China offers its people neither a spiritual nor a political public space in which to demand change from the central government. So, while China's elite may have embraced the economic laws of supply and demand, the Chinese Communist Party continues to believe that demand for political change can be suppressed or ignored.

There's another law that authoritarian left-side-of-the-J-curve states ignore. For every action, there is an equal and opposite reaction. For every state attempt to quash calls for reform, there is renewed demand for resistance. That's why there were 87,000 demonstrations in China in 2005—and why that number will probably continue to rise for the foreseeable future.

POLICY

The Chinese Communist Party is trying to beat the J curve.

In essence, economic reform represents the party's attempt to engineer a move from the left to the right side of the J curve without a fall into political instability. (See figure on page 261.) The opening of the Chinese economy *has* lifted the entire J curve so that every point on the curve is more stable than it was before reform produced broad national effects. But despite the party's best efforts, China cannot move from left to right without instability. And China is currently sliding down the left side of the curve.

The Communist elite has long sought to develop a "rational" and "scientific" means of political decision-making. It argues that democracy is a source of inefficiency and instability, and that engineers, not politicians, should govern the state. The party now recognizes that it must move beyond an emphasis on growth at all costs to policies that both promote con-

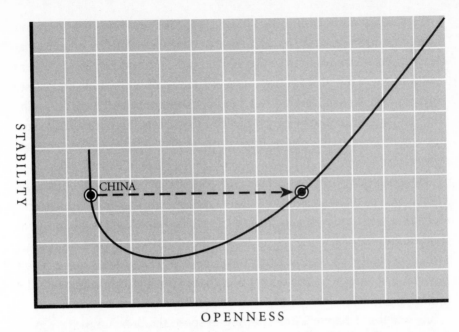

STABILITY

OPENNESS

China's Attempt to Beat the J Curve: Chinese leaders are attempting a move from the left to the right side of the J curve without a fall into the depths of instability.

tinued economic expansion and cushion the blow for those who might take to the town square and push China down the curve toward political chaos. Today, Chinese leaders speak less of "rapid growth" and more of "harmonious, coordinated, and sustainable development."

The party also recognizes that limited experiments in village self-government and a new pluralism within the party have created pressure for a more substantial decentralization of decision-making. China's Communist elite will only undertake reforms that may fuel demand for change if these reforms can be rationally engineered in a way that allows the central government to maintain political control of the country. This is work for political scientists, they argue, not for politicians.

But politics is more than a science or a product of rational decision-making. It is a process by which interests are weighed and values accommodated, an art that cannot be perfected. In the end, the Chinese people will not leave politics to the state. They will demand that the state adapt and evolve to meet their needs.

The international community has every incentive to hope China can reform its politics and move toward a more open, representative political system without descending into widespread violence and chaos. A Chinese civil war would have catastrophic effects on the global economy and on security in Asia. As in all left-side-of-the-curve states, the best hope for political change comes from within the country, from the nation's citizens. Policymakers in other nations have a role to play. But the Chinese people will change China.

How can outside actors enable reform in China? The worst choice the United States and others could make in trying to bring China through instability toward the right side of the J curve is the choice Washington has made in its relations with North Korea and Cuba. Isolating the Communist leadership will only encourage China's leaders to tighten their grip on power and to suppress the energy for change already forming inside the country.

As noted in Chapter Three, hoping to speed the breakup of the Soviet Union, Boris Yeltsin famously called on Russia's regions to "take all the sovereignty [they could] swallow." Beijing should similarly be encouraged to absorb all the elements necessary for continued economic growth that it can digest. China should be invited to make the necessary sacrifices of sovereignty to join all the multilateral international institutions it dares. Indeed, China should be allowed—perhaps even encouraged—to compete for the purchase of Western assets at fair market prices. The party should also be encouraged to build the most prosperous, globally connected middle class it can. These are the forces that will open China: prosperity, citizens' access to information, and membership in multilateral institutions with the leverage to enforce rules on China's economic, legal, and political systems. These forces are already at work.

There are those within the Chinese Communist Party who believe China's security can only be guaranteed by maximizing the strength of the People's Liberation Army. They insist Western influence be sharply limited. They suggest Beijing should adopt a hard line in its foreign policy and meet every ten protesters with a thousand soldiers. Others believe China must join the international community as fully as possible, that reform is the key to modernization, that modernization is the key to greatness, that greater openness is inevitable, and that economic growth, which depends on economic openness, is paramount. U.S. and other policymakers can help move China to the right side of the J curve by doing everything possible to ensure that the latter group wins the argument and that the Chinese people have every tool possible to build a new China whose stability is grounded in political openness.

CHAPTER SEVEN

Conclusion

All conservatism is based upon the idea that if you leave things alone you leave them as they are. But you do not. If you leave a thing alone you leave it to a torrent of change.

—G. K. Chesterton

All states are in constant movement on the J curve. Some states fluctuate within a relatively narrow range. Others, particularly those closest to the bottom on either side of the curve, experience wider swings. Left alone, a left-side state will slide toward instability because authoritarianism must be continuously reconsolidated. Kim Jong-Il, Robert Mugabe, Alexander Lukashenko, the clerics who rule Iran, the military junta that dominates Burma, the autocrats of Central Asia, the Saudi royals, the Kremlin elite, the Chinese Communist Party leadership, and all the people who enable their autocratic rule spend enormous time and energy reinforcing regime stability and resisting the natural pull of greater political, economic, and social openness.

As the energies of globalization open up the least politically and economically developed areas of the world, as the citizens of closed states learn more about life beyond their borders and discover they don't *have* to live as they do, tyrants must expend more and more effort to isolate their societies. These states can now fall more swiftly and suddenly into instability than at any time in history. That's why right-side states must be more concerned than ever by the internal developments within left-side states. Social unrest in China, the Saudi education system, a security vacuum in Afghanistan, ethnic tensions in Nigeria's oil-rich Niger Delta, and market volatility in Argentina each have a more immediate impact on geopolitics and economics than ever before.

The countries on the right side of the J curve have a collective political, economic, and security interest in working together to help move left-side states through instability to the right side of the curve. But they must recognize that the most powerful agents for constructive, sustainable change in any society are the people who live within it. Strategies that empower groups within closed states to challenge the authoritarian status quo can create strong momentum for democratic change.

In policy terms, that means right-side states have an opportunity to craft an approach toward North Korea that enables the North Korean people to learn more about the outside world and to communicate directly with one another. It means helping people like dissident Khin Maung Win build his Democratic Voice of Burma television station, which broadcasts programming from Norway into Burma. Just as the West offered Cold War–era support for Czechoslovakia's Charter 77, right-side states can now aid and abet Belarus's dissident group Charter 97. Multilateral institutions that represent the interests of right-side states—and of global stability—can certainly insist that elections everywhere in the world are conducted freely and fairly. But it is the gradual infiltration of used cell phones, VCRs, videos, and text-messaging equipment from China and South Korea into North Korea that will, over time, help undermine authoritarian rule in Pyongyang. Further isolation of Kim's regime, on the other hand, will only simplify the work of his security police and propaganda machine.

Beyond empowering responsible local opposition movements and dissident groups, the establishment of even limited trade ties between left- and right-side states enables more direct communication between peoples within and across national boundaries. It allows them to share ideas and information, and puts money in the pockets of private citizens. It gives people in both states a stake in the stability of their country's relations with other states.

By inviting states like China, Russia, Saudi Arabia, and Iran to join the World Trade Organization and to adhere to its rules, right-side states help reinforce the growth of middle classes and create rising expectations for further opening of the political cultures within those states. WTO membership alone cannot open a closed society. Cuba and Burma, after all, have been members for more than a decade. But as part of a comprehensive effort to bind these states to international norms of political and economic behavior and to provide their citizens the opportunity to build wealth beyond their government's reach, it's a solid first step.

Yet, globalization, for all the reasons listed above, can also be tremendously destabilizing. Not all states on the left side of the J curve are equipped to survive the potential chaos of the transition from left to right. There is pressure for change within every closed society, a pressure that exists naturally. But, in the short term, demands for far-reaching political change should be fully supported only in those states that have a fighting chance of surviving the passage through the depths of the curve. If a country that is unprepared for such instability falls, or is pushed, into the dip in the curve, there are two possible outcomes. Both are geopolitically dangerous.

First, when a state suddenly becomes unstable, its citizens may demand a restoration of stability at the expense of all meaningful reform. When the Soviet Union collapsed, the government of the new Russian Federation took steps to establish Russia on the right side of the curve. Boris Yeltsin's government subjected Russian society to economic "shock therapy." At the same time, opposition parties and the national media, which had up to that point been completely under state domination, were freed to do and say virtually anything. The combination of spiraling inflation, social insecurity, Chechen separatist attacks, unchecked crony capitalism, and heightened public awareness of all these problems created a frightening sense of chaos across the country. The widespread sense that society was in freefall prompted many Russians to support moves to hit the brakes on Russia's reform-driven politics. In other words, the deep social anxiety provoked by so much reform all at once created demand for an imposed order, for closed politics. That's an important reason why Russia has retreated over the last half-decade to the left side of the curve.

A natural desire for security in an unstable environment has helped produce electoral success for groups like Hamas in the Palestinian territories and Hezbollah in Lebanon, organizations that are less interested in openness to the outside world than in capitalizing on anti-Western sentiment and in consolidating ideological control of a closed society. To some extent, the 2005 election of Mahmoud Ahmadinejad in Iran represents a similar impulse toward the certainties of anticorruption campaigns and populist politics over the anxieties produced by social change and ill-conceived attempts at political reform.

The other possible consequence of a premature slide into instability is even more dangerous—total state failure. Twenty years ago, a country that played no geopolitical or global economic role could simply fail, with severe consequences for its people but little negative impact on the rest of the world. But we now live in a world in which a vacuum of power in Afghanistan can create the conditions for catastrophic events in New York and Washington. In a world in which terrorists and the proliferation of weapons of mass destruction threaten transnational upheaval, the risks created by state failure—even in states once considered of marginal geopolitical importance—can be unacceptably high.

The Bush administration has now moved beyond the "axis of evil" focus of the post-9/11 period toward a new strategy based on the active promotion of democratization in states Condoleezza Rice has called "outposts of tyranny." In part, this shift reflects Washington's recognition that military regime change—even credible military pressure—is prohibitively expensive as a major component of U.S. foreign policy. The administration lacks both the material resources and the political capital to continue to use these tools in all but the most extreme cases. In essence, the policy is an attempt to undermine authoritarian states and to push them toward the right side of the J curve with a less costly mix of political pressure and public diplomacy.

But the strategy is dangerous precisely because the Bush administration hasn't fully articulated how states that aren't ready for the transition can withstand the buffeting they'll face in the depths of the curve. Foreign policymaking is not an abstraction, and a one-size-fits-all approach is doomed to failure. The twelve states visited in this book demonstrate nothing so clearly as that each country has developed a political, intellectual, economic, and social culture that is unique.

In an authoritarian state, opposition political organizations are suppressed, their activities are outlawed, their leaders are jailed or killed, and their supporters are intimidated into silence. As a result, opposition within these states becomes radicalized; opposition activism becomes, by defini-tion, antistate activity. To suddenly hold open elections in such a state is usually to pit the most extreme elements of society directly against one an-other in a contest in which both sides know the vanquished will lose every-thing they value. In such a case, moderate parties may not have had the time or the resources to build a political base in support of responsible reform-oriented governance and to offer voters an alternative to the bitterly op-posed extremes.

The damaging effects of pushing for comprehensive change in a society that isn't ready for it can last for years. Having scheduled open elections for early 1991, the Algerian government recognized in late 1990 that an Islamist party associated with terrorist cells was set to win. The state canceled the elections and declared a state of emergency that still exists today. Because the groundwork for stability based on openness was not prepared before elections were to be held, the Algerian government suspended the nation's constitution in order to prevent a collapse into the depths of the J curve. A number of right-side-of-the-curve states had supported the premature elections. Faced with a geopolitically destabilizing result, they found them-selves backed into support for the suspension of civil liberties—the oppo-site of what they had intended.

As the leaders of states like Saudi Arabia, Kuwait, Egypt, Jordan, and others experiment with limited local-level democratization, the lessons of Algeria should not be far from our minds. All those states are home to substantial numbers of radical Islamists who prefer the restoration of the Muslim Caliphate to the establishment of liberal parliamentary democ-racy. The stability of these countries is important for the establishment of a comprehensive Middle East peace. Kuwait and, especially, Saudi Arabia are key oil-producing states on which global growth and security continue to depend. The United States can no longer offer unconditional long-term support for these authoritarian regimes in the name of geopolitical sta-bility. But it would be a mistake to believe that comprehensive political re-form can be force-fed to their peoples. Until South Korea, China, and the United States have developed a plan to mitigate the worst effects of North Korean collapse, it would be premature for Washington to push policies that might quickly destroy Kim Jong-Il's regime. Iran's political culture is rich and varied enough that responsible opposition parties could relatively quickly and smoothly replace the current ruling elite. That is not the case in North Korea. It is a distinction that makes an enormous difference.

How can right-side countries help prepare a left-side state for the destabilizing transition? By implementing policies designed to raise the left-side state's entire J curve. When a country becomes more stable at every possible level of openness, that country is better fortified to withstand the stresses of change. That's why, for example, the United States government acted wisely in rising above partisanship to renew most-favored-nation trading status for China during the 1990s.

The images of tanks crushing unarmed student demonstrators in Tiananmen Square in 1989 created intense political pressure within the United States, in particular, for "punishment" of the "butchers of Beijing."* But the best way to undermine China's police state remains a strategy that helps build a Chinese middle class and binds China's economic future and political stability to rules-based international institutions. Helping the Chinese Communist Party create prosperity within China fortifies its citizens to demand change from their government and increases the probability that China can survive its transition with as little instability as possible. Raising China's J curve means raising (the stability of) the lowest points on the curve by enriching not only China but the Chinese people.

In practical terms, raising the curve means that, as the Chinese Communist Party fails to satisfy the Chinese people's rising expectations for greater influence over their own lives and the future of their country, the people have a greater stake in protecting both—by limiting the chaos that ends single-party rule. Hundreds of millions of Chinese people, thanks to the

---

* "Butchers of Beijing" became a standard phrase for many who sought to punish the Chinese leadership following the Tiananmen Square crackdown. Representative Don Ritter said the following on the floor of the U.S. House of Representatives on June 13, 1989: "The butchers of Beijing is an apt way to describe those who head the Communist Party at this time. Not only is rejection of most favored nation status in order, but the President should call for an immediate convening of the United Nations to discuss and to denounce and to seek ways to support those Chinese who believe in peace and freedom, human life and human dignity as opposed to those butchers of Beijing."

economic reforms that have lifted them toward a middle class, now have a greater stake in protecting China's future, even as they dismantle China's past. Raising the curve also means that a new government will have the resources to maintain a new political order as China goes about the difficult business of opening and restructuring its society. In other words, economic reform prepares the ground for stable political reform.

When, on the other hand, a closed regime attempts ambitious economic and political reforms simultaneously, the resulting shocks to the system can be too great. Mikhail Gorbachev (and later Boris Yeltsin) learned that lesson the hard way. When a left-side state tries to reform its politics under conditions of high unemployment and without the support of an economically sturdy middle class, the resentments unleashed produce a dangerous backlash.

There is a direct relationship between instability and demand within society for authoritarianism. A people who fear economic insecurity will defer calls for freedom and representative government in favor of support for (or at least submission to) a single clear voice promising food, jobs, and social guarantees. The purpose, therefore, of lifting the entire J curve through economic reform and the creation of a broad middle class is to reduce demand for authoritarianism and to build the necessary public confidence that increases demand for an opening up of society. The Bush strategy of universal democratization and the elimination of "outposts of tyranny" targets *supply* of autocratic rule without addressing the underlying *demand* for it. The formulation of a comprehensive strategy that addresses both sides of the problem is vitally important.

DEMAND-SIDE GEOPOLITICAL STRATEGY

To understand how a demand-side approach to the J curve challenge can work, it is useful to consider the successes and failures of the U.S. approach to some other complex, long-term foreign-policy undertakings. The so-called war on drugs has produced two decades of policy failure. Strategies to win the ongoing global war on terror threaten to follow the same path. The foreign-policy approach the United States and its allies created to win the Cold War, on the other hand, offers a useful model for the kind of demand-side strategy that the United States and its allies used to contain Soviet Communism and to undermine its power from within.

America's war on drugs has never yielded the hoped-for results because the clear majority of resources devoted to winning it has been focused on combating drug supply—at the expense of efforts to lower demand. In fact, drug abuse in America today is worse than when the drug war officially began in 1989.[1] The United States has targeted those who grow the crops, the cartels that process and transport narcotics, and the dealers who sell the final product. But the war effort has failed to provide the consumers of illicit drugs with sufficient opportunities for treatment and rehabilitation to substantially reduce demand. The suppliers of drugs have strong financial incentives to find new places to grow their product, new soldiers to fight their wars, and new street vendors to peddle their wares. Where there is demand, there will always be supply. By the same token, when the people of a left-side state demand security, protection, and order, there will always be a supply of authoritarianism. Only a strategy that targets both supply and demand can succeed.

It is precisely on this supply-side principle that the United States risks losing the war on terror. There is demand for terrorism in parts of the Muslim world. There are growing numbers of angry young Muslims willing to surrender their lives in exchange for an outlet for their anger and a sense of pride and purpose. These men have little stake in the success of their nations. They have little hope of lawfully altering their fates. If this or that Al Qaeda captain is captured or killed, a young Muslim looking for a war will find another officer to enlist him. When bin Laden is finally captured or killed, those who demand a champion to lead the terrorist *jihad* will create a new leader.

The U.S. government has developed a strategy for both the war on drugs and the war on terror that is based on two assumptions. First, the Bush administration believes rightly that, without public support, a democracy cannot win a costly war. Second, it believes wrongly that the devotion of overwhelming resources to achieving high-profile victories over the suppliers of drugs or terrorism is an effective way to build and maintain that support. Because the wars on drugs and terror sometimes seem abstract, those who wage them try to show tangible, consistent progress: high-profile arrests, infrastructure destroyed, "bad guys" slain. The patient, methodical work of reducing demand for drugs and terrorism doesn't make the men who wage the war any more popular with their electorates. But it is precisely that effort, combined with the continuation of an aggressive strategy to bring to justice the purveyors of drugs and terrorism, that will bring change from within the troubled societies that produce them. By extension, working to undermine demand for isolation and authoritarianism can help ease left-side states toward the right side of the J curve.

Cold War–inspired strategies can help right-side states accomplish exactly that. Western governments chose the right combination of weapons to win the Cold War. They used *every means at their disposal*—military, diplomatic, cultural, economic, and social—to help open Communist-bloc states and to undermine both the Soviet supply of Communism and the demand for it from within Soviet satellites, the USSR itself, and the developing world.

Following the end of the Second World War, the United States actively promoted open governance in Europe. As America's wisest Cold War strategists recognized, the Soviet system had within it "the seeds of its own decay."* Indeed, the J curve illustrates that all states on the left side contain the elements that will one day combine to create change. Through the Marshall Plan, America helped spark a broad and sustained economic recovery across much of Europe and fed the postwar U.S. economic expansion in the process. Through deft diplomacy, the Western powers persuaded the Soviet-bloc nations to sign the 1975 Helsinki Accords, which committed all parties to respect human rights within their countries and provided a generation of Soviet and East European dissidents a platform from which to speak directly to their own peoples.

As General Wesley Clark has written, "Western labor unions, encouraged by their governments, aided the emergence of a democratic trade-union movement, especially in Poland. Western organizations provided training for a generation of human-rights workers. Western broadcast media pumped in culture and political thought, raising popular expectations and undercutting Communist state propaganda. And Western businesses and financial institutions entered the scene, too, ensnaring command economies in Western market pricing and credit practices."[2] In

---

* George Kennan wrote that often-repeated phrase in his famous *Foreign Affairs* article "The Sources of Soviet Conduct" in July 1947.

essence, the United States used every means at its disposal to open these closed societies, to replace demand for Soviet Communism with demand for political reform. The former Warsaw Pact countries did not become democracies because America imposed democracy from the outside. In fact, the United States never invaded a country under Moscow's control. The former Warsaw Pact states embraced democracy because they wanted democracy.

The West contained the advance of Communism successfully enough and long enough for reformist forces inside the Soviet Union and Communist-bloc countries to unravel the fortress mentality of their closed societies. If such an achievement were possible in the effort to open other authoritarian states from within, the results would bring more global stability than a dozen successful military regime changes, each of which might be prohibitively expensive in terms of money and lives, and each of which might produce terrible unforeseen consequences.

Winning the global war on terror is imperative for the right-side states that are under attack. But the dismantling of terror cells with transnational reach also serves the larger goal of bringing left-side states to the right side of the J curve. The Bush administration has not entirely ignored the demand side of the global conflict with terrorists. It has announced substantial increases in conditional foreign aid; a Millennium Challenge Account has been established that ties U.S. development assistance to economic and political reform progress with "clear, concrete and objective" criteria; the U.S.-funded Alhurra satellite television network has begun beaming its signal in Arabic to a Middle Eastern audience; free-trade agreements have given a number of developing states access to U.S. markets. All these initiatives help to open closed societies.

Winning the war on terror has everything to do with the challenges posed by the J curve. The greatest immediate threat to global stability can be found at the intersection of terrorism and the proliferation of weapons of mass destruction (WMD). Terrorism and WMD proliferation account for much of the risk associated with the depths of the J curve, because failed states (and areas of states not under government control) can provide the ground where terrorists and WMDs come together. Indeed, ridding a state of well-organized terrorist cells is one important means of lifting a state's entire J curve. And the instability produced by terrorism increases demand for (or at least acceptance of) authoritarian rule. A number of the regimes that rule left-side states—from China to Mauritania, Russia to Saudi Arabia, Egypt to Uzbekistan—have used the war on terror as cover for the further consolidation of domestic political power. Right-side states should not support this practice.

Some countries are better prepared than others to make the transition from authoritarian rule to open society. Certainly, the nations of the Warsaw Pact, which shared a history of Enlightenment and constitutionalism with the states of Western Europe, were better prepared for that transition than the states of the Arab world are today. But the growing desire for individual freedom and for more open societies becomes more obvious in the Arab world with each passing year. Democracy can only come to an authoritarian state when its people demand it. Feeding that demand for open society should be paramount in both winning the war on terror and in pursuing the larger struggle to move left-side states to the right side of the J curve.

THE GATED COMMUNITY

Insecurity creates demand for short-term stability in *all* states, not just those on the left side of the J curve. Terrorist attacks inside the United States and in several European countries have provoked calls for limits on immigration—essentially for the establishment of the United States and EU as "gated communities," protected by a security perimeter that keeps outsiders outside. The September 11 terrorist attacks have led some politicians to push legislation that keeps out some of the very people who might come to America, absorb Western values and ideas, and return with them to their own authoritarian countries.*

The impulse is understandable, if unwise. Anyone who could have blocked the entry into the United States of the 9/11 hijackers would have done so without hesitation, even if it meant excluding a thousand students who might have returned home following graduation from an American

---

* As Joseph Nye likes to remind audiences and readers, Alexander Yakovlev, one of the architects of *glasnost* and *perestroika,* is one of the many Soviet reformers who once studied in the United States.

university to work for political and economic reform. Many Europeans fear that admitting Muslim Turkey into the EU will make it easier for would-be terrorists to blend into European society as they move unchecked across EU borders and plan attacks on European civilians.

But willingness to trade openness for security is based on a false choice. If the vast majority of would-be immigrants from Muslim countries are denied access to the United States, if the European Union demonstrates to the Muslim world that Europe is a Christians-only club, demand in the Muslim world for terrorism and Islamist authoritarianism will surely grow. Left to their own devices, a few who are excluded from globalization's benefits will turn to the only widely practiced methods of leveling the global playing field available to them: insurgency and terror. The two sides of the divide will understand each other's worldviews even less than they do now. The dip in the J curve that separates left- and right-side states will become even more treacherous to traverse.

Changes to the global economy produce deep anxiety within all states that are plugged into it. But ill-considered protectionist economic and security policies in the United States, Europe, or anywhere else are merely another form of self-imposed isolation. No gated community, even one that was wealthy when the gates were first installed, can long remain prosperous and dynamic in a globalized world. There have been a number of disturbing signs that gated-community political logic has taken hold in the United States. A growing U.S. trade deficit with China has led some U.S. lawmakers to press Beijing to substantially revalue its currency—and to threaten a 27.5 percent tariff on Chinese imports should it refuse. A political firestorm erupted when U.S. media reported in early 2006 that the Committee on Foreign Investments in the United States had approved a deal to give a state-owned Arab firm, Dubai Ports World, the rights to operate several U.S. ports. Political shortsightedness scuttled the deal, and some U.S. lawmakers demanded changes to the process by which such transactions are investigated. National security should remain the federal government's primary responsibility. But the danger is growing that excessive security concerns will needlessly damage U.S. commercial and foreign-policy interests and ultimately America's own stability.

Protectionist legislation can also undermine U.S. efforts to open left-side states. In 2006, some lawmakers threatened to block a merger between the French firm Alcatel and the American company Lucent over concerns that Alcatel enjoys commercial ties with Iran. Alcatel has upgraded Iran's telecom network and provided the country with its first high-speed DSL Internet connections. Blocking a proposed investment in the United States by a foreign firm that helps Iran's people communicate with one another and with the outside is a very poor way of undermining Iran's conservative regime.

As the authoritarian countries of the Communist bloc discovered, all closed states eventually wither or explode. The walls that isolate them merely hide their potential instability from the outside world. Only stability based on an openness that links citizens within and across national boundaries can help left-side states meet the primary challenge of the J curve. Openness enables change. Change is an essential ingredient in growth and prosperity. Only the free exchange of information, values, ideas, and people can build a sustainable global stability that enriches all who take part in it.

Acknowledgments

I had been kicking around the idea for *The J Curve* for a number of years, but finding time to do it (outside my day job) required the sort of self-discipline that pushes people into the gym at six every morning—and too often kept me from joining them. Quite a few friends and colleagues were persistent in prodding me forward. I'd like to thank them here.

Gary Hart convinced me from the very early stages that the J curve was an idea that needed to be a book. And before I could offer a coherent objection, he introduced me to his agent. Which led me to the personally delightful Flip Brophy, who has been a pleasure to work with and has proven my indispensable guide to the publishing industry.

My editor at Simon & Schuster, Alice Mayhew, has been tremendously supportive. My thanks to her, and to Roger Labrie.

Lionel Barber, Andrew Hill, and Serge Schmemann helped me bridge the gap between academe and popular writing. I am thankful for their time and effort.

Alex Motyl kept me honest as I was thinking through the initial outline for the book. Willis Sparks has worked with me as a research associate for some time now, and his thoughtful and incisive input make this a far better book than it otherwise might have been. Thanks to Nina Khrushcheva and Steve Sestanovich for convincing me to hire him.

My dearest friends in (and around) the field have generously given their counsel, enthusiasm, and support—David Fromkin, David Gordon, Nick Gvosdev, Scott Horton, Steve Mann, Ed Morse, Tom Pickering, Kitty Pilgrim, Juan Pujadas, Joel Rosenthal, Kirsten Sandberg, Marci Shore, and Enzo Viscusi. Thanks to my buddy Ken Griffin for his seemingly unlimited willingness to jet off and explore the world on a moment's notice. Our treks to the far corners of the globe have informed many of these pages. To Lisa

Anderson, for getting me back in the classroom after a ten-year hiatus (I can barely believe it)—and to my students at Columbia University's School of International and Public Affairs, for keeping me sharp. And especially to James Chace, whom I miss very much.

I thank my colleagues at Eurasia Group, a brilliant bunch of analytic sharpshooters second to none in their intellectual honesty and curiosity, who keep me grounded and informed on just about everything: Seto Bagdoyan, Anna Belkina, Allyson Benton, Sijin Cheng, Tanya Costello, Philippe de Pontet, Amitabh Dubey, Patrick Esteruelas, Ben Faulks, Chris Garman, John Green, Bob Herrera-Lim, Ana Jelenkovic, Preston Keat, Daniel Kerner, Peter Khalil, Jason Kindopp, Bruce Klingner, Cliff Kupchan, Jon Levy, Alex Lloyd, Firaz Maksad, Denis Maslov, Kaan Nazli, Jun Okumura, Anu Patil, Wolfango Picoli, Geoff Porter, Libbie Prescott, Nick Rey, Ross Schaap, Sebastian Spio-Garbrah, Pamela Starr, Peijean Wu, and Rochdi Younsi. I single out Harry Harding, whose intellectual rigor and careful eye were indispensable. And lest I not forget, Amanda Remus and Leila Tachmamedova, whose demanding work requires them to tolerate me most every day.

Maureen Miskovic convinced me to write, write, write, and that persistence pays off. She's very convincing.

And to my mum. I dedicate this to her.

Notes

1. Stability, Openness, and the J Curve

1. Secretary Rice's Interview with Rick Nieman of RTL TV of the Netherlands, February 10, 2005, http://www.state.gov/secretary/rm/2005/42084.htm.
2. For illustrations of this and complementary ideas based on considerable research, see: Edward D. Mansfield and Jack Snyder, *Electing to Fight* (Cambridge, Mass.: MIT Press, 2005); Jack Snyder, *From Voting to Violence* (New York: Norton, 2000); Fareed Zakaria, *The Future of Freedom* (New York: Norton, 2003).

2. The Far Left Side of the J Curve

1. Lutz Kleveman, *The New Great Game: Blood and Oil in Central Asia* (New York: Grove Press, 2003), p. 150.
2. For more on Turkmenistan, see Kleveman, *The New Great Game*, pp. 144–64.
3. James Brooke, "How Electronics Are Penetrating North Korea's Isolation," *New York Times*, March 15, 2005, http://www.nytimes.com/2005/03/15/international/asia/15 north.html.
4. Simon Romero, "Oil Finds Open Door to a Less Dependent Cuba," *International Herald Tribune*, January 12, 2005, http://www.energybulletin.net/3974.html.
5. Charles Tripp, *A History of Iraq* (Cambridge: Cambridge University Press, 2000), p. 206.
6. Ibid., p. 214.
7. Ibid., p. 217.
8. Saïd Aburish, *Saddam Hussein: The Politics of Revenge* (New York: Bloomsbury, 2000).
9. Mark Bowden, "Tales of the Tyrant," *Atlantic Monthly*, May 2002.
10. Tripp, p. 237.
11. http://hrw.org/reports/1993/iraqanfal/ANFAL3.htm.
12. Tripp, p. 234.
13. http://www.historyofwar.org/articles/wars_iraniraq.html.
14. Tripp, p.251.
15. Ibid., p. 253.
16. Ibid., p. 261.
17. Ibid., p. 262.
18. Iraq Survey Group, http://www.cia.gov/cia/reports/iraq_wmd_2004/Comp_Report_Key_Findings.pdf.
19. Douglas de Bono, *Point of Honor: Prelude to the Second Gulf War*, excerpt at http://metropolisink.com/debono/poh/extract.htm.

3. The Slide Toward Instability

1. For a full elaboration of this idea, see Bernard Lewis, *The Crisis of Islam* (New York: Modern Library, 2003).

2. Nancy Birdsall and Arvind Subramanian, "Saving Iraq from its Oil," *Foreign Affairs,* July–August 2004.

3. United Nations Arab Human Development Report 2002, http://www.rbas.undp.org/ahdr.cfm.

4. Stephen Kinzer, *All the Shah's Men* (Hoboken, N.J.: John Wiley & Sons, 2003).

5. Afshin Molavi, "Buying Time in Tehran," *Foreign Affairs,* November–December 2004.

6. See UPI story at http://usti.net/home/news/clari/news/wed/da/Uiran-oilincome.Rm4u_EOC.html.

7. Molavi.

8. Ibid.

9. According to the 9/11 Commission. Dan Eggen, "9/11 Panel Links Al Qaeda, Iran," *Washington Post,* June 26, 2004, http://www.washingtonpost.com/wp-dyn/articles/A6581-2004Jun25.html.

10. Kinzer.

11. Elaine Sciolino, *Persian Mirrors* (New York: Simon & Schuster, 2000), p. 353.

12. Ibid., pp. 349–350.

13. From the U.S. Energy Information Agency, http://www.eia.doe.gov/emeu/cabs/saudi.html.

14. "What If?" *The Economist,* May 27, 2004, http://www.economist.com/business/displayStory.cfm?story_id=2705562.

15. http://www.country-data.data.com/cgi-bin/query/r-11593.html.

16. From *Jane's Intelligence Review,* May 2004.

17. U.S. Department of Energy statistics, http://www.eia.doe.gov/emeu/cabs/carbonemiss/chapter5.html.

18. USEIA, http://www.eia.doe.gov/emeu/cabs/saudi.html.

19. World Bank, *World Development Report 2000/2001* (New York: Oxford University Press, 2000), p. 295.

20. Michael Doran, "The Saudi Paradox," *Foreign Affairs,* January–February 2004.

21. Doran.

22. For an interesting analysis of Saudization, see Robert Looney, "Saudization and Sound Economic Reforms: Are the Two Compatible?" http://www.ccc.nps.navy.mil/si/2004/feb/looneyFeb04.asp.

23. *Los Angeles Times,* http://207.44.245.159/article3412.htm.

24. Strobe Talbott, *The Russia Hand* (New York: Random House, 2002), p. 106.

25. American Russian Law Institute, http://www.russianlaw.org/palmer.htm.

26. Andrew Jack, *Inside Putin's Russia* (New York: Oxford University Press, 2004), p. 62.

27. For in-depth analysis of China's influence in Russia's far east, see Dmitri Trenin, *The End of Eurasia* (Washington, D.C.: Carnegie Endowment for International Peace, 2002).

28. Ibid., p. 131.

4. The Depths of the J Curve

1. *Cape Business News,* May 2005, http://www.cbn.co.za/issues/months/May2005/5_2005_1412.htm.

2. From a speech, "The Effect of Sanctions on Constitutional Change in South Africa," given by Dave Steward on behalf of former President F. W. de Klerk to the Institut Choiseul in Paris, June 14, 2004.

3. John Williamson, Institute for International Economics, "What Should the Bank Think About the Washington Consensus?" A paper for the World Bank's *World Development Report 2000,* http://www.iie.com/publications/papers/williamson0799.htm.

4. From a speech, "The Effect of Sanctions on Constitutional Change in South Africa," given by Dave Steward on behalf of former President F. W. de Klerk to the Institut Choiseul in Paris, June 14, 2004.

5. Lewis, Stephen R., Jr., *The Economics of Apartheid* (New York and London: Council on Foreign Relations Press, 1990), pp. 27–28. From the Institute for International Economics' "Case Studies in Sanctions and Terror," http://www.iie.com/research/topics/sanc tions/southafrica3.htm.

6. Rodman, A. Kenneth, "Public and Private Sanctions Against South Africa," *Political Science Quarterly*, Summer 1994, p. 314. From the Institute for International Economics' "Case Studies in Sanctions and Terror," http://www.iie.com/research/topics/ sanctions/southafrica3.htm.

7. Christopher Bennett, *Yugoslavia's Bloody Collapse* (New York: New York University Press, 1995), p. 34.

8. Bennett, p. 35.

9. Ibid., p. 46.

10. Case study: Serbia and Montenegro Sovereign Debt, http://www2.gsb.Columbia.edu/ ipdlj_bankruptcy_serbia.html.

11. Laura Rozen, "The Balkans: Failing States and Ethnic Wars," http://64.233.161.104/ search?q=cache:TTFVaYVxddQJ:permanent.access.gpo.gov/websites/nduedu/www.ndu .edu/inss/books/Books_2001/Global%2520Century%2520-%2520June%25202001/C48 Rozen.pdf+Tito+%22Yugoslav+economy%22+remittances+oil&hl=en.

12. Bennett, p. 69.

13. Ibid.

14. Ibid.

15. From "Institutional Origins of Contemporary Serbian Nationalism," The Balkan Repository Project, http://www.balkan-archive.org.yu/politics/papers/history/vujacic2 .html.

16. Bennett, pp. 76–77.

17. Bennett, p. 108.

18. Coalition for International Justice, http://www.cij.org/index.ctm?fuseaction=view Report&reportID=309&tribunalID=1.

5. The Right Side of the J Curve

1. Andrew Mango, *The Turks Today* (New York: Overlook Press, 2004), pp. 236–237.

2. Mango, p. 35.

3. http://concise.britannica.com/ebc/article-9374253/Ottoman-Empire.

4. Mango., p. 21.

5. David L. Phillips, "Turkey's Dreams of Accession," *Foreign Affairs*, September–October 2004.

6. Mango, pp. 20–22.

7. Mango, pp. 25–26.

8. http://www.moreorless.au.com/heroes/ataturk.html.

9. Mango, p. 27.

10. Phillips.

11. Ibid.

12. Ibid.

13. Ibid.

14. "Rebel Move 'Sends Mixed Signals,' " BBC News, September 2, 2003, http://news.bbc.co .uk./2/hi/europe/3202645.stm.

15. http://www.voiceforeurope.org/Info/Info/Arguments.

16. "Revamped Party's Date with Destiny," BBC News, October 31, 2002, http://newswww .bbc.net.uk/2/hi/europe/2383693.stm.

17. Phillips.

18. Phillips.

19. See Eurobarometer 63, pp. 154–162, http://europa.eu.int/comm/public_opinion/ archives/eb/eb63/eb63_en.pdf.

20. http://www.esib.org/projects/equality/EQhandbook/ch1.html.

21. Thomas Friedman, *From Beirut to Jerusalem* (New York: Anchor Books, 1989), pp. 253–255.

22. Ibid., p. 259.

23. http://www.freedomhouse.org/inc/content/pubs/fiw/inc_country_detail.cfm?

24. Freedom House, http://www.freedomhouse.org/template.cfm?page=22&year=2005& country=6759.

25. Ibid.

26. Ibid.

27. Bank of Jerusalem 2003 Annual Report, http://64.233.161.104/search?q=cache: EjsEyBBP5hIJ:www.bankjerusalem.co.il/site/mazan-e-31122003.pdf+%22Israelis+traveled +abroad%22+2004&hl=en&start=8.

28. CIA World Factbook, http://www.cia.gov/cia/publications/factbook/geos/is.html.

29. "Israeli Coach Wins Women's Day Award," *Jerusalem Post*, March 7, 2005, http:// www.jpost.com/servlet/Satellite?pagename=JPost/JPArticle/ShowFull&cid=111016554 2177&p=1078027574097.

30. "Israel's Economic Growth: Success Without Security," *Middle East Review of International Affairs*, September 2002, http://meria.idc.ac.il/journal/2002/issue3/jv6n3a3.html.

31. June Thomas, "Vote Early and Often," Slate Magazine, November 30, 2000, http://slate.msn.com/id/94368/#ContinueArticle.

32. "Restitution vs. Resettlement," *Jerusalem Post*, n.d., http://info.jpost.com/C003/Supple ments/Refugees/10-11.html.

33. "A Regional Peace Forecast," *The Guardian*, December 17, 2003, http://www.guardian .co.uk/israel/comment/0,10551,1108812,00.html.

34. Aluf Benn, "You Can Count on Them," *Haaretz*, January 28, 2005, http://www.haaretz .com/hasen/objects/pages/PrintArticleEn.jhtml?itemNo=533294.

35. Ibid.

36. Shashi Tharoor, "Democratic Maturity," *The Hindu*, May 23, 2004.

37. Shashi Tharoor, *India: From Midnight to the Millennium* (New York: Arcade Publishing, 1997), p. 29.

38. http://encarta.msn.com/encyclopedia_761577072/Nehru_Jawaharlal.html.

39. Ibid., p. 29.

40. http://ns.indnet.org/demog/0031.html.

41. Sunil Khilnani, "States of Emergency," *The New Republic*, http://www.tnr.com/ doc.mhtml?i=20011217&S=Khilani121701&C=3.

42. http://countrystudies.us/India/117.htm.

43. Tharoor, *India*, p. 162.

44. Tharoor, *India*, p. 166.

45. Jennifer Morrow, "Fervor, Furor, Fiasco: India's Telecom Privatization on Hold," *Indian Economy Overview*, http://www.ieo.org/jen001.html.

46. "Happy Anniversary?" *The Economist*, August 14, 1997, http://www.economist.com/dis playstory.cfm?story_id=153844.

47. Soutik Biswas, "India Architect of Reforms," BBC News Online, http://news.bbc.co .uk/1/hi/world/south_asia/3725357.stm.

48. "Mobile Users Figure Crosses 100 Million Mark," *Asian News International,* April 13, 2005, http://in.news.yahoo.com/050413/139/2kqgy.html.

49. Tharoor, *India,* p. 172.

50. James Madison, *Federalist Papers,* No. 10, http://thomas.loc.gov/home/histdox/ fed_10.html.

51. Tharoor, *India,* pp. 113–14.

52. Tharoor, pp. 54–56.

53. http://www.indiaonestop.com/tradepartners/japanoverview.html.

54. Tharoor, *India,* p .105.

55. http://www.hrw.org/reports/1999/india/India994=04.htm.

56. "US and India Seal Nuclear Accord," BBC News, March 2, 2006, http://news.bbc.co .uk/2/hi/south_asia/4764826.stm.

6. China's Dilemma

1. George Gilboy, "The Myth Behind China's Miracle," *Foreign Affairs,* July/August 2004, http://www.foreignaffairs.org/20040701faessay83405/george-j-gilboy/the-myth-behind -china-s-miracle.html.

2. *China Daily,* http://www.chinadaily.com.cn/english/doc/2005-03/01/content _420724 .htm.

3. Reuters, February 18, 2005, http://story.news.yahoo.com/news?tmpl=story2&u=/nm/ 20050218/od_nm/china_messages_dc.

4. "Breaking Down the Great Firewall," BBC News, April 30, 2005, http://news.bbc.co .uk/1/hi/world/asia-pacific/4496163.stm.

5. http://www.country-studies.com/china/reform=of=the=economic=system,=beginning =in=1979.html.

6. http://www.china.org.cn/e=china/openingup/sez.htm.

7. *OECD Observer,* August 2003, http://www.oecdobserver.org/news/fullstory.php/aid/ 1037/China _ahead_in_foreign_direct_investment.html.

8. U.S. Department of State, http://www.usconsulate.org.hk/uscn/trade/sprpt/2005/ics .htm.

9. Gilboy.

10. Gilboy.

11. Ibid.

12. Ross Terrill, *The New Chinese Empire: And What It Means for the United States* (New York: Basic Books, 2003), p. 310.

13. Nicholas Kristof and Sheryl WuDunn, *China Wakes: The Struggle for the Soul of a Rising Power* (New York: Vintage Books, 1994), p. 49.

14. Kristof and WuDunn, pp. 49–50.

15. China Digital Times, http://chinadigitaltimes.net/2005/08/regulations_on.php.

16. FRONTLINE/World, http://www.pbs.org/frontlineworld/stories/china401/facts.html.

17. Kristof and WuDunn, p. 134.

18. *New York Times,* http://www.nytimes.com/reuters/international/international-china -xinjiang.html?pagewanted=print.

19. Cleaner Production in China, http://www.chinacp.com/eng/cpfactories/cpfact_lun nan_oilfield.html.

20. http://www.uighurlanguage.com/logs/2005/01/introduction.php.

21. Terrill, pp. 234–237.

22. Ibid., p. 243.

23. "The Real Enemy Within," *The Economist,* April 29, 1999, http://www.economist.com/displaystory.cfm?story_id=321367.

24. "A Day of Saints and Sinners," *The Economist,* October 5, 2000, http://www.economist.com/displaystory.cfm?story_id=387368.

25. The Congressional-Executive Commission on China, http://www.cecc.gov/pages/virtualAcad/gov/judind.php.

26. Stanford University, WAIS Forum on Freedom of the Press, http://wais.stanford.edu/China/china_freedomofthepress103002.html.

27. Reporters Without Borders, http://www.rsf.org/article.php3?id_article=10749.

28. "Breaking Down the Great Firewall," BBC News, April 30, 2005, http://news.bbc.co.uk/1/hi/world/asia-pacific/4496163.stm.

29. http://news.bbc.co.uk/2/hi/business/4237122.stm.

30. "China Net Café Culture Crackdown," BBC News, February 14, 2005, http://news.bbc.co.uk/1/hi/technology/4263525.stm.

31. Kristof and WuDunn, pp. 79–80.

32. Murray Scot Tanner, "China Rethinks Unrest," *Washington Quarterly,* Summer 2004, pp. 138–140.

33. "China Sets Up Riot Police Units," BBC News, August 18, 2005, http://news.bbc.co.uk/2/hi/asia-pacific/4162254.stm.

34. Hannah Beech, "Inside the Pitchfork Rebellion," *Time,* March 13, 2006, http://www.time.com/time/archive/preview/0,10987.1169902,00.html.

35. Philip P. Pan, "Civil Unrest Challenges China's Party Leadership," *Washington Post,* November 4, 2004, http://www.washingtonpost.com/wp=dyn/articles/A23519-2004Nov3.html.

36. Tanner, p. 144.

37. Terrill, pp. 306–307.

38. Elizabeth Economy, "Economic Boom, Environmental Bust," October 22, 2004, http://www.cfr.org/publication/7548/economic_boom_environmental_bust.html.

39. "Safe as Houses?" *The Economist,* April 21, 2005, http://www.economist.com/displaystory.cfm?story_ID=3894857.

40. "Official: Beijing Sees Jump in Wealth Gap," *BusinessWeek,* March 8, 2006, http://www.businessweek.com/ap/financialnews/D8G7BH600.htm?campaign_id=apn_home_down&chan=db.

41. Terrill, p. 317.

42. This info can also be found at http://servihoo.com/channels/kinews/afp_details.php?id=96149&CategoryID=47.

43. "The Chinese Get the Vote, If Only for 'Super Girl,' " Jim Yardley, *New York Times,* September 4, 2005.

7. Conclusion

1. For documentation from U.S. government sources, see the following representative samples of the evidence: http://www.whitehousedrugpolicy.gov/publications/factsht/druguse; http://oas.samhsa.gov/NHSDA/2k3NSDUH/2k3results.htm#ch2; http://www.ojp.usdoj.gov/bjs/dcf/tables/emerg.htm.

2. Wesley Clark, "Broken Engagement," *Washington Monthly,* May 2004, http://www.washingtonmonthly.com/features/2004/0405.clark.html.

Index

287

About the Author

IAN BREMMER is president of Eurasia Group, the political risk consultancy. His publications include *New States, New Politics: Building the Post-Soviet Nations,* and over two hundred articles and essays in *International Affairs,* the *Harvard Business Review, Survival,* the *New Republic,* the *Financial Times, Fortune,* the *Los Angeles Times,* the *Wall Street Journal,* the *International Herald Tribune,* and the *New York Times.* He is a columnist for *Slate,* contributing editor at the *National Interest,* and a political commentator on CNN, FOX News, and CNBC. He lives in New York and teaches at Columbia University.

"More than forty years of quadriplegia has underscored to me the matchless value of knowing—really knowing—the doctrines of the Christian faith. *Dug Down Deep* reveals how biblical doctrine provides a pathway to understanding the heart and mind of God. If you're looking for 'that one book' that will push you farther down the road to faith than you've ever journeyed before, *Dug Down Deep* is it. I highly recommend it!"
—JONI EARECKSON TADA, author; founder and CEO,
International Disability Center, Agoura Hills, CA

"In *Dug Down Deep* my longtime friend Joshua Harris explains the basics of Christian theology in a way all of us can understand. He is a humble man and teaches humbly. If you are tired of hyped promises and want essential truth, this book is for you. As religious fads come and go, the truths in this book will last."
—DONALD MILLER, author of *Blue Like Jazz*

"When the apostle Peter says, "Humble yourselves under the mighty hand of *God*...casting all your anxiety on Him," he implies that humble people are fearless. They have the courage to stand up for truth humbly. I love the term "humble orthodoxy." And I love Josh Harris. When they come together (Josh and humble orthodoxy), as they do in this book, you get a humble, helpful, courageous testimony to biblical truth. Thank you, Josh, for following through so well on the conversation in Al Mohler's study."
—JOHN PIPER, author of *Desiring God;* Pastor for Preaching
and Vision, Bethlehem Baptist Church, Minneapolis

"Via vivid autobiography, Pastor Harris takes readers on a personal journey into the biblical theology that, belatedly, he found he could not manage without. A humbling, compelling, invigorating read."
—J. I. PACKER, author of *Knowing God*

"Josh says that this book is his 'reveling in theology in my own simple way.' Having read it, I can say that it is also a popular defense of the importance of theology and, at the same time, an introduction to it. I enjoyed reading it. And my mind immediately began to go to how I could use this book. Josh has given me a new tool! It is interesting, well written, and excellently illustrated. Josh has succeeded again in giving us a book that is clear, engaging, direct, solid, easy to read, sound, God centered, balanced, humorous—and it even has pictures!"

—MARK DEVER, author; Senior Pastor, Capitol Hill
Baptist Church, Washington DC

"*Dug Down Deep* is an incredible book! It's a tangible and incarnate look at theology. I would give it to any young Christian who wants to understand their faith."

—LECRAE, hip-hop artist

"As two young guys who have been deeply blessed and influenced by Josh's books and example, we couldn't be more excited about *Dug Down Deep* and how God is going to use it to transform a generation. It's a gripping and honest read. In it we learned things about our older brother that we had never, in twenty-one years, been told before! But more importantly, we learned things about our Savior that caused us to fall more deeply in love with him and his Word. Get this book. Read it. And join us on a journey to rediscover what has always been true."

—ALEX AND BRETT HARRIS, authors of *Do Hard Things*

"At *Boundless*, we've enjoyed watching young adults cultivate a fresh desire to go 'further up and further in' as followers of Christ. Few writers fuel that desire quite like Joshua Harris. With humility, humor, and honesty, *Dug Down Deep* shows the difference that a foundation can make—how vulnerable you can be when it's weak and how transformed you can be when you're willing to go deep."

—TED SLATER, editor, Boundless.org; Focus on the Family

DUG
DOWN
DEEP

DUG
DOWN
DEEP

*Unearthing What I Believe
and Why It Matters*

JOSHUA
HARRIS

Multnomah
BOOKS

DUG DOWN DEEP
PUBLISHED BY MULTNOMAH BOOKS
12265 Oracle Boulevard, Suite 200
Colorado Springs, Colorado 80921

ISBN 978-1-60142-151-7
ISBN 978-1-60142-259-0 (electronic)

Published in the United States by WaterBrook Multnomah, an imprint of the Crown Publishing Group, a division of Random House Inc., New York.

MULTNOMAH and its mountain colophon are registered trademarks of Random House Inc.

Library of Congress Cataloging-in-Publication Data
Harris, Joshua.
   Dug down deep : unearthing what I believe and why it matters / Joshua Harris. — 1st ed.
      p. cm.
   Includes bibliographical references.
   ISBN 978-1-60142-151-7 — ISBN 978-1-60142-259-0 (electronic) 1. Theology, Doctrinal—Popular works. I. Title.
   BT77.H2835 2010
   230—dc22
                                        2009028885

Printed in the United States of America
2010—First Edition

10 9 8 7 6 5 4 3 2 1

SPECIAL SALES

Most WaterBrook Multnomah books are available at special quantity discounts when purchased in bulk by corporations, organizations, and special-interest groups. Custom imprinting or excerpting can also be done to fit special needs. For information, please e-mail SpecialMarkets@WaterBrook Multnomah.com or call 1-800-603-7051.

To Emma Grace, Joshua Quinn, and Mary Kate

Your father loves you very much. One day when you're older
I hope you'll read this book and realize that I wrote it for you.
I have no greater hope for each of you
than to see you build your life on Jesus.

CONTENTS

MY RUMSPRINGA

"We're all theologians. The question is whether what we know about God is true."

IT'S STRANGE TO SEE an Amish girl drunk. The pairing of a bonnet and a can of beer is awkward. If she were stumbling along with a jug of moonshine, it would at least match her long, dowdy dress. But right now she can't worry about that. She is flat-out wasted.

Welcome to *rumspringa*.

———

The Amish, people who belong to a Christian religious sect with roots in Europe, practice a radical form of separation from the modern world. They live and dress with simplicity. Amish women wear bonnets and long, old-fashioned dresses and never touch makeup. The men wear wide-rimmed straw hats, sport bowl cuts, and grow chin curtains—full beards with the mustaches shaved off.

My wife, Shannon, sometimes says she wants to be Amish, but I know this isn't true. Shannon entertains her Amish fantasy when life feels too

1

complicated or when she's tired of doing laundry. She thinks life would be easier if she had only two dresses to choose from and both looked the same. I tell her that if she ever tried to be Amish, she would buy a pair of jeans and ditch her head covering about ten minutes into the experiment. Besides, she would never let me grow a beard like that.

Once Shannon and her girlfriend Shelley drove to Lancaster, Pennsylvania, for a weekend of furniture and quilt shopping in Amish country. They stayed at a bed-and-breakfast located next door to an Amish farm. One morning Shannon struck up a conversation with the inn's owner, who had lived among the Amish his entire life. She asked him questions, hoping for romantic details about the simple, buggy-driven life. But instead he complained about having to pick up beer cans every weekend.

Beer cans?

"Yes," he said, "the Amish kids leave them everywhere." That's when he told her about rumspringa. The Amish believe that before a young person chooses to commit to the Amish church as an adult, he or she should have the chance to freely explore the forbidden delights of the outside world. So at age sixteen everything changes for Amish teenagers. They go from milking cows and singing hymns to living like debauched rock stars.

In the Pennsylvania Dutch language, *rumspringa* literally means "running around." It's a season of doing anything and everything you want with zero rules. During this time—which can last from a few months to several years—all the restrictions of the Amish church are lifted. Teens are free to shop at malls, have sex, wear makeup, play video games, do drugs, use cell phones, dress however they want, and buy and drive cars. But what they seem to enjoy most during rumspringa is gathering at someone's barn, blasting music, and then drinking themselves into the ground. Every weekend, the man told Shannon, he had to clean up beer cans littered around his property following the raucous, all-night Amish parties.

———

When Shannon came home from her Lancaster weekend, her Amish aspirations had diminished considerably. The picture of cute little Amish girls binge drinking took the sheen off her idealistic vision of Amish life. We completed her disillusionment when we rented a documentary about the rite of rumspringa called *Devil's Playground*. Filmmaker Lucy Walker spent three years befriending, interviewing, and filming Amish teens as they explored the outside world. That's where we saw the drunk Amish girl tripping along at a barn party. We learned that most girls continue to dress Amish even as they party—as though their clothes are a lifeline back to safety while they explore life on the wild side.

In the documentary Faron, an outgoing, skinny eighteen-year-old sells and is addicted to the drug crystal meth. After Faron is busted by the cops, he turns in rival drug dealers. When his life is threatened, Faron moves back to his parents' home and tries to start over. The Amish faith is a good religion, he says. He wants to be Amish, but his old habits keep tugging on him.

A girl named Velda struggles with depression. During rumspringa she finds the partying empty, but after joining the church she can't imagine living the rest of her life as an Amish woman. "God talks to me in one ear, Satan in the other," Velda says. "Part of me wants to be like my parents, but the other part wants the jeans, the haircut, to do what I want to do."[1] When she fails to convince her Amish fiancé to leave the church with her, she breaks off her engagement a month before the wedding and leaves the Amish faith for good. As a result Velda is shunned by her family and the entire community. Alone but determined, she begins to attend college.

Velda's story is the exception. Eighty to 90 percent of Amish teens decide to return to the Amish church after rumspringa.[2] At one point in the film, Faron insightfully comments that rumspringa is like a vaccination for Amish

3

teens. They binge on all the worst aspects of the modern world long enough to make themselves sick of it. Then, weary and disgusted, they turn back to the comforting, familiar, and safe world of Amish life.

But as I watched, I wondered, *What are they really going back to? Are they choosing God or just a safe and simple way of life?*

———

I know what it means to wrestle with questions of faith. I know what it's like for faith to be so mixed up with family tradition that it's hard to distinguish between a genuine knowledge of God and comfort in a familiar way of life.

I grew up in an evangelical Christian family. One that was on the more conservative end of the spectrum. I'm the oldest of seven children. Our parents homeschooled us, raised us without television, and believed that old-fashioned courtship was better than modern dating. Friends in our neighborhood probably thought our family was Amish, but that's only because they didn't know some of the really conservative Christian home-school families. The truth was that our family was more culturally liberal than many homeschoolers. We watched movies, could listen to rock music (as long as it was Christian or the Beatles), and were allowed to have Star Wars and Transformers toys.

But even so, during high school I bucked my parents' restrictions. That's not to say my spiritual waywardness was very shocking. I doubt Amish kids would be impressed by my teenage dabbling in worldly pleasure. I never did drugs. Never got drunk. The worst things I ever did were to steal porn magazines, sneak out of the house at night with a kid from church, and date various girls behind my parents' backs. Although my rebellion was tame in comparison, it was never virtue that held me back from sin. It was lack of opportunity. I shudder to think what I would have done with a parent-sanctioned season of rumspringa.

The bottom line is that my parents' faith wasn't really my faith. I knew how to work the system, I knew the Christian lingo, but my heart wasn't in it. My heart was set on enjoying the moment.

Recently a friend of mine met someone who knew me in early high school. "What did she remember about me?" I asked.

"She said you were girl crazy, full of yourself, and immature," my friend told me.

Yeah, she knew me, I thought. It wasn't nice to hear, but I couldn't argue. I didn't know or fear God. I didn't have any driving desire to know him.

For me, the Christian faith was more about a set of moral standards than belief and trust in Jesus Christ.

———

During my early twenties I went through a phase of blaming the church I had attended in high school for all my spiritual deficiencies. Evangelical mega-churches make good punching bags.

My reasoning went something like this: I was spiritually shallow because the pastors' teaching had been shallow. I wasn't fully engaged because they hadn't done enough to grab my attention. I was a hypocrite because everyone else had been a hypocrite. I didn't know God because they hadn't provided enough programs. Or they hadn't provided the right programs. Or maybe they'd had too many programs.

All I knew was that it was someone else's fault.

Blaming the church for our problems is second only to the popular and easy course of blaming our parents for everything that's wrong with us. But the older I get, the less I do of both. I hope that's partly due to the wisdom that comes with age. But I'm sure it's also because I am now both a parent and a pastor. Suddenly I have a lot more sympathy for my dad and mom and the pastors at my old church. Funny how that works, isn't it?

At the church where I now pastor (which I love), some young adults remind me of myself when I was in high school. They are church kids who know so much about Christian religion and yet so little about God. Some are passive, completely ambivalent toward spiritual things. Others are actively straying from their faith—ticked off about their parents' authority, bitter over a rule or guideline, and counting the minutes until they turn eighteen and can disappear. Others aren't going anywhere, but they stay just to go through the motions. For them, church is a social group.

It's strange being on the other side now. When I pray for specific young men and women who are wandering from God, when I stand to preach and feel powerless to change a single heart, when I sit and counsel people and it seems nothing I can say will draw them away from sin, I remember the pastors from my teenage years. I realize they must have felt like this too. They must have prayed and cried over me. They must have labored over sermons with students like me in mind.

I see now that they were doing the best they knew how. But a lot of the time, I wasn't listening.

During high school I spent most Sunday sermons doodling, passing notes, checking out girls, and wishing I were two years older and five inches taller so a redhead named Jenny would stop thinking of me as her "little brother." That never happened.

I mostly floated through grown-up church. Like a lot of teenagers in evangelical churches, I found my sense of identity and community in the parallel universe of the youth ministry. Our youth group was geared to being loud, fast paced, and fun. It was modeled on the massive and influential, seeker-sensitive Willow Creek Community Church located outside Chicago. The goal was simple: put on a show, get kids in the building, and let them see that Christians are cool, thus Jesus is cool. We had to prove that being a Christian is, contrary to popular opinion and even a few annoying passages of the Bible, loads of fun. Admittedly it's not as much fun as partying and having sex but pretty fun nonetheless.

Every Wednesday night our group of four-hundred-plus students divided into teams. We competed against each other in games and won points by bringing guests. As a homeschooler, of course I was completely worthless in the "bring friends from school" category. So I tried to make up for that by working on the drama and video team. My buddy Matt and I wrote, performed, and directed skits to complement our youth pastor's messages. Unfortunately, our idea of complementing was to deliver skits that were not even remotely connected to the message. The fact that Matt was a Brad Pitt look-alike assured that our skits were well received (at least by the girls).

The high point of my youth-group performing career came when the pastor found out I could dance and asked me to do a Michael Jackson impersonation. The album *Bad* had just come out. I bought it, learned all the dance moves, and then when I performed—how do I say this humbly?—I blew everyone away. I *was* bad (and I mean that in the good sense of the word *bad*). The crowd went absolutely nuts. The music pulsed, and girls were screaming and grabbing at me in mock adulation as I moonwalked and lip-synced my way through one of the most inane pop songs ever written. I loved every minute of it.

Looking back, I'm not real proud of that performance. I would feel better about my *bad* moment if the sermon that night had been about the depravity of man or something else that was even slightly related. But there was no connection. It had nothing to do with anything.

For me, dancing like Michael Jackson that night has come to embody my experience in a big, evangelical, seeker-oriented youth group. It was fun, it was entertaining, it was culturally savvy (at the time), and it had very little to do with God. Sad to say, I spent more time studying Michael's dance moves for that drama assignment than I was ever asked to invest in studying about God.

Of course, this was primarily my own fault. I was doing what I wanted to do. There were other kids in the youth group who were more mature and who grew more spiritually during their youth-group stint. And I don't doubt the good intentions of my youth pastor. He was trying to strike the balance between getting kids to attend and teaching them.

Maybe I wouldn't have been interested in youth group if it hadn't been packaged in fun and games and a good band. But I still wish someone had expected more of me—of all of us.

Would I have listened? I can't know. But I do know that a clear vision of God and the power of his Word and the purpose of Jesus's life, death, and resurrection were lost on me in the midst of all the flash and fun.

———

There's a story in the Bible of a young king named Josiah, who lived about 640 years before Christ. I think Josiah could have related to me—being religious but ignorant of God. Josiah's generation had lost God's Word. And I don't mean that figuratively. They *literally* lost God's Word. It sounds ridiculous, but they essentially misplaced the Bible.

If you think about it, this was a pretty big deal. We're not talking about a pair of sunglasses or a set of keys. The Creator of the universe had communicated with mankind through the prophet Moses. He gave his law. He revealed what he was like and what he wanted. He told his people what it meant for them to be his people and how they were to live. All this was dutifully recorded on a scroll. Then this scroll, which was precious beyond measure, was stored in the holy temple. But later it was misplaced. No one knows how. Maybe a clumsy priest dropped it and it rolled into a dark corner.

But here's the really sad thing: nobody noticed it was missing. No search was made. Nobody checked under the couch. It was gone and no one cared. For decades those who wore the label "God's people" actually had no communication with him.

They wore their priestly robes, they carried on their traditions in their beautiful temple, and they taught their messages that were so wise, so insightful, so inspirational.

But it was all a bunch of hot air—nothing but their own opinions. Empty ritual. Their robes were costumes, and their temple was an empty shell.

This story scares me because it shows that it's possible for a whole generation to go happily about the business of religion, all the while having lost a true knowledge of God.

———

When we talk about knowledge of God, we're talking about theology. Simply put, theology is the study of the nature of God—who he is and how he thinks and acts. But theology isn't high on many people's list of daily concerns.

My friend Curtis says that most people today think only of themselves. He calls this "me-ology." I guess that's true. I know it was true of me and still can be. It's a lot easier to be an expert on what I think and feel and want than to give myself to knowing an invisible, universe-creating God.

Others view theology as something only scholars or pastors should worry about. I used to think that way. I viewed theology as an excuse for all the intellectual types in the world to add homework to Christianity.

But I've learned that this isn't the case. Theology isn't for a certain group of people. In fact, it's impossible for anyone to escape theology. It's everywhere. All of us are constantly "doing" theology. In other words, all of us have some idea or opinion about what God is like. Oprah does theology. The person who says, "I can't believe in a God who sends people to hell" is doing theology.

We all have some level of knowledge. This knowledge can be much or little, informed or uninformed, true or false, but we all have some concept of God (even if it's that he doesn't exist). And we all base our lives on what we think God is like.

So when I was spinning around like Michael Jackson at youth group, I was a theologian. Even though I wasn't paying attention in church. Even though I wasn't very concerned with Jesus or pleasing him. Even though I was more preoccupied with my girlfriend and with being popular. Granted I was a really bad theologian—my thoughts about God were unclear and often ignorant. But I had a concept of God that directed how I lived.

I've come to learn that theology matters. And it matters not because we want a good grade on a test but because what we know about God shapes the way we think and live. What you believe about God's nature—what he is like, what he wants from you, and whether or not you will answer to him—affects every part of your life.

Theology matters, because if we get it wrong, then our whole life will be wrong.

———

I know the idea of "studying" God often rubs people the wrong way. It sounds cold and theoretical, as if God were a frog carcass to dissect in a lab or a set of ideas that we memorize like math proofs.

But studying God doesn't have to be like that. You can study him the way you study a sunset that leaves you speechless. You can study him the way a man studies the wife he passionately loves. Does anyone fault him for noting her every like and dislike? Is it clinical for him to desire to know the thoughts and longings of her heart? Or to want to hear her speak?

Knowledge doesn't have to be dry and lifeless. And when you think about it, exactly what is our alternative? Ignorance? Falsehood?

We're either building our lives on the reality of what God is truly like and what he's about, or we're basing our lives on our own imagination and misconceptions.

We're all theologians. The question is whether what we know about God is true.

———

In the days of King Josiah, theology was completely messed up. This isn't really surprising. People had lost God's words and then quickly forgot what the true God was like.

King Josiah was a contemporary of the prophet Jeremiah. People call Jeremiah the weeping prophet, and there was a lot to weep about in those days. "A horrible and shocking thing has happened in the land," Jeremiah said. "The prophets prophesy lies, the priests rule by their own authority, and my people love it this way" (Jeremiah 5:30–31, NIV).

As people learned to love their lies about God, they lost their ability to recognize his voice. "To whom can I speak and give warning?" God asked. "Who will listen to me? Their ears are closed so they cannot hear. The word of the LORD is offensive to them; they find no pleasure in it" (Jeremiah 6:10, NIV).

People forgot God. They lost their taste for his words. They forgot what he had done for them, what he commanded of them, and what he threatened if they disobeyed. So they started inventing gods for themselves. They started borrowing ideas about God from the pagan cults. Their made-up gods let them live however they wanted. It was "me-ology" masquerading as theology.

The results were not pretty.

Messed-up theology leads to messed-up living. The nation of Judah resembled one of those skanky reality television shows where a houseful of barely dressed singles sleep around, stab each other in the back, and try to win cash. Immorality and injustice were everywhere. The rich trampled the poor. People replaced the worship of God with the worship of pagan deities that demanded religious orgies and child sacrifice. Every level of society, from marriage and the legal system to religion and politics, was corrupt.

The surprising part of Josiah's story is that in the midst of all the distortion and corruption, he chose to seek and obey God. And he did this as a young man (probably no older than his late teens or early twenties). Scripture gives this description of Josiah: "He did what was right in the eyes of the LORD and walked in all the ways of his father David, not turning aside to the right or to the left" (2 Kings 22:2, NIV).

The prophet Jeremiah called people to the same straight path of true theology and humble obedience:

Thus says the LORD:
"Stand by the roads, and look,
 and ask for the ancient paths,
where the good way is; and walk in it,
 and find rest for your souls." (Jeremiah 6:16)

In Jeremiah's words you see a description of King Josiah's life. His generation was rushing past him, flooding down the easy paths of man-made religion, injustice, and immorality.

They didn't stop to look for a different path.

They didn't pause to consider where the easy path ended.

They didn't ask if there was a better way.

But Josiah stopped. He stood at a crossroads, and he looked. And then he asked for something that an entire generation had neglected, even completely forgotten. He asked for the ancient paths.

———

What are the ancient paths? When the Old Testament prophet Jeremiah used the phrase, he was describing obedience to the Law of Moses. But today the ancient paths have been transformed by the coming of Jesus Christ. Now we see that those ancient paths ultimately led to Jesus. We have not only truth to obey but a person to trust in—a person who perfectly obeyed the Law and who died on the cross in our place.

But just as in the days of Jeremiah, the ancient paths still represent life based on a true knowledge of God—a God who is holy, a God who is just, a God who is full of mercy toward sinners. Walking in the ancient paths still means relating to God on his terms. It still means receiving and obeying his self-revelation with humility and awe.

Just as he did with Josiah and Jeremiah and every generation after them, God calls us to the ancient paths. He beckons us to return to theology that is true. He calls us, as Jeremiah called God's people, to recommit ourselves to orthodoxy.

The word *orthodoxy* literally means "right opinion." In the context of Christian faith, orthodoxy is shorthand for getting your opinion or thoughts about God right. It is teaching and beliefs based on the established, proven, cherished truths of the faith. These are the truths that don't budge. They're clearly taught in Scripture and affirmed in the historic creeds of the Christian faith:

There is one God who created all things.

God is triune: Father, Son, and Holy Spirit.

The Bible is God's inerrant word to humanity.

Jesus is the virgin-born, eternal Son of God.

Jesus died as a substitute for sinners so they could be forgiven.

Jesus rose from the dead.

Jesus will one day return to judge the world.

Orthodox beliefs are ones that genuine followers of Jesus have acknowledged from the beginning and then handed down through the ages. Take one of them away, and you're left with something less than historic Christian belief.

———

When I watched the documentary about the Amish rite of rumspringa, what stood out to me was the way the Amish teenagers processed the decision of whether or not to join the Amish church. With few exceptions the decision seemed to have very little to do with God. They weren't searching Scripture to see if what their church taught about the world, the human heart, and salvation was true. They weren't wrestling with theology. I'm not implying that the Amish don't have a genuine faith and trust in Jesus. But for the teens in the documentary, the decision was mostly a matter of choosing a culture and a lifestyle. It gave them a sense of belonging. In some cases it gave them a steady job or allowed them to marry the person they wanted.

I wonder how many evangelical church kids are like the Amish in this regard. Many of us are not theologically informed. Truth about God doesn't define us and shape us. We have grown up in our own religious culture. And often this culture, with its own rituals and music and moral values, comes to represent Christianity far more than specific beliefs about God do.

Every new generation of Christians has to ask the question, what are we actually choosing when we choose to be Christians? Watching the stories of the Amish teenagers helped me realize that a return to orthodoxy has to be more than a return to a way of life or to cherished traditions. Of course the Christian faith leads to living in specific ways. And it does join us to a specific community. And it does involve tradition. All this is good. It's important. But it has to be more than tradition. It has to be about a person—the historical and living person of Jesus Christ.

Orthodoxy matters because the Christian faith is not just a cultural tradition or moral code. Orthodoxy is the irreducible truths about God and his work in the world. Our faith is not just a state of mind, a mystical experience, or concepts on a page. Theology, doctrine, and orthodoxy matter because God is real, and he has acted in our world, and his actions have meaning today and for all eternity.

———

For many people, words like *theology, doctrine,* and *orthodoxy* are almost completely meaningless. Maybe they're unappealing, even repellent.

Theology sounds stuffy.

Doctrine is something unkind people fight over.

And orthodoxy? Many Christians would have trouble saying what it is other than it calls to mind images of musty churches guarded by old men with comb-overs who hush and scold.

I can relate to that perspective. I've been there. But I've also discovered that my prejudice, my "theology allergy," was unfounded.

This book is the story of how I first glimpsed the beauty of Christian theology. These pages hold the journal entries of my own spiritual journey—a journey that led to the realization that sound doctrine is at the center of loving Jesus with passion and authenticity. I want to share how I learned that orthodoxy isn't just for old men but is for anyone who longs to behold a God who is bigger and more real and glorious than the human mind can imagine.

The irony of my story—and I suppose it often works this way—is that the very things I needed, even longed for in my relationship with God, were wrapped up in the very things I was so sure could do me no good. I didn't understand that such seemingly worn-out words as *theology, doctrine,* and *orthodoxy* were the pathway to the mysterious, awe-filled experience of truly knowing the living Jesus Christ.

They told the story of the Person I longed to know.

2

IN WHICH I LEARN TO DIG

"Underneath was a deeper question: what would I build my life on?"

DO YOU REMEMBER the story Jesus told about the wise and foolish builders? Simple story. The wise man dug in the ground and built his house on the rock. When storms came, his house stood firm. The foolish man built his house on the sand. When the wind and waves arrived, the house was swept away. As children we used to sing the story in Sunday school, complete with hand motions. Now that I think of it, this is really quite a traumatic concept for children to sing about—houses toppling and all. But it never really scared me because I went to church, and of course I was a "rock person."

At least that's what I thought.

Recently I reread the parable of the two builders in Luke 6:46–49 as I was sitting on a beach in Florida. I was on vacation with my family, and I'd woken up early to read my Bible and pray by the water. Doing your devotions with the sun rising behind you and an ocean at your feet makes everything you read and think seem really deep and expansive and spiritual. I wish

I could read my Bible by the beach every morning. But there is no beach in Gaithersburg, Maryland. I have a clock radio that makes ocean sounds, but it's not the same.

I've read this story about the two builders countless times. I've read it so many times that I almost don't read it anymore when I come across it in the Gospels. I skim it. I gulp down three sentences at a time because I already know what they say. I don't want to read my Bible like that, but, honestly, sometimes I do. That morning on the beach I almost skimmed right past the two builders. Almost. Maybe it was the sand between my toes. Maybe it was the soundtrack of the lapping waves. But for some reason I made myself slow down.

And as I did, I saw something I hadn't seen before. In the past I thought the point was simply that being a Christian is better than not being a Christian. And I suppose on a very rudimentary level, that is what it means. But I never thought about the specifics of what digging down to rock represents.

Jesus started his story with a piercing question. He asked, "Why do you call me Lord but don't do what I say?" That question makes me uncomfortable because I can't pretend I don't understand it. And I feel that he's talking to me, that he's talking to religious people—people who claim to belong to God, people who say that Jesus is Lord. This is interesting because it clues us in to the fact that Jesus isn't just contrasting religious and nonreligious people. He's not just saying that atheists get their houses knocked down. He's talking to people who claim to believe in God.

Jesus is calling the bluff of the religious. He says, Why play this game? Why call me Lord as if you care who I am or what I want when you don't bother really knowing me or doing what I say? And then Jesus tells the story about the builders and their two houses. The homes they build represent their lives—their beliefs, convictions, aspirations, and choices.

Jesus is telling us that there are stable and unstable foundations on which to construct our lives. Regardless of our intentions, it's possible to base our confidence and trust—the very footing of our lives—on what is insecure and faulty. On shifting sand.

It's easy to write off the man who built on sand as a know-nothing. But that's just because we see the bad outcome of his choice. The foolish builder didn't know he was foolish. At the time, building his house where he did probably made a lot of sense. An oceanfront view. Lots of sand for the kids to play in. And without the backbreaking work of digging, his construction time was cut in half.

I wonder how many years the foolish man lived in his beautiful house on the sand before the storm came. Should any of us assume we're above making his mistake? Would Jesus warn us of something obvious?

The wise builder chose a different approach. Jesus said he built his house on the rock. That involved work and strenuous effort. It took more time.

But listen to how Jesus describes what building on the rock symbolizes. This is what I had always missed. The wise builder is the one who comes to Jesus, listens to his words, and then puts them into practice. This activity—this faith-filled approach to Jesus, the acceptance of his truth and then the application of the truth—is what Jesus said is like a man who dug down deep and built on a solid foundation. When problems and trials and the storms of life came, the "house" of his life kept standing.

What hit me that morning on the beach is that digging down and building on the rock isn't a picture of being nominally religious or knowing Jesus from a distance. Being a Christian means being a person who labors to establish his beliefs, his dreams, his choices, his very view of the world on the truth of who Jesus is and what he has accomplished—a Christian who cares about truth, who cares about sound doctrine.

Doctrine is just a clunky word for truths to build our lives on—truths we'd all doubt or simply wouldn't know about without the Bible. Christian doctrine is Christian teaching about any number of subjects addressed in Scripture: God, sin, Jesus, heaven, hell, the resurrection…and on and on.

Maybe you've never thought about it in these terms, but coming to Jesus and listening to his words involves doctrine. It involves knowing and understanding what the Bible teaches about who Jesus is, why we need him, how he saves us and changes us. In other words, it involves knowing theological truth.

When Jesus talks about the person who listens to his words, he's referring to more than just the red letters in Matthew, Mark, Luke, and John. All Scripture is the Word of God. It's all Jesus speaking to us.

Studying these words and understanding what they mean involve effort. The wise builder digs. It is sweaty, salt-in-the-eyes work. Digging that involves studying. Digging that requires thinking and reading and grappling with sometimes challenging truths.

But the hardest work of all is putting the truth into practice. That's what Jesus pinpointed in his story (and it's the focus of the preceding verses in Luke 6). Truth requires action. Coming to him, calling him Lord, and knowing his words can never be enough. Church affiliation and a list of beliefs are never enough. Doctrine and theology are always meant to be applied to our lives—to shape and reshape not only a statement of faith but also the practical decisions of how we think and act. Book knowledge about building on rock has no value if we're still resting on shifting sand.

Once when my little brother Isaac was four years old, he grabbed a shovel and headed toward the woods. My mom asked what he was doing. He answered, "I'm going to dig for holes." The story has become a family favorite, and Isaac is tired of having it repeated. But it's a good description of what we do when we study and argue over beliefs without putting them into practice. We're digging for holes.

We need to dig for rock.

I know from experience that it's possible to be a Christian but live life on the surface. The surface can be empty tradition. It can be emotionalism. It can even be doctrine without application. I think I've done it all. I've spent my share of time on the sandy surface of superficial Christianity.

The first four years following high school brought good changes in my life—most notably in my spiritual life. Don't ask me to tell you when I was converted. Like a lot of church kids, I don't have a specific day when I repented, put my trust in Jesus, and was saved. For me there was no one breakthrough moment. God poked and prodded and shaped me through countless small, seemingly insignificant experiences and decisions and friendships. Do you know the kind of slow transformation I'm talking about? You don't really see it while it's happening. But later you look back and realize you're not the same.

I can identify a few key moments, though. When I was seventeen, I went to a Christian leadership camp in Colorado Springs. The students there were different from other Christians I'd met. They were serious, focused. That might have been the first time I was with a group of Christians who weren't simply trying to "outfun" the world. These kids wanted to outthink and out-work and outlove the world. They wanted to apply their minds to studying Scripture and gaining a Christian worldview. Many had a hunger for God and his Word that stood in stark contrast to my life.

In one session the camp director asked students to stand and recite passages of Scripture they had memorized. I misunderstood the request and at one point stood with my Bible in hand and read a passage. When I realized my mistake, I felt really dumb. I slumped back into my chair red-faced and embarrassed as others stood, one after another, and recited portions from memory. Worse than my misunderstanding was the realization that I didn't have a passage of the Bible memorized. My conscience was pricked.

Around that same time my girlfriend and I ended our two-year relationship. It was a significant moment in my spiritual life. I didn't realize till we broke up just how much our relationship, with its ongoing temptation to compromise, had been draining my spiritual passion. With the distraction and guilt of that relationship over, I began to pursue God in a way I'd never done before.

In his quiet, steady providence, God awakened in me a growing desire to know him. I just wasn't sure what to do with it. My impulse (which was a mix of godly desires and plain ambition) was to try to do something "big" for God. My hero in those days was Billy Graham, so *big* meant big crowds and big fame (all for Jesus, of course).

So at age seventeen, I followed my dad into public speaking. I also began to edit a small magazine for homeschooled teenagers. Preparing messages and writing for the magazine had a good effect on me. It drove me to dig.

Then a friend and I attended a lecture by Christian apologist Ravi Zacharias on the campus of Reed College. I was enthralled by this Indian man with his glowing white hair who was brave enough to venture onto a very secular, even anti-God campus and speak so intelligently about matters of faith. He quoted poets and philosophers as he spoke of Christian truth. He taught Scripture and built a case for the reasonableness of faith that stirred me. He asked me to think; he asked me to engage my mind with God's truth. And he did it all with a really cool accent.

I was hooked. I bought dozens of Zacharias's messages on cassette tape.

I hauled around a cardboard box of his tapes in the front seat of my car and listened to them over and over. I spent so much time with those tapes I even started pronouncing certain words with a slight Indian accent (which must have seemed very odd to people at my conferences). As I drove around listening to Zacharias, I dreamed about marrying one of his daughters and having my father-in-law train me to be the next great apologist, who could disarm atheists and skeptics with jujitsulike skill. (Of course, I wanted to marry every Christian leader's daughter in those days.)

I got hold of J. I. Packer's classic *Knowing God.* It was the first serious theological book I read. Packer taught me that it wasn't enough to know about God or know about godliness but that I needed to truly know God himself—his character and attributes. The study of these doctrines wasn't an end in itself but a means to a relationship with my Creator and Redeemer. Packer taught me that, far from being impractical or irrelevant, theology was vitally important to the living of everyday life. For the first time I began to learn theological terms such as *propitiation* and *sovereignty* and *justification.*

Unfortunately, not everything I studied was as helpful as Dr. Packer's book. Often I picked authors based on what *sounded* spiritually deep. Obscure worked too. I started reading the writings of some rather unhelpful Christian mystics. I was looking for something, anything, that was totally different from what I considered the plastic evangelical world I'd grown up in.

In terms of a church home, I found "totally different" at a large charismatic congregation that met on a hill overlooking the Columbia River. The church building itself was an architectural structure unlike any I'd ever seen— two white domes settled into the hillside. It looked as though God himself had reached down from heaven and placed two giant cereal bowls upside down.

Friends from my old church teased me about the "bubble church" with all its charismatic oddities. I didn't care what they said. I met the Holy Spirit at the bubble church, and since there were only three members of the Trinity, I thought this was fairly significant.

I loved so many things about my charismatic church. I loved the passion and emotional zeal that people had. I'd never seen people so excited about God. They raised their hands and danced during worship. They prayed for hours. They spoke about God and his Spirit with an expectation that he would break into the world at any moment. For a young man hungering for spiritual reality, this vision of God's presence and power was extremely attractive.

I wouldn't trade my time in that church for anything. I encountered God in very powerful ways and learned about the work of the Holy Spirit there. But over time the continual focus on looking for a fresh move of the Spirit began to wear thin. I couldn't shake the sense that something was missing.

I realize now that I still hadn't found what I needed most. I still hadn't uncovered the value of finding and building on bedrock. I was shuffling along the surface, poking at but not digging into sound doctrine.

If I'd been drawn to my old church for a set of friends, I began to see that in some sense my focus at the bubble church was on the latest spiritual experience. I had begun to measure my relationship with God in terms of emotional euphoria and encounters with the Spirit. I wanted to get knocked over or slain in the Spirit. I had merely gone from theology-lite, seeker-sensitive evangelicalism to theology-lite, experience-driven Pentecostalism.

———

When I turned twenty-one, my dad wrote me a letter filled with fatherly advice. One statement stood out: "Find men that you want to be like and then sit at their feet." As I launched into manhood, he was reminding me that some of the lessons I needed most wouldn't be found in a textbook; they'd be written in the heart and life of a godly man. I needed to get close enough to such a man to observe his character and to be shaped by his example. I needed a mentor.

I liked the sound of that. But finding a mentor was easier said than done. It's not as if wise, godly leaders have sign-up sheets for people to "sit at their feet." And in a lot of ways, I felt like I was doing okay. Things were going really well in my pursuit of "big" things for God. The magazine I had started had grown up to glossy, full-color splendor with more than five thousand subscribers. The teen conferences my dad had helped me start had become relatively popular. To top it off, I'd signed a contract with a Christian publisher to write a book. I was living the evangelical American dream. I was doing something big.

But big doesn't equal deep. I had a lot to learn.

One of my teen conferences was sponsored by a little church in Lancaster, Pennsylvania. In fact, that church hosted my conference two years in a row. A young woman named Debbie, who had been one of the first subscribers to my magazine, worked as the church secretary and had organized the event. After the conference I hung out with Debbie and friends from her church. They were weird, but weird in a good way. What I noticed first was the friendship and sense of community they seemed to share. The second thing was how they spoke. They talked about grace, sin, Christ's work on the cross, and sanctification with a warmth and openness that stood out to me. In their normal conversations they used some of the theological terms I'd been learning in books such as *Knowing God*. It was as if they'd taken doctrinal ideas off the high shelf, which they seemed to occupy in my mind, and put them to work in their everyday lives. I found this odd and yet appealing.

I think Debbie saw through the facade of my "success" as a young Christian speaker and writer. She saw a young man who had communication gifts but who lacked real spiritual depth. Even though she was less than a year older than I was, an almost motherly instinct kicked into gear. She was determined to help me.

Debbie's help came in the form of cassette tapes. She sent me sermons by a pastor named C. J. Mahaney, who led a church called Covenant Life in Maryland. Debbie was friends with his daughters, and C.J.'s church had helped to plant the church Debbie attended.

I had listened to dynamic, humorous preachers before, but C.J. was unique. His passion was infused with a theological depth I wasn't accustomed to. His sermons revealed his love for reading and inspired a similar love in the people he preached to. But he didn't reference the popular Christian bestsellers with which I was so impressed. Instead he quoted men like J. I. Packer, Sinclair Ferguson, John Stott, and D. A. Carson. He talked about and quoted long-since-dead pastors and theologians like Jonathan Edwards, Thomas Watson, and John Calvin as though they were still-living, personal friends. Charles Spurgeon, the nineteenth-century London pastor, whose preaching and example of gospel proclamation inspired C.J., was his "historical hero." John Owen was his tutor on the doctrine of sin.

C.J. opened up a whole universe of books and rich theology that I never knew existed. It was like finding out that the most amazing party was being held in your basement but no one had bothered to tell you. Or like a child discovering a carnival in his own backyard.

This is what I'd been longing for but had never known how to name. My soul had been craving good, solid, undiluted truth about God and the good news of his Son's life, death, and resurrection. I didn't need to be entertained. I didn't primarily need to fall over at a prayer meeting. And I didn't need lifeless information. I needed to *know* God. The authors I was discovering spoke about God in ways I'd never heard. They exulted in the God of Scripture who sovereignly ruled over the universe. He was a loving Father who saved men and women by sheer grace, all for his own praise and glory. His Son was the Savior whose atoning death rescued sinners from wrath.

And it was this message of the gospel of grace for which C.J. reserved his greatest passion. Most preachers and zealous Christians I knew got fired up over what *we* needed to do for God. But C.J.'s greatest passion was reserved for exulting in what *God* had done for us. He loved to preach about the Cross and how Christ died in our place, as our substitute.

For someone who had practically been born into church, I found this surprisingly new. The deeper I delved into Christian doctrine, the more I saw that the good news of salvation by grace alone in Jesus, who died for sin—the gospel—was the main message of the whole Bible.

I suppose it might seem completely obvious that this is the center of the Christian faith, and yet it felt new to me. I began to see orthodoxy as the treasuring of the truths that point to Jesus and his saving work. Doctrine was the living story of what Jesus did for us and what it means. Yes, caring about it involved study. Yes, it involved opening books and learning sometimes awkward words. But it was the key to truly knowing Jesus.

On a chilly February morning, I shoved the last few bags into my car—a worn, musty-smelling, baby blue 1988 Honda Civic hatchback. Not exactly a chick-magnet sort of car. My friends mockingly called it the grocery getter. When you're twenty-two and single, *grocery* is not a word you want associated with your vehicle. But I couldn't really argue with the description. I just hoped my homely little car would survive the trip.

I was moving to Maryland. C.J. had invited me to do an internship at his church. I was going to live in his basement and be trained as a pastor. It was still hard to believe it had all happened. But my parents thought the invitation was God's plan for me. "My son can learn things from you that I can't teach him," Dad had told C.J.

In the two years since I had first listened to a cassette tape of his sermons, C.J. and I had developed a personal friendship. I had visited his church, attended a conference he hosted for pastors, and stayed in his home. One late-night conversation at his kitchen table made a lasting impression. We talked about my speaking tour, the book I was writing, and my plans for the next few years. And then C.J. asked me, "What are you going to build with your life?" As we talked, he encouraged me to look past numbers as a measure of success and consider what it meant to build something that would last beyond a weekend conference or best-selling book.

Underneath everything he said was a deeper question that I didn't quite grasp at the time: what would I build my life *on*?

So much of my thinking and planning had been based on opportunity, on my feelings, and on the pragmatic—on what worked. C.J. was challenging me to take a radically different approach and base my choices on truth about God and what he was doing in the world.

Two days later, after the conference had ended and I was about to leave, I worked up the nerve to ask C.J. if he'd train me. "I want to learn from you," I told him. What I didn't know was that in the preceding months C.J. had felt God directing his attention to training the next generation of young pastors. My request was a confirmation of that new focus.

"I would be honored to serve you," C.J. said. "Go home, and if your parents and your pastors are supportive, we'll talk."

Less than seven months later, I packed my bags and headed east.

It took five days to drive from Oregon to Maryland. I got one ticket in

Idaho. I didn't even mind. I was glad to have proof that my dinky little Honda could actually break the speed limit.

———

After I got to Maryland, C.J. put me to work with a new study regimen. He gave me books by Iain H. Murray on Charles Spurgeon, including *Spurgeon v. Hyper-Calvinism* and *The Forgotten Spurgeon,* about the great pastor and his stand against the downgrading of gospel truth. He put in my hands books on practical theology, including Jerry Bridges's *The Discipline of Grace* and J. C. Ryle's *Holiness.* He assigned me messages by David Powlison, a biblical counseling expert, about progressive sanctification. I became the proud owner of Wayne Grudem's *Systematic Theology,* a textbook fatter than a phone book. And I read John Stott's *The Cross of Christ.*

It took me awhile to get used to reading meatier books about theology. Many times while reading Stott's book on the Cross, I underlined and highlighted points that I thought were good only to find at the end of the chapter that Mr. Stott had been sharing them as examples of error. I felt stupid, but I was learning.

But more than digging into the books, I studied C.J. himself. Living with C.J. and his family, I saw what he was like behind the scenes—at the end of the day when he was tired. When his four-year-old son was acting up. When people slandered him. I learned that pastoring a big church isn't glamorous. It's hard work that involves constantly carrying people on your heart—the sick, the wandering, the weak. In it all I saw C.J.'s joy—a joy always grounded in the fact that Jesus had died for his sins. I heard him confess his sin. The authenticity I witnessed in those moments made me want the knowledge of God that C.J. was building his life on.

For different reasons many Christians in my generation and older generations are leery of too much emphasis on doctrine. They have come to equate doctrine with church splits, hate mail, arrogance, and angry diatribes. They have seen how easy it is for life-giving truths to be reduced to empty formulas. No wonder that, for them, Christian doctrine can seem more hindrance than help when it comes to cultivating a vibrant relationship with Jesus.

I understand. If my heart is cold toward God, I can turn the most precious truth into an end in itself or a weapon to attack others. This is part of the reason I find the story of the wise builder so instructive. It reminds me that doctrine isn't about me or my little tribe. Jesus said that the person who digs down to the rock is the one who comes to *him*. This has to be the first and final motivation. Pursuing orthodoxy and sound doctrine has to begin with a heart drawing close to Jesus—not to a theological system, denomination, or book.

It's easy to make the mistake of thinking that since theological beliefs shouldn't be our goal, we don't need them at all. But this isn't true in knowing Jesus any more than it's true in other relationships. For example, I have a nine-year-old daughter named Emma, whom I love very much. It is absolutely true that information and facts about my daughter can never take the place of actually loving her. But this doesn't mean I should avoid knowing about her. An important part of caring for and cultivating a relationship with my little girl involves my willingness to learn her character and personality, her likes and dislikes. Details about her—the color of her hair, the music she enjoys, her gifts, fears, and dreams—are all important to me because *she* is important to me. These truths about her could be empty data, but because they describe a living person whom I love, they enrich and grow my love for her. Facts can never take her place, but I can't know her without them.

Doctrine can never take the place of Jesus himself, but we can't know him and relate to him in the right way without doctrine. This is because doctrine tells us not only what God has done but also what his actions mean to us. A theologian named J. Gresham Machen, who wrote in the early part of the twentieth century, helped me better understand all this. His explanation of Christian doctrine helped me see how it connects to the living person of Jesus. In one of his books, Machen explains that while Christians in the early church wanted to know what Jesus taught, they were primarily concerned with what Jesus had *done*. "The world was to be redeemed," Machen writes, "through the proclamation of an event."

Of course the event he's referring to is Jesus's death by crucifixion and his resurrection from the dead. The first Christians knew they had to tell people about this event. But simply telling them wasn't enough. They also had to tell them what the event meant. And this, Machen explains, is doctrine. Doctrine is the setting forth of what Jesus has done along with the meaning of the event for us.

"These two elements are always combined in the Christian message," Machen continues. "The narration of the facts is history; the narration of the facts with the meaning of the facts is doctrine. 'Suffered under Pontius Pilate, was crucified, dead and buried'—that is history. 'He loved me and gave Himself for me'—that is doctrine."[1]

Doctrine is the meaning of the story God is writing in the world. It's the explanation of what he's done and why he's done it and why it matters to you and me.

Jesus's story of the two builders ends with one house standing firm through storms and the other house being washed away. The sand didn't hold, and the house came crashing down. The wind and waves Jesus spoke about might represent difficulties and trials in life. They could also be a symbol of the final judgment when all mankind will stand before Jesus and give an account. I suppose it's best to think of both. Both are going to happen. Trials and suffering will touch us all eventually. And the final day, even though it seems distant, will eventually arrive.

And in both cases, knowing and living by sound doctrine are of utmost importance. Why? Because on the final day only those who have believed in Jesus Christ and lived for him will be rescued from the wrath of God. And because in the present when our lives are shaken by suffering, firsthand knowledge of God's character and love is the only thing that can hold us.

I saw this reality in the life of my younger brother Joel and his wife, Kimberly. Not long after they married, they found out they were pregnant. You've never seen a more excited dad- and mom-to-be. And then the ultrasound results came back with devastating news. Their little girl's heart was missing a chamber. After she was born, doctors discovered further complications with her heart. Baby Faith, as they named her, had a very small chance to survive. She fought hard to live, but her tiny heart worked at just half capacity. Only a heart transplant could have saved her. When it didn't come and when her strength began to fail, doctors attempted emergency heart surgery. But during the procedure the surgeon made a mistake. Her heart was punctured, and she died. Two months after she came into the world, little Faith went to be with the Lord.

I'm eight years older than Joel. Watching my little brother and his wife walk through the sadness of losing a child was gut-wrenching. To borrow the imagery of Jesus's parable, it was like watching from a distance as the home they lived in was hit by a tidal wave. The wind and waves of suffering crashed like a tsunami against their life.

But when the water cleared, the house of their life stood firm and strong.

Joel and Kimberly felt deep grief; they experienced deep anguish of the soul. But they stood firm because they were rooted in a deep knowledge of God. They had built their lives on truth.

Each day during those difficult weeks before Faith's passing, I would read what Joel and Kimberly had written on the Web page where they shared updates and prayer requests for Faith. Over and over again they wrote about the confidence and hope they had in the truth of God's sovereignty. And after Faith passed away, they never blamed the surgeon. They were never bitter. They wrote about God's providence, his sovereign control of the situation, their gratefulness for the gospel.

When I think about Joel and Kimberly, I can't bear to hear people speak of doctrine as a meaningless pursuit of facts and figures and formulas. There's nothing more important, more precious, more life securing than knowing and living by God's truth.

———

If doctrine is only words on a page, it can be perceived as a bunch of lifeless rules or formulas. But when you see orthodoxy in the vibrant colors of a person's life—when you observe that person applying it with joy and humility—you see that it's beautiful. When you see someone walking in the old paths and being led to a deeper knowledge of Jesus, it makes you want to walk in them too. When you witness the strength and security that come with being dug down into doctrinal truth, it makes you want to dig into truth yourself.

And that is the purpose of this book. I write in the hope that you'll catch a glimpse of how good and beautiful the old paths of orthodoxy are, how firm and trustworthy the solid rock of sound doctrine can be for your life.

I hope these pages will inspire you to dig into the richness of theology.

The past ten years of my life have been the story of uncovering the relevance, the joy, and the practical power that come from Christian doctrine. Doctrine isn't dry and boring. It isn't just for arguing. It's for knowing God and living life to the fullest.

The following chapters are reflections on various Christian doctrines that have particularly touched my life. This isn't a book on systematic theology proper. It's more like a mixtape of biblical truth that I've found personally significant.

Dug Down Deep is my reveling in theology in my own simple way—not too polished, sometimes awkward, less than scholarly, hopefully gracious and faithful. Even though these are deep truths, I don't pretend to be swimming in the deep end of the pool. I'm splashing in the shallow end. But if my splashing can inspire you to dive in, I will have succeeded.

A few years ago I was back in my hometown in Oregon to visit my family. While I was there, I saw Steve, the youth pastor from the church I'd grown up in (the big evangelical church where I danced like Michael Jackson). We bumped into each other in the produce section of the local grocery store. I hadn't seen him for years. He had known me when I was a cocky thirteen-year-old with Aqua Net–soaked hair. Now I was married, a father who drove a minivan, and had shaved my head as a preemptive strike against baldness.

Steve hadn't changed at all. He'd always loved to work out and was still ripped. His eyes were still bright with life. It was good to see him. We started talking about old times, and then he told me how things were going at the youth group now. A lot had changed since the days I was there, he said. He had learned so much in the past decade about what kids really needed. Now he had students studying doctrine from *Systematic Theology,* Grudem's hefty textbook that is normally used in seminaries. The students were undaunted by its size. In fact, they liked the challenge. "They're eating it up," he told me. "These kids are on fire for God like you wouldn't believe. They're sharing their faith with friends. It's incredible."

I left the grocery store that day smiling. I thought about God having mercy on a hypocritical punk of a church kid like me. He'd replaced my love for the world with a love for Jesus and his truth. I'd gone from scraping the surface of shallow Christianity to being a young pastor who loved digging into doctrine. I was learning how to build my life on the rock and to lead others in doing the same.

And I smiled as I imagined Steve with a new generation of church kids studying theology and finding that exciting. That made my day. I pictured Steve in one of his muscle shirts tearing into the ground with a big old shovel. I imagined him handing out shovels to all those kids in the youth group. Teaching them how to dig deep.

3

NEAR BUT NOT
IN MY POCKET

*"God is utterly different from me.
And that is utterly wonderful."*

THERE'S THIS COFFEE SHOP about ten minutes from my house where I spend a fair amount of time. I'll go there to study or work on a sermon. I usually sit at the table in the far right-hand corner, the one next to the electric outlet. If I stay long enough, the smell of roasted coffee beans soaks into my clothes. The aroma smells good while I'm there, but for some reason, after I leave, I smell like I've been chain-smoking. My wife can always tell if I've been at the coffee shop all day. When I come home, she will kiss me and say, "Hey, smoker." That always makes me smile.

One side of the coffee shop is lined with big windows that look out on a sidewalk. When I sit facing the wall of windows, I find it entertaining to watch people as they walk by, because almost every person uses the windows as a mirror. Those on the outside have to purposely focus their eyes to see inside, where the lighting is low. It's much easier just to look at their own reflections.

If you've ever watched people look at themselves in a mirror, you know how amusing this can be. I've noticed that women give themselves the once-over very quickly. Their eyes dart up and down in a millisecond. A lot of them do this funny pouty thing with their mouths. Or they purse their lips like a lipstick model. Then they tug on some part of their clothing and move on. Men are different. Some lift their heads and straighten their backs. Others tilt their heads down and narrow their eyes as if they're James Dean.

I've learned that everyone has a mirror face—that facial expression we put on when we check ourselves out in a mirror. It's the way we think we look most attractive. So we smile a certain way or arch our eyebrows or suck in our cheeks or cock our heads. The funny thing about a mirror face is that it looks ridiculous to other people. If we walked around wearing our mirror faces, our friends would laugh at us, and strangers would think we had some kind of rock-star complex.

Sitting in the coffee shop, I watch people flash their mirror faces as they pass by the windows. I find it funny that they forget people like me are inside looking out at them. They see only themselves.

People's mirror faces got me thinking about theology. But let me back up first. The study of theology encompasses many different subjects: God's church, God's plan of salvation, God's work in us to make us like Jesus, to name a few. But when we focus on God himself—who he is and what he is like—we're touching the *heart* of theology. In fact, the doctrine of God is called *theology proper,* because that's what the word *theology* means: the study of God. In this chapter we're launching into an examination of key Christian beliefs. And I think the doctrine of God, or theology proper, is a good place for us to start, because what we think about God—what we understand about his character and his attributes—shapes our understanding of every other doctrine and even life itself.

There's nothing more important than rightly knowing God and thinking true thoughts about him. But there's also nothing I find more difficult. And that's not for the reason you might assume.

You would think the hardest thing about studying the doctrine of God is that God is so immense it's impossible for our limited minds to comprehend him. And in one sense this is true. Because God is infinite and we are limited, finite creatures, we can never have a complete knowledge of him. God is incomprehensible. He is great beyond all bounds. But while we can't know God exhaustively, we can know him truly. This is only possible because God has revealed truths about himself. And while these are deep truths and God's greatness surpasses all human measurements, what God has revealed about himself in his Word is truth we can grasp.

What makes it difficult for us to see the truth about God, I think, isn't his overwhelming immensity but our overwhelming self-centeredness. Looking past ourselves is a lot harder to do than most of us realize. Many have never tried. In this way we're a lot like the people walking past the windows of the coffee shop. Instead of looking through the window of God's self-revelation and seeing him, we find it easier to admire our own reflection or to place on him the constraints of our own existence. We judge him by our standards of justice, fairness, power, and mercy. We even measure his greatness by our own ideals of greatness.

The ironic thing about these moments is that we often think we're seeing God. We think we know something about what he is like. But we're seeing mostly a reflection—a God who looks a lot like us. A God imagined in our own image.

A few years back a couple of sociologists named Christian Smith and Melinda Denton published the first results of their study on the religious beliefs of teenagers in America. I'm not really into studies or statistics. In fact, as soon as someone mentions a statistic, my eyes start to glaze over. But when I read the findings of this study, they caught my attention, because in many ways I felt they describe how I viewed and related to God in high school. And also because the findings show that most people today imagine God as they'd like him to be—a God who caters to their personal needs and desires.

In their book *Soul Searching,* Smith and Denton describe the prevalent view of God among teenagers as "moralistic therapeutic deism." Now that's a mouthful, but let me explain.

A *moralistic* outlook says if I live a moral life, do good things, and try not to do bad things, God will reward me and send me to a "better place" when I die. For most people a good life involves not killing other people or robbing old ladies and babies. The bar is not real high.

A *therapeutic* orientation to God says his primary reason for existing is to make me happy and peaceful. So God is a form of therapy, of self-help. He exists for me.

Deism says God exists but he's distant and mostly uninvolved. Or we could say *conveniently* uninvolved. He won't interrupt my plans or get in my business. He doesn't tell me what to do.

"In short," Smith and Denton write, "God is something like a combination Divine Butler and Cosmic Therapist: he is always on call, takes care of any problems that arise, professionally helps his people to feel better about themselves, and does not become too personally involved in the process."

They quote a seventeen-year-old girl from Florida who said, "God's all around you, all the time. He believes in forgiving people and whatnot and he's there to guide us, for somebody to talk to and help us through our problems. Of course, he doesn't talk back."[1]

Some of us might have a more sophisticated description of God than this seventeen-year-old. We might even have enough theological knowledge to give a very different description. But I wonder how different our functional view of God is from hers. I would never dare to call God my Divine Butler or Cosmic Therapist, but how often do I treat him as if he were? Do I live in a way that proves I have great and true thoughts of God?

"We are a modern people," writes J. I. Packer, "and modern people, though they cherish great thoughts of themselves, have as a rule small thoughts of God." He goes on to point out that just because God is personal (meaning we can speak to him, relate to him, and know him) doesn't mean he's the same sort of person that we are—"weak, inadequate, ineffective, a little pathetic." Packer says, "Our personal life is a finite thing: it is limited in every direction, in space, in time, in knowledge, in power. But God is not so limited. He is eternal, infinite and almighty. He has us in his hands; we never have him in ours. Like us, he is personal; but unlike us, he is *great*."[2]

What do I see about God when I look past my own reflection? In the Bible—the primary place God reveals himself—I behold a God who is utterly and wonderfully different from me.

I am created. *God is Creator.* I am made. God is the one who made all things, who "created the heavens and the earth" (Genesis 1:1). He spoke and created the world out of nothing.

I have a beginning. I was conceived in my mother's womb in the year 1974. Before that I didn't exist. *God is eternal.* God has no beginning and no end. He exists outside of time and space. Psalm 90:2 says, "Before the mountains were brought forth, or ever you had formed the earth and the world, from everlasting to everlasting you are God."

I am dependent. I need air to breathe, water to drink, food to eat, or my body dies. *God is self-existent.* He does not rely on anything outside of himself. He has life in himself and draws his unending energy from himself.[3] God "does not live in temples made by man, nor is he served by human hands, as though he needed anything, since he himself gives to all mankind life and breath and everything" (Acts 17:24–25).

I am limited in space. I can be in only one place at one time. *God is omnipresent.* He is everywhere always present. "God is spirit" and not limited by space (John 4:24). God says of himself, "Am I a God at hand, declares the LORD, and not a God far away? Can a man hide himself in secret places so that I cannot see him? declares the LORD. Do I not fill heaven and earth? declares the LORD" (Jeremiah 23:23–24).

I am limited in power. There are limits to how fast I can run. How much weight I can lift. How high I can jump. *God is almighty.* He is omnipotent—possessing all power. Nothing is too hard for him (Jeremiah 32:17). He can do all things, and no purpose of his can be thwarted (Job 42:2).

I am limited in knowledge. My knowledge of any subject is at best partial. No matter how much I study, it is still incomplete. I can know only what I observe, read, or am told by someone else. And my mind can forget some or all that I've learned. *God is all-knowing.* He is omniscient—he has full knowledge of all things past, present, and future. Job 37:16 tells us that God is "perfect in knowledge." And Hebrews 4:13 says, "And no creature is hidden from his sight, but all are naked and exposed to the eyes of him to whom we must give account."

God isn't a bigger, better version of me. "It is not just that we exist and God has always existed," writes Wayne Grudem, "it is also that God *necessarily* exists in an infinitely better, stronger, more excellent way. The difference between God's being and ours is more than the difference between the sun and a candle, more than the difference between the ocean and a raindrop, more than the difference between the arctic ice cap and a snowflake, more than the difference between the universe and the room we are sitting in: God's being is *qualitatively different.*"[4]

The qualitative difference of God, his "otherliness" revealed in his divine attributes, is summed up in the word *holy.* In Isaiah's vision of God on his throne, the angels covered their eyes and feet before God and cried, "Holy, holy, holy is the LORD of hosts; the whole earth is full of his glory!" (Isaiah 6:3).

I used to think of God's holiness only in terms of moral purity. But R. C. Sproul taught me that holiness primarily speaks of God being separate from his creation in his perfection and power. God's holiness means that he is transcendent—that he exceeds all limitations. That God is holy means that he is above us and beyond us.

"When the Bible calls God holy," writes Sproul, "it means primarily that God is transcendentally separate. He is so far above and beyond us that He seems almost totally foreign to us."[5]

I remember one of the first times I experienced the practical power of truth about God in my life. It wasn't long after I moved to Maryland. I was single, wanting to get married, interested in several girls (one of whom was Shannon), but unsure about when and with whom I should pursue a relationship. I was confused, impatient, and acutely aware of how little I knew about the future. I wanted God to tell me what to do. I wanted a girl's name written in the sky.

During that time I'd been studying God's attributes, in particular his sovereignty. I was learning that God had total power and authority over everything. He was sovereign over every molecule of the universe (Hebrews 1:3). Over every kingdom and earthly authority (Psalm 47:8). Over every human heart (Proverbs 21:1).

One day as I was walking and praying, I began to reflect on Romans 8:30, where Paul describes God's sovereignty in salvation: "And those whom he predestined he also called, and those whom he called he also justified, and those whom he justified he also glorified." I was overwhelmed by the thought that God knew me before I was born. The awesome implications of this truth flooded my mind. For God to see me down through time, for him to bring about my life, he had to sovereignly direct a billion countless details.

God was sovereign in the emigration of my great-grandparents from Japan. He was sovereign over the mortar in World War II that exploded near my grandfather and caused him to lose his leg, sending him to the hospital where he met my grandmother. For God to see me, he had to see both of my parents and all the moments and days of their two lives that would lead to their marriage and my birth.

The reality of God holding all human history in his hands—including my little life and my little questions—filled me with awe. God saw my past, present, and future perfectly. He had mercifully saved me. He had promised that one day I would be glorified. In light of all this, there was no reason to doubt him. I could trust him with my questions about marriage and my future.

None of my questions were answered. I still didn't know whom I was supposed to marry. I didn't know anything more about my future. But I was filled with the most amazing sense of peace as I considered the awesome God who was sovereign over all.

God's attributes are not merely a list of facts and features. They are truths that inform belief and inspire faith. God reveals truth about himself in his Word, not for the sake of knowledge, but for the sake of relationship with us. He tells us about himself so we will put our faith in him, so we will treasure and worship him and not waste ourselves on man-made idols. He wants our souls to soar in worship and communion with him—not rot in the pursuit of sin or waste away in worry and fear.

God is different from you and me. He is utterly different. And that is utterly wonderful.

There is surprising comfort in the realization that God is so unlike you and me. The fact that he's not like us is the reason we can run to him for rescue.

It's good news that God doesn't think and act the way we do. As he invites us to approach him to receive mercy and pardon, he holds out wonderful news: "For my thoughts are not your thoughts, neither are your ways my ways, declares the LORD. For as the heavens are higher than the earth, so are my ways higher than your ways and my thoughts than your thoughts" (Isaiah 55:8–9).

God is not like us. He's strong. He's unchanging. His love is steadfast (Psalm 136:1). He is full of mercy. And he does what we would never do, what we would never imagine: he dies for his enemies. "God shows his love for us in that while we were still sinners, Christ died for us" (Romans 5:8).

———

Once, as I was shopping at a mall, I noticed a woman working at a kiosk that sold beads and jewelry. She had no customers. She was leafing through a magazine. And I had a strong sense that I should talk to her about God. Trying to be bold, I walked up and said, "Excuse me, but I just felt that I was to tell you that God loves you."

She looked up from her magazine with the most bored, disinterested expression imaginable, raised one eyebrow, and said, "I know that," and immediately turned back to her magazine. I froze. I had no idea what to say next, so I turned and walked away.

I left thinking two things. First, that I stink at evangelism and that telling someone God loves them is a dumb way to start a conversation. But the second thing I realized was that, like this woman, a lot of people take lightly the idea of God loving them because they have no idea who he is.

Most people seem to assume it's God's job to love them. *Of course God loves us. What else does he have to do?* He is weak, small, and maybe even a little nerdy. He needs us. He pines for us. And if we pay him any attention— go to church, do a good deed, recycle, or maybe meditate while listening to soothing music—then we've done him a really big favor.

The love of God is wonderful news only when we understand his transcendence—when we tremble at his holiness, when we're awed by his perfection and power. God's love is perceived as amazing only when we realize that the one thing we truly deserve from him is righteous wrath and eternal punishment for our disobedience and disloyalty.

Seeing God for who he is leaves us asking with the psalmist, "What is man that you are mindful of him, and the son of man that you care for him?" (Psalm 8:4).

Careful study of the character and attributes of God should leave us feeling more amazed, more loved, and more secure in God's love. But this happens in the most surprising way. We become more confident of God's love for us as we understand we are not the center of the universe. God is. God is not centering himself around us and our worth. God is centered on his own eternal glory.

I remember the first time I heard someone articulate a biblical vision of a God-centered God. I was in Austin, Texas, listening to John Piper preach at Louie Giglio's Passion conference in 1998. The theme verse for the event was Isaiah 26:8: "Yes, LORD, walking in the way of your laws, we wait for you; your name and renown are the desire of our hearts" (NIV). The messages were focused on God's fame and renown.

The irony about my participation in a conference dedicated to God's glory was how consumed I was the whole time with my own glory. My first book had been released the year prior, and I found myself constantly wondering if people would recognize me, if they'd know who I was. I loved glory. But it wasn't God's glory that captured my heart. I wanted my own glory.

Piper's message was a stinging balm for my soul. He preached about God's passion for his glory. He explained how the major obstacle to glorifying God is a secular mind-set that begins with man as the starting point of life and reality. With this mind-set, he said, problems and successes are defined by us and our goals and priorities.

But the biblical mind-set, as Piper called it, is completely opposite. Here the starting point is God. His rights and goals define reality. We talk of human rights and civil rights, Piper said, but never of Creator rights. I'd never thought of that before. The implication was that what constitutes a problem in this universe is not what upsets my itsy-bitsy world of clothes, sex, food, relationships, traffic, and television. No, what constitutes a problem is anything that contradicts the goals and plans of this Creator.

Then Piper asked what the basic riddle of the universe really is. Is it the question, why is there suffering in the world? No, said Piper, not for the person with a biblical mind-set. The question for this God-centered person is, why is there any goodness for a sinner like me? How can God—a holy and righteous God—pass over the sins of man? Why doesn't he wipe us out?

I was ashamed to admit the question never kept me up at night. I had a small view of God's holiness and righteousness and an inflated view of my worth and value.

Piper continued to press the question, how can God be good and forgive sinners? He used the hypothetical illustration of a failed attempt by terrorists to destroy the White House and kill the president. If the terrorists are brought to trial and the judge forgives them, gives them a vacation, and sends them on their way, what will other nations assume about this judge? They'll think he is crazy or has been bought off. Or at least assume he has no respect for the law.

So it is with God's glory, Piper explained. If God passed over sin and brought no punishment, what else could we assume about his character except that he was less than perfect?

Then Piper pointed to the Cross. On Calvary, God displayed his justice and his love. He was glorified in the death of his Son. He loves his glory that much! And how great was the glory of the death and resurrection of the one and only Christ—the very Son of God! "The foundation of your salvation," Piper said, "is God's love for His own glory."

I'd never heard anyone speak that way about Jesus's death on the cross. I had always heard it explained in terms of my great worth. I am so valuable that God would send Jesus to die. The question Piper closed his message with deeply challenged me. "Do you love the Cross because it makes much of you?" he asked. "Or do you love it because it enables you to enjoy an eternity of making much of God?"

I left Austin with an unsettling thought that has never left me. If I love the Cross only for what it does for me, I will have reduced it to a monument to myself. But the greatest glory of the Cross is what it tells me about God. A God of justice and mercy. A God who loved helpless sinners like me so much that he came to die so we could be free to know and worship him for eternity.

In my high school youth group, we used to sing a song about how God is transcendent but also immanent and close to us. Actually, at the time I didn't know what the song was about. I didn't understand it. The words said,

> This is what the high and lofty one says,
> He who lives forever, holy is his name.
> "I dwell in a high and lofty place
> And with the lowly in spirit."

Our worship leader would have the guys and girls sing it as a round. That always sounded pretty cool. But I didn't know what it meant. Somehow I missed that the words of the song were drawn from Isaiah 57:15, which says,

> For thus says the One who is high and lifted up,
>   who inhabits eternity, whose name is Holy:
> "I dwell in the high and holy place,
>   and also with him who is of a contrite and lowly spirit,
> to revive the spirit of the lowly,
>   and to revive the heart of the contrite."

What this verse is saying, and what we used to sing about, is the incredible reality that the God who "inhabits eternity" and who is holy and transcendent—that is, totally separate and different from us—is also the God who draws close to men and women who are contrite and humble before him. God is immanent; he is near. Jesus is called Emmanuel, God with us.

I wish I'd understood the richness and wonder of the doctrine I was singing. The lofty One of heaven is also the near-at-hand One who revives the hearts of the lowly. The awesome God who transcends all creation condescends to dwell with the weak and helpless in the person of his Son. This is amazing.

We have to hold these two truths about God together. If we lose our grasp on either one, our vision of God will be distorted. If we focus only on God's transcendence, we push him out of the picture of human life. We end up acting as though God is so far away that he's nowhere to be seen. Or that, being so distant, he won't mind if we ignore him.

The opposite extreme is to bring God so close that we strip him of his "godness." These days I would guess it is the more common error. Most people I talk to aren't afraid of or even in awe of God. They think they have him figured out. So God becomes our pal, our buddy, our Divine Butler. His nearness isn't so much celebrated as it is taken for granted. He is close and familiar and commonplace. God is near, but we've made him small—so small that we can carry him around in our pocket like a good-luck charm.

To know and relate to God as we should, we must remember that God is both *transcendent* and *immanent*. God is so far above us in power and glory. But not far-off, disinterested, or disengaged. He is, as the psalmist says, at our right hand, upholding those who trust in him (Psalm 16:8).

I knew a girl who used to think the stars were tiny specks of light just over her head. I'm not kidding. And she wasn't in grade school when she believed this. She was in college. She was a really sweet, kind redhead who spoke almost perfect Spanish. She was intelligent in many ways. But one day in a conversation, she mentioned that she had just learned that stars in the night sky were actually really far away. I asked her what she meant.

She said, "You know, they're not just right up there. They're not just tiny little dots. They're really far, far away."

I was incredulous.

"What did you think they were before?" I asked.

"I thought they were, you know, just right up above us."

If you were to ask me why it matters that we study the doctrine of God, I'd say for the same reason that it's worth knowing that stars are not tiny pinpricks of light just above our heads. When we know the truth about God, it fills us with wonder. If we fail to understand his true character, we'll never be amazed by him. We'll never feel small as we stare up at him. We'll never worship him as we ought. We'll never run to him for refuge or realize the great love he's shown in bridging the measureless distance to rescue us.

There is a right way and a wrong way to approach the doctrine of God. We can study God with a microscope or a telescope. A microscope makes something very small look big. But this isn't the way we are to magnify God. When we do, we're like scientists in a sterile laboratory magnifying something miniscule for the sake of scientific categorization. But we're not bigger than God, capable of numbering and naming his parts.

Instead we should study God's attributes the way an astronomer studies a heavenly body—through a telescope. Its lenses enable us to see just how much bigger and more awesome something is than we first imagined.[6]

When we study the doctrine of God, there should be a sense of awe in our hearts. We should be like children with a telescope under a starry night sky. Then we will be filled with amazement that Someone so great—so transcendent—can be known and seen by us. We will rightly feel small and insignificant as we realize how great and powerful the God we're beholding really is.

The more you learn of who God truly is, the more incredible his invitation to know him becomes. When you know him as the infinite, almighty, holy, eternal God of heaven, the announcement that he loves you takes on a whole new meaning. It's not expected. It's not commonplace. It is cause for astonishment.

The high and lofty One offers to draw near to those who are humble. He sent his Son to die so that the One of perfect holiness could dwell among us. God is near. But we don't manage or contain him. He's not in our pockets. The almighty One is holding us in *his* hands.

4

RIPPING, BURNING, EATING

"When we read the Bible,
it opens us up. It reads us."

A. J. JACOBS MAKES a living being a human guinea pig. He puts himself through offbeat, strange life experiments, then he writes about them. Once for an article in *Esquire* called "My Outsourced Life," Jacobs hired a team of people in Bangalore, India, to live his life for him. They answered his e-mails, called his co-workers, argued with his wife, and read bedtime stories to his son. His first book was about the year he spent reading the entire *Encyclopedia Britannica* in a quest to become the smartest person in the world.

A more recent book entitled *The Year of Living Biblically* follows a similar pattern. It's the story of how Jacobs attempted to follow every rule in the Bible as literally as possible for an entire year. You should know that Jacobs is an agnostic. "I am officially Jewish," he writes, "but I'm Jewish in the same way the Olive Garden is an Italian restaurant. Which is to say: not very."[1]

Jacobs started his experiment with a visit to a Christian bookstore in midtown Manhattan. He needed to purchase a Bible and supplemental study tools. A soft-spoken salesman named Chris helped him sort through the different sizes of Bibles and linguistic options. Then he pointed out a unique Bible version for teenage girls that was designed to look exactly like a *Seventeen* magazine. "This one's good if you're on the subway and are too embarrassed to be seen reading the Bible," said Chris. "Because no one will ever know it's a Bible." Jacobs's response is one of my favorite lines in the book: "You know you're in a secular city when it's considered more acceptable for a grown man to read a teen girl's magazine than the Bible."[2]

Jacobs left the store with two shopping bags filled with Scripture. He then proceeded to read through the entire Bible in four weeks. As he read, he wrote down every rule or direction that he came across—big and small. That included obvious ones like the Ten Commandments and "love your neighbor" but also lesser known Old Testament laws for diet and ritual cleanliness. His goal was to take the Bible at face value, as literally as possible, and put it all into practice.

As you can imagine, the outcome was often hilarious.

For example, because the book of Leviticus says men should leave the edges of their beards unshaven, Jacobs stopped shaving. Within a few months he looked like a lost member of ZZ Top. He stopped wearing clothing made of mixed fibers. He played a ten-string harp. He refused to shake hands with women who might be ceremonially unclean because they were having their periods, which involved his asking every woman he knew about her monthly cycle. (Oddly enough, the women in his office were happy to supply him with their information on Excel spreadsheets.)

Possibly his most outlandish activity was his attempt to stone adulterers. He accomplished this by trying to fling tiny pebbles at strangers without their noticing. Evidently Jacobs assumed that just about any New Yorker is an adulterer.

His book is a gimmick, but it also raises serious questions about what it means to live by the Bible. Do growing a beard and playing a harp equal living biblically? More important, how should we think about the Bible? Does Scripture have the authority to tell us how to live? Or is the Bible just a bunch of archaic rules and rituals that have no meaning in our modern world?

———

In one sense I think the Bible would be easier to understand, easier to manage, if it were just a rule book about diet and facial hair and sexual behavior. I don't know if you've ever thought about this, but we humans do rule books quite well. And I don't mean just religious books. Every year a new stack of books about diet and lifestyle and time management tells us exactly what to eat, how to exercise, and how to spend our time. We dutifully buy these books and then obey them like slaves. For a month or two—till we realize we're still fat and disorganized. Then we go looking for a new book to boss us around.

Basically Jacobs approached the Bible as the ultimate rule book. But while he submitted his life to an ancient book, he didn't encounter the Person speaking through the book. He didn't know or even believe in the God of the Bible—the God who comes looking for us through his living Word.

The Bible is much more wonderful and dangerous and radically life transforming than a mere book of instructions. But you won't understand it or gain any benefit from it until you believe what the Bible claims about itself. The Bible presents itself as a living communication from a personal God to the human race—more specifically to *you*.

Stop and think about that for a moment. God speaking to you.

What an incredible claim. And yet this is what the Christian faith is built on—what it asserts without apology. God is. He exists. And as Francis Schaeffer expressed it in the title of a book, "He is not silent." God speaks. He communicates. And he has ordained that his words be recorded in the signs and symbols of our human languages—written and printed on paper in a book that we can hold in our hands.

———

When we talk about the *doctrine of Scripture,* we mean all that the Bible teaches us about itself: what the Bible is, where it comes from, what its characteristics are, and how we're to read it and obey it. Getting the doctrine of Scripture right is essential for having a solid foundation as a Christian. If you don't understand that God has spoken through the Bible, or don't trust the Bible, how can you know him or cultivate a real relationship with him?

The doctrine of Scripture is uniquely important among Christian doctrines because it touches every other Christian belief. What we know about God and salvation we know because God reveals it to us in the Bible. In other words, we only have a doctrine of God and a doctrine of the atonement if we believe that Scripture can be understood and that it's true (without error).

So Scripture is the foundation of every other Christian belief. Ephesians 2:20 tells us that the church is "built on the foundation of the apostles and prophets, Christ Jesus himself being the cornerstone." While Jesus is always the cornerstone of God's church, the church also rests on the solid foundation of the teaching and preaching of the apostles and prophets that are recorded in the Bible. God commissioned the prophets; Jesus commissioned the apostles. They were the appointed spokesmen for God. And that's why we honor their teachings. Their words written down for us in Scripture form the basis of our faith and practice as followers of Jesus Christ.

Hebrews 1:1–2 says, "Long ago, at many times and in many ways, God spoke to our fathers by the prophets, but in these last days he has spoken to us by his Son." God's communication to mankind—first through the prophets and then through Jesus—is what the Bible records. It tells us who God is and how he has acted in human history. Then it explains the meaning of his actions.

While we can learn some things about God by observing his creation (Romans 1:19–20), this knowledge is limited. We are dependent on divine revelation from God in Scripture. We need God to speak and to reveal himself to us.

This is why we have the Bible. It's not just a relic of an ancient religion. Apart from the communication of God in the Bible, apart from revelation, we could not know God or understand his activity in the world. This is called the *necessity* of Scripture, meaning that Scripture is necessary for us to know and obey God.

There is no genuine spirituality apart from God's Word. We need God's self-revelation to know what he is like. We need revelation to know who we are and why we exist. We need revelation to explain our purpose and the eternal significance of life on this planet. We need revelation to know we're sinners and deserving of judgment. And we need revelation to know the good news of salvation through faith in Jesus.

Without the Bible there is no saving knowledge of God. Without the Bible we would not know or understand the meaning of the Cross and Resurrection. Without the Bible there is nothing for us to put our faith in. Romans 10:17 says, "So faith comes from hearing, and hearing through the word of Christ."

———

My earliest memories of the Bible involve comic books. As a kid I had been given a set of three paperbacks that presented the Bible in comic-book form. I would pore over them.

I especially loved the Old Testament. Even as a kid I had a sense of it being slightly illicit. As though someone had slipped an R-rated action movie into a pile of Disney DVDs. For starters Adam and Eve were naked on the first page. I was fascinated by Eve's ability to always stand in the Garden of Eden so that a tree branch or leaf was covering her private areas like some kind of organic bikini.

But it was the Bible's murder and mayhem that really got my attention. When I started reading the real Bible, I spent most of my time in Genesis, Exodus, 1 and 2 Samuel, and 1 and 2 Kings. Talk about violent. Cain killed Abel. The Egyptians fed babies to alligators. Moses killed an Egyptian. God killed thousands of Egyptians in the Red Sea. David killed Goliath and won a girl by bringing a bag of two hundred Philistine foreskins to his future father-in-law. I couldn't believe that Mom was so happy about my spending time each morning reading about gruesome battles, prostitutes, fratricide, murder, and adultery. What a way to have a "quiet time."

While I grew up with a fairly solid grasp of Bible stories, I didn't have a clear idea of how the Bible fit together or what it was all about. I certainly didn't understand how the exciting stories of the Old Testament connected to the rather less-exciting New Testament and the story of Jesus.

This concept of the Bible as a bunch of disconnected stories sprinkled with wise advice and capped off with the inspirational life of Jesus seems fairly common among Christians. That is so unfortunate, because to see the Bible as one book with one author and all about one main character is to see it in its breathtaking beauty.

Since I started caring about theology, I've learned that an important part of being grounded in truth is not only believing that the Bible is God's Word but also understanding the story line of the Bible from start to finish. The Bible is both doctrine and narrative. It not only presents us with true principles and propositions but also uses the power of story to show us how God works and acts in human history.

I've been helped by books like Graeme Goldsworthy's *Gospel and Kingdom* and Vaughan Robert's *God's Big Picture* that unpack what is called biblical theology. Unlike systematic theology, which pulls together the teaching of Scripture on specific topics, biblical theology is concerned with what we learn about God and his plan of salvation through the story line of the Bible. Biblical theology shows us how it all connects, how God's plan unfolds from Genesis to Revelation.

Ironically, one of the most helpful books I've read on biblical theology is one for children called *The Jesus Storybook Bible* by Sally Lloyd-Jones. Here's part of the introduction from that book, which I think is beautiful:

> Now, some people think the Bible is a book of rules, telling you what you should do and shouldn't do. The Bible certainly does have some rules in it. They show you how life works best. But the Bible isn't mainly about you and what you should be doing. It's about God and what he has done.
>
> Other people think the Bible is a book of heroes, showing you people you should copy. The Bible does have some heroes in it, but (as you'll soon find out) most of the people in the Bible aren't heroes at all. They make some big mistakes (sometimes on purpose). They get afraid and run away. At times they are downright mean.
>
> No, the Bible isn't a book of rules, or a book of heroes. The Bible is most of all a Story. It's an adventure story about a young Hero who comes from a far country to win back his lost treasure. It's a love story about a brave Prince who leaves his palace, his throne—everything—

to rescue the one he loves. It's like the most wonderful of fairy tales that has come true in real life!

You see, the best thing about the Story is—it's true.

There are lots of stories in the Bible, but all the stories are telling one Big Story. The Story of how God loves his children and comes to rescue them.

It takes the whole Bible to tell this Story. And at the center of the Story, there is a baby. Every Story in the Bible whispers his name. He is like the missing piece in a puzzle—the piece that makes all the other pieces fit together, and suddenly you can see a beautiful picture.[3]

I remember the night I first read this passage to my kids. I was so moved that tears filled my eyes. My kids, of course, were bewildered. "Daddy, are you crying?" they asked. I tried to explain that I was and it was because I was overwhelmed with gratefulness for God's Word and for Jesus. I kept saying, "I wish you could understand how good this is!"

The Bible is one story—the story of God's purpose to save sinners through the sacrifice of his Son in place of those sinners. The laws and rituals of diet and cleanliness given in Leviticus, which A. J. Jacobs attempted to obey so fastidiously, were never given to save but were given to point to mankind's inability to save itself.

Only Jesus can perfectly obey. And in the Bible every page, every story whispers his name. When God tells Abraham not to sacrifice his only son, Isaac, but promises to supply the sacrifice, Jesus, "the lamb of God," is anticipated. When David defeats Goliath, it's a preview of Jesus—the ultimate Champion who will one day conquer death itself on behalf of his people.

The Bible is the story of Jesus (John 5:39–40, 46–47). And it's the truth of Jesus. All of Scripture is given to us so we can know him and love him. Revelation is for relationship.

In his book *God Has Spoken,* J. I. Packer asks why God speaks to us through his Word. "The truly staggering answer which the Bible gives to this question is that God's purpose in revelation is to *make friends* with us." He goes on to explain that God created us in his image so we could commune with him in a two-sided relationship of affection and love. This was God's purpose when he created Adam and Eve. This is his purpose in overthrowing the curse of sin—enabling us to be his children, to relate to him as Father. "God's friendship with men and women begins and grows through speech," Packer continues. "His to us in revelation, and ours to Him in prayer and praise. Though I cannot see God, He and I can yet be personal friends, because in revelation He talks to me."[4]

When God tells us truth about himself *through stories* and *through doctrine,* his purpose is relationship. The statements "God is love" and "God is holy" are propositional statements—they're doctrinal truths. But they're also deeply relational. Only by knowing truth about who God is can we have a real relationship with him. But God also uses stories to teach us and reveal himself to us. The Bible isn't limited to one or the other, and they're not at odds. Through both, God is speaking and revealing himself to us so we can truly know him.

———

In 2 Timothy 3:16 the apostle Paul says, "All Scripture is God-breathed" (NIV). It's hard to imagine a phrase that could more strongly communicate the connection between God and Scripture. It is not merely God-blessed or God-sanctioned. Scripture is God-breathed. "It is not a matter of God adding to what men had written," Sinclair Ferguson explains, "but of God being the origin, the source of what has been written."[5] As if when we read, he himself were speaking again, his breath rustling past us.

The process of inspiration—the way in which God directed the writing of Scripture—wasn't always the same. In some cases, as with the apostle John, God said, "Write this down" and then gave specific instructions (Revelation 21:5). But most of the time, God worked through seemingly normal means. Nehemiah wrote a first-person account. A scribe named Baruch wrote down Jeremiah's prophecies. Paul wrote letters. Luke documented eyewitness testimony in writing his gospel, then spent time traveling with Paul to write his history of the early church, found in Acts.

Yet 2 Peter 1:21 says, "For no prophecy was ever produced by the will of man, but men spoke from God as they were carried along by the Holy Spirit." God used human beings to write words, but he guided their minds and even life experiences and backgrounds to accomplish the final result. So although the human writers were very much in control of themselves, the Holy Spirit was guiding them to write the very words God wanted them to write.

Some people question the Bible because they say the church merely voted on what books to include in the New Testament. But this is a distortion of how we came to have the Bible as it is today. When the church affirmed the books that made up the Bible, they were simply acknowledging what had always been affirmed by the church from the earliest days—that the Old Testament and the writings of the apostles and their close associates whom Jesus commissioned to be his witnesses held a unique authority and were inspired. These books were acknowledged as the *canon,* a Greek word that means "staff or straight rod." *Canon* came to be used as a word for "measure" or "rule" and "came to be applied to the contents of the New Testament: together they formed the 'rule of faith and life' by which the whole Church and Christians individually governed their lives."[6]

While the ultimate affirmation of Scripture as God's Word is the testimony of Scripture itself, a second and important testimony is that of the church and individual believers down through the ages. When we read the words of Scripture in the Old and New Testaments, the Holy Spirit bears witness in our hearts that these words are unlike any others. Paul saw this effect when he preached to the Thessalonians. They received his apostolic teaching, not as the word of men, but "as what it really is, the word of God, which is at work in you believers" (1 Thessalonians 2:13). Believers everywhere can relate to this experience. Scripture speaks to our souls with a depth and intensity that is unmatched.

Hebrews 4:12–13 says, "For the word of God is living and active, sharper than any two-edged sword, piercing to the division of soul and of spirit, of joints and of marrow, and discerning the thoughts and intentions of the heart. And no creature is hidden from his sight, but all are naked and exposed to the eyes of him to whom we must give account." When we read it, the Bible opens *us* up. It reads us. It searches us in the deepest way possible. It reveals our hearts and motivations. It convicts and comforts us. When we read it, the Holy Spirit confirms in our hearts that it is not the word of men but the very Word of God himself. They are words unlike any other words on earth. They are true and eternal. Proverbs 30:5–6 says, "Every word of God proves true.... Do not add to his words, lest he rebuke you and you be found a liar."

And Jesus said, "Heaven and earth will pass away, but my words will not pass away" (Luke 21:33).

———

God honors those who revere and respect him and his Word—those who treat Scripture not as mere words on a page or human invention but as the holy, God-breathed, powerful, and authoritative words of the Almighty. God says in Isaiah 66:2, "But this is the one to whom I will look: he who is humble and contrite in spirit and trembles at my word."

My favorite story of humility before the authority of God's Word comes from the life of King Josiah. In his day the law of God had been lost—forgotten for decades. But 2 Kings 22 tells the story of the day when the lost scroll was discovered and brought before the king. Josiah was twenty-six years old. It was the defining moment of his life.

The Bible says that when Josiah heard the words of God—when he heard of God's holiness and the promises of blessing and judgment he gave to his people—he tore his royal robes. In ancient times to tear your robes was a symbol of deep anguish and grief. For the king to tear his robes was an act of humiliation—as if to say, "My position, my role mean nothing." It was a statement of sorrow and penitence. "You are God; you are right, and I am wrong."

Josiah tore his robes. And he wept.

God was watching. And the Bible says that God was pleased. God said to Josiah, "Because you humbled yourself, because you were penitent, because you wept, I have heard you." He promised to show Josiah mercy (see 2 Kings 22:18–20).

I guess all humans have wondered, *When I pray, does God hear me?* But what this story teaches is that the questions we should ask are, *Am I hearing God through his Word? Am I listening to him? Am I trembling before his Word?*

———

"I asked God for a sign," she told me. My fellow pastor Isaac and I were meeting with a young woman in the church who was ensnared in an immoral relationship with a non-Christian boyfriend. "I know that God brought him into my life for a reason," she kept saying.

"How do you know this?" I asked.

"I just know it," she said.

We were meeting to plead with her to turn from sin. I read three passages from the Bible that forbid sex outside of marriage, or sexual immorality (1 Corinthians 6:18; Ephesians 5:3; 1 Thessalonians 4:3). "Do you see that God says what you're doing is wrong?" I asked.

"Yes, I see that," she said. "I know it's immoral. I'm just asking God to show me what to do," she said. Earlier that week she had woken up in the middle of the night plagued with doubt about her relationship. Maybe she should break it off. "God, please give me a sign," she had prayed.

That day was their "anniversary." As she drove to work, she had the thought that her boyfriend had never sent her flowers at work. Then she walked into her office to a beautiful bouquet of roses.

"Was that a message from God?" she asked through tears. "Is that my answer?"

I found it ironic and sad that she was consumed with discovering a sign from God—an anniversary, flowers, being awake in the middle of the night—when God was speaking to her clearly in the Bible. Jesus said, "If you love me, you will keep my commandments" (John 14:15).

The doctrine of Scripture teaches us about the authority of God's Word. Scripture must be the final rule of faith and practice for our lives. Not our feelings or emotions. Not signs or prophetic words or hunches.

What more can God give us than what he's given in Scripture? The question is, will we listen? Will we obey when we don't like what the Bible has to say?

This is a moment when our belief about Scripture meets reality. What we *say* we believe makes very little difference until we act on our belief. I suppose most Christians would say that the Bible is the authoritative Word of God. But until this authority actually changes how we live—how we think and act—talk of the authority of Scripture is nothing but a bunch of religious lingo. We're treating the God-breathed Word of God like a lot of hot air.

Scripture is always meant to work in our lives. When Paul said Scripture is God-breathed, he didn't stop there. He said, "All Scripture is God-breathed and is useful for teaching, rebuking, correcting and training in righteousness, so that the man of God may be thoroughly equipped for every good work" (2 Timothy 3:16–17, NIV).

God's Word teaches us how to think. It teaches us truth. It rebukes and corrects our old, self-centered ways of thinking. It trains us in righteousness. God's Word has authority, and when we submit ourselves to it, Scripture equips us for good works. It gives us what we need to love, serve, and sacrifice.

The Bible has limited value as merely an esoteric, spiritually inspiring book of ancient wisdom. It was given to be obeyed and lived. Josiah let the Word of God *reform* him. He ripped his robes—a visual symbol that said, "I'm the one who needs to change." He didn't twist God's words to fit his agenda; he let God's words reshape his life.

I want to be like Josiah. When my life disagrees with the Word of God, I want to say, "This Word is true, and I must change."

———

How we relate to Scripture reveals how we view God himself. The Bible tells a story of a man whose regard for God was so low that he actually burned God's Word. Sadly, this man named Jehoiakim was the son of the godly King Josiah. Jehoiakim became king of Judah less than a year after his father's death. He was twenty-five and went on to reign for eleven years. Second

Kings 23:37 sums up his life by simply saying, "And he did what was evil in the sight of the LORD."

Jeremiah 36 tells the grievous tale of Jehoiakim's rejection of God's Word. A scroll with all of Jeremiah's prophecies written on it was brought to King Jehoiakim. He was staying at his winter house, and a fire was burning in a fire pot by his side. He listened as the prophecy was read, but his heart was unmoved. He didn't tremble. He despised the Word of God. As three or four columns of the prophecy were read, the king cut them off with a knife and threw them into the fire. He did this until the entire scroll was reduced to ashes. Jeremiah 36:24 states, "Yet neither the king nor any of his servants who heard all these words was afraid, nor did they tear their garments."

It's a chilling picture of blatant disregard for God and his Word. And the contrast between Josiah and his son Jehoiakim couldn't be more clear.

Josiah tore his robes. Jehoiakim cut up the words of God.

Josiah was penitent. Jehoiakim was cold-hearted.

Josiah reformed his life after hearing God's words. Jehoiakim burned God's words.

The young woman sitting in my office was burning God's Word as she heard it and refused to obey. How many times have I done the same thing? I've read God's Word, known what it called me to, but refused to turn in a new direction.

Every generation and every person can burn God's Word in their own way. Sometimes this is crass. But at other times this burning is sophisticated, nuanced, scholarly.

The most common way people cut and burn God's Word is to strip it of the qualities it claims for itself. So if I say that although Scripture is inspired, it has errors, I can claim a great regard for the Bible, but I've essentially made myself the judge over it. If it's possible for some part of it to be untrue, then I am now in the role of choosing what I will and won't listen to in Scripture.

The technical study of Scripture engaged in by academics can, when used humbly, further our understanding of God's Word. But it can also be a guise for exalting man's wisdom and opinions above the Word of God. The inerrancy of God's Word is thrown out, but the inerrancy of man's historical, textual, and scientific knowledge is assumed. Scripture is doubted, questioned, and edited until only a shell is left. The tools and words have changed since Jehoiakim's knife and fire pot, but the result is no different. God's Word is burned.

Can you trust what you're reading in Scripture? Is it clear enough that you can understand what God wants you to understand? Is the Bible all that you need? These aren't questions for pastors and professors; these are questions that every Christian who reads the Bible needs to answer. A handful of crucial words can help us think rightly about Scripture.

Inerrancy: The orthodox teaching of the Christian church down through the centuries has been that God's Word in its original manuscripts is inerrant. This means that it is totally true—free from error—in all it affirms. This is built on the Bible's testimony that God never lies (Titus 1:2). Proverbs 30:5 states, "Every word of God proves true; he is a shield to those who take refuge in him."

In his book *Bible Doctrine,* Wayne Grudem points out that when Jesus prays in John 17:17, he doesn't say, "Sanctify them in the truth; your words are *true.*" Instead he prays, "Sanctify them in the truth; your word is *truth.*"

"The difference is significant," writes Grudem, "for this statement encourages us to think of the Bible not simply as being 'true' in the sense that it conforms to some higher standard of truth, but rather to think of the Bible as itself the final standard of truth."[7]

Clarity: Another important quality of God's Word is its clarity. The Holy Spirit illuminates our hearts, as believers, to understand its message and apply it to our lives. It is straightforward in its meaning. And in those cases where a portion of Scripture is difficult to understand, we can test our viewpoint against other parts of Scripture. This means Scripture is self-interpreting. Psalm 19:7 says, "The testimony of the LORD is sure, making wise the simple." Though studying God's Word requires diligence and careful thought, no one can claim that it is unclear as an excuse for ignoring or disobeying it.

Sufficiency: In the Bible, God has given us all we need to know for salvation and eternal life (John 5:24). The Bible is sufficient. This doesn't mean God has told us all we could know or all that he knows; it means he has told us all *we* need to know in order to truly know him, find the forgiveness of sins, and be assured of everlasting life with our Creator and Redeemer. When Paul wrote Timothy, he said the "sacred writings" that Timothy had learned as a child "are able to make you wise for salvation through faith in Christ Jesus" (2 Timothy 3:15).

God doesn't want our view of his Word to be supported by sentimental attachment or mere emotion. He wants us to be confident in the Bible because he wants us to be confident in him. Taking time to study the doctrine of Scripture is a practical and spiritually enriching endeavor because it strengthens our trust in God's Word.[8]

Eating God's Word. It's an odd picture. Yet that's what the prophet Jeremiah describes when he says to God, "Your words were found, and I ate them, and your words became to me a joy and the delight of my heart, for I am called by your name, O LORD, God of hosts" (Jeremiah 15:16).

When I read these words, I imagine someone tearing out the crinkly, tissue-thin pages of a Bible and stuffing them in his mouth. Of course I know Jeremiah is speaking metaphorically. He's describing his wholehearted embrace of God's Word. We should have the same appetite.

That's how I want to be. But I still have a long way to go. I do love God's Word. I've tasted that it's good. But sometimes I only nibble on it. Sometimes I don't feel like eating at all. I want to delight in it the way Jeremiah describes. I want to be hungrier than I am.

Jeremiah's example is inspiring. He feeds on God's Word. He wants its truth and life *in* him. It is his joy. It is his delight. And if we didn't look more closely, we could assume that Jeremiah couldn't relate to the apathy and spiritual dryness that we lesser mortals experience.

But when we read Jeremiah's story and the context of his statement of delighting in God's Word, we make an interesting discovery. Jeremiah is in the midst of dark depression and anguished complaint. He is so discouraged, so disheartened, that he wishes he had never been born (Jeremiah 15:10). He lists all the ways he has suffered as a result of speaking God's truth. Jeremiah 15:17–18 says,

I did not sit in the company of revelers,
    nor did I rejoice;
I sat alone, because your hand was upon me,
    for you had filled me with indignation.
Why is my pain unceasing,
    my wound incurable,
    refusing to be healed?
Will you be to me like a deceitful brook,
    like waters that fail?

It turns out that Jeremiah's spiritual life isn't one mountaintop experience after another. Instead, he's often discouraged and depressed. He's tempted to question God's goodness. At this low moment of his life, he is more aware of what he's done for God than he is of what God has done for him.

This sounds terrible, but, honestly, it encourages me. It tells me that God's Word meets us where we are. It meets us in the midst of doubt. It speaks to us in the midst of spiritual struggle. Maybe that's where you are. The teaching of a college professor has you feeling like a fool for trusting in an "outdated, flawed book." Or maybe you're just tired. Reading the Bible feels like an empty exercise.

God can meet you and me in these moments of life. The Bible isn't just for people who feel strong. I'm grateful we don't have to lead perfect lives to read God's perfect Word. Jeremiah's life teaches us this. Jeremiah suffered. He was discouraged. God's Word isn't just for the happy people of the world. We can find joy in God's Word and in the trustworthiness of his promises even when we lack joy in our hearts.

Sometimes we have to work to find delight in God's Word. Jeremiah said that when he ate God's words, they became a joy. They don't become a joy sitting on a shelf. We have to taste and receive them. The fact that this requires effort shouldn't discourage us. As we grow in our knowledge of how trustworthy and powerful Scripture is, our love for it will increase.

———

God responded to Jeremiah's complaint with a loving rebuke, telling him to stop uttering worthless words. Jeremiah was more focused on his own performance and all that he had done for God.

God understands our weakness, but he doesn't make allowance for distrust and disbelief. He gave Jeremiah this wonderful promise: "I am with you to save you and deliver you" (Jeremiah 15:20, NASB).

God saves. God delivers. It was true for Jeremiah. It was true for the people of Judah. It's true for you and me. God alone can save.

That is the central message of the Bible. And it's the key to understanding the Bible and learning to love it as God wants us to. The Bible is the story of what God has done for us. We don't come to it to receive instructions on saving ourselves. It's not a list of rules and guidelines that we must follow perfectly in order to earn our way into God's favor. The Bible is the story of what he has done. It's the story of how every man-made effort at salvation fails and only the grace of God can rescue and redeem sinners.

Too often we read the Bible the way A. J. Jacobs did when he attempted to spend a year "living biblically." We read it and look for all the things we have to do. And while there are things God commands us to do, we first need to read the Bible looking at all he has done for us. It's the story of his champion, his Son, who came to die for us.

My kids' children's Bible says it best. Every story whispers his name. Jesus came looking for us. He came to deliver us. When you understand that, reading the Bible becomes a delight.

GOD WITH A BELLYBUTTON

"Jesus is unique. And he came to accomplish something that no one else could."

SOME DAYS AN early-morning mist settles on my backyard. It's as though a cloud loses its way and comes to rest there before floating back to the sky. On those mornings my backyard, with its two towering oak trees and flat stretch of grass, has a hazy glow. It looks mystical and enchanting.

I read my Bible and pray in a room that looks out over the backyard. One morning when the mist hung over the yard, I couldn't seem to focus on a single thing I read. My prayers were listless.

I stared out the window. The thought struck me that this quiet time would be better if Jesus would walk across my backyard and come talk to me. That would give my faith a boost. I imagined his bare feet sinking into the dew-wet grass. I don't know why I pictured him barefoot. He just was. He would walk up to the side door, right across from where I was sitting, and knock gently.

"That's what I wish would happen," I said out loud. "I wish you'd step out of that mist and sit right there." The armchair in the corner was empty. I imagined Jesus stepping into the quiet room and sitting down.

I am alive approximately 1,975 years after Jesus walked the earth. On some days that seems like a long time.

Once while surfing the Internet, I came across a Bible-themed video game that pitted Bible characters against each other in brutal combat. You could choose to fight as Moses, Noah, Eve, Mary, Satan, or Jesus. It was a sacrilegious version of the old Street Fighter II game we used to play at 7-Eleven. Besides basic kicking, punching, and jumping abilities, each character had his or her own special powers. Moses could hail down frogs. Eve threw apples and whipped a snake at her foes. Noah could call out a herd of animals to run over people. Jesus threw loaves and fish. I am not making this up.

The game was clever but obviously created by secular people who had little regard for the sacred. Sadly, I've heard of youth groups who celebrate the game as a way to teach teenagers the Bible. Somehow I don't think that Noah beating up Eve is the kind of Bible knowledge we need today.

While most people wouldn't feel comfortable playing this irreverent game, I wonder if it captures a common way of thinking about Jesus—as just one person in the pantheon of Bible heroes. He did miraculous things, but then so did Moses and Elijah. We know he's special, and we have a sense that we should be indebted to him for all the trouble of dying on the cross, but at the end of the day, he's just another Bible character.

C. S. Lewis famously said that Jesus is either the true Son of God, a demon, or else a madman.[1] The all-or-nothingness of that statement always gives me chills. Jesus is either who he claims to be—the God-man who came to redeem humanity—or he's completely insane, even sick. You can't have it somewhere in the middle. He can't be a great teacher and a wonderful moral example and at the same time a liar and a charlatan. He can't be enlightened and be a trusted source of spiritual guidance and at the same time be wrong about his identity.

This seems like an airtight argument to me, but countless people find a way to wriggle out of it. They hold on to Jesus in some form, but they deny that he is the Son of God who should be obeyed and worshiped. The intellectual gymnastics required for this remind me of pictures of people doing yoga who are able to wrap both feet around their heads and tie them in a knot. I don't know why they want to do that, and it looks painful.

I have a friend who holds to the "Jesus isn't really God, but he's still a really good thing" viewpoint. In his opinion Jesus was an enlightened and wonderful man (I would put Mr. Rogers in this same category). More than any other human, Jesus achieved a connection with what my friend calls the "Christ spirit." He thinks all the supernatural elements of the New Testament—from miracles to the resurrection—were fabricated by Jesus's followers. He believes that, while the Bible is a great work of literature and spiritual comfort, it's merely the result of human imagination and error. So he picks through the Bible as if he's at the grocery store buying green beans. He passes over what he views as the "brown and shriveled" displays of supernatural power and claims of divinity and grabs only the moral teaching, the acts of compassion, and the heroic suffering displayed in Jesus's life.

"So what do you believe was happening when Jesus died on the cross?" I asked him one day.

"I think Jesus was opposing injustice," he answered. "He was demonstrating the power of love."

I love my friend, but his beliefs befuddle me. Not because I don't understand them, but because I can't see why he bothers having them at all. To turn the old saying on its head, it's as if he's thrown out the baby but kept the bathwater. Christianity without a supernatural, divine, all-powerful Jesus seems pointless to me—less useful than old bathwater.

My question is, Why spend time figuring out a way to hold on to church attendance and Christian tradition and even Christian morality while not believing much of anything about Jesus except that he was a really great guy? I know a lot of really great guys, but I sure wouldn't spend every Sunday morning singing about them. I can find plenty of other compelling examples of suffering. I can find moving moral teaching from any number of gurus and religious teachers.

If Christianity is a tradition built on the fable of a man we know about only through reports we can't trust, why in the world would a person waste time with any part of it?

In this chapter I want to explore what theologians call the doctrine of the person and work of Christ. His *person* addresses who Jesus is, his *work*, what he has done for us. The person and work of Christ are meant to be kept together. You can't grasp the significance of either without the other. As we study both, we'll learn that Jesus is unlike anyone in the Bible or in world history. He is fully God and fully man. And he came into this world to accomplish something that no one else could.

Jesus Christ is known by some people as the founder of the Christian religion. Technically, of course, this is true. But for a Christian, who believes that Jesus is the eternal Son of God who became a man, it seems odd to call him the founder of anything. For that matter he's also the founder of the universe, having created the world and all living things.

But in strictly historical terms, the Christian faith does start with Jesus.

He claimed to be, and his followers acknowledged him to be, the fulfillment of the Jewish faith and all the promises of the Old Testament prophets. Jesus presented himself as the Messiah, the "anointed one," one who is chosen and empowered by God for a specific task. The Greek form of *messiah* is *Christ,* which explains the title Jesus is known by. For Jesus to be the Christ means that he is the specially chosen one of God, sent for a very specific purpose.

Jesus lived in Palestine during the reign of Augustus Caesar. The Jewish people were humbled and distressed by the presence of the pagan occupiers. Seeing the holy city of Jerusalem overrun with Roman soldiers grated on their souls. They longed for freedom and self-rule.

Jesus, a descendant of the great King David of old, was born in Bethlehem but raised in Nazareth. Every region has some city or town that it looks down on and considers backwoods or hick. It seems that Nazareth was on the bottom rung of that ladder in Galilee. It had no prestige or distinction. In several places in the Gospels, people snidely comment on Nazareth for its lack of sophistication, describing it as a place nothing good could come from (John 1:46).

Jesus, like his adopted father, Joseph, was a carpenter by trade. He worked in Nazareth until he was around the age of thirty. Then he started his public ministry of teaching and healing. For three years he traveled through various cities in Judea. He trained a small band of disciples. He taught in synagogues and eventually before large crowds. People mobbed him when word spread of his miraculous powers to heal sickness and cast out demons.

While Jesus gained many followers, he also made enemies. The religious leaders of the day conspired to kill him. They were jealous of his popularity, outraged by his claims to be equal with God, and offended by his rejection of their man-made traditions and laws.

Jesus was sold out by one of his closest associates, falsely accused, flogged, and executed by crucifixion at the hands of the Romans.

On the third day, in fulfillment of ancient prophecy and his own promise, Jesus rose from the dead. He appeared to his followers over the course of more than a month. He commissioned them to take the news of his death and resurrection to the world. And then he ascended into heaven.

Today, two thousand years later, a man who never traveled more than a hundred miles from his hometown has reached people in every continent of the world. The empire of Rome, under whose shadow Jesus was born and murdered, long ago crumbled to ruins. But the number of those who swear allegiance to Jesus and call him Lord has grown through every century. In the West we divide human history by his birth. Nearly two billion humans describe themselves as his followers.

Jesus Christ is the most famous, most powerful, most controversial and revolutionary figure in all human history. And he has promised to return.

———

The question that divides the human race is, who is Jesus? That's a question Jesus asked his own followers. It wasn't enough for them to list the ideas and opinions of other people. "Who do *you* say that I am?" he asked (Matthew 16:15, emphasis added).

During Jesus's ministry some thought he was a great teacher, others a prophet. Not surprisingly, false teaching about Jesus's nature spread easily in the early church.

One teacher named Apollinaris taught that Jesus had a human body but not a human mind or spirit. He asserted that while Jesus was a man, he had received a mind/spirit transplant of divinity. On one level this might seem like a nice way to fit Jesus together as both God and man, but church leaders saw a serious problem. Jesus had come to save the whole man—body and spirit. In order to represent us and thus fully save us, Jesus had to be fully human as Scripture claims. Scripture says Jesus was made like us in every way (Hebrews 2:17). And after his death Jesus was raised to life with a physical body; he didn't abandon it and return to spirit-only form (Luke 24:39).

Another teacher, named Nestorius, argued that Christ was made up of two separate persons. In this view the divine person and human person were like roommates sharing the same space or like Siamese twins who could argue with each other and have different agendas. But nowhere in the Bible is Jesus presented as two persons. He is always and only one person in his thoughts and actions.

A third erroneous view presented Jesus as a sort of divine-human hybrid. His divine nature came together with his human nature and morphed into a totally new nature that was neither God nor man but a mixture of both. This idea that Christ had only one nature is called Monophysitism or Eutychianism, after a man named Eutyches, who spread it. Why was this view a problem? Because it left us with a less-than-biblical Jesus who was not really God or man.

At the Council of Chalcedon in AD 451, the church fathers laid out a declaration designed to correct the false teachings and clearly delineate and protect the biblical teaching about Jesus's nature.[2] The Chalcedonian Creed stated that Jesus has two natures in one person. He is both "perfect in Godhead and also perfect in manhood; truly God and truly man" with a real human soul and body. So whatever is true of God's nature is true of Jesus's nature. And whatever is true of human nature is also true of Jesus's nature. Jesus is in every way like us in our humanity, except without sin, even as he is of the same essence as God the Father. These two natures are "to be acknowledged...inconfusedly, unchangeably, indivisibly, inseparably." In other words, Jesus's two natures are not mixed together, they're not morphing, neither one is diminished by the other, they can't be divided, and they can't be separated. Jesus is fully God and fully man in one person forever.[3]

———

Let's consider Jesus who is "truly God." Scripture points to Jesus's divine nature in many ways. The first is his virgin conception. Before Jesus was conceived, his mother, Mary, had never had sex with a man. Her first question when the angel announced her pregnancy reveals her innocence and womanly practicality: "How will this be, since I am a virgin?" (Luke 1:34).

The angel's answer leaves this miracle shrouded in mystery, but it makes one thing unmistakably certain: the child conceived in Mary's womb would be of divine, heavenly origin. "The Holy Spirit will come upon you," the angel told her. "And the power of the Most High will overshadow you; therefore the child to be born will be called holy—the Son of God" (Luke 1:35).

John the Baptist was a witness to Jesus as the Son of God (Luke 3:16). John said of Jesus, "The one who comes from above is above all; the one who is from the earth belongs to the earth, and speaks as one from the earth. The one who comes from heaven is above all" (John 3:31, NIV). And when John baptized Jesus, God spoke from heaven and said to Jesus, "You are my beloved Son; with you I am well pleased" (Luke 3:22).

Jesus also revealed his divine nature through the supernatural miracles he performed. He demonstrated his power over the human body in healing (Luke 4:40), over demonic powers (Mark 1:25), and over the natural elements. "Who is this man?" his disciples once asked themselves after he quieted a violent storm. "Even the winds and the waves obey him!" (Matthew 8:27, NIV).

Unlike any other prophet in the Bible, Jesus made claims of equality with God. He said, "I and the Father are one" (John 10:30). And once he said to the religious leaders, "I tell you the truth, before Abraham was born, I am!" (John 8:58, NIV). This was an audacious claim to divinity. Not only was Jesus saying that he existed before the patriarch Abraham, who had lived thousands of years before; he also referred to himself in a clear echo of the divine name: I AM. This was the name God had told Moses to give to the children of Israel when they asked who sent him. "Tell them I AM sent you," God instructed Moses (see Exodus 3:13–14). The point Jesus made wasn't lost on his listeners. They knew he was claiming equality with the eternal God and picked up stones to kill him.

In his book *Salvation Belongs to the Lord,* theologian John Frame points out how incredible it is that Jesus's disciples came to believe that he was God. They were all Jews who had been raised to believe that there is one God and only God should be worshiped. They were not primed to look for God in the form of a man. The idea was preposterous. "Somehow," Frame writes, "during the next three years or so, all these Jewish disciples, and many more people besides, are convinced that Jesus is God and deserves to be worshiped as God. They have known him intimately as a man, have walked and talked and eaten with him; yet, they have come to worship him. That is quite an amazing thing."[4]

Frame goes on to talk about the fact that Jesus's deity wasn't debated by Christians in the early church (although they were more than ready to argue about other theological issues). They didn't argue about it, Frame says, because the whole Christian community agreed that Jesus was God.

The apostle Paul, who encountered the risen Jesus Christ, said, "He is the image of the invisible God, the firstborn of all creation" and "in him the whole fullness of deity dwells bodily" (Colossians 1:15; 2:9).

Once when Jesus was on a mountain with Peter, James, and John, he was transfigured, or changed in form, before their eyes (Mark 9:2–13). The three disciples saw a preview of the eternal glory Jesus would possess after his resurrection. His clothes became dazzling white. Jesus stood and spoke to Moses and Elijah—the two greatest prophets of the Old Testament. When Peter beheld the sight, he was awestruck (unfortunately, not enough to refrain from speaking). He offered to set up three tents, one for each of the men. But then God the Father spoke from heaven and made something very clear: this wasn't about three great heroes of faith coming together for a reunion tour. God said, "This is my Son, whom I love. Listen to him!" (Mark 9:7, NIV).

This is my Son. Unlike any other. Greater than anyone else who has ever walked this earth. Not merely a servant or prophet of God but the one and only Son of God.

———

Jesus is "perfect in Godhead and also perfect in manhood." Have you ever taken time to reflect on the reality of Jesus's human nature? The world has had two millennia to get used to the concept of God becoming a man. But even after all that time, the idea of God being a human—a bundle of muscle, bones, and fluid—is scandalous. Hands. Arms. Feet. Body hair. Sweat glands. How can this possibly be?

This is, without question, the greatest miracle recorded in Scripture. The parting of the Red Sea is nothing in comparison. Fire from heaven that consumed Elijah's altar? No big deal. Even the raising of Lazarus from the dead takes a backseat to a moment that no human eye saw. In the womb of a virgin, a human life was conceived. But no human father was involved. The Holy Spirit, in a miracle too wonderful for the human mind to comprehend, overshadowed a young woman (Luke 1:35). And in a split second that the cosmos is still reeling from, God "incarnated." He took on our humanity.

God the Son, existing for all eternity, now became dependent, floating in the amniotic fluid of a female womb. The One by whose power the whole world is sustained, now nourished by an umbilical cord. The God-man would have a bellybutton.

And then he had to be born. He had to come out. Think about that. When the angels announced Jesus's birth to shepherds outside the town of Bethlehem, they said, "Born this day in the city of David a Savior, who is Christ the Lord" (Luke 2:11). When we read this account, we're often distracted by the fact that angels have appeared. We imagine them shining, and we picture the shepherds and sheep. But none of this is truly incredible. What is incredible is this word *born*.

God has been *born*.

Born in what sense? Carried-down-from-the-sky-by-angels, pink-and-chubby-and-wrapped-in-white-blankets born? No. Born in the painful, screaming, sweaty, pushed-out-between-the-legs-of-a-woman sense. Born in all the bloody, slimy mess of real human birth. Squeezed and prodded from the darkness of his mother's womb by the powerful, rhythmic contractions of her uterus.

And there he is, the Son of God, covered in fluid and blood. His lungs filling with oxygen for the first time. Crying. Helpless.

————

That Jesus was fully man is clearly taught in the Bible. Not only did he have a human mother; he grew and developed like any child (Luke 2:52). He was hungry (Matthew 4:2). He was thirsty (John 4:7). He experienced human emotions: he was troubled (John 12:27) and sorrowful at the death of a close friend (John 11:35). He also grew tired and needed sleep (Luke 8:23).

And beyond these examples, the response to Jesus from those who knew him was, well, normal. For years his brothers didn't believe he was the Messiah

(John 7:5). People in his hometown of Nazareth thought of him as simply "Joseph's son" and rejected him as a prophet (Matthew 13:53–58). Evidently Jesus's very normal human life and behavior had not prepared them for the idea that he could be the divine Messiah.

For thirty years Jesus lived an everyday human life in first-century Palestine. He learned the trade of a carpenter. His hands would have been calloused and rough from working with wood. He knew the salty sting of sweat in his eyes. He knew the relief of resting tired muscles after a full day of work.

Why does all this matter? The Bible tells us that Christ's full humanity is important because of the unique purpose of his mission. Jesus came to represent the human race before God. Part of his work on earth was to be our priest. In the Old Testament a priest's role was to stand before God on behalf of the people. He had to be someone from their midst—one of them—so that the sacrifices he offered before God would be counted toward his people.

Hebrews says that Jesus, who came to be our priest and representative before God, "had to be made like his brothers in every respect, so that he might become a merciful and faithful high priest in the service of God, to make propitiation for the sins of the people" (2:17).

The requirement of full humanity not only made it possible for Jesus to offer himself for our sins, but it also assures us of being cared for by a priest who understands our plight. Hebrews 4:15 says, "For we do not have a high priest who is unable to sympathize with our weaknesses, but one who in every respect has been tempted as we are, yet without sin."

Jesus is like us in every aspect of our humanity—in all the mundane, glorious, and impolite aspects of the human existence. He had all the weakness and desires that make us human; he was tempted in every respect as we are. The difference is that Jesus was without sin. And it was his sinless perfection that made it possible for him to pay for our sins.

This means we can be assured that we pray to and hope in a High Priest who knows us. He sympathizes with us. He has a friendly, personal understanding of our weaknesses. He says to us, "I've been there," and he actually means it. John Frame writes, "God, who has no body, has taken to himself a body in the person of Jesus Christ. God, who cannot suffer, has taken to himself a human nature, in which he can suffer, in Christ."[5]

———

Jesus is the center, the focal point, of the Christian faith. But it's odd how averse we Christians can be to studying and defining a clear "doctrine" of Jesus. That just doesn't seem relational. We don't want to study Jesus. We want to experience him.

I see this tendency in my own life. When I think about Jesus, I'm not inclined to ask, "What truth does the Bible tell me about Jesus? What does Jesus want me to think and believe about him?" Instead I'm more inclined to try to work my way into a certain emotional state. To "feel" a certain way about Jesus.

I'm not even sure how to describe the feeling that I believe I should have about Jesus. All I know is that I want a really deep and meaningful feeling. I want something to wash over me. I wouldn't even mind crying. Actually crying is good. The feeling I'm after definitely needs to be passionate and profound. A touch of melancholy works too. Sad and austere feel very spiritual. I want to feel like Jesus is my closest friend, like we could hang out. I want to feel that he likes me—my tastes, my sensibilities, my music, my food. I want a deep bond—the kind that doesn't even need words to communicate.

Putting all my desired "Jesus feelings" into words makes me sound like an emotional seventh-grade girl about to leave summer camp. That is not good.

I think many Christians are more interested in chasing a feeling about Jesus than pursuing Jesus himself and reviewing and thinking about the truth of who he is.

The irony of this feeling-driven approach to Jesus is that ultimately it produces the opposite of what we actually want. Deep emotion in response to Jesus isn't wrong. It can be good. But to find it, we need more than imagination and introspection.

One of the most valuable lessons C.J. has taught me about the Christian spiritual life is that if you want to feel deeply, you have to think deeply. Too often we separate the two. We assume that if we want to feel deeply, then we need to sit around and, well, *feel*.

But emotion built on emotion is empty. True emotion—emotion that is reliable and doesn't lead us astray—is always a response to reality, to truth. It's only as we study and consider truth about Jesus with our minds that our hearts will be moved by the depth of his greatness and love for us. When we engage our minds with the doctrine of his person and his work, our emotions are given something to stand on, a reason to worship and revel in the very appropriate feelings of awe and gratefulness and adoration.

Knowing Jesus and feeling right emotions about him start with thinking about the truth of who he is and what he's done. Jesus never asks us how we feel about him. He calls us to believe in him, to trust in him. The question he asked his disciples is the same one he confronts us with: "Who do you say that I am?" The real questions when it comes to Jesus are, Do you believe he is who he says he is? Do you believe he's done what he said he came to do?

———

We've been considering the person of Christ. But now let's look at how this relates to the work he came to do. During the early 1900s there was intense pressure in academic circles and in many churches to deny Jesus as a supernatural person. People emphasized his teaching and example instead. But J. Gresham Machen argued that Jesus was far more than "the fairest flower of humanity,"[6] as some presented him. True Christian faith had always involved looking to Jesus as a supernatural Person, indeed "a Person who was God."[7] Jesus did not just inspire faith; he was the *object* of faith for the apostles and the early church. He was the one in whom they put their faith.

"If Jesus was merely a man like the rest of men," Machen wrote, "then an ideal is all that we have in Him. Far more is needed by a sinful world. It is small comfort to be told that there was goodness in the world, when what we need is goodness triumphant over sin."[8]

Is Jesus just an ideal? Is he just a goal for which we're to aim? The Bible presents a very different narrative. In Scripture the story of Jesus is not the story of goodness cropping up in the world. It is the story of goodness conquering sin. It is the story of wickedness and death being pushed back, thrown down, and defeated by the supernatural man who came from heaven but was born on earth.

This is the work Jesus came to do. And it's only when we realize how big, how massive, the mission of Jesus truly is that we begin to understand how unique he is. The work he came to accomplish is nothing less than the setting right of all that is wrong—in our relationship with God, in our hearts, in creation, in the whole of the universe.

We can adopt small thoughts of Jesus if we limit our view of his work to our tiny self-interests. But to truly see the glory of God's purpose in Jesus, we have to look beyond our own front porch, our town, our country, even our lifetime. God's purpose is so much bigger. Jesus didn't come only to save me, forgive my sins, and improve my life. He does all this, but this is only a small part of a much larger picture.

In the book of Ephesians, Paul glories in the cosmic implications of Jesus and his work. He lists the spiritual blessings we have in Jesus: adoption by God as his children, redemption through his blood, the forgiveness of our sins (1:3–8). But then he explains the ultimate purpose to which they point.

What is this purpose? God's purpose, Paul says, is to unite all things in Jesus, things in heaven and things on earth (1:9–10). What does this mean, and what's the big deal?

Let me explain it this way. Let's say I ask you what the big deal is about Abraham Lincoln. Why does he get to have his picture on the penny and the five-dollar bill and have a big memorial in downtown Washington DC? What would you say? You'd most likely say that he is one of America's greatest presidents because he emancipated the slaves and preserved the union. But what if I asked, "Why is that so special?" You'd try to give me some historical perspective. You'd explain that this was extremely significant because of the terrible injustice and wickedness of slavery. You'd describe the great turmoil and division of the Civil War—how a whole country was being ripped apart, how hundreds of thousands of men died in the conflict.

The point is that people can't appreciate Lincoln and his unique gifts and accomplishments until they understand the circumstances of his presidency. In a similar way, we can't grasp the significance of God's plan to unite all things in Jesus until we understand the disunity and chasm between heaven and earth brought about by man's sin.

When man first sinned, it was an act of treason against almighty God. It was earth revolting against heaven. And it plunged humanity and the whole world into death and disarray. The result of sin was that mankind was separated from God. Our fellowship with the Creator was broken. And the division didn't stop there. Sin created division within humanity. It tore apart families. It turned man against woman. It created hatred and animosity among the races. The wars and genocide and ethnic cleansing that continue to this day are the tragic legacy of sin.

The Bible tells us that creation itself was affected by mankind's fall into sin. When we see earthquakes and hurricanes, it can seem as though creation is at war with itself. And in a very real way it is. Our world is, in a sense, cut off from God and under a curse (Genesis 3:17; Romans 8:20–21).

The questions that humans have asked for thousands of years are, How can this broken, sin-scorched, divided world be made right? Who can save us? Who can fix all this?

God always had a plan. But he took his time unveiling it. In the Old Testament he hinted at it. He gave clues. But his ultimate purpose was a mystery. It was hidden. The prophets of old searched and searched, seeking to glimpse God's plan and to determine the timing of the salvation he promised. They asked, "Who will bring harmony? How can sinful man make peace with a holy God? What sacrifice will cleanse us? Who can reconcile the nations? Who can bring lasting peace?"

The Bible tells us that, at just the right time, God enacted his plan. "But when the fullness of time had come, God sent forth his Son, born of woman, born under the law, to redeem those who were under the law, so that we might receive adoption as sons" (Galatians 4:4–5).

In Jesus, the eternal Son of God became a man. Heaven and earth came together in one person—fully God and fully man. And he came not to condemn but to save. How does he make peace? He gives himself in the place of sinners. How can he do this? Because he's one of us. But how can he face the wrath of God for millions upon millions of sinners? Because he is the eternal God. By his death he removes our guilt. He appeases the wrath of God the Father. And through his death and resurrection, he reverses death itself. Jesus's resurrection shows that God's purpose is to make all things new—not just spiritually, but also physically. The promise of a new heaven and a new earth is glimpsed in the risen, glorified human body of Jesus Christ. In the new earth that God will create, all things are remade (Revelation 21:1–5).

The unity that Jesus brings is total power over all things. Ephesians 1:21 says that God has placed Jesus "far above all rule and authority and power and dominion, and above every name that is named, not only in this age but also in the one to come." In other words, he's in charge. His enemies are crushed, the sinful are punished, and every knee bows to him (Revelation 21:8; Romans 14:11). The world is united because everyone is obeying Jesus.

When you glimpse the big-picture perspective of who Jesus is and what he has come to do, it takes your breath away. His person and work are unlike any other. Abraham was simply a servant of God. Moses was only a prophet for God. Muhammad was just a man. Buddha was just a teacher. Confucius, more a social philosopher. Joseph Smith, who founded Mormonism, and Charles Taze Russell, who founded the Jehovah's Witnesses, and L. Ron Hubbard, who founded Scientology, are flawed sinners like you and me. None of these people and none of their philosophies and ideas can save us. Just like us they're guilty before a holy God.

Only Jesus can rescue. Only Jesus offers the world outside help. And that's what our world needs. We need God to come down to earth to save us. Only Jesus claims this for himself. Only Jesus died and rose again. And only Jesus can and will unite all things in himself.

First Timothy 2:5 says, "For there is one God, and there is one mediator between God and men, the man Christ Jesus." A mediator is someone who stands between and reconciles two opposing parties. Jesus is the one mediator who can stand between God and man. Only Jesus, by his death on the cross, can reconcile heaven and earth.

Jesus said, "I am the way, and the truth, and the life. No one comes to the Father except through me" (John 14:6).

Have you ever wondered if believing in Jesus would be easier if you could somehow push your way back in time toward him? If you could be, chronologically speaking, closer?

I've had that thought. If I could just be nearer to the actual moment when God invaded our space and time, I'm sure my faith would be unbreakable. Or at least it would be really strong. Maybe.

But then I wonder how far back in time I'd have to go for it to make any real difference. Going back just a thousand years definitely wouldn't be enough. It's not as though living in the tenth century would make me feel much closer to Jesus. Besides, who wants to live in the Dark Ages?

I'm not even certain that living a few hundred years after Jesus would help. I live a little more than two hundred years after America's first president, George Washington. I handle money with his picture on it. Every night I toss into my change jar quarters imprinted with his likeness. Good grief, I live outside Washington DC, which is named after him. I can drive over to his old house at Mount Vernon anytime I want. But I can't say I feel much of a connection with George. I believe in him in the sense that I know he was here. But he still feels far removed and unreal.

So I guess I'd really be happy only if I met Jesus in person. To be someone who was healed by him or perhaps be that kid whose lunch he multiplied. That would be cool.

But even then I'm not sure this business of faith would be simple. Because those who were close to Jesus—people who camped with him, touched him, spoke to him, listened to him preach—also struggled with unbelief and doubts. The disciple Thomas, just *one day* after the resurrection, refused to believe Jesus had risen again unless he saw and touched the wounds in Jesus's hands (John 20:24–29). Some people give Thomas a hard time because of his doubts. But honestly, would any of us have done differently?

I understand how Thomas must have felt. I'd want to see and touch Jesus's hands too.

I think this says something about the makeup of the human soul. No matter how close in time we are, no matter how immediate and intimate the testimony about Jesus is, we want more. We want to remove the need for faith.

So you and I are living almost two thousand years after the historic moment when Jesus performed miracles, died, and rose back to life. We have to trust the testimony of the apostles that is recorded in the Bible. We have to trust that God enabled people to faithfully preserve and translate his words. We have to trust that the message has been accurately transmitted through time and culture. And at times it feels like that requires a lot of faith.

But think of Thomas. He didn't have to trust something he read in a book. No translation was required. No strangers were involved. No, the people he had to trust were his best friends. His closest friends were eyewitnesses of Jesus's resurrection. And they had seen him alive *yesterday*. And yet, even with all that, Thomas felt like believing required a lot of faith. More faith than he could muster at the moment.

Jesus was patient with Thomas. Just like he's patient with us. And when he appeared to Thomas, he said, "Have you believed because you have seen me? Blessed are those who have not seen and yet have believed" (John 20:29).

I like reading those words because I know Jesus is talking about me—me and you and all the other followers he has called to himself in the years since. It's as though he's saying, "I know it takes a lot of faith. I know you'd prefer to have been here. I know you'd like to be with me now. To see me. To have me walk through your backyard and sit in your chair. But I've spoken to you in my Word. I've told you about me. I've given you my Holy Spirit as a promise of what is to come. One day your faith will be sight. One day you'll see me and touch me."

In the verses right after this story of Thomas, the apostle John wrote, "Now Jesus did many other signs in the presence of the disciples, which are not written in this book; but these are written so that you may believe that Jesus is the Christ, the Son of God, and that by believing you may have life in his name" (verses 30–31).

I've never seen Jesus. But I do believe that Jesus is the Christ, the Son of God. And by grace, I know I've found life in his name.

6

A WAY TO BE GOOD AGAIN

*"For too long the news that Jesus died
for my sins had no real meaning."*

THE WEIGHT OF GUILT felt like it would press me into the ground. Crush me. Part of me wanted it to. Maybe then I wouldn't have to feel this way. I lay down on the bed. I longed for sleep—not to rest but to escape. I didn't want to be awake. I didn't want to be conscious, to have to think about what a stupid, hypocritical sinner I was.

I'd watched a pornographic video once before when I was thirteen years old. I had found the VHS tape while baby-sitting at the home of a Christian family. The parents were gone. The kid I watched was napping, and I just sat there, drinking in the defiling images that played out on the television screen. I remember going home that day feeling like I was covered head to foot with a grimy film. I wanted to take the most scalding hot shower possible, to scrub myself clean.

That was six years earlier. I felt dirty then, but this was worse. So much worse. At age thirteen I didn't care about God. I didn't pretend to want to please him. But this time I was different. I loved God. I was serious about serving him.

I'd flown all the way to San Juan, Puerto Rico, to be a volunteer at a Billy Graham Crusade. I had come to do God's work and be part of a historic moment in Christendom. The evangelistic crusade was being broadcast around the world, simultaneously translated into dozens of languages. Well-known Christians had gathered from many nations. There were training sessions for young evangelists. I got my picture taken with apologist Ravi Zacharias, Korean evangelist Billy Kim, and Billy Graham's famous music director, Cliff Barrows. I stood just a few feet from Graham himself and listened to him preach. I was on holy ground.

But one night, when the pastor I was staying with left the house for a meeting, I plopped down on his couch and turned on the television. I mindlessly channel-surfed. Then I clicked past a channel that was all static—the images blurred and hard to identify. I clicked back to it. When I did, the static cleared for several seconds, and the images sharpened. It was a pornographic cable channel.

I didn't turn it off. I could have. I kept thinking that later as I lay on my bed. *I could have turned it off.* Instead, I gave full vent to my lustful desires. I spent the next hour clicking back to the channel for five-second glimpses. For some reason that made it even worse. I hadn't just watched pornography. I had worn out my thumb on the remote control and strained my eyes to make out the vulgar images.

When I finally turned off the television and went to my room, the conviction I'd been holding at bay came rushing into my heart. I'd traveled all this way to sit in a pastor's house and watch porn. I was there to do God's work. I wanted to learn so God could use me. What a joke. I was nothing but a disgusting hypocrite. As I lay there staring at the ceiling, I couldn't even bring myself to pray. I finally slipped into a fitful sleep.

That's when I had the dream.

I don't remember most of my dreams. But I doubt I'll ever forget this one. It was the most vivid and powerful dream I've ever had—before or since.

I dreamed I was in a room filled with index card–size files. They were like the ones libraries used in the past. When I opened a file, I discovered that the cards described thoughts and actions from my life. The room was a crude catalog system of everything, good and bad, I'd ever done.

As I browsed the cards under the headings "Friends I've Betrayed," "Lies I've Told," and "Lustful Thoughts," I was overwhelmed with guilt. Long-forgotten moments of wrongdoing were described in chilling detail. Each card was in my handwriting and signed with my signature. Sadly, my misdeeds woefully outnumbered my good deeds. I tried to destroy a card, desperate to erase the memory of what I'd done. But the past couldn't be changed. I could only weep in the face of my failure and shame.

Then Jesus entered the room. He took the cards and, one by one, began signing his name on them. His name covered mine and was written with his blood.

When I woke from the dream, I was overcome with emotion. I had never been so aware of my guilt before God and, at the same time, the reality of my forgiveness by God. The dream helped me see that my failure and sin were so much worse than one lustful hour of watching pornography. But incredibly, God's grace and love toward me in Jesus were also much more powerful than I had ever realized.

On the cross Jesus took my place. He took every one of my sins upon himself. As never before, the incredible implications of the Son of God dying in *my* place for *my* sins flooded my soul.

Christians say that Jesus died for our sins. But what does this mean? Why did he have to die? What did Jesus accomplish through his death on the cross? What was happening as he hung there between heaven and earth? And what effect does his death have on you and me today? What does it change?

These questions bring us to the very heart of the Christian faith. They bring us to the awe-inspiring subject of the atonement. The word *atonement* speaks of how sinful, guilty men and women can have a restored relationship with a perfectly good and righteous God—how we can be united or "at one" with our Creator.

"Atonement means making amends," writes J. I. Packer, "blotting out the offense, and giving satisfaction for wrong done; thus reconciling to oneself the alienated other and restoring the disrupted relationship."[1]

The Bible teaches that our relationship with God has been disrupted by our disobedience. We are not only separated from him because of the vileness of our sin; we're guilty before him and worthy of his punishment.

The most confounding theological question humanity has ever faced is the question of how a truly good and righteous God could love and forgive guilty people. If God ignores human sin, then he is immoral and unjust. Or he is an amoral force with no standards at all. And yet God has promised to rescue us and accept us. How can this be? The answer is the Cross.

———

I grew up being told that Jesus died on the cross for me. But for too long this information had no real meaning. Of course it was really nice of him and everything. But it was like someone spending a lot of money on a gift you don't really want or need. It made no sense to me. Even after I chose to give my life to God, the Cross was a blurry concept in my thinking.

I have a vivid memory from this period in my life. I was a young teenager. I was walking into our brown duplex on Kane Road in Gresham, Oregon. As I opened the door from the carport to the kitchen, I had the thought, *I don't understand why Jesus had to die.* This matter-of-fact statement just ran through my mind.

It's odd to me that such a fleeting moment would be so clear in my memory. Maybe I was slightly discomforted by my confusion. Sadly, I wasn't distressed enough by my lack of understanding to do anything about it. I didn't ask anyone to explain the Cross to me. I didn't go read my Bible. And there was no sense of urgency in my heart, no sense I needed Jesus's death to occur.

I wonder how many people in churches today have the same unclear thoughts about the Cross. When you compare this modern fuzzy thinking with the sharp focus on Christ's death in the pages of Scripture, you can't help but think that something is very wrong.

Jesus anticipated the time and manner of his death (Matthew 20:17–19). He taught his followers that his death would be the climax of the earthly mission he had come to accomplish. Jesus said, "For even the Son of Man came not to be served but to serve, and to give his life as a ransom for many" (Mark 10:45).

The Cross wasn't the tragic upending of Jesus's plan; it was the fulfillment of his plan. The hour of his greatest anguish was the hour for which he had come (John 12:27). And on the night of his betrayal, Jesus instituted what we call the Lord's Supper—a ceremony he gave to the church by which we are to remember his death. When we eat the bread and drink the cup together as a reminder of his body broken and his blood poured out for us, we proclaim his death until his return (1 Corinthians 11:26). John Stott points out that this commemorative act "dramatizes neither his birth nor his life, neither his words nor his works, but only his death." Stott writes of Jesus,

"It was by his death that he wished above all else to be remembered. There is then, it is safe to say, no Christianity without the cross. If the cross is not central to our religion, ours is not the religion of Jesus."[2]

In the book *In My Place Condemned He Stood,* authors J. I. Packer and Mark Dever say that we can't understand the atonement without a grasp of three things: first, the Trinitarian nature of God; second, the holiness and justice of God; and, third, our own guilt and sin before God.

This helps me understand my confusion about the Cross and Jesus's atoning work. As a teenager, I certainly had not given careful thought to God as Trinity. And if you don't understand that God is one and yet three distinct persons in the Father, Son, and Holy Spirit, then the death of Jesus on the cross seems like nothing but a tragic example of injustice. Or even worse, it could be viewed as the ruthless action of a God who punishes his unsuspecting, somewhat clueless Son.

One of the few times I remember the Cross being clearly presented during high school youth group was when a speaker told a story about a train conductor who was responsible for lowering a bridge so a commuter train could safely pass. One day the conductor's young son came with him to work and, while playing, got trapped in the gears that lowered the bridge. As the train approached, the conductor realized his son's plight. Without enough time to rescue his son and with the train rushing toward the bridge, the conductor made the heart-wrenching decision to lower the bridge on his son so the people on the train could be saved. "And that," the speaker said, "is what God did for you." I remember thinking, *God is a jerk.*

I hated that story. I was mad at the conductor for bringing his son to work. Mad at the son for playing in the gears. And mad at the guy for telling me the stupid story. It didn't make me appreciate the Cross more. It made the Cross seem like some sort of cosmic accident that was supposed to make me feel indebted and guilty.

Many years later I learned how inaccurate and unhelpful the analogy of the conductor is for explaining the Cross. At the root of its error is an absence of the Trinitarian nature of God.

The Father is God, the Son is God, and the Spirit is God. God is one in three distinct persons. The Father, Son, and Holy Spirit have perfect communion, and they worked together to save mankind. The work of salvation on the Cross was the united work of all three persons of the Trinity. Many places in Scripture point to this teamwork. Hebrews 9:14 says, "How much more will the blood of *Christ,* who through the eternal *Spirit* offered himself without blemish to *God,* purify our conscience from dead works to serve the living God" (emphasis added).

Jesus was no victim trapped in the gears of Roman injustice. Jesus was God himself, who willingly laid down his life. God the Father was no cruel, abusive deity who lacked pity for his child. Instead, in the mystery of the Godhead, Father and Son chose together to redeem mankind through substitution. Human sin demanded a price be paid. But God would pay the price. With his own life.

The Son became sin in that he represented mankind and stood in the place of sinful humanity. God the Father administered justice. The righteous wrath and punishment that human treason and rebellion deserved was poured out on God the Son. At the Cross, God himself both delivered and received the blow.

Jesus wasn't trapped. He was in control. And he chose, because of love, to lay down his life for us. Jesus said, "For this reason the Father loves me, because I lay down my life that I may take it up again. No one takes it from me, but I lay it down of my own accord. I have authority to lay it down, and

I have authority to take it up again. This charge I have received from my Father" (John 10:17–18).

Jesus laid down his life. He loved his Father's glory. The Father loved his Son. And together, out of love for a lost world, they paid the greatest price to atone for sin.

———

To atone means to make amends for wrong that's been done. Most people can admit they've done wrong. The easiest, most common confession in the world is "I admit I'm not perfect." But the idea that our sins and "imperfections" need the gruesome death of an innocent—much less the Son of God—seems a little over the top. We've done wrong, but in most cases we don't think it's that big a deal.

We feel this way because we don't truly know God. We don't understand that he is holy and righteous, that he hates and must punish all sin and wickedness. Scripture says that God's eyes are so pure he cannot look on evil (Habakkuk 1:13).

Maybe you've noticed in the Bible that when people encounter God, their common response is to fall down as though dead (see, for example, Revelation 1:17). You never get the sense that they're being melodramatic. They are sure they are going to die. Their actions convey pure terror. Why? Because they behold a God who is not only overwhelming in his power and glory but who is also completely righteous. The Bible uses the word *holy* to describe him. We usually think of holiness in terms of moral purity, and God is holy in that sense. But the word *holy* primarily describes God's "otherness." He is completely separate from us. God is completely different and exalted above mankind. There is no sin or darkness in him. He is completely good, true, and righteous.

Do we have any concept of what it means to encounter the holy, righteous, pure God of heaven? When Isaiah beheld God, he was instantly aware of his guilt and cried, "Woe is me! For I am lost; for I am a man of unclean lips, and I dwell in the midst of a people of unclean lips; for my eyes have seen the King, the LORD of hosts!" (Isaiah 6:5). When Job heard God speak, he despised himself and his arrogant demands (Job 42:6). When Peter first met Jesus and saw his supernatural power and holiness, he fell at Jesus's knees and begged, "Depart from me, for I am a sinful man, O Lord" (Luke 5:8). In the presence of the Holy God, Peter was undone by an awareness of his own sinfulness.

If we don't feel the need for atonement, it's probably because we assume God has the same nonchalant attitude toward evil that we do. But he doesn't. God has a total, unremitting hatred for sin and injustice. His response to sin is extreme righteous anger. The Bible calls this God's wrath. Some people are repulsed by the idea of God being a God of wrath. But if you think about it, a God who doesn't hate evil is terrifying. True goodness hates evil. True righteousness and justice must stand in opposition to injustice and unrighteousness. God's wrath, writes John Stott, "is in fact his holy reaction to evil."[3]

This is hard for me to grasp. Too often I place sin and injustice on a scale. Sin is less sinful if everyone is doing it. Injustice is less a problem if it's not against me or someone I love. If I can't see it or feel the effects of it, I don't lose sleep.

God is so different from me. He sees sin for what it is—an affront to his rule and reign. All human sin—even when it's done against another person—is ultimately also a sin against God. It's a violation of his laws (Psalm 51:4). And he sees the death and destruction and sorrow that sin brings about in people's lives. You and I have no idea how connected and consequential our sin is. We see most of our sins as insignificant—a small match dropping on the grass or at worst a tiny brush fire. God sees what the small flames lead to. He sees the forest fire that devours the countryside and ravages homes and takes lives.

God sees the devastation that human sin has wrought in the world. And in his perfect justice, he has promised to punish it all.

This is the most comforting and yet the most terrifying truth in the world: because God is holy and just, no one will get away with anything in this life. At the end of time, there will be a final and perfect accounting before him (Romans 14:12). What human judges and human courts couldn't prosecute, God Almighty will prosecute. There will be no unsolved crimes. No cold cases. He will judge the living and the dead (1 Peter 4:5). All sin—from genocide and murder to gossip and slander, from rape and human trafficking to lust and immorality—will be punished.

The irony of all this is that a God of perfect justice is both the one for whom we long and the one whom we dread. We long for someone to set things right, to punish those who terrorize, molest, kill, and enslave the innocent. We want someone to judge and punish evil. We want a judge with total power and a piercing commitment to righteousness.

But when his eyes turn on us, we realize that we, too, are guilty. We, too, deserve his judgment.

———

The night I had my dream about the room of files, I woke up sobbing. I turned on the light, grabbed my laptop, and began to write about my dream. I wept as I wrote. At times I could barely see the screen through the tears.

I called the story "The Room" and a few months later printed it in the small magazine I published at the time.[4] Maybe you've read it before. After it was printed, the story made its way around the Internet as one of those forwarded "Read this!" e-mails that clog your in-box.

I'm still amazed at the response the dream generated. I received stories of it being read by chaplains at prisons and by pastors to their congregations and being performed as a drama. Since then it's been printed in various magazines and even turned into a short film. A few years later I included "The Room" in a chapter of my first book. That chapter was the most frequently referenced by readers who wrote to me. What has surprised me most is the reaction it elicits from non-Christians. Many have told me how moved they were by the story. Many times they've said, "I began to cry as I read it."

Why does the dream connect with so many different people on a deep level? I think the answer is that it touches on the universal theme of guilt and redemption. We all carry around some sense that we've done wrong, that we haven't measured up to the standards of others or to our own standards—much less the standards of God.

Most of us attempt to find peace from past sins by trying to forget and move on. We find comfort in the distance that comes with the passing of time. The further we are from our sins, the less we feel they mark our lives and the less guilty we feel. I can tell you the story of watching pornography fourteen years ago. But do I want to confess the sin I committed last week? And do I even remember half of the wrongs I've done? The truth is that I've conveniently forgotten most of my violations.

I read a newspaper story about a woman named Jill Price who has a rare condition doctors call "superior autobiographical memory." Jill can recall in vivid detail every day of her life since age fourteen. Experts at the University of California studied her for six years to confirm her ability. If you've ever wished you had a better memory, you might want to reconsider. Jill views it as a blessing and a curse. She has warm memories that comfort her in difficult times, but there's also a dark side. She recalls every bad decision, every insult, and every excruciating embarrassment. Over the years, Jill said, the memories have eaten her up. She feels paralyzed and assaulted by them. Peaceful sleep is rare.[5]

We all want to think of ourselves as basically good people. But we can believe that illusion only because we forget most of our past decisions and actions and thoughts. But what if we remembered them perfectly? God does.

It's an uncomfortable thought, isn't it? I guess that's why my dream about the room filled with cards has such an emotional impact on people. We all have things in our lives that we don't want to remember. Things we know should be made right. Things that should be atoned for.

———

The Bible teaches that sin requires death. When Adam and Eve rebelled against God, his judgment on them and all mankind was physical death (Genesis 3:19).

But even in the garden, God spoke of his plan to rescue and restore mankind (Genesis 3:15). He didn't unveil his purpose or plan. Instead over the course of centuries, God began to teach his people the principle of atonement through substitutionary death.

When God rescued his people from slavery in Egypt, he punished the pride of Pharaoh by striking down the firstborn of every Egyptian family. But he showed mercy to the people of Israel by giving them a way to escape this death. Through Moses, the Lord instructed his people to sacrifice a spotless, unblemished lamb and mark the doorpost of their homes with its blood. In Exodus 12:13 God said, "The blood shall be a sign for you, on the houses where you are. And when I see the blood, I will pass over you, and no plague will befall you to destroy you, when I strike the land of Egypt." Judgment and death passed over the homes with doorposts wet with blood, the symbol of life poured out. A lamb had already died. A substitute had been offered.

After God brought his people out of Egypt, he established an elaborate system of animal sacrifices that provided a means of forgiving and removing their sin. The sacrificial system taught them that sin is serious and can only be covered by the shedding of blood. Leviticus 17:11 says, "For the life of the flesh is in the blood, and I have given it for you on the altar to make atonement for your souls, for it is the blood that makes atonement by the life."

Blood symbolizes a person's life. To shed blood means to give up life, to die. When a lamb or bull was killed in the blood sacrifices of the Old Testament, it was a vivid, graphic portrayal of paying for sins by the sacrifice of life. An Israelite man would choose a lamb without defect and bring it before the Lord. He would lay his hands on the animal, a symbol of it bearing his guilt. Then the animal would be sacrificed and its blood sprinkled on the altar.

Besides the ongoing sacrifices prescribed in the Law, there was also a special day each year called the Day of Atonement (Leviticus 16). One ritual of this day involved two goats. The first goat was sacrificed in the normal way. But the high priest laid his hands on the second animal, confessed the sins of the nation, and then sent the goat outside the camp into the wilderness. The second goat portrayed what the sacrifice of the first goat accomplished. God had provided a way for the people's sins to be removed, carried away by the sacrifice of a substitute. This is the origin of the term *scapegoat,* which refers to someone who is blamed for the wrongs and misdeeds of others so they can escape punishment.

The two goats on the Day of Atonement and all the blood sacrifices practiced over the centuries gave God's people a language and vivid imagery for their need for atonement. God wanted them to understand that they needed to be cleansed, to be forgiven. But the sacrifice of bulls and lambs and goats was merely a foreshadowing of the only sacrifice that could truly remove guilt. These blood sacrifices pointed ahead to Jesus. They were given so that one day God's people would grasp the meaning of Jesus Christ and his bloody death on a cross.

Jesus was betrayed on the night of the Passover celebration. On that night he gave his followers a new ceremony to recount God's redeeming work (Matthew 26:17–29). They would not shed the blood of a lamb; instead they would remember Jesus's body broken and his blood poured out.

Like the scapegoat that bore the sins of the people, Jesus was taken outside the city when he was crucified. He bore our sins and carried them away. Hebrews 13:12 says, "So Jesus also suffered outside the gate in order to sanctify the people through his own blood."

And of all the names used for Christ, few are as powerful as "the Lamb of God." Why is Jesus called by this name? It isn't because Jesus was cute and adorable and fluffy. He is called the Lamb of God because he was sacrificed by God for our sins. John the Baptist said of Jesus, "Behold, the Lamb of God, who takes away the sin of the world!" (John 1:29). And in his vision of heaven, the apostle John saw Jesus being worshiped by countless multitudes. And how does Jesus appear in his glory? As a lamb, standing as though slain (Revelation 5:6).

This is a staggering thought. Why would God need a lamb? He has no sin of his own to pay for. Why would God offer a sacrifice? The answer is that God offers his Son, and his Son willingly lays down his life, to atone for mankind's sins. We can never pay for our own sins. The debt we owe to God and the guilt we carry before God are too great. Only God himself can remove the stain of guilt and shame.

In Jesus's death God provided the lamb. Instead of you and me facing the wrath and punishment our sins deserve, Jesus took our place. He is our substitute. He shed his blood, he gave his life, so that our sins are removed and God's wrath is turned away.

Khaled Hosseini's novel *The Kite Runner* is a powerful portrayal of the human longing for atonement. The book tells the story of Amir, a newly married Afghan immigrant living in California who is haunted by an act of betrayal from his childhood. When he was a young boy growing up in Kabul, he stood by as his best friend, Hassan, was beaten and raped by a vicious older boy named Assef. Instead of rushing to his friend's aid, Amir cowered in fear and watched from the shadows.

Afterward Amir was racked with guilt. His shame was compounded by Hassan's continued kindness and loyalty. Hassan, whose father worked as a servant for Amir's wealthy father, continued to selflessly serve Amir. Even though he knew of Amir's cowardice, Hassan refused to retaliate or even utter a harsh word. Eaten up by his guilt, Amir falsely accused Hassan of stealing a new watch. Eventually Amir's behavior forced Hassan and his father out of the home.

The story picks up years later when Amir is grown and living in America with his elderly father. He's a world away from the land of his childhood, but the moment in the alley still plagues him. "That was a long time ago," he says, "but it's wrong what they say about the past, I've learned, about how you can bury it. Because the past claws its way out. Looking back now, I realize I have been peeking into that deserted alley for the last twenty-six years."[6]

When one of his old friends who knew of his shameful act calls from Pakistan and asks him to visit, Amir knows it isn't just his friend on the line but his "past of unatoned sins" calling. Before the old friend hangs up, he says, "There is a way to be good again."[7]

A way to be good again. Isn't that what we all long for? We want forgiveness and cleansing—a way to make up for and cover our wrongdoings and acts of selfishness. In *The Kite Runner* Amir finds this opportunity when he eventually returns to Afghanistan to face his past. He learns that his friend Hassan is dead but that his orphaned son is alive and in need of rescue. But saving the young boy requires that Amir face the same sadistic Assef who violated Hassan so many years before.

The story finds resolution as Amir reenacts the moments from his past in which he miserably failed. This time when he faces Assef, he doesn't back down. To gain his old friend's son, he accepts a brutal beating from Assef. His ribs are broken. His jaw is crushed. He chokes on his own blood. And yet in the midst of his beating, he begins to laugh. He laughs as he is battered and bruised. He finally feels that he is paying for his wrongs.

Amir risks his life to save the son of his friend Hassan. By showing kindness to the boy and adopting him, Amir finds a way "to be good again."

But can any of us ever atone for our past wrongs like this? What if the people we've sinned against are gone? Whom do we repay? What if there's nothing we can give to make up for what we stole? What if a beating isn't enough to salve our conscience? What can we give to pay for the wrongs we've done?

The Bible teaches that for us the problem is even more serious. Our sin isn't just against our friends and family members. Ultimately, all the wrong we do is an act of hatred and disobedience toward God himself. Our sin is the breaking of his law. It is not just our conscience that needs to be satisfied; it is the holy wrath of God that demands payment. Our problem is far greater than we imagine. How can an act of rebellion against an infinitely holy God, who must by his very nature judge wickedness and remove it from his good creation, be forgiven? First Samuel 2:25 says, "If someone sins against a man, God will mediate for him, but if someone sins against the LORD, who can intercede for him?" God's anger burns against us.

Even if we could somehow revisit and repay all the wrongs we've done (which we can't), we'd still have God to deal with. How do we make peace with a God of perfect righteousness and justice?

How does God make us good again before him? How does he deal with our guilt and sin? The unimaginable message of the Bible is that God's love for us is so great that he has made a way for us to be good again through the atoning life and death of his Son.

Jesus did for us what we could not do ourselves. He came to intercede for the human race that had sinned against God. He lived and died on our behalf.

Whereas we disobeyed God's law, Jesus perfectly obeyed it. Just as Adam's sin plunged the world into guilt, Jesus's obedience makes all who trust in him righteous (Romans 5:19). This is "the righteousness from God that depends on faith" (Philippians 3:9).

Instead of abandoning us and condemning us, God came looking for us. He so loved the world that he sent his only Son to save the world (John 3:16–17). Jesus came to reconcile us to God.

How does he reconcile us? By paying the penalty for our sins. This is what theologians call *penal substitution.* On the cross Jesus became our substitute and took our penalty. Just as Jesus obeyed in our place, he also died in our place. Galatians 3:13 says that Jesus became "a curse for us." The prophet Isaiah described Jesus's substitutionary, atoning death when he wrote:

> But he was wounded for our transgressions;
>> he was crushed for our iniquities;
> upon him was the chastisement that brought us peace,
>> and with his stripes we are healed.

All we like sheep have gone astray;

we have turned—every one—to his own way;

and the LORD has laid on him

the iniquity of us all. (Isaiah 53:5–6)

We transgressed. We committed the iniquity. But Jesus was wounded for us. He was crushed in our place. God laid on him our guilt so we could be forgiven. Second Corinthians 5:21 says, "For our sake he made him to be sin who knew no sin, so that in him we might become the righteousness of God."

What was happening when Jesus hung between heaven and earth? First Peter 2:24 says, "He himself bore our sins in his body on the tree." Apart from the unthinkable physical suffering of crucifixion, Jesus endured the torment of God's wrath toward sin.

The result of Christ's substitution is that God's wrath is satisfied and turned away. This is called *propitiation.* Romans 3:25 says that God put Christ forward "as a propitiation by his blood." God's justice demands death for sin. Jesus's blood poured out, his life given in our place, satisfies that demand. First John 4:10 says, "In this is love, not that we have loved God but that he loved us and sent his Son to be the propitiation for our sins."

"It is God himself who in holy wrath needs to be propitiated," writes John Stott. "God himself who in holy love undertook to do the propitiating, and God himself who in the person of his Son died for the propitiation of our sins."[8]

At the cross God's wrath was satisfied. Our sins were paid for so we could be forgiven and accepted by God. First Peter 3:18 says, "For Christ also suffered once for sins, the righteous for the unrighteous, that he might bring us to God."

A few years ago I was told that there was a Muslim version of my story "The Room" on various Islamic Web sites.[9]

A girl named Jenny, who had grown up in a religious, fundamentalist Muslim family, wrote to tell me how she'd read the story of my dream at a week-long camp for Muslim girls. On the emotional final evening around the campfire, Jenny was asked to read the story of the room filled with files. But she said the Muslim version of the dream had been edited. Jesus never appeared. There was no assurance of forgiveness. It ended with this paragraph:

> And then the tears came. I began to weep. Sobs so deep that the hurt
> started in my stomach and shook through me. I fell on my knees and
> cried. I cried out of shame, from the overwhelming shame of it all.
> The rows of file shelves swirled in my tear-filled eyes. No one must
> ever, ever know of this room. I must lock it up and hide the key.

After she read the story, the other girls left the campfire crying. But the effect was much deeper for Jenny. She was consumed by a sense of desperation and hopelessness. Throughout her life she had been a devout follower of Islam. Along with her family, she memorized the Koran, prayed five times a day, and had even visited Mecca. She did her best, but she was constantly aware of her shortcomings. She was distracted during prayers. She sometimes lied.

In high school Jenny had begun to have vivid nightmares of hell. She would wake up in a cold sweat with a desperate sense of hopelessness. "I was no longer so confident in my admittance to heaven," she said.

The Muslim version of "The Room" had been read around the campfire to spur the girls to be better and live moral lives, but it left Jenny exhausted and disillusioned. *I can't try any harder,* she thought, *and I know I am not good enough.* She began to look for God outside of Islam.

Several years later, after many stories of God's mercy in her life, Jenny came to a saving faith in Jesus Christ as her Savior. After she became a Christian, someone e-mailed her the complete Christian version of "The Room." When she opened the e-mail, she immediately recognized the beginning of the story. She was curious how she would feel reading the story now that she was a Christian.

"As I got to the end of the part that I remembered, I did not feel the deep sadness that I had before," Jenny told me. But the surprise for her was that the original version had a different ending. The version she had read at camp ended with terror and fear. But in this conclusion Jesus entered the room. Jenny read the words about Jesus that had been deleted from the story:

He looked at me with pity in His eyes. But this was a pity that didn't anger me. I dropped my head, covered my face with my hands and began to cry again. He walked over and put His arm around me. He could have said so many things. But He didn't say a word. He just cried with me.

Then He got up and walked back to the wall of files. Starting at one end of the room, He took out a file and, one by one, began to sign His name over mine on each card.

"No!" I shouted rushing to Him. All I could find to say was "No, no," as I pulled the card from Him. His name shouldn't be on these cards. But there it was, written in red so rich, so dark, so alive. The name of Jesus covered mine. It was written with His blood.

He gently took the card back. He smiled a sad smile and began to sign the cards. I don't think I'll ever understand how He did it so quickly, but the next instant it seemed I heard Him close the last file and walk back to my side. He placed His hand on my shoulder and said, "It is finished."

I stood up, and He led me out of the room. There was no lock on its door. There were still cards to be written.

Do you see how essential the atonement is to the Christian faith? Apart from the Cross of Jesus Christ, our lives dead-end in hopelessness and terror. We stand guilty before a God we can't please. We know our best efforts are inadequate. And the gnawing guilt for our wrongs can't be shaken.

That's where man-made religion leaves us—not just Islam, but every religious system (including some that claim to be Christian) that excludes the atoning sacrifice of the Cross. Without the blood of Jesus Christ shed for sins, there is no atonement, no forgiveness, no reconciliation. No hope.

But the story doesn't end with our guilt. Isn't that incredible? Jesus enters the picture. He walks into the reality of our failure and shame and guilt. Think of the worst card in your room full of files and consider this: Jesus died so your worst moment could be covered. He took the blame so you could stand before God forgiven and accepted.

There is a way to be good again. It is to trust in Jesus and his atoning death. To receive by faith his rescue. There is nothing you and I can do to pay for our sins. Our good deeds cannot cover them. Time will not make them fade. Only the blood of the Lamb of God can cleanse us, cover us, and rescue us from judgment.

HOW JESUS SAVED GREGG EUGENE HARRIS

"How does redemption accomplished outside Jerusalem give life to a young man on a California beach?"

GREGG PLAYED THE GUITAR and sang on the beach for tips. With his tattered bell-bottom jeans, mustache, and wispy, shoulder-length brown hair, he was the quintessential hippie troubadour. Laguna Beach, California, circa 1970, was a magnet for artists and musicians. They came from every corner of the country. Peace, love, and a steady supply of drugs made the beach town an idyllic setting.

"Would you like to hear a song?" Gregg would ask people lounging in the sun. He learned to read people—their style, age, and interests—and then did his best to sing a song to match them. He sang only original songs. His music was his art, and he refused to be a human jukebox playing songs heard on the radio.

Once he played a song for José Feliciano, the blind, lightning-fingered guitarist whose song "Light My Fire" had been a big hit. Gregg didn't recognize the rock star, but afterward Feliciano told him to come to his concert that night. He said he wanted to buy Gregg's song.

But Gregg didn't show that evening because he couldn't "prostitute" his art. Besides, he planned to make it big with his music on his own. He didn't know that God had bigger plans for him than musical stardom.

One day on the beach, Gregg was approached by two hippies. "Hey, man, what do you know about Jesus?" one of them asked him. It was the last question Gregg expected. He'd run all the way from Ohio to get away from Jesus and the stifling religion of his childhood. He knew everything about Jesus, and he despised him.

He decided to have a little fun with the two Jesus freaks. He would use his Bible knowledge to skewer them. He'd ask them questions they couldn't answer. He'd overpower them with his arguments. So he launched into a rant right there on the beach.

But they weren't overpowered. They just listened and smiled. Then, when he was done, they talked about Jesus in a way Gregg had never heard before. They said Jesus was a king who had come to redeem a world ruined by sin. In Jesus, God himself had invaded the planet. Jesus died on the cross, not as a victim, but to conquer death itself. He had shown the real meaning of love. And one day very soon Jesus would return. He would judge the whole world and rule the nations. Today was the day to turn from sin and believe in him.

In spite of himself, Gregg listened. Their words, their answers to his questions, their description of Jesus sank into his soul and tugged on something deep within him. It was as though someone was calling him from far off.

When the conversation ended, he tried to play it cool. He didn't let on how deeply affected he was by their words. He didn't kneel and pray or even say he would think more about what they'd said. The two men said goodbye and walked off down the beach.

"Somehow," Gregg says, "I knew my life would never be the same."

If someone digs a well and taps a spring of the purest water, it's no use to anyone unless the water is channeled to dry soil and carried to parched lips. To be told that such a well exists or merely to see it from a distance will not quench your thirst. You have to drink from it yourself.

Jesus once described the salvation he offers as living water. He told a woman he met by a well that if she drank the water he could give her, she would never be thirsty again (you can read the story in John 4). Jesus said that his water would become a spring welling up inside her, giving eternal life. He was speaking of the new spiritual life that he came to bring.

Of course, she didn't understand all that at first. She thought he was talking about normal water. She liked the idea of not being thirsty and not having to break her back pulling up buckets from the well.

But eventually the woman did come to understand that the water Jesus spoke of was a metaphor for spiritual life—for knowing and believing in him. And she did drink this living water. She trusted in Jesus as the promised Savior.

The Bible tells us that Jesus died and rose again so that sinners could have their sins forgiven and be reconciled to God (1 Corinthians 15:1–4). This message is what Christians call the gospel, a word that means "good news." Many people have heard this message of good news, but obviously not all have been saved by it. It's possible to learn about the events of Jesus's life, death, and resurrection from a distance—to be told of their meaning, their power, and their hope—and yet receive no personal benefit from them.

Somehow, Jesus's great work of salvation has to reach us. Not only the news of it but the real spiritual power of it has to touch us and change us. So how does that happen?

Theologian John Murray has a helpful way of describing God's saving work. He uses the terms *redemption accomplished* and *redemption applied*. *Redemption accomplished* is what Jesus has already done for us—his life of perfect obedience, his substitutionary death on the cross, and his resurrection.

It's the second aspect of God's redemption—the applied part—that I want us to reflect on here. *Redemption applied* is how Jesus's accomplishment connects to us. How it reaches us and saves us. Another name for this is the *doctrine of salvation.*

The doctrine of salvation answers the questions "How does Jesus's saving work translate into our salvation? What does it mean to get saved? How do we go from being sinners who are spiritually dead and alienated from God to being spiritually alive, righteous children of God?"

Or, to put the question in terms that are much more personal to me, how does Jesus's redemption accomplished on a hill outside Jerusalem reach down through the centuries to the year 1970 and to a young man playing his guitar on a California beach?

There are many ways to explore the doctrine of salvation, but I'd like to consider it by sharing the story of how Jesus applied his mighty salvation to one person. His name is Gregg Harris, and he's my father.

———

His parents named him Gregg Eugene. His first name was spelled with two *g*'s on the end because that's how Grandma saw it on a nameplate at a doctor's office. His middle name, Eugene, was his father's name. He never liked his middle name, but for some reason he passed it on to me. I've mostly forgiven him for that.

Dad was born on October 23, 1952, in Dayton, Ohio, at the Miami Valley Hospital. He appeared to be a normal, healthy baby, but the doctor shared devastating news with Gene and Francis. "Nature forgot to finish her work," he said. Their little boy had three very serious internal birth defects. For there to be any hope of his survival, he had to undergo three major surgeries within forty-eight hours of his birth. In 1952 the procedures were dangerous, bordering on experimental. If he survived, the doctors said, he probably wouldn't make it past six years old. And if he did, he would be confined to a wheelchair and need constant care.

Grandma never stopped praying. My grandmother was a devout Christian who had given her life to Jesus when she was eight years old. Her family lived a mile from the church. She read her Bible and went to church every time the doors were open. Her father played the organ. He could make the organ talk. Every day Grandma asked God to grow her faith "daily, monthly, and yearly."

Her one major lapse in Christian faithfulness was dating and marrying Gene. My grandfather was a quiet World War II veteran who worked at the Frigidaire plant in Dayton, loved horses, and always had a pouch of Red Man chewing tobacco handy. He was born in Alabama and lived most of his life in Tennessee. Grandma knew he wasn't a genuine believer. During their courtship he went to church and feigned enough interest in the Bible to convince her to marry him. But afterward his church attendance slowly dropped off. Church just seemed to make him mad. When he did go with her, they would argue on their way home from the meeting. Finally he stopped going altogether.

But Grandma's faith sustained her in the difficult years after my dad's birth and the surgeries. They had only partially solved his problems; he couldn't pass solids normally. Grandma would spend hours each day, pumping him full of oil, trying to help him go to the bathroom.

Caring for him consumed every ounce of her energy, leaving her physically and emotionally exhausted. Worst of all she was alone in the endeavor.

Grandpa couldn't handle his son's disability. Wanting to pretend it away and looking for any excuse to get out of the house, he spent most of his free time at ball games and racetracks.

The daily stress was almost too much for Grandma to handle. She contemplated suicide. "I know that's wrong," she told God. And when she thought of little Gregg, she knew she had to keep living, if only for him. "My life is like a jigsaw puzzle that's all confused, and I can't put it together," she prayed. "God, only you can fix this."

Another major surgery was planned when Dad was seven. The doctors said it might make things worse instead of better, but they had to try something. Then on the day of the operation, while they were waiting at the hospital, he went to the bathroom by himself. This had never happened naturally before. The surgery was called off. Grandma knew it was a miracle from heaven.

But even with this progress, Dad still faced significant challenges. His childhood was shaped by his disability. For fear that a blow to his stomach could kill him, he was isolated and kept from any kind of rough play or sports. "I was treated like an egg," Dad remembers. And because most of his early years were spent with his mother, he had a warped view of his place in the world. Grandma was so intent on keeping him in good spirits that she treated him like a little prince. She made him believe that his every word was brilliant and his every joke was sidesplittingly funny.

When he got to school, the illusion was shattered. He wasn't brilliant or funny. And when the other kids didn't laugh at his jokes, Gregg just tried harder. To make matters worse, his disability led to several occasions when he soiled himself in class. In elementary school that's not the sort of thing you live down. For years he was ostracized and mocked.

A story from sixth grade epitomizes Gregg's elementary school years. One day a popular girl named Marilyn announced in the cafeteria that she was having a party at her house later that afternoon. Everyone was invited. Gregg thought "everyone" included him. After school he rushed home, flush with excitement. He put on his Sunday best—a crisp white shirt and clip-on bow tie—and marched off to Marilyn's house. She was standing at the door smiling as she welcomed all the kids. But when she saw Gregg, her smile turned to a scowl. "I don't remember inviting you," she sneered.

"I know," he quickly lied. "I was just coming here to meet a friend."

"Oh," Marilyn replied coolly. She went inside and shut the door.

Gregg stood there a moment listening to the sounds of the party in the house. Kids were talking and laughing. He was sure they were laughing at him. He turned and ran all the way back home, into his room, and threw himself on his bed. He buried his face in his pillow and screamed.

Throughout his childhood Gregg was a church kid. Each week Grandma dragged him and his brother and sister to First Baptist in Centerville. Look-ing back, Dad says that exposure to religion acted like a flu shot—it immu-nized him from genuine faith. He got just enough to develop a deep-rooted disdain for Christianity and the church.

But as a young child, he tried to please his mom by learning to parrot reli-gious phrases and recite Bible facts. And he dutifully got himself "saved" dozens of times. Weekly attendance at Sunday school and Vacation Bible School every summer gave him countless opportunities to pray the sinner's prayer. He didn't mean any of it, and it didn't do anything for him. He had no real understanding of what it meant to trust in Jesus. And no real desire to get what the church offered.

Pastor Snoddy was a nice enough man, but the women really ran the place. In Gregg's eyes Jesus was just a long-haired version of Pastor Snoddy—

mild, gentle, and a bit of a pushover. The Jesus he saw in the painting on his Sunday school wall had a glowing face and doe eyes. And he was a little too pretty for comfort.

His Sunday school teachers said that Jesus loved him, that Jesus wanted to come into his heart. But that only made Jesus seem more clingy and desperate. And what did it really mean for Jesus to come into your heart?

———

You would think that something as important as how one gets saved would get more careful attention from Christians. But I think a lot of us share Dad's hazy conception of salvation. For many, getting saved is simply a matter of praying a prayer or responding to an altar call. But if you press Christians for the specifics of what our prayer means or what actually occurs inwardly when someone believes, our understanding starts to break down. Our "doctrine of salvation" is premised on a string of undefined religious clichés: God loves me. I gave my life to Jesus. I have a personal relationship with Jesus. I invited Jesus into my heart. I got saved. I became a Christian.

It seems that most Christians think of getting saved as something *we* do. We drive the action. We do the choosing. We find God. We invite Jesus in. We become Christians. In America, salvation is a lot like shopping for a new flat-screen television.

The odd thing about this "we do it" emphasis in our view of salvation is how different it is from the way the Bible talks about salvation. Scripture does command us to respond to Jesus, to turn to God in faith and repent of sin (Acts 2:38). But when the Bible speaks of the powerful, mysterious work of salvation in the human soul, it always emphasizes what God does. It always talks about God's grace and God's power.

God's grace, as Jerry Bridges defines it, is "God's kindness shown to the ill-deserving."[1] Because of our disobedience and rebellion toward God, we're not just undeserving of kindness; we're actually ill-deserving. We're guilty. The only thing we deserve is punishment. Salvation isn't something we earn or buy. Ephesians 2:8–9 says, "For by grace you have been saved through faith. And this is not your own doing; it is the gift of God, not a result of works, so that no one may boast." Salvation is not our doing. It is a gift. Only God can pay for our sins and make us worthy to relate to him. And this is what he's done through the death of his Son. This is why God's kindness toward us can be described as amazing grace.

Power is the ability to do or accomplish something. The Bible insistently denies that we have the spiritual power to save ourselves or even contribute to the process. We are not just weak; we are spiritually lifeless, dead (Ephesians 2:1). Salvation is accomplished not by our striving but by God's power. In Romans, the apostle Paul states that the work of Jesus in dying and rising again is "the power of God for salvation" for all who believe (1:16). Elsewhere Paul says that while the message of a crucified Savior seems foolish to many, for those who are saved, it is "the power of God" (1 Corinthians 1:18).

Even the analogies God uses in the Bible to describe salvation emphasize that it is his work. Look at how God describes the ways he redeems his people. Think about Israel's great rescue from Egypt, told in the book of Exodus. That mighty act of salvation from slavery foreshadowed Christ's salvation of sinners. Who made that happen? The mighty Israelites? No, the power of God working through his servant Moses.

Or consider the Old Testament prophet Ezekiel. God gave him the incredible vision of a valley filled with dry bones (Ezekiel 37:1–14). It was an open graveyard of human skeletons. The bones were dry and lifeless. God asked, "Can these bones live?" (verse 3). Then God told Ezekiel to prophesy to the bones, to speak God's word over them. Ezekiel spoke, and as he did, God's mighty word breathed life into the bones. They flew into alignment.

They were wrapped in sinew and muscle and flesh. The word of God transformed a valley of dry bones into a mighty, living army.

Dead bones brought to life. That's a picture of how God saves people. We have no life in ourselves. No human desire or effort can impart life. How can we live? Only by the bidding of God. Only by the power of the mighty Word of God breathing life into dead people.

Jonah 2:9 says, "Salvation belongs to the LORD!" It's true. Salvation is the supernatural work of God in the human soul. It is owned by God. Only he can give it. It depends solely on the power of God and the grace of God.

This perspective of salvation is incredibly humbling. If salvation isn't ultimately because of my spiritual insight, my discovery, my inner goodness, my effort, or my religious work, then I cannot save myself. It doesn't matter what family or church I've been born into. It doesn't matter how moral or religious or respected I am. In this sense the message of the gospel is very bad news for human ingenuity and pride.

But at the same time, it's very good news for people whom Jesus described as "the poor in spirit" (Matthew 5:3)—people who know they can't save themselves, people who realize their spiritual poverty and helplessness. For these people, the gospel imparts hope. Because if God is truly the central figure and actor in salvation—if his choosing, his searching, his calling, his grace, his regenerating power giving new life is what makes salvation possible—then *no one* is beyond hope.

And this is incredibly good news. It means God can save anyone.

Even me. Even you. Even my dad.

———

Things got a little better for Dad after elementary school. The family moved from Kettering to Miamisburg. More significantly, he got a guitar.

He had found some success writing poetry when he was younger. One of his poems had even been published in the newspaper. That got the girls' attention. Now he tried his hand at putting his poems to music. He learned a few chords and had a decent voice. He had finally found his niche. He had always been a loner. But now he was a loner with a guitar. It wasn't a bad mystique to possess.

The counterculture movement of the 1960s was in full swing. The Beatles had invaded America. Jefferson Airplane and Big Brother and the Holding Company with Janis Joplin were on the radio. Thousands had gathered in Haight-Ashbury for the Summer of Love. Dad started hanging out at the coffeehouse on Bigger Road. He started smoking pot. He grew his hair long. He found an identity among the freaks, the hippies. The song on the radio said, "If you're going to San Francisco, be sure to wear some flowers in your hair."[2] Dad dreamed of escaping the suffocating backwoods town of Miamisburg and heading west.

If he didn't already have enough reasons to leave Miamisburg, he got another one when he became a target of the Orchard Hill boys. This hillbilly gang was known for binge drinking, stealing, reselling car parts, and maliciously beating anyone who crossed them. Dad made the mistake of singing a song to a girl one of the Orchard Hill boys liked. After that whenever they saw him, they would jump him. One day at the county fair, a thug named Marvin Boleyn belted him from behind with a tire iron.

That was the last straw. Under the guise of taking his sister to a movie, he headed to downtown Dayton. He ditched his sister at the theater and, guitar in hand, headed to the bus station. He found a used ticket on the ground, put his thumb over the hole punched in it, and rode away. He was sixteen years old.

The bus took him to Cincinnati. From there he hitchhiked to Chicago, then St. Louis, where he made two dollars an hour loading crates for a shipping company. He wrote his parents from the road, trying to assuage his mom's fears. He was eating well. He was happy. He said that now that he didn't have anyone to tell him what to do, he felt like doing all they'd always told him to. (That was a lie.) He told his mom that he had Sundays off and would go to church. (That was a lie too.) He told his sister, Leslie, that he was sorry for leaving her stranded at the movie theater. (That was sincere.)

After he worked a few weeks in St. Louis, a trucker took him as far as Colorado Springs. That's when he saw his first mountain, Pikes Peak. A cop picked him up hitchhiking and asked, "Where you headed, son?"

"Home," Dad said.

"Where ya live?"

"Just over those mountains."

"There ain't nothin' on the other side of those mountains," the officer replied.

He was caught. They shipped him back to Ohio.

Dad ran away again a few months later. He asked to borrow the car, but his dad wouldn't let him. He was indignant. "I don't need a car to get where I want to go," he said to himself. Two days later he called his parents from Clearwater Beach, Florida.

In Clearwater he found a vibrant hippie scene down on the pier. He survived by panhandling and playing his guitar for spare change. He also stole purses. After emptying out their contents, he would bury them in the sand.

His life of petty crime in Florida was cut short when he was caught stealing at a convenience store. Dad wasn't the smartest thief. He walked into the store with money in his pocket but decided to steal a powdered sugar doughnut. The evidence of his crime wasn't hard for the store's owner to spot. The police arrived, and he was put in jail for three days.

His short stint in jail shook him up. He was surrounded by drunks and winos who snored at night and cussed and scuffled during the day. He was absolutely miserable and terrified.

A Baptist preacher visited the jail and asked where Dad was from and if his parents knew where he was. He shared the gospel with Dad, and although Dad listened, he didn't find it particularly compelling. They were the same words he had heard hundreds of times growing up. But then the preacher did something that did grab his attention. He paid Dad's fine for shoplifting, got him out of jail, and bought him a one-way plane ticket back to Dayton, Ohio.

That act of kindness had a profound effect on Dad. It made him want to be good. He was so filled with gratitude that he decided he was going to change. He was going to be a Christian—and not just any Christian. He was going to be a great Christian.

The only problem with his plan was that he could no more make himself a Christian than dry bones can will themselves to live.

———

Jesus said that in order to be saved, in order to be part of his kingdom, a person has to be "born again" (John 3:3).

Jesus liked to speak in ways that piqued people's curiosity, even shocked them. Two thousand years after Jesus's earthly ministry, we've worn the edges off most of his shocking statements and smoothed them like stones in a rock polisher. So now when we hear the phrase *born again,* we picture a certain type of person, or we think of a voting bloc. People who followed the news in the late 1970s might think of Jimmy Carter, a former peanut farmer from Georgia who became president and was famous for stating that he was a born-again Christian.

But when Jesus first said "born again," no one pictured Jimmy Carter or any other stereotype of a Christian. Instead they pictured the sticky mess of human birth, and then they imagined having to go through that process again.

That's how the Pharisee Nicodemus reacted when he heard Jesus talk about being born again. He asked, "How can a man be born when he is old? Can he enter a second time into his mother's womb and be born?" (John 3:4). Jesus explained that the spiritual life required to live in his kingdom is a *brand-new* life. It requires a change so radical, so transformational, that it could be described as new birth. The change is as powerful and fresh as when a child enters the world.

The new birth Jesus described is called *regeneration*. John Frame writes that regeneration is "a sovereign act of God, beginning a new spiritual life in us."[3] In regeneration God gives a person a new nature, a new heart, and new spiritual life.

Apart from regeneration, we are all dead spiritually (Ephesians 2:1–2). Not sick. Not weak. Not disabled. We are dead. Dead like dry bones. This means we are unable to know or respond to God. We don't just need a little shove, a kick-start, or resuscitation; we need spiritual resurrection and regeneration.

Paul speaks of regeneration in terms of a Christian being a "new creation" (2 Corinthians 5:17). This new life is what God foretold to the prophet Ezekiel hundreds of years before Jesus came. God said, "And I will give them one heart, and a new spirit I will put within them. I will remove the heart of stone from their flesh and give them a heart of flesh" (Ezekiel 11:19).

New birth. New creation. Heart transplant. You can't help but see the emphasis on salvation being the work of God. In fact, the point of Jesus's phrase *born again* is not only new life but new life brought about by the work of God's Spirit. In John 3:6–8 Jesus said, "That which is born of the flesh is flesh, and that which is born of the Spirit is spirit. Do not marvel that I said to you, 'You must be born again.' The wind blows where it wishes, and you hear its sound, but you do not know where it comes from or where it goes. So it is with everyone who is born of the Spirit."

Only the Holy Spirit imparts life. This isn't under our control. Like the wind, the Spirit blows where it wishes. We see its effect, we hear its sound, but we don't know where it comes from, and we can't control its direction. So the new birth, God's act of regenerating power, is solely dependent on God's will. We can't will ourselves to be born again any more than we could have willed ourselves to be born the first time. None of us had any control over the timing of our physical conception and birth. In the same way, our spiritual birth is utterly and completely a work of God's Holy Spirit. Before God does this work in us, we don't possess the inner desire to believe in him, seek him, repent of sin, or genuinely pray for salvation.

The problem with Dad's decision to make himself a "good Christian" at age sixteen was that he hadn't experienced the miracle of regeneration. He hadn't been born again. His pseudoconversion after his jail stint was an attempt at self-reform. It was an effort to be, by his own willpower, a better, more moral person.

It wasn't by the power of God; it wasn't really even about God. Dad didn't acknowledge his sin and guilt before God. He didn't repent. He didn't place his trust in Jesus, who died to absorb God's wrath for his sin. Instead, Dad simply decided to stop being bad and start being good. He was going to "do" religion like no ever had. He was going to try harder than anyone before him.

When he got home from Florida, he went back to school and started going to church. He cut his hair. He stopped smoking cigarettes and doing drugs. He stopped messing around with girls. He even started a Christian club at his school called Teens for Christ. His mom and all the ladies from church were thrilled.

It worked pretty well…for a while. Then, like one of the seeds in Jesus's parable of the soils, Dad's growth spurt was interrupted and proven to be superficial.

His Christian club hosted a talent show at school. They put it on so a Christian band in the area could play and share the gospel. Because it was a school-sponsored event, other, non-Christian bands were also invited to perform. When a few of the secular bands had some fun during the concert and gently mocked the Christian-themed event, the members of the Christian band were offended and refused to participate.

Dad was so mad, so outraged at being let down by these Christians that he decided he wanted nothing more to do with Christianity. (The timing of his outrage may have had something to do with a girl from school he'd been eyeing.) And just as he had turned his self-generated Christianity on, he turned it off.

After rejecting Christianity, Dad went back to his old ways. He hit the road again and hitchhiked to Florida. Most of his friends were gone, so he headed to California. On his way he spent a month in Austin, Texas, where he joined up with the antiauthoritarian Youth International Party, or Yippies, as they were called. He became instantly popular with the Yippies because he wrote and sang protest songs. He joined them when they invaded the LBJ Library, an act which got them on national television. But the weather in Austin was too hot, so he moved on.

He arrived in San Diego, then headed up the coast till he landed in Laguna Beach. The sleepy little beach town had its requisite surfers but was also known as an arts community that hosted two major arts festivals. It was populated by dancers, painters, jewelry craftsmen, singers, and poets. Dad felt like he had finally found a home with his own tribe. He got a three-dollar-a-night room at the Laguna Hotel and started working.

By this time he had an established routine. He would go to a nice restaurant and ask if he could serve as a troubadour, walking among the tables singing songs. All he wanted was a meal at the end of the night and whatever tips he made from singing. He wrote songs for children, songs for elderly couples, songs for couples. If he sang the right song, he could sometimes get a twenty-dollar tip. The money he made enabled him to buy a used Volvo P1800 and rent a room in a nice house with a friend. They even had a pool. He and a friend founded the Laguna Beach Free Poets Society, a little group that would gather at a local coffeehouse and read their poetry. He'd never been happier or experienced more success.

Then came his fateful conversation on the beach. Dad was sitting on one of his favorite rocks, working on a new song, when the two Christian hippies approached him.

Dad remembers that the way the two hippies talked about Jesus was unlike anything he had ever heard before. I don't know that what they said that day on the beach was a clearer or more powerful presentation of the gospel than he'd heard in Sunday school or from the Baptist preacher in the Florida jail cell. Maybe it was. But ultimately the eloquence or persuasiveness of the messenger doesn't save a person. It's the work of God's Spirit in a person's heart. That day on the beach, God's Spirit opened Dad's heart to listen. Through the message of the gospel, God called him. It's this "heavenly calling," as Hebrews 3:1 refers to it, that distinguishes all genuine Christians. No matter how a person hears or who tells him the message of Jesus crucified for sins and risen from the dead, behind it all is God, summoning a sinner to himself. Calling him, calling her "into the fellowship of his Son, Jesus Christ our Lord" (1 Corinthians 1:9).

Dad doesn't think he was saved that day on the beach, but as he puts it, "the hook was set." Like a fish on a line, he sensed God drawing him from that moment forward.

A few days after he heard the gospel on the beach, there was a drug bust at the home where he was living. He was gone when police raided the house and arrested several of his roommates. Even though the cops ransacked the house, they didn't find the bag of marijuana hidden underneath a trash bin in his room. But he figured they might come back and arrest him for his connection to his roommates. So he packed up his car that day and drove out of town.

The timing of the raid so soon after hearing the gospel wasn't lost on Dad. He was sure it was more than coincidence. He felt God chasing him. The question that kept ringing in his mind was, *What if it's true? What if Jesus is the Son of God?*

The songs he wrote in those days were different. They were songs filled with questions and yearning for meaning in life. One was called "There Are No Words to Say."

What can I say to a mountain
Can I tell it of some time it has not known
What can I say to a mighty redwood tree
Lest I speak to it how little I have grown
I have so many stories
Stories of my time as living clay
I have so many stories, but I have no words to say

He made his way to Colorado and found a restaurant to work at in Vail, but nothing seemed to go right. In a drunken fog, his landlord threw a brick through the window of his car. Only after he reported the incident to the police did he learn that his landlord was a major contractor who had built half of the city. The next day he lost his job at the restaurant.

He kept running, traveling east. In Indianapolis he started singing and playing rhythm guitar in a band. The group needed a lead singer, and they liked the songs he wrote. They got a good gig that paid each band member $125 a night. But then Dad got a bad cold and started to lose his voice after the first set. Suddenly his band mates stopped being so friendly. They pushed him to sing. They were losing money and were unsympathetic to his plight.

That was Dad's breaking point. He and the other members of the band lived together in an old farmhouse. One night Dad went into the bathroom, the only room where you could be alone, locked the door, and did something he hadn't done in a long time. He prayed.

"God," he said, "if you're really there, I want to know. I don't want to psych myself up believing in something that's not true. But if you really are there, then you are the most important thing and the reason I'm here. I don't know if you're allowed to do this, but will you please show me?"

Dad says he was born again right there in the bathroom. "I know God doesn't always do this," he told me recently. "But when I prayed that night, it sounded like a thousand voices all started cheering, 'Surprise! Welcome home!' It was just in my head, but it was deafening. It was like I had walked into a room and there was a surprise party for me."

He began to weep. The welcome and deep sense of acceptance he felt were the extreme opposite of all the rejection he had experienced in his life. In that moment he knew the love of God for him. He believed that Jesus was the Son of God who had died for his sins. As he sat on a bathroom floor in

Indiana, God changed his heart. And in response he repented of his sin and gave his whole life to Jesus.

———

The Bible teaches that we must respond to the gospel in repentance and faith (Acts 3:19). Most of us understand the faith part. We trust that what Jesus did was for us, and we entrust our lives to him. But we often overlook the repentance part. To repent means to turn away from something, to renounce it. Genuine repentance involves a sorrow over sin as an offense against God. But this sorrow is not hopeless. It is a sorrow that turns and believes that Jesus can forgive and, by his death, cleanse us from all our guilt.

When God saved my dad that night in Indiana, Dad's view of his sin was so different from what it had been before. A few years earlier when he tried making himself a Christian, he simply wanted to be good. But now there was a real sorrow, even hatred for his rebellion. And there was a new-found humility.

For a long time he hadn't wanted to become a Christian in large part because he didn't want his mom to win. She could seem so smug in her confidence that God would one day save him. He just knew that if he ever became a Christian, she'd say, "I always knew you would." In the past the thought of her gloating drove him crazy. But now that didn't matter anymore. God had saved him. He didn't care if that made his mom right. He had been wrong. He wanted to live for Jesus. His repentance was real.

Repentance and faith are inseparable—two sides of the same coin. When people are genuinely converted, they don't simply turn away from sin and bad behavior; they turn toward the person of Jesus Christ and his lordship. They believe that his death atoned for sins. They believe that he alone can save. They turn to him as King, and in so doing they turn their back on a life of sin and self-rule.

It's easy to mistakenly think that because we're commanded to have faith, our faith saves us. But this isn't the case. Faith is not the grounds for our salvation. Salvation is always and only by grace alone (Ephesians 2:8–10). Our faith doesn't merit anything; it is simply the instrument by which God's grace flows to us. "Faith," writes Jerry Bridges, "is merely the hand that receives the gift of God, and God through His Spirit even opens our hand to receive the gift."[4]

Jesus has earned everything for us. It is his work, his obedience, his death in our place that saves us. We are called to trust him, to rest in his work, and through that trusting to receive all he has accomplished.

My father wasn't saved because he cleaned himself up morally and presented himself to God. He wasn't saved because he did acts of kindness as penance for his wrongdoing.

No, like every other sinner who is saved from destruction, my dad was saved by grace through faith. He was saved by Jesus Christ, whom he clung to. That is how God saves people. That is what it means to be a Christian, to know salvation. God saves people by joining them or uniting them with Christ. All the spiritual blessings of salvation—redemption from sin, new life, forgiveness of guilt—come through Christ and in Christ and because of Christ (Ephesians 1:3–14).

Jesus has done all the work. Salvation comes by getting in on what he's done. This is how Jesus's accomplishment of redemption gets applied to us. Through faith and the work of the Holy Spirit, we are united with Christ and receive all the saving benefits of Jesus's life, death, and resurrection.

When my dad trusted in Jesus, God viewed him as though all that Jesus had earned and accomplished belonged to my dad. God declared him righteous, because Jesus is righteous. And God adopted him as a son, because Jesus is his Son. These important aspects of God's saving work are called *justification* and *adoption.*

In justification, God gives sinners a new legal status. Because of our sin, we are guilty before God. In the courtroom of his justice, we rightly deserve punishment. We've violated his truth by lying. We've dishonored his plan for our sexuality by immorality, adultery, and homosexuality. We've ignored his commands to honor our parents. We've rejected his place as the only God by worshiping false gods. We've robbed, cheated, and abused others. Worst of all we've lived as though we were ultimate—we've substituted ourselves for him. All these acts of sin, all these violations of his law, make us guilty.

For God simply to overlook these real sins would make him unjust. Justice must be served. Someone has to pay; someone has to receive the punishment for sin.

And this is why Christ had to die. The only way we can be righteous is for God to give us a righteousness we don't possess in and of ourselves. The only way for our sins to be paid for (apart from our spending an eternity in hell) is for God himself, in Christ, to receive the punishment.

This has been called the blessed exchange. All who trust in Jesus are given Jesus's righteousness. And Jesus takes on the guilt of their sin. We are "justified by his grace as a gift, through the redemption that is in Christ Jesus, whom God put forward as a propitiation by his blood, to be received by faith" (Romans 3:24–25).

The Cross shows God to be just, in that he punishes all sin. And the Cross shows God to be the gracious "justifier" of all who have faith in Jesus (Romans 3:26).

When my father trusted in Jesus, God declared him justified. He was no longer Gregg Eugene Harris, the lying, immoral, selfish thief. He became Gregg Eugene Harris, who is united by faith to Jesus Christ—the holy One, the perfect keeper of the law, the righteous One.

———

While justification borrows the language of the courtroom to help us understand God's work of salvation, *adoption* uses the language of family to help us see that behind all of God's saving work is a deeply relational and personal motive of love. God tells us that when we trust in Jesus, God adopts us as his sons and daughters (Ephesians 1:5). More than anything else this should convince us of God's love. "See what kind of love the Father has given to us, that we should be called children of God; and so we are" (1 John 3:1).

Justification gives us a new legal status. Adoption gives us a new family and a new father. This is another expression of our union with Christ. Because Jesus is the only begotten Son of God, as we trust in him, we receive his status as a child of God. John 1:12 says that to all who receive Jesus, to all who believe in his name, "he gave the right to become children of God."

In Christ, we are not forgiven servants. We are given all the rights and privileges of natural-born children. We are adopted and welcomed into the warmth of relationship with God as our loving Father. Romans 8:15–16 describes the Holy Spirit as "the Spirit of adoption" who enables us to cry to God as our Abba—an intimate Hebrew term akin to *dad*. It combines intimacy and respect. The Holy Spirit bears witness with our spirit "that we are children of God."

"What is a Christian?" asks J. I. Packer. "The question can be answered in many ways, but the richest answer I know is that a Christian is one who has God as Father."[5] And Sinclair Ferguson writes, "You cannot open the pages of the New Testament without realizing that one of the things that makes it so 'new', in every way, is that here men and women call God 'Father'. This conviction, that we can speak to the Maker of the universe in such intimate terms, lies at the heart of the Christian faith."[6]

———

The first question Dad asked God after he was saved was, "What do you want me to do?" The unmistakable impression he sensed was, "Go home." And so Dad obeyed his new Lord.

If ever there was sure evidence that Gregg Harris was a new creation, it's that he was happy to be heading back to Miamisburg, Ohio. He began attending First Baptist Church. There was a new pastor and a new wave of young people whom God had saved. One of them was a beautiful Japanese American girl named Sono Sato. She had just been saved that summer.

Dad and Mom's first date was to go witnessing in a park together. My dad was truly transformed. He had a newfound love for the Bible. He had never been good at study, but now, even though he was still a slow reader, he couldn't get enough of Scripture. And he loved to tell others about Jesus. He even had a near run-in with the police when he and a friend stood in a crowded mall and began to preach the gospel. They were a little too effective in gathering a crowd, and the police arrived to usher the zealots away.

Mom says she fell in love with Dad because his faith in God was the most important thing in his life. Less than a year after they were married, I was born. My dad was twenty-one; my mom was twenty. They'd been saved only a short time, but they brought me into a Christian home.

———

I've often wished I could go back in time and listen in on that conversation on Laguna Beach when the two Christian hippies talked to my dad about Jesus. What I wouldn't give to hear Dad's best arguments as an amateur atheist and then to hear their presentation of the gospel. It's impossible to measure how much that moment has shaped my life.

Mostly, I'd just like to find the two men and thank them. I'd thank them for being bold that day and for telling my dad the truth even when he didn't want to hear it. The Bible says that without the proclamation of the gospel, without everyday Christians bearing witness to Jesus, people can't hear the good news; they can't believe in and can't call upon God (Romans 10:14).

I'd tell them how much God has used their faithfulness to share the gospel. I'd tell them about all the great things God has done through Dad in the years since. I'd tell them how over the years Dad has literally taught hundreds of thousands of parents about the importance of teaching their children to know and love God. I'd tell them about all the people who have told me that God used my dad to give them a vision for building a godly Christian home.

I'd tell them that everything I've been able to do as a pastor and writer is directly tied to my dad and the godly heritage he passed on to me and my six siblings. He raised us to seek and trust Jesus.

I guess that conversation will have to wait for heaven. I look forward to it.

———

Recently my dad, mom, and younger siblings came to Maryland. Our church hosted a conference featuring my younger brothers Alex and Brett, both of whom are skilled speakers and writers. They were challenging teens to "do hard things" for the glory of God. My brother Joel was leading the crowd in worship.

The building was packed with more than thirty-five hundred teenagers and their parents. People sat in the aisles and on the floors. I sat on the front row with Shannon and our kids. The whole time I felt as if I were about to explode with joy and gratefulness. I was so proud of my brothers. I was so thankful for God's kindness toward our family. He was letting us encourage other Christians and share truth from his Word.

And then my dad got up and spoke. He shared a simple but profound message about what it means to be saved, to truly be a Christian. He talked about how people can be saved only by the power of God giving them a new heart and a new nature. He preached like I've never heard him preach before.

And as I sat there, I couldn't help thinking how mighty God's salvation really is. I had seen its power at work in this man, my father. Over the years, like any child, I saw his weaknesses and his flaws. To be honest, we haven't always had the best relationship. Since I was the oldest child, Dad was still finding his way in the maze of parenting. By his own admission he made many mistakes. Of course, I added my sin to the relationship. I didn't honor and appreciate him the way I should have.

We've talked about those regrets, and we've forgiven each other. But more important, we both know the forgiveness of God. My dad and I are very different in many ways, and we disagree about a number of issues, but we have one thing—the most important thing—in common. We've both been saved by grace alone.

As I listened to my father preach the wonderful gospel of salvation by grace, I rejoiced in the truth that both his sins and mine had been dealt with on the Cross. The mighty work of Jesus that brought my dad to life and made him God's son is the same power that saved me.

And God's work isn't done in either of us.

My dad's story encourages me. It reminds me of God's faithfulness and goodness. Not just for my dad, but for me and every other person who looks to Jesus for salvation.

I've told you my dad's story. But his is just one story among countless millions.

Pick a believer and trace his or her story. Retell your own. And consider how much God loves us.

He chose us.

He called us.

He regenerated our hearts.

He justified us.

He adopted us.

He's sanctifying us day by day.

And one day, when Jesus returns, we'll receive glorified bodies. We will rise with him, and our lowly, feeble bodies will be transformed. And his mighty salvation will be complete.

On that day a man named Gregg Eugene Harris will rise to meet his Savior. A man born with a broken, flawed body—a man born dead in sin— will rise with a perfect, pain-free, sinless, glorified body.

He will rise as a child of God to live with his Father in heaven for eternity.

CHANGED, CHANGING, TO BE CHANGED

"Sanctification is work. But it's good work—
the privilege of the redeemed."

A FRIEND E-MAILED ME, "You're on the latest episode of *This American Life.*"

My heart leaped. I couldn't believe it.

This American Life is a weekly radio show produced by Chicago Public Radio. I really like this show. Okay, it's more than that. I'm a slightly obsessed fan. One of my fantasies is to write something good enough to be featured on the show. But I seriously doubt that will ever happen. Not after this.

The show has a simple format: each week the producers choose a theme and then tell a variety of stories on that theme. The stories are real-life slices of life—sometimes humorous, sometimes tragic, but always intriguing. The writing is topnotch. The storytelling and production are brilliant. The host, a guy named Ira Glass, has a kind of geek chic aura. I don't know how to explain it. He's a nerd but in a really cool way. He wears big chunky glasses (I know this because he has a television show too). His voice is nasal, even whiny, but somehow he comes off sounding good. His delivery is so natural, his cadence so nonchalant that when I'm driving around listening to him, I feel like he dropped out of the sky into the passenger seat and is chatting with me. He is low-key in the most brilliantly hip way imaginable.

As I said, I'm a fan. So when I heard I was featured on the show, I was ecstatic.

I went online to the show's Web site and began to play the newest episode. The theme was the Ten Commandments.

I knew immediately which of the commandments I was going to be a part of: thou shall not commit adultery. Two years earlier I had written a Christian book about lust and sexual temptation. That's when it hit me that being featured might not be a good thing. A feeling of dread spread through my body as I considered what part of my book would be quoted. I didn't bother listening to the beginning of the show but skipped ahead to the part on adultery.

The segment featured a guy named Dave telling his story. Dave was raised as an evangelical Christian in Tucson, Arizona. Evangelical Christians, Dave explained, believe that looking at a woman lustfully is as bad as committing adultery with her in your heart. He spoke of evangelicals as though he were narrating a *National Geographic* special and describing an exotic tribe of naked cannibals.

Dave said that, growing up, he desperately tried to please God. Since he didn't want to commit adultery, he decided as a young, hormone-infused teenager that he would try to never think a lustful thought. It didn't go so well. In fact, it nearly drove him crazy.

Dave became more and more preoccupied with sex. He began to spend hours wandering his college campus and even the local grocery store, checking out women and hoping to catch a glimpse of one leaning over so he could look down her shirt. As he put it, he was like a very timid stalker with incredibly low standards. His grades began to suffer. He finally asked his pastor for help. His pastor, very unhelpfully, sent him to a meeting of Sex Addicts Anonymous. He was twenty-two and a virgin, and none of the people there could relate to him.

My cameo in the story came when Dave began to talk about the abundance of Christian books on the topic of sex. "The first thing these books always tell you," Dave said, "is that sex is a beautiful gift from God. But even though it's a gift, they don't want you to touch it or even think about it because you're gonna ruin it with your filthy paws."[1]

I smiled at his description, knowing it was partly true. But I was having trouble enjoying Dave's story because I was bracing myself for my appearance in the story. I just knew he was going to quote something about lust from my book—a book that Dave no doubt considered silly, repressive, and the cause for many a grocery-store-wandering sex addict. Actually, it was worse than that. Dave didn't quote me. He played a clip of *me* reading from my book.

As I listened to my voice, I was sure that Dave, filled with malice, had picked the worst possible sentences to feature. I talked about controlling your eyes and looking away from women on the street. Then he cut to me talking about the temptation that clothing catalogs featuring scantily clad women can present. I said guys should get their wives or mothers to help by throwing these catalogs away when they arrive.

My tone was indignant, and without any context my words sounded so uptight and backward—like some old church lady railing against the dangers of liquor and rock 'n' roll music. And my voice sounded terrible. I remembered that I'd had a slight cold the day I recorded the book. My voice was nasal. But not nasal in a cool, Ira Glass sort of way. Just nasal.

I was on *This American Life*. My dream had come true. And it was a nightmare.

After I got over the trauma of sounding hopelessly uncool on my favorite radio show, I was able to see the humor in it all and laugh at myself. It was good for me. God knows I take myself too seriously.

Later I went back and listened to the show again. Instead of worrying about how I sounded, I just listened to Dave and his story. I thought about the questions he raised and the real struggle he faced. My heart went out to the guy. I could relate to his turmoil. He said he wanted to please God. But sadly, he didn't seem to understand the concept of grace and forgiveness. Instead he was eaten up by guilt because he couldn't stop doing "M," as he called it. He felt like a monster walking around campus, ogling the girls. He felt powerless to change. And none of the tips and tricks for being good— trying to control his thoughts, only looking at girls' faces, having a quiet time every morning—seemed to work for him. So he stopped trying. He concluded that a person could try too hard to obey God, "that you could lead yourself astray by following the Bible's rules." He eventually found a Christian counselor who told him to give himself permission to do the big M to his heart's content. So Dave went home that day with a copy of *Playboy* magazine. He said his life was forever changed. He was free. "It felt like a miracle," Dave said. "It was so fast, so life changing that it was like converting all over again."

Dave's story saddened me. I don't know what he believes about God today or whether he would still consider himself a Christian. I doubt his *Playboy*-sponsored conversion has led to lasting fulfillment; my own experience of indulging in lust is that it only leaves me dissatisfied and craving something more. I pray that Dave will one day escape the slavery of that so-called freedom.

Can you relate to Dave's story? We each have parts of our lives where obeying God seems really difficult. Have you ever wondered why you still want to sin? Or maybe you've started to think that the Bible's whole promise of change is exaggerated. Is it a bunch of hype? Does God really change people?

He absolutely does. God's Word promises it. And the life of every true believer proves it. If you're a Christian, your life proves it. Maybe you haven't noticed how God has changed you, because you're preoccupied with your weaknesses and areas of failure. Don't overlook what God has done in you. He wants to increase your faith as you see his work in you.

We live in a world that endlessly longs for personal, physical, relational, and political change. People search for change everywhere. But ultimately, only the gospel of Jesus Christ offers real hope for radical, lasting change because only through faith in Jesus can a person's *nature* be changed. Second Corinthians 5:17 says, "Therefore, if anyone is in Christ, he is a new creation. The old has passed away; behold, the new has come." All other sorts of man-made change are outward and superficial. Only God can give a man or woman a new, spiritually alive heart (Ezekiel 36:26). Only God can cause a person to be born again (John 3:3–8).

But if we're new, why do we so often act old? If we're changed by faith in Christ, why do so many parts of our lives still need renovation? Why do we still face temptation? Why do we still sin?

The questions surrounding how Christians deal with sin, obey God, and become more holy all relate to something that Scripture calls *sanctification.* That is the ongoing process of change that begins the moment a person is saved and continues until that person's last breath. Sanctification is the journey of becoming holy, becoming like God. Wayne Grudem defines sanctification as "a progressive work of God and man that make us more and more free from sin and like Christ in our actual lives."[2]

I like his phrase "actual lives." If you think about it, while there is a radical inward and spiritual change the instant a man or woman is saved, nothing in their "actual lives" has been altered. She might still be living with her boyfriend. He might still have a salty vocabulary. They will definitely still have old habits of thinking and speaking that they developed over the years. The process of sanctification doesn't end with the initial dramatic breaks we make with sin when we first believe—it continues for the rest of our lives. The process of becoming more like Jesus isn't a "one and done" deal. It is progressive. And it involves our effort. God doesn't leave us alone in this work; he empowers us and enables us by his Spirit. But it's still work.

While I believe all Christian doctrine is practical in that all of it affects the way we think and live, I think it's safe to say that no doctrine is more practical than sanctification. This is where we live and breathe. No matter how young or old we are, no matter how long we've been disciples of Jesus, if we're still alive, then we're still being sanctified.

Understanding sanctification is important because of its daily relevance. But it's also important because if we get this wrong, we can end up sidetracked by multiple problems—from laziness and apathy to self-sufficiency and legalism. And if our expectations aren't informed by Scripture, we can end up unnecessarily discouraged, even tempted to give up on our faith altogether. How many people have turned their backs on Christianity—grabbed a *Playboy* and headed off the narrow road—because they didn't understand the doctrine of sanctification? Too many.

I used to think that sanctification was a matter of personal style. Like some sort of spiritual hobby that certain Christians were really into. Some Christians are into holiness, while others might make evangelism or Scripture memory or potlucks their thing.

But that's not how the Bible talks about sanctification. God's Word teaches that sanctification isn't optional for believers. Hebrews 12:14 says, "Strive for…holiness without which no one will see the Lord." That verse always sobers me. It says that if there isn't some degree of holiness in our lives, there's a real question of whether we've truly experienced God's saving work. If we don't love what Jesus loves, if we don't want to be like him, then maybe we've never really met him.

This isn't to say that our good works earn our salvation—we are saved only by grace (Ephesians 2:8). But the way we live proves the reality of our salvation. If a person has truly been saved, truly been justified by grace, it shows in a new lifestyle. Every genuine Christian is being sanctified. The process might be slow, it might move ahead in fits and starts, but if we've been justified, we will also begin to be sanctified.

God's saving work through Jesus's life, death, and resurrection has practical, real-world implications for our lives. It is truth that can't be kept on a page or in a house of worship. It follows us home. To our school. To our work. To our bedrooms. It grabs hold of every detail of our lives. Our thoughts. Our sexuality. Our money. Our leisure. Our relationships. Our desires. Our dreams.

A big question a lot of us have is, Why is this process of changing so stinking hard? Why is it so painful? Why do Christians still struggle with sin?

Encountering sin as a believer can be one of the most confusing and potentially disillusioning aspects of the Christian experience. You become a Christian and are reveling in the fact that you've been reborn, transformed, forgiven, justified, and filled with God's Spirit. But then one day you wake up and realize you're still tempted to_____ (fill in the blank). Get angry. Get drunk. Look at pictures of naked people. Lie. Gossip. Sleep with your boyfriend. Swear like a sailor. Or maybe you seem morally upright on the outside, but inside you know you lack any real passion for prayer or God's Word. Or you lack compassion and genuine care for others. Your heart is filled with pride. The list of potential "old you" behaviors seems endless.

How could you still want any of that? You turned your back on the old you. In fact, you hate the old you and your empty former way of life. So why are you still enticed by what you left behind?

This paradox is why it's important to know what Scripture teaches about what does and doesn't change in people's relationship to sin after they're saved. The Bible teaches, and our experience confirms, that while Jesus's death freed us from the reign and absolute rule of sin in our lives (Romans 6:11, 14), we haven't yet been completely freed from the presence and influence of sin. James 3:2 states, "For we all stumble in many ways." And 1 John 1:8 says, "If we say we have no sin, we deceive ourselves, and the truth is not in us."

The analogy is flawed, but we're like prisoners of war who have been freed from captivity but are still behind enemy lines. In a real sense we have been rescued—we're no longer locked up and at the mercy of the enemy. But at the same time, the war isn't over. We're waiting for our captain to return and completely vanquish the enemy. The fallen world, the devil, and our own wandering hearts put us at risk. Like never before, we have to be on our guard.

In a similar sense we live between two moments in salvation history—

between the arrival of salvation through Jesus's first coming and the ultimate fulfillment of our salvation when Jesus returns and establishes his eternal kingdom. Theologians call this in-between reality the "already" and the "not yet" aspects of our salvation.

Jesus has *already* brought salvation by his substitutionary death on the cross and his resurrection. Jesus has *already* made us new creatures with new desires and the power to obey (2 Corinthians 5:17). He has *already* freed us from slavery to sin (Romans 6:6).

But we've *not yet* arrived. He has *not yet* fully vanquished sin and Satan. Jesus has *not yet* freed us from the presence and consequences of sin. He has *not yet* banished death, wiped away every tear, punished all injustice, and established everlasting peace (Revelation 21:1–7).

The *already* and *not yet* reality of our salvation helps us keep things in perspective. We shouldn't be surprised that even though we've been changed, we still have to struggle with weaknesses and imperfections. We still have to deal with the ugliness of life in a fallen world where people let us down and disappoint us and where sickness and death break our hearts. So we shouldn't despair over ongoing struggles with sin. This is part of the deal. Jesus has already brought salvation. But he's not yet taken us home.

It helps me to think about this process in three parts. First, God has *changed* us. When we believed, we were given new life, new desires, and a new identity as God's children (Ephesians 2:4–5; John 1:12). Second, right now as we live the Christian life, we're still *changing*. As we cooperate with God's Spirit, turn away from sin, and learn to obey God's Word, we're being conformed to God's image and becoming holy (Colossians 3:8–10). But we don't expect sinless perfection in this life. There's a third and final installment to God's work of change in us: Christians await Jesus's return *to be changed* fully and forever. Then we will be made like Christ with glorified bodies free from sin and all its corrupting effect. "For the trumpet will sound, and the dead will be raised imperishable, and we shall be changed" (1 Corinthians 15:52).

We've been changed. But we're still changing. And yet we're also waiting to be changed.

Until the final day, until we're changed and freed forever from our struggle against sin, we have to deal with the ongoing presence and influence of sin—what theologians call *indwelling* or *remaining sin. Indwelling sin* refers to the fact that even as Christians we can still be enticed and tempted by our old desires, what the Bible often refers to as "the flesh." Galatians 5:17 says, "For the desires of the flesh are against the Spirit, and the desires of the Spirit are against the flesh, for these are opposed to each other, to keep you from doing the things you want to do."

Romans 13:14 says, "But put on the Lord Jesus Christ, and make no provision for the flesh, to gratify its desires." Once when I was working on a sermon on Romans 13:14, I started doodling on my notepad (a habit that helps me think but that sometimes annoys other people when I'm supposed to be paying attention in a meeting). Anyway, I drew some cartoons to try to illustrate the Christian's relationship to the flesh. My kids liked the pictures, so the following is my first-grade-friendly explanation of "the flesh." (Feel free to color.)

1. **This is you.** Or us. We're humans made in God's image (Genesis 1:26–27). Ladies, sorry you have to identify with a little guy.
   And I'm not sure why he doesn't have on a shirt. That's just
   how I drew him.

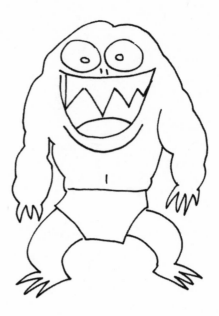

2. **This is the flesh.** He's kind of Jabba the Hutt meets WWE
   wrestler. The flesh represents the sinful, corrupted desires of
   our hearts. It's not a reference to our bodies—our bodies are
   created by God and are good. And though my cartoon can't
   do this justice, the flesh isn't something outside us or just a part
   of us. It's who we are apart from Christ. The flesh represents
   our sinful cravings to live for ourselves and disobey God's laws
   and commands (Romans 7:18).

3. **Before Jesus saves us**, we all relate to the flesh this way. The
   Bible says we are slaves to our sinful desires (John 8:34; 2 Peter
   2:19). Our flesh is boss. It controls us (Proverbs 5:22). Even the
   good things we do are stained by sin and selfishness.

4. **This is what happens when we trust in Jesus**. Because Jesus
   died on the cross and conquered sin and rose again, we are
   freed from the power or dominion of sin (Galatians 2:20). It
   no longer dominates us (Romans 6:22). It's no longer our boss.
   See how the chain is broken? And we get clothes, which is
   really great.

5. **But our flesh doesn't disappear.** It no longer reigns, but it's
   still a reality (Galatians 5:16–17). It still hangs around to entice
   us. After we become Christians, we're no longer slaves to sin,
   but the flesh can still tempt us. We can choose to give in to
   temptation and indulge the flesh. Jesus broke the power of sin,
   but until we're in heaven, we still live with the presence and
   influence of sinful desires. Don't think it's a stalemate. The
   Holy Spirit indwells believers and empowers us to say no to
   the flesh. He is at work in us, transforming us to be like Jesus
   (2 Corinthians 3:18).

6. **That's why the Bible is full of encouragement to fight our fleshly desires.** We can't live at peace with the flesh. We have to attack it and deny it and kill it (Romans 8:13; 13:12). In hindsight, I guess drawing a sword of the Spirit would have been a bit more biblical. Oh well. This is the "stick" of the Spirit.

7. **The problem is that too often Christians make friends with their flesh.** In fact, they *feed* their flesh. That's what "making provision" means (Romans 13:14). We feed our flesh when we do things that encourage or foster our old sinful desires. This is choosing to live like who we used to be. Giving in to temptation, dwelling on sinful thoughts, and spending time with people and in places that celebrate sin are like giving our flesh three well-rounded meals a day with snacks and dessert. We might think that since we've been freed by the Cross, it's okay to indulge the flesh, but that's not true (Galatians 5:13, 24). And there's a real problem. When we feed the flesh...

8. **Our flesh can grow!** And before we know it, the flesh is bigger
   and stronger than we are and starts to push us around (Romans
   6:12). This is why even genuine Christians, who are no longer
   wearing the chains of sin, can feel like their flesh is bullying
   them (Galatians 6:7–8). That's why Paul tells us in Romans
   13:14 that we need to...

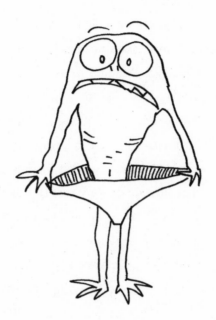

9. **Starve our flesh!** This is what we want our flesh to look like.
   We want the flesh gaunt and feeble (2 Corinthians 7:1). We
   should never expect it to be completely gone until Jesus returns and forever frees us from the presence of sin. Even a
   weak, wimpy flesh can try to trip us up (1 Corinthians 10:12).
   But when we starve the flesh, it's easier to resist temptation and
   walk in obedience.

Again, one problem with my cartoons is that they could give the impression that the flesh is an outside force attacking us. But it is called indwelling sin because it's *in* us. It resides in our hearts.

The reality of remaining sin should cause us to walk humbly, to live dependently on God, and to seek the help of other Christians. The truth is, we can be deceived. Our motives are not perfectly innocent. We need the power of the Spirit and the Word of God to search us.

I read the transcript of a television interview that Tom Brokaw did with pastor Ted Haggard several years ago.[3] At the time Haggard was at the height of his popularity and influence. His church and ministry were thriving. Brokaw insightfully asked why there was so little mention of sin in his church. Haggard said that since Jesus took care of our sin at the Cross, the church's emphasis was on fulfilling the destiny God had called them to.

Sadly, just a few years later, Haggard was forced to resign when a serious pattern of sexual immorality in his life was revealed. His casual, even flippant attitude toward sin in light of these dismaying revelations underscores the danger of neglecting the ongoing fight against sin. Yes, Jesus dealt with our sin at the Cross; those who trust in him will never face the wrath of God. But that doesn't mean we can ignore the fight against remaining sin. We ignore it to our own spiritual peril.

You and I are no better than Ted Haggard. We can be ensnared in sin just as easily. We're all susceptible to temptation. The reality of God's grace should never be an excuse to be unconcerned about holiness. The Bible says that God's grace is "training us to renounce ungodliness and worldly passions, and to live self-controlled, upright, and godly lives in the present age" (Titus 2:12). Grace doesn't lull us into indifference toward righteousness. It trains us and compels us toward self-control and godliness.

I once heard John Piper say in a sermon that sanctification isn't necessarily progressive. If we're not careful, it can be regressive. If we choose to feed our sinful desires and indulge our cravings, we make them stronger. We can backtrack in holiness.

That's why we aren't equally holy. While one Christian is not more justified than another, some Christians are more like Jesus than others. Those who hear God's Word and strive to obey it in the power of the Spirit will be more like him. Those who actively put off sin and put on the behavior of the Savior will grow in holiness. Those who give attention to communion with God through prayer and study of his Word will be more conformed to the image of Jesus Christ. We all desperately need God's help to do this. Philippians 2:12–13 urges, "Work out your own salvation with fear and trembling, for it is God who works in you, both to will and to work for his good pleasure."

I have friends who think that talking about sin and giving attention to the details of fighting sin is defeatist. I know it's possible to be morbidly introspective about sin. And that's not what I'm advocating. I think we should all be more aware of Jesus's saving work than we are of our shortcomings. Robert Murray McCheyne's advice is worth repeating: "For every one look at your sins, take ten looks at Christ."[4]

But I don't think that being aware of sin has to be an exercise in despair. In fact, though it might seem counterintuitive, I've found that facing the reality of remaining sin gives hope when connected to the gospel. First, it explains life. It explains why becoming a Christian doesn't mean we're free from temptation. It also engenders patience with other Christians. Remaining sin explains why even in the church and among Christians, we let each other down and experience relational strife. None of us has arrived. We're all still being sanctified. We all have blind spots and ways we can grow. We all need each other's mercy and patience.

Understanding what the Bible teaches about the flesh and our ongoing propensity to sin also fosters a healthy sense of humility. I don't mean a crippling sense of utter worthlessness that causes us to doubt God's love. I mean a humility that allows us to second-guess ourselves when necessary. Not to assume we're right but to listen to the constructive criticism of other people because there's a good chance we got something wrong.

If anything has turned the world off to Christianity, it's self-righteousness and arrogance that pretend our religious observance makes us better than other people. But a biblically informed view of indwelling sin and sanctification sweeps away self-righteousness. Christians who are being sanctified don't have time to be sanctimonious. They're aware of how far they have to go. They're aware of their weakness and God's ongoing grace toward them. This is what enables them to be gracious toward others.

———

Our pursuit of sanctification is complicated by the reality that we live in a world that has effectively pretended away sin. We've lost a clear, Bible-informed view of sin. We don't think of it as a violation of God's laws and character. We don't define it as a rejection of his rule in our lives. We don't acknowledge that sin is rebellion, a willful choice from the heart to make something besides God our ultimate concern. We don't call sin "sin." We excuse it, overlook it, and rename it.

Think about how we apologize. How rare it is, even among Christians, for a person to say, "I was wrong. I sinned, and I'm fully responsible. My sinful desires motivated me, and what I did dishonored God and hurt you. Please forgive me."

When was the last time someone asked your forgiveness with such words?

The normal approach is to talk about ourselves and our actions in sin-free categories. We like to think of ourselves as victims. We blame-shift. We add a "but…" after "I'm sorry." So we say, "I'm sorry I did that, but you made me so mad!" Or, "I'm sorry I broke our marriage vows, but I have self-esteem issues and sexual addictions." An even more subtle Christian apology is, "I'm sorry you took it that way." We like to keep the problem outside ourselves; it's someone else's fault. It's not something that needs to be repented of; it's a condition that needs to be understood and possibly medicated.

If you pretend, blame, and excuse all sin away, sanctification gets replaced by therapy. It becomes a vague, self-centered pursuit of self-improvement. And all we're left with is the hope of new drugs, new therapy, and better circumstances so our better self can emerge.

God's Word gives us a radically different picture of ourselves. It pinpoints our hearts as the source of the problem. James 1:14 says, "But each person is tempted when he is lured and enticed by his own desire." And James 4:1–2 asks, "What causes quarrels and what causes fights among you? Is it not this, that your passions are at war within you? You desire and do not have, so you murder. You covet and cannot obtain, so you fight and quarrel."

Acknowledging sin and our guilt stings our pride, but if we aren't honest enough to call sin what it is, we'll never receive the power God provides to overcome it. First John 1:8–10 says, "If we say we have no sin, we deceive ourselves, and the truth is not in us. If we confess our sins, he is faithful and just to forgive us our sins and to cleanse us from all unrighteousness. If we say we have not sinned, we make him a liar, and his word is not in us." When we think and speak as if we're only victims and never sin, we're lying to ourselves. And we're missing out on the cleansing grace of God that is available daily.

Martin Luther said that the "whole life of believers should be repentance."[5] Repentance isn't just for getting saved. It should be a normal, even daily part of the Christian's life. We're going to sin in a multitude of ways every day. Repentance is simply agreeing with God about sin, turning away from it, and accepting the redeeming grace of God through the Cross.

When you know God's cleansing grace, repentance doesn't have to be a traumatic thing. The author Tim Keller notes that some people view admitting they're wrong as an earth-shattering experience.[6] That shouldn't be the case for Christians. We already admitted we were wrong when we trusted in Jesus and acknowledged that we had no means by which to save ourselves. So it shouldn't be too hard to do this day by day as we become more like Jesus.

What do we do when Christians disagree about what obedience looks like? All around us are different opinions and standards, and they can be a significant diversion from sanctification.

I learned as a child that Christians had different standards for any number of issues. For example, some of our more conservative Christian friends thought all movies were wicked. When I was around them, I was supposed to refrain from mentioning that our family watched movies. I had to act as if I'd never heard of Darth Vader or Indiana Jones.

Other Christian friends were on the opposite end of the spectrum. They watched everything—even the bad movies I was never allowed to see. When

I was with them, I was supposed to refrain from mentioning that they were a bunch of filthy pagans dangling over the fires of hell.

I think a lot of Christians look around, see the diversity of standards, and assume that since nobody agrees, maybe it doesn't really matter. So they do whatever works for them. Sadly, few check in with God.

Other people just adopt the standards and practices of the Christians around them. This can give the appearance of holiness and growth, but it's superficial and can lead to bigger problems later. They can get sidetracked in their faith because they never took the time to cultivate personal convictions about Christian obedience. They never took the time to search God's Word for themselves. At some point, following a rule without real reference to God becomes an unwanted burden, and they start to chafe under the restriction. Obedience becomes joyless and wearying.

They know the rules but don't really know God. It's possible to know the restrictions of righteousness but never learn to appreciate the beauty and goodness of righteousness. Of course the problem is that their obedience is not motivated by a desire to please God. They're not being guided by his Word. They're just conforming to someone else's practice. As God describes in Isaiah 29:13, this brand of worship is "made up only of rules taught by men" (NIV).

Eventually people practicing rules taught by men get fed up and over-react by throwing out all restraint. I know a lot of people who were so burned by what they call their fundamentalist upbringing that they spend their life bucking every rule they can find. They start seeing legalists under every rock. If they once had blinders to all that Scripture says about grace and freedom, they have exchanged them for blinders that shut out all the Bible says about the danger of sin and the priority of holiness.

Any attitude that causes us either to *add to* our Bibles or *edit* our Bibles and live in reaction to someone besides God is unhealthy. Christian growth can't be defined by whom we don't want to be like. It has to be defined by becoming like Jesus. It has to be rooted in relationship to him. And it has to be built on real, Bible-rooted conviction.

When I use the word *conviction*, I'm talking about a heart-level, settled belief before God that doesn't change with our environment. Conviction is something we believe, not because someone is making us, not because we have to, but because we are convinced it's what *God* would have us believe.

Compliance isn't conviction. Conformity to other people's standards isn't conviction. Adapting to a church culture isn't conviction. Biblical conviction is the result of the study of Scripture, careful thought, discussion, and the search for wisdom. It requires work. It requires the humility to test the results of our choices and change our actions when necessary. Most important it requires a laser focus on God.

The solution here isn't to throw out all rules. It's to embrace God's rules and obey them out of a desire to honor him. If there's a rule in your life that you obey solely because of someone else and that person's opinion, take the time to study Scripture for yourself. See if your rule is really biblical. Sometimes you'll find that it is—either because Scripture directly commands it or because biblical principles convince you of its wisdom. But other times you might find that it's man-made and you could leave it behind.

Sometimes I make my relationship with God more about the sin I need to avoid than the good I'm called to pursue. Recently I wrote Galatians 5:22–23 in the front page of my journal: "But the fruit of the Spirit is love, joy, peace, patience, kindness, goodness, faithfulness, gentleness, self-control."

I wrote the words in big bold letters. These are the words that are to define and mark my life. I want them to call out to me every time I commune with God. This is who he's called me to be. This is what his Spirit wants to produce in me. I want to spend as much time seeking to be defined by love, joy, and peace as I do seeking to rid my life of anger, lust, and complaints.

Becoming like Jesus isn't just a matter of not doing wrong. It's a matter of actively "doing" righteousness. It's pursuing obedience. Romans 13:14 (the passage I cartooned earlier) tells us to avoid feeding the flesh, but it starts by telling us to "put on the Lord Jesus Christ." The New International Version says, "Rather, clothe yourselves with the Lord Jesus Christ." Paul is saying that the Christian life is about constant trust and dependence and identification with Jesus Christ. Just as the clothing we wear may identify our job or nationality, so our behavior shows our identification with Jesus. We're to "put on" righteous behavior that matches his. We're to live in a way that identifies us as his disciples. The Christian life is about putting on new behavior, clothing ourselves with Jesus himself.

Recently I've been learning how important it is for sanctification to be fueled by my status as God's child. Ephesians 5:1 says, "Therefore be imitators of God, as beloved children." Sanctification is all about imitating our Father. It's not conforming to a group or a religious culture. It's about modeling our lives and actions after the character of our heavenly Father and Jesus our brother and coheir (Romans 8:17).

When God saves us, he doesn't merely forgive us or ransom us from sin; he adopts us (Ephesians 1:4–5). In love, he makes us his children. He grants us all the rights and privileges of natural-born children. The apostle John viewed this truth as one of the greatest proofs of God's profound love for his people. He wrote, "See what kind of love the Father has given to us, that we should be called children of God; and so we are" (1 John 3:1).

Once my fellow pastor Mark pointed out that when I prayed, I rarely addressed God as Father. "I've noticed that you usually say 'Lord' or 'God' when you pray," he told me. At first I thought Mark had joined the prayer police or something. I wasn't sure why he was nitpicking words. But as we talked, and as I've learned since, it's not a matter of quibbling over words. Jesus himself taught us to pray to God as Father (Matthew 6:9). What we call God reveals how we think about him. And how we think about him shapes how we relate to him. And how we relate to him determines how we interpret his work in us and his purpose for us.

Knowing God as Father matters because he wants us to know how much he truly loves us. And that his love for us isn't the changing, professional, or skittish variety. It is real and deep and familial.

All the imagery God uses about salvation is designed to assure us how real his love for us is, how comprehensive his restoration of us is. So when we feel overwhelmed by guilt, God uses the legal language of the court and tells us that through Christ we're justified, declared completely righteous before him (Romans 5:8–9). When we feel enslaved and unworthy, he uses the language of the marketplace and tells us that he has bought us, ransomed us from sin (1 Peter 1:18–19).

And God uses the language of adoption to encourage us in the hard, ongoing work of learning to obey and follow Jesus as we wait for his return. God doesn't just point back to his love in forgiving us and redeeming us in the past. He uses the language of the family to say, "I love you *right now.* You have a relationship with me that isn't changed by your performance. I am your dad. You are my son. You are my daughter. Nothing can change that. I love you. I am always your Father."

This is the truth we need when we fall down. When we mess up again. When we do for the millionth time what we said we wouldn't do again.

Living in the present reality of God as Father will radically change your view of the Christian life. I'm in process on this. I can't say I've completely got it. But I'm learning to view my obedience and my struggle with sin through the lens of being a child of God. I have a Father in heaven who has promised to give me his Holy Spirit (Luke 11:11–13). He's promised to provide me with all the power I need to obey him (2 Peter 1:3).

Holiness is just not a list of rules. It's about imitating my Father (1 Peter 1:15–16). He is loving, he is kind, he is pure, he is truthful, he is patient, and he is gentle. And because I'm his kid, I want to look like him and please him.

Turning away from sin isn't about what I'm not allowed to do. I don't want what displeases my Father. I want to love what he loves. How can I take joy in what grieves the One who has loved me with an everlasting love (Jeremiah 31:3)?

Righteousness in relationship is what pleases my Father. I'm not trying to live up to some church standard or self-imposed standard. I want to grow in honoring and knowing and blessing the heart of my Father.

The truth of God's adopting love for me means I'm not obeying to get into his family or even to stay in the club. I obey because I'm already in. Because of Jesus, I'm family. There's incredible safety in that.

Jesus said, "If you love me, you will keep my commandments" (John 14:15). Those words always bring me back to the simplicity of sanctification. This is why I obey. This is to be my motivation. People who love Jesus do what he says. They learn to obey him in the big and small parts of their lives.

Dave, the guy on the radio show, decided you could try to obey God too much. Maybe that's true if you're chasing perfection or obeying rules taught by men. But if obeying is really about loving Jesus, can you love him too much? When we finally see Jesus face to face, will any of us regret the times we said no to our own desires and said yes to him?

I know I'll never obey God perfectly this side of heaven. Even though I've been changed, I'm still changing. I have a long way to go. I'll fail many times along the way. I'll need to repent and seek my Father's gracious forgiveness countless times between today and the final day—the day when I'm ultimately and forever changed by the power of God.

I'm really looking forward to that day.

Until then, I've got work to do. Yes, sanctification is work. But it's good work. It's work enabled by the Holy Spirit. It's the privilege of the redeemed. It's the great honor of God's adopted children to work to be like their Father.

I BELIEVE IN THE
HOLY SPIRIT

"I longed to know that God was present,
that I was doing more than singing songs to the ceiling."

I WAS SEVENTEEN when I learned about my parents' secret life: they were closet charismatics. I suppose it could have been worse. I've heard of people who discovered that their parents were Nazis or in the Mafia. Still it surprised me. It wasn't what I expected to hear the night I came home from the church I'd been visiting and boldly announced that I was now a Spirit-filled, tongue-talking charismatic.

I considered this shocking news. I expected sparks to fly. I imagined their eyes widening, jaws dropping. Maybe a lip trembling. I realize now that this was immature. But at the time, I had a mischievous delight in feeling that I was living on the edge spiritually and that my new "Holy Spirit experience" would slightly scandalize my comfortably evangelical dad and mom. Since I was a good, Christian, homeschooled kid, this was the closest I would ever come to announcing that I'd joined a biker gang and gotten a skull tattooed across my chest.

But Dad and Mom just smiled and said, "Oh, honey, that's wonderful."

Then they told me the story of their own involvement in the charismatic movement as young Christians and the work of the Spirit in their lives ever since. My dreams of creating panic fizzled. It was as if Dad and Mom lifted their shirt sleeves to show off their own tattoos and told me they had two Harleys hidden in the garage.

———

I've come a long way in my beliefs about the Holy Spirit since the night I burst through the door and made my dramatic announcement. I hope my motivation has matured and my understanding has deepened. Some people might say I'm less charismatic. But I believe I've become more passionate about and more grateful for the person and work of the Holy Spirit.

In case you're feeling nervous about where I'm headed, let me assure you that I'm no longer interested in shocking people when it comes to discussing the Holy Spirit. In fact, I'm going to do my best to skirt the controversial issues associated with him. My goal isn't to prove or disprove the ongoing function of spiritual gifts; I don't want to argue about prophecy or speaking in tongues. So whether you think the miraculous gifts ended with the last apostles (referred to as the *cessationist* position) or you think the miraculous gifts continue today (sometimes called the *continuationist* viewpoint), I want to focus on our common ground.

That common ground begins with the historical, orthodox Christian belief that there is, in fact, a Holy Spirit. One line of the Apostles' Creed states, "I believe in the Holy Spirit." All orthodox Christians can affirm this statement. But what comes next? Doesn't it follow that it's important to know who the Holy Spirit is? To know what he's doing and how we're to relate to him? Jesus said in John 14:16 that the Spirit would be our "Helper." Shouldn't we understand how he wants to help us?

The reason my parents turned their backs on their charismatic roots is an interesting story. They were both saved during the Jesus movement in the early 1970s. Back then thousands of hippies across America were coming to faith in Jesus. Around the same time many Christians were experiencing a dramatic renewal of interest in the work of the Holy Spirit. Beliefs that had once been confined to Pentecostal churches—the idea of a second experience "baptism of the Spirit" and present-day manifestations of the Spirit in prophecy, tongues, and healing—began to sweep through other Christian denominations. This became known as the charismatic movement (the term *charismatic* is based on the Greek word *charisma* and refers to the "grace gifts" of the Spirit).

Many people saw the charismatic movement as a genuine and much-needed renewal of mainline denominations that were dead, formal, and lacking zeal in worship and evangelism. Skeptics saw it as unbiblical, out-of-control emotionalism and possibly the lingering effects of all those drugs. Looking back, I think both sides were partially right. Like many revivals in church history, this one had a mix of good and bad.

What isn't in question is that there was a good deal of controversy. Some churches left their denominations over the issue. Other churches split. Charismatics claimed they were teaching the "full gospel" and described themselves as "Spirit-filled." The implication was clear: Christians who didn't adopt their beliefs about the Holy Spirit had a "partial gospel" and were "Spirit-empty." Not the best way to win friends.

On the other hand, noncharismatics often judged all charismatics by the worst, most extreme examples of excess in the movement. To them it was all a chaotic mess. In their opinion, the gifts of the Spirit were imagined or faked at best, the work of demons at worst.

My dad and mom met in a Baptist church that fully embraced the charismatic renewal. The church became a magnet for young people. Many young men, my dad among them, sensed a call to full-time ministry. The church started a small Bible college, and Dad was in the first class.

But as time went by, Dad and Mom became disillusioned with certain unbiblical aspects of the church. They watched as "spiritual gifts" were used to manipulate people. At times the emphasis on gifts and anointing was used to shut down questions or concerns about the character of leaders. Then a woman in the church was diagnosed with cancer, and the pastor promised the congregation that she would be healed. When she wasn't, he publicly blamed the woman's husband, implying that there was sin or a lack of faith in the home.[1] Not long afterward the church split, and my parents left.

I don't think there was a moment when my parents changed their beliefs about the Holy Spirit. But they edged further and further away from the charismatic practice they'd seen in those early years. While they continued to depend and rely on the Spirit in their personal lives, they shed the label of charismatic and avoided churches that made the Holy Spirit and the spiritual gifts their calling card. By the time I was a teenager, they had edged so far away from that aspect of their spiritual heritage that I had no idea it had ever been part of our family history.

———

I tell my parents' story because it's a narrative shared by many. To one degree or another, a lot of us have had bad experiences or run-ins with "charismaniacs." This could be as involved as growing up in a charismatic or Pentecostal church or as limited as having a friend who was charismatic and who weirded us out. Maybe your bad experience was just watching a few minutes of an oily-haired televangelist wearing pancake makeup who broke into tongues and claimed to heal people over the airwaves (for a small donation).

Let's face it: the Holy Spirit has gotten a lot of bad press. A good bit of tacky, strange, and just plain wrong things have been done in his name. Of course the same could be said about Jesus. But I think it's easier to sort through the good and bad with Jesus. The Holy Spirit is a little more complicated. Maybe because he is a Spirit, it's easier to blame weird stuff on him. Or maybe because not enough is said about him outside charismatic circles, some people are left with mainly negative impressions.

This isn't a healthy state of affairs. Whenever we live some part of our faith in reaction to anything other than God's Word, we become unbalanced and misguided. We shouldn't neglect the person and work of the Holy Spirit just because other people have misrepresented him.

Making the decision to give careful thought and attention to the Holy Spirit isn't a decision to become a charismatic. It's a decision to be a faithful disciple of Jesus Christ and a student of God's Word.

———

Thinking rightly about the Holy Spirit begins with right thoughts about the Trinitarian nature of God. John Frame writes, "The Holy Spirit is God, and he is a person of the Trinity, distinct from the Father and Son."[2] The Holy Spirit is not merely a ministering angel that God sends on missions. He is not mere power from God. The Holy Spirit *is* God.

The Bible reveals that the Holy Spirit is God in passages such as Acts 5:3–4, where Peter equates lying to the Spirit with lying to God. First Corinthians 2:10–11 states that the Spirit comprehends and knows the thoughts of God. The Spirit's equality with the Father and Son is expressed in various benedictions in Scripture, including 2 Corinthians 13:14, which says, "The grace of the Lord Jesus Christ and the love of God and the fellowship of the Holy Spirit be with you all." It's also evident in Jesus's instruction that his followers be baptized in the triune name of God—"in the name of the Father and of the Son and of the Holy Spirit" (Matthew 28:19).

Like the Father and Son, the Holy Spirit is a person. Members of the Jehovah's Witnesses cult deny the Holy Spirit's personhood (they think he's a force like electricity). But ask them how they know the *Father* is a person. How do we determine personhood? The answer is that persons are those who do personal actions (speak, hear, think, feel, etc.). The Bible reveals that the Spirit engages in these personal actions. He speaks (Acts 13:2). He has a mind (Romans 8:27). He can be grieved by our sin (Ephesians 4:30). So the Holy Spirit is not an impersonal force or power. The Holy Spirit is a "he" not an "it" (John 14:17; 1 Corinthians 12:11).

And just as there could be no salvation apart from the ministry of the Father and Son, there would be no salvation apart from the work of the Holy Spirit in our lives. In perfect fellowship and unity, the members of the Godhead partner in the great work of salvation. Though equal in power and deity, each plays a unique role. What the Father planned, and the Son purchased by his death, the Holy Spirit activates or applies in our lives. It is the Holy Spirit who gives us a new spiritual heart (John 3:5–8; Romans 8:9–11). It is through the Holy Spirit that we are washed, sanctified, and justified (1 Corinthians 6:11). It is the Holy Spirit who empowers us to become like Jesus (Romans 8:14; Galatians 5:16–18).

I don't remember the charismatic church my parents attended when I was a child. That's probably a good thing. But the downside of my parents' leaving that church tradition behind was that by the time I graduated from high school, I had next to no concept of who the Holy Spirit was or why he mattered.

Then when I was seventeen, I visited a big charismatic church in Portland. The passion I saw in the people kept drawing me back. There was an emotional reality to the way people talked about God. They spoke about him as if he were *right there*—like right next to them.

And the singing! Worship was a full-body experience. I'd grown up in churches where you sang with your hands by your side or in your pockets. These people not only raised their hands; they moved their whole bodies. They danced. I remember the first time I saw the whole congregation, including the pastors in their suits, begin to hop, jump, and two-step everywhere in the auditorium. They were dancing in church! It felt like the whole building was shaking.

On one level I guess it looked silly. But that's not how it struck me. I felt like everyone around me was saying, "This is how excited we are about God! He is so real, so good that we can't hold in our joy!"

I remember the day I finally joined in the dancing. I shut my eyes tight and just started jumping in place with total abandon. For the first time I didn't care how I looked or what anyone around me thought. My heart was bursting with an awareness of how worthy God was of all the passion of my life. God felt more real and nearer than he ever had before. For a long time I'd been aching for a sense that God was present and active in my life. I wanted to know that my faith was more than just reading a book. That I was doing more than singing songs to the ceiling.

After a few months of visiting the church, I approached Bob, the youth pastor. He was a short, stocky man who looked like Fred Flintstone in a suit. He was quick to smile and was always very kind to me.

"I hear you guys talk about the Holy Spirit and being filled with the Spirit," I told Bob. "But what does that mean? How do I get that?"

I was half expecting (and hoping) that Bob would put his hand on my forehead and shout a fiery prayer over me. But he didn't.

"Do you have a pen?" he asked. Then as I scribbled furiously, he rattled off a list of references from the Old and New Testaments. "Those are passages that talk about the Holy Spirit," Bob told me. "Go read them. Pray over them. Then come talk to me in a few weeks."

I went home and began to read the passages Bob had pointed me to. I read how the Spirit equipped Joseph, Moses, and David for leadership (Genesis 41:38; Numbers 11:17; 1 Samuel 16:13). How he gave Joshua wisdom and Gideon courage (Deuteronomy 34:9; Judges 6:34). How the Spirit instructed and taught God's people (Nehemiah 9:20).

In the New Testament I read Jesus's promise to send another Helper, whom he called the "Spirit of truth" (John 14:15–17). I read Acts 2 about the Day of Pentecost when the Holy Spirit came like a wind on the men and women waiting and praying in the upper room. I saw Peter transformed from a man who cowered before a servant girl to a man of courage who stood boldly before a crowd of thousands to preach about Jesus.

I spent the next two weeks reading those scriptures and praying for God to give me what the men and women I read about had. I remember praying at night in the hallway outside the bedroom I shared with my younger brother. I would kneel in front of the window and reach my hands up toward the night sky. "God, give me your Holy Spirit!" I would pray over and over. I wasn't even sure what that meant, but I had an overwhelming sense that I needed God's Spirit. I kept praying and waiting for something, anything, to happen.

Since then I've come to believe that I already had what I was asking for. As I've studied God's Word, I've become convinced that all Christians are indwelt by the Holy Spirit when they first believe (1 Corinthians 2:12). So I don't think there is a "baptism in the Spirit" separate from regeneration.

Instead, I believe God invites us to continually seek to be filled with the Spirit. We should all desire more of the Spirit's presence and influence in our hearts and lives. Ephesians 5:18 tells us to "be filled with the Spirit." I see now that God was stirring in me a good desire to be filled. God's Spirit was working in me, illuminating his Word and showing me my need for more of his work. Those weeks of studying Scripture and seeking God in prayer were very important for me as my sense of need and dependence grew.

Not long afterward Pastor Bob and a guy named Quinn took time to pray for me after a meeting. I had what you could describe as a dramatic spiritual experience in which I spoke in tongues. That was the night I drove home and told my parents about my Holy Spirit encounter.

———

J. I. Packer says that for many charismatics their experience is better than their theology.[3] I think that was true of me. My experience the night Pastor Bob prayed for me and my experiences in the years that followed were real. As I continued to attend the charismatic church, God moved in my life and empowered me to serve him in specific ways. But often my experience outpaced my biblical understanding.

Today, in hindsight, I'd say that I had a very narrow understanding of how and why the Holy Spirit works in people's lives. I basically confined him to a certain emotional experience in church meetings. In my view the Holy Spirit was moving when I felt a surge of emotion while we sang or when I had a dramatic experience during times of prayer. While I believe the Spirit can move in those ways, confining his work to those moments is sort of like thinking that a fork can be used only to eat peas. It's not that my knowledge about the Holy Spirit was false; it was just woefully incomplete.

A few years after I joined the church, it was abuzz with word that a special "move of the Spirit" had started in a church in another city. People from our church flew out for special meetings with them and claimed to come back with some of whatever they had there. A few zealous but not always wise people began to steer meetings in strange directions that had less and less rooting in Scripture. The work of the Spirit became more about odd manifestations—uncontrollable laughter and extended times of prayer where half the people would be laid out on the ground "under the influence."

At first it seemed exciting. Then after a while, I started to feel like we were chasing our tails—seeking emotion and experience for their own sake. It became increasingly less clear to me what the point of it all was. People appeared to be measuring their relationship with God by how dramatic or odd their encounters with the Holy Spirit were.

Part of my spiritual journey has involved sorting through the good and the not-so-good of those days. This has taken time. I'm not willing to discount all that happened during my years at the church, nor am I willing to endorse it all as biblical. It's been a process of learning to define my ideas about the Holy Spirit by God's Word, not my good or bad experiences.

———

These days I find myself less interested in the labels of charismatic and noncharismatic, less interested in arguing about whether there is a distinct "baptism of the Spirit" or only ongoing fillings of the Spirit throughout a Christian's life, less interested in whether gifts like tongues and prophecy still function today.

Personally, I do speak in tongues. And I've been encouraged by it. But honestly, I often forget to use it. It's not the apex of my relationship with God. I know a lot of Christians (my wife among them) who have never received the gift of tongues, and they're doing just fine.

I believe in the gift of prophecy (carefully defined), but it is clearly not to be equated with Scripture or prophecy in the Bible. It's not God speaking infallibly as he did through the prophets in the Old Testament or through the apostles. So no one is adding to Holy Scripture today. The canon of Scripture is closed. I'd rather have two words of Scripture than a hundred words of prophecy. Only Scripture is perfect and authoritative (Proverbs 30:5–6).

I don't feel comfortable with people who are anxious to claim a prophetic gift or who place too much emphasis on its importance. In our church we discourage people from sharing prophetic words that are predictive or directive. It's just too easy for people's own ideas and thoughts to get mixed up in prophecy.

That being said, I've seen this gift used to edify others. And I've been encouraged by it personally. Most of the times I see prophecy function, it serves to remind people of truths and promises from God's Word. It's not revealing the future or imparting fresh revelation but affirming and applying God's already-revealed truth to specific people and situations. When prophecy is genuine, it points people to Jesus, reminds them of his faithfulness, and directs them to his priorities. True prophecy always confirms and accords with God's Word.

In a similar way, while I believe God still heals, I'm less concerned about identifying a particular person as having a gift of healing. Even the apostles didn't have a gift that ensured healing on every occasion. I believe God can and does heal and that he is glorified when we ask him to heal (James 5:13–15). But we shouldn't do this as a demand or think that a lack of healing reveals a lack of faith.

When people ask me how to discover their spiritual gifts, I say, "Just serve." Don't overspiritualize spiritual gifts. There's a good chance the gifts God has given you to serve your church are the same ones you use in your daily work. Don't worry about whether or not you have a gift that appears in one of the lists of spiritual gifts in the Bible. (See Romans 12:6–8; 1 Corinthians 12:7–10, 28; Ephesians 4:11.) Those lists aren't exhaustive. Instead, just look around you for needs, and then try to meet them. If what you do is helpful and other people are encouraged by your service, maybe you have a gift. But you don't need a badge to be useful. Just serve. It's not about you and your gift; it's about serving the needs of others and glorifying Jesus through your life.

I've come to see that you can limit God in different ways. You can limit him by thinking he can *never* work in spectacular ways. But you can also limit him by thinking that *only* the spectacular is meaningful.

The Spirit's power and work are much broader, much more multifaceted than we often think. And it's all meaningful.

What's the biggest thing you've ever asked God for? Think of all the outrageous pleas you've prayed. Have you ever stopped to realize that by giving you his Holy Spirit, your Father in heaven has presented you a gift that infinitely surpasses your greatest request? To be indwelt by the Spirit of the living, eternal God is a greater gift, a more overwhelming honor than any position, any possession, any amount of wealth, or any human achievement.

There is no greater gift that God bestows than the gift of his Spirit. Are you aware of how he is working in you?

The Holy Spirit is presently at work in the life of every Christian, reshaping and reforming us to be like Christ (2 Thessalonians 2:13; Titus 3:5). We're called to cooperate and welcome this work by obeying Jesus, treasuring his Word, and doing the things that honor him. This is what the Bible describes when it says, "If we live by the Spirit, let us also walk by the Spirit"

(Galatians 5:25). It calls qualities like love, joy, peace, patience, goodness, and self-control the "fruit of the Spirit" (Galatians 5:22–23).

The Bible also tells us that the Spirit empowers us with boldness to share the truth about Jesus with others. Before Jesus ascended to heaven, he told his disciples, "You will receive power when the Holy Spirit has come upon you, and you will be my witnesses in Jerusalem and in all Judea and Samaria, and to the end of the earth" (Acts 1:8). Repeatedly in the book of Acts, whenever the Spirit fills believers in a pronounced way, the result is their courageous witness to others about Jesus's death and resurrection (see, for example, Acts 2; 4:31).

The Spirit also gives grace gifts to believers so we can serve and build up the church of Jesus. These gifts are diverse and, oftentimes, seemingly common. And yet Scripture informs us that the Spirit empowers Christians to use them for the good of other believers. "Now there are varieties of gifts, but the same Spirit; and there are varieties of service, but the same Lord; and there are varieties of activities, but it is the same God who empowers them all in everyone. To each is given the manifestation of the Spirit for the common good" (1 Corinthians 12:4–7).

When the Holy Spirit is working in our lives, there will be a dynamic quality of holiness, evangelistic boldness, and an otherworldly willingness to play the role of a servant to others.

I'm not arguing against the supernatural and spectacular. But I think we need to broaden our definition of both. The truth is that there is no such thing as normal or nonsupernatural Christian living. Every day of faith is a day of the supernatural work of the Spirit in our lives. Every time we're filled with love for God, every time we become aware of how glorious Jesus is, every time we read God's Word and understand and believe it, every time we choose to obey God and turn away from sin, every time we selflessly use our abilities to serve others—the Holy Spirit is powerfully working in us.

Ironically, one of the most compelling pieces I've read about the Holy Spirit is an essay written by a noncharismatic New Testament professor from Dallas Theological Seminary named Dan Wallace.

In some ways Dan's story is a lot like my parents'. As a young Christian he came into contact with a charismatic church. It was a time of intense passion for the Lord, expressed in fervent prayer, study of Scripture, and a boldness in evangelism that was uncharacteristic of his normally shy disposition.

But he noticed practices in his charismatic church that didn't line up with Scripture and eventually left. He went to a Christian college and then to a seminary that took a strong stand against the gifts of the Spirit. Over time Dan slipped away from his early vibrant contact with God. While his understanding of Scripture was heightened, he says his walk with God slowed to a crawl.

Then his eight-year-old son was diagnosed with a rare and deadly form of cancer. The boy lost weight. His hair fell out. He was so weak he had to be carried everywhere, even to the bathroom. The months of watching his son suffer and waste away during chemotherapy treatments shook Dan to the core of his being. He was in an emotional wasteland. He was angry. God seemed distant.

For the first time Dan realized that all the restrictions he had placed on the Spirit were suffocating his faith. He writes:

I needed God in a personal way—not as an object of my study, but as friend, guide, comforter. I needed an existential experience of the Holy One.… I found the scriptures to be helpful—even authoritatively helpful—as a guide. But without *feeling* God, the Bible gave me little solace.… I found a longing to get closer to God, but found myself unable to do so through my normal means: exegesis, scripture reading, more exegesis. I believe that I had depersonalized God so much that when I really needed him I didn't know how to relate.[4]

Mercifully, Dan's son recovered from his cancer. But the lessons Dan learned about his relationship with God during that excruciating time stayed with him.

He decided to radically rethink his attitude and perspective on the Holy Spirit. While he still believed the miraculous or sign gifts had died in the first century, he realized he needed to acknowledge that the Holy Spirit had not. What could he affirm that the Holy Spirit was doing today?

Dan began to consider what it meant when Jesus said, "My sheep listen to my voice" (John 10:27, NIV). "I am increasingly convinced," Dan writes, "that although God does not communicate in a way that opposes the scriptures, he often communicates in a non-verbal manner to his children, giving them assurance, bringing them comfort, guiding them through life's rough waters. To deny that God speaks verbally to us today apart from the scriptures is not to deny that he communicates to us apart from the scriptures."[5]

Dan realized that a Christian can depersonalize God by making him the object of investigation rather than the Lord to whom we are subject. The vitality of our faith gets sucked out when our stance toward God changes from "I trust in" to "I believe that."

He acknowledged that part of his own motivation for depersonalizing God was a craving for control. "What I despised most about charismatics was their loss of control, their emotionalism," he says. "But should we not have a reckless abandon in our devotion to him? Should we not throw ourselves on him, knowing that apart from him we can do nothing?"[6]

The apostle Paul prays a fascinating prayer in Ephesians. It's a prayer for Christians. It's a prayer for their inner lives. It's a prayer for a powerful work of the Spirit in their lives. But consider the focus and purpose of this request for the Spirit's power. Paul prays that through the Spirit they will be strengthened with power in their inner beings, that Christ will dwell in their hearts through faith, and that they will "be filled to the measure of all the fullness of God." And what is the end result of all this? A greater awareness of the depth of God's love for them (Ephesians 3:14–19, NIV).

The phrases Paul uses are different ways of describing the same thing. He is praying that the Holy Spirit will work in the inner lives of his Christian friends so they will be brought into a deeper union with Jesus, a greater awareness of his presence with them, and a fuller knowledge of his love for them. He doesn't want God to be an impersonal truth, a vague idea or philosophy.

Isn't this what we need more than anything else—to know that God truly loves us? Isn't this the only thing that can ultimately sustain us when we experience suffering and doubt and discouragement? when we feel alone in the world? when our child has cancer? The power we need in those moments is the power to believe that everything Jesus did two millennia ago really is for us.

This is what the Spirit does in God's people. He works in our hearts, in our affections and emotions. *The Spirit mediates the presence of Jesus Christ to us.* The Spirit is why Christians can say when we gather, "Jesus is with us right now" (see Matthew 18:20).

The Spirit shows us that Jesus is with us and loves us. He takes us from being people who know theoretically that God is our Father to being people who know experientially in our hearts that we are his children—people who can cry "Abba! Father!" to God (Galatians 4:6). This isn't something we can write down in easy steps. It's not a neat formula. It's the wonderful, mysterious work of God's Spirit in our hearts.

Do you see how important this is? Without the work of his Spirit in our hearts and minds, the truth of Scripture will be just words on a page. Paul understood that. Before his prayer for the Ephesians, he spent three chapters expounding some of the richest doctrinal truths about God's plan of salvation known to mankind. But he knew that apart from the Spirit, his words would be nothing more than lifeless facts, dead orthodoxy.

It's not enough that we simply know truth. God wants us to feel it, to believe it, and to apprehend it in the deepest, most personal way. He wants us to be able to say, "The cross is for me. The empty tomb is for me. Forgiveness and adoption and redemption are mine because I am united with Jesus Christ! Jesus loves me! Jesus is with me!"

This is living truth. It is impassioned orthodoxy—truth set on fire in our hearts.

Sound doctrine is so important. But we can never settle for merely knowing doctrine. God has given us his Holy Spirit, and he invites us to ask to be continually filled with his Spirit afresh so that doctrine becomes the living story of God's great love for us. So that it melts our hearts. So that this truth sets us on fire with love for the Savior who loved us first. The glorious truth of God's love for us in the giving of his Son isn't something we can grasp through mere knowledge or bigger books. We need the power of God's Holy Spirit to give us "strength to comprehend" how big and wide and deep God's love for us is (Ephesians 3:18–19).

Do you know what Jesus spent extended time teaching his disciples in the hours leading up to his arrest and crucifixion? He spent those final moments teaching them about the Holy Spirit (John 14–16). What does that tell us, as followers of Jesus, about how important it is to learn about the person and work of the Spirit? Jesus called the Spirit another Helper or Counselor. Jesus had fulfilled this role during his earthly ministry, but soon he would send another Helper. The Greek word he used was *paraclete,* which refers to one who advocates for, defends, counsels, encourages, comforts, and helps. What a powerful summary of the Spirit's work in our lives.

And what is the ultimate aim of the Spirit's encouragement, comfort, and help? To enable us to know and see the glory of the Savior. The Holy Spirit is all about glorifying Jesus. To glorify something is to exalt it, to show it to be wonderful and worthy and good. When Jesus told his disciples about the Holy Spirit the night before his death, he said of the Spirit, "He will glorify me" (John 16:14).

J. I. Packer taught me that understanding this is the key to understanding the Holy Spirit's work. Packer says that the Holy Spirit in his "Jesus glorifying" work is like a spotlight behind us that shines forward and throws an illuminating light on Jesus. The Spirit's goal is to show us Jesus in all his perfection, holiness, and mercy. As we read Scripture, as we meditate on Christ, the Spirit cuts through the darkness of our sin-dulled minds and lights up the person and work of Jesus.

The Holy Spirit isn't interested in drawing attention to himself. His role is to point away from himself and to Jesus. Packer writes, "The Spirit's message to us is never, 'Look at me; listen to me; come to me; get to know me,' but always, 'Look at *him,* and see his glory; listen to *him,* and hear his word; go to *him,* and have life; get to know *him,* and taste his gift of joy and peace.' "[7]

The point of a spotlight is not to stand in front of it and stare into its bright light (that would blind you). A spotlight is useful only when it's pointed at others, enabling us to see them more clearly. And that's what the

Spirit does. That's the most loving, powerful thing he can do in our lives—help us to see and treasure Jesus Christ.

You know the Spirit is working if you're more amazed by Jesus, more desirous to serve and obey him, more ready to tell other people about him, more ready to serve the church he loves.

THE INVISIBLE
MADE VISIBLE

"God's plan has always been a group plan—
he reveals himself through his people."

I HEARD A STORY on the radio about a summer camp for atheist middle-school children. Some guy decided that it wasn't fair for religious kids to have all the fun camps and programs while atheist kids got nothing. So he started a camp. I found this fascinating. It was a place where students could play and swim, do crafts, and sit around campfires talking about evolution and how ludicrous religion is. I wondered what you had to do to get into trouble at that camp. Maybe sneak a peak at a Bible or whisper about the merits of Intelligent Design theory? I don't know.

One part of the story featured a few of the atheist kids railing against religion. One girl was pretty fired up. She said something like, "And if there is a God, why doesn't he come out and show himself? Why doesn't he just appear and say, 'Hello, I'm God. Believe in me!' Why doesn't he do that? It doesn't make any sense."

I laughed because I could relate to her question. Sometimes I wish God would do that. Once a year he could hold a big rally for the whole world, with television coverage, satellite links, and streaming Internet, and come out and—*boom!*—just do something really massive. Maybe turn a well-known, nasty, angry atheist into a donkey or something. Of course he could change him back at the end if he wanted. But it would need to be impressive so everybody would say, "Wow! There is a God. I want to sign up."

But when I really think about it, I know this idea is silly. Partly because I know that unless God opens people's spiritual eyes, they wouldn't believe even if he did this every week. Jesus said that if people don't accept the testimony of God's Word, even having someone come back from the dead wouldn't convince them to believe (Luke 16:31). And that's true. Jesus came back from the dead, but that wasn't enough for his enemies or even some of his friends. Some still doubted (Matthew 28:17).

And besides, what kind of stories would we have to tell in heaven if God just showed up and made everybody believe?

Imagine those conversations.

"So when did God save you?"

"Oh, it was the year he came out and turned Christopher Hitchens into a turtle."

"Snapping turtle, wasn't it?"

"Oh, right. That was clever. Yep, that's when I believed."

That's not a conversation that leads to worship. That's not a story that makes you shake your head in amazement. God is too great a storyteller to settle for something so plain.

Instead, he's chosen to write a story in human history that will, at the end of time, leave the universe speechless. It's the story of his great rescue mission in Jesus. The story of how he redeemed—made new—all that human sin had ruined.

But this is the incredible part. God is writing his story through his people. Through his children. Through his church. Through us.

So God doesn't come out on a big stage once a year to prove himself to the world. He does something so much riskier and more daring and, on the face of it, so preposterous that it makes you bite your lip—he makes *us* the show. He proves himself and displays himself through his church.

Most Christians neglect the doctrine of the church. That's not really surprising. This subject by necessity involves people. Real, annoying, infuriating, obnoxious, stubborn people, whose preferences and styles and smells can bring soaring theological ruminations crashing to the ground.

You can study the doctrine of justification and think only about our perfect Savior and his cross. But if you think about the church, chances are you'll start thinking about a specific group of people, a specific pastor, a specific denomination, and all the specific mistakes, deficiencies, and problems that go with them. And this is where a lot of us get tripped up. We don't hear what God has to say about the church because his voice is drowned out by the noise of our own experiences, perceptions, and disillusionment.

Pushing past all this can be difficult. But we have to try. We need to care about the church for own spiritual good and for the sake of the world that needs us to be the church. But an even simpler motivation for caring is because God does. Every metaphor used in Scripture to describe the church shows how deeply God cares. He calls the church his *bride* (Ephesians 5:25–32). He calls it his *household* or *family* (2:19). He says we are his *temple* in which he dwells by his Spirit (2:21–22). He says we are his *body* (1:22–23).

How can we claim to know and love Jesus and yet be indifferent toward his bride, his temple, his family, his own body? Can I say that I love Jesus but hate the wife he cherishes? Can I say I enjoy spending time with him but refuse to enter his house? Can I claim friendship with Jesus but think his body is repulsive? It's not possible.

———

For the first two decades of my life, I didn't give much thought to the "us" aspect of the Christian faith. I viewed faith in a very individualistic way. It was about *me* and *my* Jesus. I didn't consider Christianity's corporate or group nature.

Of course I *went* to church. That's what Christians do—we have meetings. But it was just tradition. It was a habit like sleeping, breathing, and all the other things we can do without thinking. In my more cynical moments, I viewed church suspiciously, as a way for pastors to give themselves jobs and exert power. But, really, I didn't give it much thought. So while church attendance played a big part in my life growing up, the church didn't have much of my heart.

I treated the church like a gas station. Everybody needs a gas station, right? You stop in (usually when you're in hurry) to get filled up. You go to the one that's most convenient for you. You get what you need, then you move on. I stopped by the church for the spiritual fuel that comes from worship, teaching, and relationships with other Christians. But then I hit the road and got back to my own plans—my own destination.

I think that describes a good number of Christians today, and they are abandoning the church. Some drop out completely. Others attend meetings but lack a real commitment and engagement in any one church. This leads to the church-hopping syndrome. I know a guy who used to go to one church for the singing and then drive to another church for the sermon. He had this timed so perfectly that he could stop by McDonald's in between for coffee and a breakfast sandwich. I think the only thing he missed was the offering, in both churches.

So why is this happening? If we're the body of Christ, why are so many body parts not showing up to play their part? No doubt some are burned out or disillusioned by the corruption or poor leadership they've seen. Others feel that the church is cumbersome and that there are more effective ways to get things done.

But my guess is that a vast majority of Christians who have lost their vision for the church are like I was: they've never taken the time to study what the Bible says about God's purpose and plan for the church. Instead, they're living their lives guided by their feelings or experience. They're pragmatic, so they're focused more on what "works" than on what Scripture dictates. They're consumers who approach church asking, "What's in it for me?"

But what if we saw that the church is more than a human program, more than what we disparagingly refer to as organized religion? What if we saw that it originated in the heart and mind of God himself and that his plan began before the dawn of human history and stretches into eternity? What if we learned that the church was so precious to Jesus that he was willing to shed his own blood to obtain it? What if the church is the means by which God has chosen to accomplish his purpose for us and for the world? And what if it is irreplaceable?

If we could see this, then we'd realize that rejecting the church is rejecting God himself.

———

God's plan for glorifying himself in the world has always been a group plan. He has always planned to redeem a *people*. And he's always revealed himself to the world through a nation. That was the past perfection in the first pages of the book of Genesis. That is the future described in the closing pages of Revelation—God dwelling among his people.

I'm not sure how I went so long without seeing this. Part of my problem was that I read my Bible as a collection of stories about isolated, outstanding individuals. But when you look more closely, you realize that while the Bible does tell the story of individuals such as Abraham, Sarah, Joseph, Moses, Ruth, and David, their stories and the significance of their lives are always directly tied to what God is doing in the family and the nation of which they're a part.

The history of the Jewish nation in the Old Testament is a preview of God's ultimate purpose to save a people for himself through Jesus. Down through the centuries God kept hinting at and pointing toward the coming of Christ and the establishment of his eternal kingdom to which people of every tribe and tongue would belong.

When God called Abraham, he promised him that one day his family would be a great nation. He said that through Abraham's descendants all the nations of the world would be blessed (Genesis 12:2–3). God was announcing the worldwide nature of his purpose in Christ.

Hundreds of years later God used Moses to rescue Abraham's descendants, the Israelites, from slavery in Egypt. God demonstrated his saving power and led them out of bondage toward the Promised Land. Through a weak and insignificant people, God displayed his power to the nations.

God gathered the people of Israel at the foot of Mount Sinai and spoke to them in a thundering voice (Exodus 19–20). He announced that if they obeyed his commandments and were faithful to the covenant he made with them, they would be his "treasured possession among all peoples," a "kingdom of priests," and a "holy nation" before him (Exodus 19:5–6).

Deuteronomy 9:10 calls the day when God spoke to the people "the day of the assembly." In Hebrew the word *assembly* is *qahal,* which is sometimes translated *congregation.* The Greek version of this word, *ekklesia,* is the basis of our word *church.* John Frame points out that this was, in an important sense, the beginning of the church. "It was on this day," he writes, "that the nation of Israel became, by covenant, God's holy nation, distinguished from all the other nations of the world."[1]

This amazes me. An unseen, eternal God chose to join himself to a ragtag group of humans. He set them apart as his special people and gave them the privilege of representing him to the world.

If you lived in the days of Moses and wanted to know what God was like, you wouldn't find the answer in the temples of Egypt or the sorcery of the Canaanites. The only way to glimpse the living God was to go to the desert, to an unimpressive group of nomads called the Israelites. In their worship, in their obedience to God's laws, in their rituals and commitment to holiness, the character of God was displayed.

The same thing can be said of the church today. Frame notes that thousands of years later, after the coming of Jesus Christ, the apostle Peter would use the words of Exodus 19:4–6 about Israel to describe Christians in the New Testament church. First Peter 2:9 says, "But you are a chosen race, a royal priesthood, a holy nation, a people for his own possession, that you may proclaim the excellencies of him who called you out of darkness into his marvelous light."

What is the church? It is the fulfillment of God's promises to Abraham to bless all the nations of the world. The church, comprised of men and women from every nationality and ethnicity, is now God's chosen people in the world. The church is how God makes himself known in the world.

Back when I lived in Oregon and was just learning to care about theology, one of the first set of sermons I listened to by C. J. Mahaney concerned God's purpose for the church. I was twenty years old, and that was the first time I was confronted with a biblical, century-spanning, world-shaking vision of the church. I loved Jesus and wanted to accomplish great things for God, but I still treated the church like a gas station. In my mind the real action and spiritual excitement were somewhere else.

Then I listened to that sermon series. It was called *Passion for the Church.* I remember thinking that was the oddest pairing of words. In my mind passion and church had no connection. It might as well have been called *Passion for the Laundromat.* But for some reason I listened.

C.J. preached from the book of Ephesians, a book that's been described as the apostle Paul's masterpiece on the church. He showed that, in the church, God was creating a whole new humanity—those who were reconciled to him and to each other (Ephesians 2:13–16). He showed from Matthew 16:18 that the church was the only institution Jesus had promised to sustain forever. The church was what God was using to teach Christians to know and obey him and to advance his mission around the world.

C.J. read a quote by John Stott that stopped me in my tracks: "If the church is central to God's purpose, as seen in both history and the gospel, it must surely also be central to our lives. How can we take lightly what God takes so seriously? How dare we push to the circumference what God has placed at the centre?"[2]

I couldn't shake that question. How could I take lightly what God took so seriously? How could I be so nonchalant, so belittling about the church that Acts 20:28 says Jesus "obtained with his own blood"?

For the first time I began to realize that God's purpose for the Christian's involvement in the church was radically different from my gas-station approach. The church wasn't merely a place to swing by for a fill-up. The journey of the Christian faith was supposed to be made *with* other believers.

The church isn't a gas station, I realized. It's the bus I'm supposed to be traveling on.

———

Some people throw the word *church* around as if anytime two Christians are in the same room, they are a church. So exactly what makes a church a church? I've heard performers at Christian concerts say, "We're gonna have church in here tonight!" as though church were merely a matter of Christians singing certain songs together. Christians will describe their campus ministry or neighborhood Bible study or even online group as a church. All these groups can be good and wonderfully encouraging, but that doesn't make them churches.

Since the Reformation, protestant Christians have agreed that a church requires two essential elements: the right preaching of God's Word and the right practice of baptism and communion.[3] These two marks of a true church tell us several important things about the church's character and purpose.

First, we learn that the church is to be a congregation of people who are submitted to the truth and authority of the Bible to teach, train, reprove, and correct them (2 Timothy 3:16). And the right teaching of the Word means presenting the good news of Jesus's substitutionary death and resurrection for sinners as its central message (1 Corinthians 15:1–3). Thus the church is built on a specific message, not just any random idea or philosophy.

Second, the priority of baptism and communion reemphasizes the necessity of the church being a *defined* community fixated on the gospel of Jesus Christ. Both are ways for God's people to act out and remember who we are and what we have through faith in Jesus's death and resurrection for us. And both distinguish who is and who is not part of God's people.

Baptism is the entry point into the church. It symbolizes a Christian's death to sin, resurrection with Jesus to new life, and entry into God's family (Matthew 28:19). It occurs one time, when a person first believes.

Communion is repeated many times throughout a Christian's life. Jesus instructed his followers to partake of the bread and the cup in remembrance of his broken body and blood poured out in his atoning death on the cross (1 Corinthians 11:23–26). As members of a local church eat and drink together, they proclaim Jesus's death as the source of their salvation. And they say to each other and the watching world, "We're still here. We're still pressing forward in faith. We're connected to Jesus and to each other because he died for our sins and made us God's children."

The New Testament is filled with practical instruction about what local churches are supposed to be and do. We see that churches are organized under the leadership of men who meet clearly defined character qualifications. They must manage their own families well and practice and teach healthy doctrine (1 Timothy 3; Titus 1:5–9). These qualities are important because a primary purpose of the church is to teach and train Christians to know and obey God. The church is also the place where Christians receive care and nurture from other believers. In the local church Christians put into practice the Bible's commands to love, serve, honor, pray for, and encourage one another (John 13:34; Galatians 5:13; Romans 12:10; James 5:16; 1 Thessalonians 5:11).

Does it matter that we belong to a specific local church? Evidently it does. This is illustrated in passages of Scripture that encourage Christians to honor and obey the leaders in their local church (Hebrews 13:17), to accept the discipline of the community (Matthew 18:15–19; Galatians 6:1), and not to neglect gathering with other believers (Hebrews 10:25).

What all this adds up to is that the New Testament assumes believers will participate in a local church where they can be baptized, partake of communion, be taught God's Word, worship, use their gifts to serve, be cared for spiritually by qualified leaders, be held accountable by a loving community, and bear witness to nonbelievers of Jesus's saving death. Christians are to join an assembly not just for their own spiritual health but so that the world around them can clearly see the reality of Jesus Christ.

Getting on the bus of God's plan for the church involved a more dramatic change of course for me than it does for most people. I ended up moving across the country to be part of C.J.'s church. I curtailed my conference speaking schedule so I could throw myself into the life of the church. I stopped publishing my magazine so I could work as an intern in the youth ministry and be trained as a pastor.

Looking back, I realize that my internship wasn't just training for ministry. It was an internship in understanding what church life is all about. In many ways it was a jarring experience. I learned that life in a local church wasn't anything like putting on a conference. On the conference circuit it was relatively easy to sweep into a city for a weekend, look impressive to people who didn't know me, and sound good as I taught a message I'd given a hundred times before.

Being a pastor in a local church was totally different. I didn't look impressive when people saw me day in and day out. And it wasn't enough to have a few inspiring messages. I needed to search God's Word and help people apply it to real-life situations and challenges. I had to learn how Jesus's death and resurrection made a difference in the dark valleys of pain—things I didn't have to face when I jumped from one city to another doing conferences.

Life in the local church was harder and less glamorous. But it was also sweeter and more rewarding than anything I'd been part of before. I saw the gospel change people. Not just tears and promises of change at altar calls, but sustained, true change in individuals and families.

I saw the body of Christ living and breathing and moving. I saw the love of Jesus made real as members wept with one another at the death of a child, as they carried one another in times of need, as they nurtured one another in times of temptation and doubt. As the well-worn saying goes, the church isn't a building or a meeting—it's people. But you never get to actually see this if your involvement is limited to meetings in one building. The real beauty of people being a church in a local community is only seen when you hang around long enough to watch them loving and serving one another through good times and bad.

Although I lost the adulation that comes with being a visiting speaker and author, I gained something so much better. I gained friends who really knew me—my strengths and my weaknesses. I gained brothers and sisters who were willing to challenge me when I was proud and comfort me when I was discouraged.

For the first time I realized that growing as a Christian wasn't something I could do on my own. Progress as a disciple required relationships and community. Studying the Bible on my own and even hearing good preaching weren't enough by themselves. I needed relationships in the church to practice what I learned. And I needed relationships in the church to help me see all the ways I wasn't practicing what I claimed to believe. I had no idea how inaccurately I saw myself. I didn't have blind spots; I had blind patches. Or, maybe more accurately, blind acres.

I'm a proud man. And I'd like to pretend that whatever maturity I have is the result of my wisdom, good breeding, and superior spiritual effort. But I can trace every example of growth and change in my life to the help of fellow Christians. And most often they were Christians in my local church. That's not surprising, is it? The people who know us best are the ones who can help us the most. It's impossible to calculate all that I've gained from their examples, their loving correction, their encouragement and prayers for me.

I learned that God's purpose for me is inextricably tied to his purpose for his people. My faith isn't all about me. It isn't only about my story and my journey. Being a Christian is about *us* belonging to God and to each other and then together fulfilling God's mission in the world.

What is God's mission for his church? "The task of the church," writes J. I. Packer, "is to make the invisible kingdom visible through faithful Christian living and witness-bearing."[4]

I love that statement. The church makes the invisible kingdom visible. The world can't see God. They can't see his reign in our hearts. But we join our lives together in the church so they can see him. They see him when we obey his commands. When we love one another. When we preach his Word and proclaim his gospel. When we do good works and serve the poor and the outcast. On earth everything we do—our worship, our building of Christian community, our service, our work—is to be done with an eye to spreading the fame and glory of Jesus Christ so the nations might know and worship him with us.

In John 20:21, Jesus said to his disciples, "As the Father has sent me, even so I am sending you." And in his final words before he ascended into heaven, Jesus gave all his followers an assignment that we call the Great Commission:

All authority in heaven and on earth has been given to me. Go therefore and make disciples of all nations, baptizing them in the name of

the Father and of the Son and of the Holy Spirit, teaching them to observe all that I have commanded you. And behold, I am with you always, to the end of the age. (Matthew 28:18–20)

The purpose of Christian community in the church is not only our joy and spiritual growth. The purpose is also mission—displaying and advancing God's reign and rule in the world.

———

I'll be honest. The mission Jesus has given us scares me. I'm much more comfortable being called out of the world than I am being sent into it. As a pastor I can devote myself to the concerns of the church, spend most of my time with other Christians, and shut myself off in the safety of church life like a hamster in a plastic rolling ball.

But that impulse to wall myself off from the world isn't always motivated by a love for holiness. Too often I separate myself from the world because I'm afraid or just plain lazy. Unbelieving people think I'm weird. They're different from me, and different can be uncomfortable.

In those moments I have to remind myself: it's not enough for me to be holy. When Jesus left, he didn't say, "Stay on this hill and be holy." He told his followers to be holy and to go share the gospel with the world. For the church to be faithful, we need both a concern for holiness and a heart to reach the world. Each of us has to continually evaluate our motives, our lifestyle choices, and our efforts to befriend people who don't know Jesus.

I once heard John Piper share the story of being invited as a young boy to attend a movie with his classmates. His very godly but very conservative parents frowned on movie watching. But while his mother would have preferred he not go, she didn't forbid him. Instead she explained her own convictions and let him make the choice. "Do what you think is right," she told him. "We have standards, Son, but they have to come from the inside." Reflecting on the story, Piper said, "There's a world of difference between separation and consecration. The issue is not separating rules but consecrated hearts."[5]

There's a lot of wisdom for the church in those words as we wrestle with questions about engaging and influencing a godless culture. To consecrate something means to set it apart for God's use. True consecration is an inward reality, not a matter of physical proximity or outward regulation.

There's no contradiction between consecration and evangelistic mission. If our hearts are consecrated, we can live in the darkest culture and powerfully shine forth the truth of the gospel. If our hearts are not consecrated, no amount of separation or man-made rules will keep us from the influence of worldliness (1 John 2:15–17). It will be in us no matter how high we build the walls around ourselves.

Jesus said that Christians are to be like salt and light in the world (Matthew 5:13–16). John Stott writes, "So Jesus calls his disciples to exert a double influence on the secular community, a negative influence by arresting its decay and a positive influence by bringing light into its darkness. For it is one thing to stop the spread of evil; it is another to promote the spread of truth, beauty and goodness."[6] The church is called to engage the world around us with countercultural lives and countercultural truth from God's Word—to arrest the decay brought about by human rebellion and spreading the life-giving light of God's truth.

Notice that both analogies Jesus uses assume contact. Salt is a natural preservative. It halts decay. But it won't work if it's diluted. And it has no effect if it's isolated. Salt has to come into contact. So it is with the church. We have to be in the world, engaging and influencing every aspect of culture with the truth of the gospel.

In the same way Jesus doesn't call his people to be just a city. We're to be a city on a hill that shines forth light to a dark world. "Flight into the invisible is a denial of the call," writes Dietrich Bonhoeffer. "A community of Jesus which seeks to hide itself has ceased to follow him."[7]

If we would obey Jesus, we must go into the world. I've been challenged by the example of other churches to study my local community with the evangelistic intentionality of a missionary. To ask questions like "If I were a missionary to another nation, how would I view my life? What decisions would I make about where I live or how much I need to live on? Where would I spend my time so I could form friendships with unbelieving people? What would I seek to learn about the culture so I could befriend and clearly communicate the gospel? What are the idols and false gods people are worshiping?"

Ask these questions, and then apply them to your current location. The mission field is right in front of you. Imagine how this kind of evangelistic urgency could be used by God to touch your campus, workplace, neighborhood, and community.

———

God's people can't reach the world if we hide. And we can't reach the world unless we're distinct from the world. We need to recapture the connection between holiness and mission. God calls his people to be distinct and holy, not so we can feel morally superior to our sinful neighbors. He calls us to be holy so that our neighbors will see the transforming power of the crucified, risen Jesus Christ.

It's not enough simply to go to the world. In Genesis, Abraham's nephew Lot went to the city of Sodom. Scripture states that Lot was a righteous man (2 Peter 2:7). But he lost his family to the sinful culture of the city. When God visited it in judgment, none of Lot's extended family and none of his neighbors would leave with him. Even after fire rained down on Sodom, Lot's wife looked back with longing eyes on the city and was punished (Genesis 19).

The world needs a church that will engage it, go to it. But how will we go to the world? Lot went to the world, but the world reshaped him. Jonah was a missionary, but he preached to Nineveh without love or compassion. He burned with rage when God showed the city mercy (Jonah 4:1).

Jesus is our model of love-motivated mission. Jesus wept over the sin of Jerusalem (Matthew 23:37–39). He stopped for the blind, the lame, and the outcasts. He ate with sinners. He scandalized the religious by befriending prostitutes and tax collectors. He went to the world with love and a saving message that countered everything the world stood for. He was willing to suffer and die at the hands of the people he came to save.

It was love that motivated God to send his Son on a mission of salvation (John 3:16). The same must be true of us. Only the great commandments to love God with heart, soul, mind, and strength and to love our neighbor as we love ourselves can push us outside ourselves and our narrow self-interests (Mark 12:28–34). Only this love can compel us to lay down our lives caring for the poor, marginalized, and oppressed of the world.

Only this love will give us the sustained courage to go into the world to speak the foolish, unwanted, yet saving message of a crucified Messiah. Love has to fuel mission. We can't go to the world because we want their approval; we can't go for power or to prove ourselves right. Mission has to be the overflow of a love for God that aches to see others experiencing his grace, love, and compassion for people who are lost and destined for hell.

Admittedly, the mission Jesus has given us would be easier if we didn't have to love, if we didn't have to care. It would be so much easier if we could either hate the world or just not care.

When I read about the violent, radical strain of Islam that has led to terrorism, I'm repulsed by it. But I can also see its appeal. There's something very straightforward, very doable about the assignment to hate the modern world, fight it, and try to blow it up. That's a relatively simple job description. I could do that. Blow myself up and then die and go to heaven.

But Jesus asks something much harder of his followers—something that takes much more courage and sacrifice. It's a mission that requires divine empowerment. He tells us to die to ourselves and live for him. He tells us to lay down our lives in the service of people who often despise us. He tells us to fully engage in a world that wants to seduce us and that hates us when we resist. He sends his church to plead with a culture that loves its sin.

Jesus asks us to die. But this is a sort of slow death. It's not a death that takes away life but a death that gives others life. It's the death of taking up a cross and walking in the footsteps of our crucified Savior. It's suffering for the message of the gospel. It's dying to popularity and being a church that stands for righteousness. This is something much more painful and terrifying than a split-second decision to press a button and become a human bomb. But it is the way of Jesus, and it leads to everlasting life.

What's your definition of success for the church? Numbers? Political power? The acceptance of Christianity in popular culture? We all carry around some concept of what it would look like if the church were really making progress.

Each year a Christian magazine publishes a list of the one hundred biggest churches as well as the one hundred fastest-growing churches in

America. Now, there's nothing wrong with this idea, and I'm sure it's of service to many people. But I had to stop reading that particular issue because I found it wasn't good for me. I started to feel like I was ogling other churches across the country. I felt like I was lusting after success and numbers and acclaim and that it was distorting my motivation for being a pastor. So I put the magazine aside.

When I find myself discouraged about the church, I have to stop and think about God's definition of success. It helps me to remember what Jesus taught about the nature of his kingdom and how it would grow. Jesus said the kingdom was like the tiniest of seeds that grows into the largest of plants (Luke 13:18–19). At first it doesn't look impressive. Nobody cares about it. But over time and so slowly you hardly notice, it grows and expands.

For Christians who want to see God's kingdom come with convincing, awe-inspiring power, a tiny, slow-growing seed can be something of a letdown. Have you ever sat and tried to watch a plant grow? That's how it can feel with God's kingdom. It's growing, but you can perceive it only over long stretches of time.

Jesus said the kingdom was like yeast used to make bread (Luke 13:20–21). Yeast is small and seemingly insignificant in quantity compared to the other ingredients, yet when it's worked into the dough, it causes the whole loaf to rise. It fundamentally changes the composition of the whole.

The kingdom of God isn't impressive to human eyes. It's outnumbered. In some ways it seems to be swallowed up by the world around it. But ever so slowly it's permeating the world around it and effecting change in ways no one anticipates.

The advance of God's kingdom takes time. And contact. The yeast does nothing sitting in a bowl removed from and unmixed with the dough. People of God's kingdom accomplish nothing when we're separated and have no contact with the world around us.

Jesus told another story about seeds being planted in different kinds of soil (Matthew 13:1–23). Most of the seeds didn't grow. They were eaten, trampled, or choked, or they withered. But a few grew and produced a great harvest. Growth and advance in God's kingdom should be expected amid seeming setbacks, even failure. Sometimes God draws big crowds. But not always. Maybe not often.

Jesus said that the kingdom was like a banquet held by a king that no one respectable or successful wanted to attend (Luke 14:15–24). All the beautiful people turned down the invitation and made up excuses for their absence. So the king sent his servants into the streets and gathered in the lowlifes, the poor and uneducated and overlooked of the world. It wouldn't make a very good ad campaign, but that's your basic description of the church. It's a huge party for losers. Losers who realize that only Jesus can save them.

I think when Christians talk about reaching the culture, we sometimes don't want to reach it for the sake of God as much as for ourselves. We want to win for winning's sake. We want acceptance because we're tired of looking foolish. We want success as the world defines it. We want a loser-free church that is hip and sophisticated.

But none of this squares with what Jesus told us about his kingdom. He didn't tell us to aim for numbers or adoring crowds or cultural acceptance. He told us just to love him, love each other, and love the world by telling them about him.

I want to learn to be faithful to the two Great Commandments and the Great Commission and leave the results to God. I want to reach the world because I really love God and I really love my neighbor.

I'd like to be part of a church that makes God's list of the most faithful.

Paul says that "through the church" God is making known the truths he had kept hidden for centuries. He says heaven itself leans down to watch in wonder the "manifold wisdom of God" on display in the church (Ephesians 3:9–11).

This part of God's plan leaves me speechless. He chooses to include us. With our flaws—with all our weaknesses, petty jealousies, blind spots, and ignorance—he lets us play a part in his story.

Why are we still here? Why hasn't he brought us home? Why has he given us a mission that seems so hard? so impossible? Because he wants to give us stories to tell around the campfires of heaven. Stories of how he empowered us when we thought we couldn't go on. Stories of how he enabled us to love in the face of opposition, hatred, and even death. Stories of how he used our weak and feeble voices to announce the saving message of the gospel. Stories of how he saved people we thought were beyond saving. Stories of how he orchestrated the crashing chaos of world history so people from every nation and tribe and tongue would be represented in his family on the final day. Stories of how our ineffective churches still managed to put his glory on display.

11

HUMBLE ORTHODOXY

"Here's what deflates my arrogance faster than anything else: trying to live the truth I have."

A FEW YEARS AGO I was in Seattle with an old friend who had written a popular book about his personal reflections and experiences with the Christian faith. He began telling me about the letters he was getting from readers. He said the harshest ones were from people who presented themselves as "caring about doctrine." Their e-mails were vitriolic, pointing out the theological errors and inconsistencies of what he had written.

My friend isn't a pastor or Bible scholar. He's a poet and a storyteller. That's part of what makes his writing appealing. Honestly, he did get some things wrong in his book. I think he knows that. But I saw how hard it was for him to admit that when the information was coming from people whose words and attitudes were ugly.

As we've learned, *orthodoxy* means right thinking about God. It's teaching and belief based on the established, proven, cherished truths of the faith. And *doctrine* is simply Christian teaching. But one of the problems with the words *orthodoxy* and *doctrine* is that they're usually brought up when someone is being reprimanded. So they've gotten something of a bad reputation, like an older sibling who is always peeking around the corner, trying to catch you doing something wrong.

I think every generation of Christians faces the temptation to buck orthodoxy for just this reason. Even if we know something is true and right, we don't like others telling us we have to believe it. And if youthful pride weren't enough, the temptation to abandon orthodoxy really intensifies when its advocates are unlikable and meanspirited.

I don't know any other way to say this: sometimes it seems like a lot of the people who care about orthodoxy are jerks.

But why? Does good doctrine necessarily lead to being argumentative, annoying, and arrogant?

We've reached the end of this book. If you're new to the Christian faith, some of the Christian beliefs we've explored may have been unfamiliar to you. Or if you've studied doctrine before, perhaps the chapters were mostly a review. But whether our theological knowledge is great or small, we all need to ask a vital question: what will we *do* with the knowledge of God that we have?

Will it lead us to an ever-growing desire to know and love the Lord? Will it practically affect the way we think and live? Will we have the courage to hold on to the truth even when it isn't popular? And how will we express our beliefs? With humility—or with pride?

I don't want to be like the people who wrote angry letters to my friend. At the same time, I don't want to be like well-intentioned people I know who are careless, almost unconcerned about Christian truths. They'd never make others feel uncomfortable about their beliefs, but that's because they believe hardly anything themselves.

Do we have to choose between a zeal for truth and kindness? Does embracing deeply held beliefs require that we let go of humility?

Most people want to choose between the two, but the Bible doesn't give us that option. It tells us that we need both. We need conviction, and we need gentleness. We need orthodoxy, and we need humility.

———

He was young and afraid. What business did he have being a pastor? He wondered sometimes. How could he lead a church being torn by opposition? He wanted to be bold. He wanted to be fearless. He prayed that God would make him so. But he felt so isolated, so completely alone. And then the letter came. Its message must have hit him like a blow to the stomach, knocking the air out of him.

His friend, mentor, and father in the faith was writing to say good-bye. The end was near.

Today we call the letter 2 Timothy. We read it as one of the twenty-seven books of the New Testament. We see crisply printed text divided into four chapters with neatly numbered verses and descriptive subheadings. We read it as someone else's story in a faraway place and time.

But I wonder what it was like for Timothy to read the letter. For him it wasn't someone else's story. It was *his* story. It wasn't long-past history. Timothy read it in the uncertain, terrifying present. "For I am already being poured out as a drink offering," the apostle Paul wrote. "And the time of my departure has come" (4:6).

This time Paul wasn't going to be released from prison. He was going to be executed.

Few things clear away the cobwebs in your mind like the words of a godly man who knows he is about to die. In 2 Timothy, Paul is looking back on a life that will soon be over. He is looking ahead to the unknown future of the fledgling church, which must now struggle on without his guidance. No wonder there is such urgency and emotion in his words.

And what does he choose for his final message? Paul's driving concern is the preservation of the gospel—the heart of Christian orthodoxy. For Paul this isn't about proving someone else wrong, winning an argument, or adding people to his little club. For Paul, orthodoxy makes the difference between life and death, heaven and hell. Whether or not it is faithfully communicated determines if the world will know the saving truth about Jesus Christ.

Paul urges Timothy to stand unashamed on the truth about Jesus's life, suffering, and bodily resurrection. "Remember Jesus Christ, risen from the dead, the offspring of David, as preached in my gospel," he wrote (2:8).

You might think that telling a Christian to "remember Jesus" borders on the unnecessary. Can Christians really forget him? Paul knew they could. And even worse, he knew that they could claim allegiance to Jesus but lose sight of the real meaning of his life and death.

The true message of the gospel was under attack. False teachers parading as Christians had denied it, distorted it, and twisted it to serve their own selfish desires. Paul compared their teaching to gangrene—a disease that rots human flesh into a guacamole-colored open sore and is often remedied by amputation (2:17–18). For Paul the analogy was no exaggeration. A distorted gospel rots the soul.

The only antidote for Timothy, Paul said, was to keep teaching the orthodox truths of the faith that had been passed down to him. "Follow the pattern of the sound words that you have heard from me, in the faith and love that are in Christ Jesus," Paul urged. "By the Holy Spirit who dwells within us, guard the good deposit entrusted to you" (1:13–14).

Some people think of orthodoxy as something lifeless and restrictive—

a paint-by-numbers guide that stifles creativity. But Paul saw it as a treasure. It wasn't a canvas for self-expression. It was a "good deposit," something so precious it needed to be guarded and protected.

Now it was Timothy's job to put on display the beauty of this treasure, to preserve it, and to pass it on unaltered to those who would follow. "What you have heard from me," Paul wrote, "in the presence of many witnesses entrust to faithful men who will be able to teach others also" (2:2).

Reading 2 Timothy reminds me of the sad reality of falsehood and lies. I wish I lived in a world where beliefs were like different flavors of ice cream—no wrong answers, just different options. But that's not the world we live in. We live in a world of truths and lies. We live in a world in which God's true revelation and the smooth words of charlatans and false prophets compete for our attention. A world where there is murder, genocide, and the worship of idols. A world where teachers and writers offer empty hope in human achievement and material possessions (3:1–9). A world filled with evil and an Evil One who is bent on distorting and destroying the truth and those who believe it (1 Peter 5:8).

Love for God and love for neighbor require opposing falsehood. There is nothing more unloving than to be silent in the face of lies that will ruin another person. Sometimes love demands that we say, "This philosophy, no matter how plausible or popular, is not true. This person, no matter how likable, gifted, or well-intentioned, is teaching something that contradicts God's Word; therefore, it is untrue."

Paul modeled this type of love-infused courage—courage that was willing to contend for God's unchanging truth that has once and for all been "delivered to the saints" (Jude 3).

You and I need to be willing to contend for truth. But there's a fine line between contending for truth and being contentious. I think this is why, in his final instruction to Timothy, the old apostle goes out of his way to tell Timothy that even though orthodoxy is important, it's not enough by itself.

Truth matters, but so does our attitude. We have to live and speak and interact with others in a spirit of humility. Paul wrote:

> Have nothing to do with foolish, ignorant controversies; you know that they breed quarrels. And the Lord's servant must not be quarrelsome but kind to everyone, able to teach, patiently enduring evil, correcting his opponents with gentleness. God may perhaps grant them repentance leading to a knowledge of the truth, and they may come to their senses and escape from the snare of the devil, after being captured by him to do his will. (2 Timothy 2:23–26)

I find these words amazing in light of Paul's circumstances. He's about to die. He sees false teachers working to destroy the church. He has been betrayed and abandoned. You would expect him to say, "Nuke the heretics, and don't worry about civilian casualties!" But he doesn't. Instead he says, "Don't be a jerk."

Don't be quarrelsome.

Don't get sidetracked on secondary issues.

Be kind.

Be patient.

When other people are evil, endure it while trusting in God.

When you need to correct someone, do it with gentleness.

Even when Paul was opposing false teachers—the enemies of orthodoxy—he hoped that his correction would bring them to their senses. Maybe he pictured himself standing by as Stephen was murdered (Acts 7:54–60). On that day no one could have imagined that Saul, the destroyer of the church, would become Paul, the defender of the church and an apostle of Christ Jesus. But the risen Lord had rescued him and commissioned him to announce the gospel across the world.

Paul had been shown grace by the Lord. So he did the same toward others, even opponents. He genuinely cared about people who disagreed with him. Even when he fiercely opposed them, he didn't just want to beat them in an argument; he wanted to win them to the truth.

———

My buddy Eric says that what Christians need today is humble orthodoxy. I like that phrase. I think it's a good description of what Paul was telling Timothy to practice. Christians need to have a strong commitment to sound doctrine. We need to be courageous in our stand for biblical truth. But we also need to be gracious in our words and interaction with other people.

Eric says that a lot of Christians today are turned off by orthodoxy because they've never seen it held humbly. I think that's true. Many Christians, especially younger ones, are running from orthodoxy, not so much because of doctrine, but because of the arrogance and divisiveness they associate with those who promote it.

So why do people who care about orthodoxy and doctrine often have a harsh streak? Why is there so much arrogant orthodoxy in the church? The Bible says that " 'knowledge' puffs up, but love builds up" (1 Corinthians 8:1). Ever since the first man and woman in the garden turned from God to gain the sweet, forbidden knowledge offered by the serpent, there has been an inclination in every human heart to pursue knowledge to inflate the self rather than to glorify God.

In his book *The Reason for God,* Tim Keller says that all sin is attempting to find a sense of identity and meaning apart from God. "So, according to the Bible," he writes, "the primary way to define sin is not just the doing of bad things, but the making of good things into *ultimate* things."[1]

Applied to the topic at hand, Keller's point is that if we make a good thing like right theology ultimate—if being right becomes more important to us than God—then our theology is not really about God anymore; it's about us. It becomes the source of our sense of worth and identity. And if theology becomes about us, then we'll despise and demonize those who oppose us.[2]

Knowledge about God that doesn't translate into exalting him in our words, thoughts, and actions will soon become self-exaltation. And then we'll attack anyone who threatens our tiny Kingdom of Self.

If we stand before the awesome knowledge of God's character and our first thought isn't *I am small and unworthy to know the Creator of the universe,* then we should be concerned. Too many of us catch a glimpse of him and think, *Look at* me, *taking this all in. Think of all the poor fools who have never seen this. God, you're certainly lucky to have me beholding you.*

It's regrettable that human sin can distort sound teaching just as it can mess up anything else that's good in the world. But should this cause us to abandon the pursuit and defense of biblical truth?

Paul didn't think so. He spent his last moments of life urging Timothy to hold to the truth about Jesus. And the problems of pride and turf wars wouldn't go away even if we tried to avoid orthodoxy. We'd just find something else to throw at each other. We'd find something else to be proud about.

The solution to arrogant orthodoxy is not less orthodoxy; it's more. If we truly know and embrace orthodoxy, it should humble us. When we know the truth about God—his power, his greatness, his holiness, his mercy—it doesn't leave us boasting; it leaves us amazed. It doesn't lead to a preoccupation with being right but to amazement that we have been rescued.

Genuine orthodoxy—the heart of which is the death of God's Son for undeserving sinners—is the most humbling, human-pride-smashing message in the world. And if we truly know the gospel of grace, it will create in us a heart of humility and grace toward others. Francis Schaeffer, a Christian writer and thinker from the twentieth century, modeled this kind of profound compassion. He genuinely loved people. And even as he analyzed and critiqued the culture, he did so "with a tear in his eye."[3]

That is humble orthodoxy. It's standing for truth with a tear in our eye. It's telling a friend living in sexual sin that we love her even as we tell her that her sexual activity is disobedient to God. It's remembering that angry, unkind opponents of the gospel are human beings created in the image of God who need the same mercy he has shown us. It's remembering that when we're arrogant and self-righteous in the way we represent orthodoxy, we're actually contradicting with our lives what we claim to believe.

But while we shouldn't be mean and spiteful in representing biblical truth, neither should we apologize for believing that God has been clear in his Word. The humility we need in our theology is first and foremost a humility before God. As pastor Mark Dever puts it, "Humble theology [is] theology which submits itself to the truth of God's Word."[4] This is a good reminder for me. Because I think it's possible for me, or anyone for that matter, to overreact to arrogant orthodoxy with a brand of squishy theology that believes others are arrogant if they think the Bible teaches anything clearly.

But truth can be known. And what the Bible teaches should be obeyed. Just because we can't know God exhaustively doesn't mean we can't know him truly (Psalm 19:7–10; John 17:17). Just because there is mystery in God's Word doesn't mean we can pretend God hasn't spoken clearly in the Bible.

"Christian humility," Dever writes, "is to simply accept whatever God has revealed in His Word. Humility is following God's Word wherever it goes, as far as it goes, *not* either going beyond it or stopping short of it.... The humility we want in our churches is to read the Bible and believe it.... It is not humble to be hesitant where God has been clear and plain."[5]

I won't pretend that I've arrived at humble orthodoxy. When I gain a bit of theological knowledge, I all too frequently can get puffed up with pride. But I'll tell you what deflates my arrogance and self-righteousness faster than anything else: trying to live whatever truth I have.

Do you want to keep your orthodoxy humble? Try to live it. Don't spend all your time theorizing about it, debating about it, or blogging about it. Spend more energy living the truth you know than worrying about what the next guy does or doesn't know. Don't measure yourself by what you know. Measure yourself by your practice of what you know.

Do I know something of the doctrine of God? Can I list his attributes of sovereignty, omnipotence, and love? Then I should live that truth and stop worrying and complaining and being anxious.

Do I know something of the doctrine of justification? Can I tell you that I'm justified by grace alone through faith alone in Christ alone? Good. Then I should live that truth by repenting of my worthless efforts to earn God's approval. I should weep over my self-righteousness when I think and act toward others as if I'm anything but the recipient of pure, unmerited grace.

Do I know something about the doctrine of sanctification? Do I know the priority of holiness and the reality of remaining sin in my life? Then why attack or look down on another Christian who seems less sanctified? I have enough areas where I need to grow to keep me busy. I should pray for more of the Holy Spirit's power to enable *me* to grow in obedience.

Here's a useful exercise. Go back over the doctrines we've studied in this book, and think about the real-world, real-life implications of each truth for your life. What would it look like to live the truth of each one? What would change about your relationships, your words, your attitudes, and your actions?

I think this is what Paul was telling Timothy to do when he said, "Watch your life and doctrine closely. Persevere in them, because if you do, you will save both yourself and your hearers" (1 Timothy 4:16, NIV). It's not enough to get our doctrine straight. Life and doctrine can't be separated. Our lives either put the beauty of God's truth on display, or they obscure it.

It helps me to remember that one day in heaven there will be only one right person.

I'm sorry, but it won't be you. Or me.

It will be God.

Everybody else in heaven will be wrong in a million different ways about a million different things. The Bible tells us that only those who trusted in Jesus Christ, who turned from sin and believed in him, will be in God's presence. But on a host of secondary matters, we'll all discover how much we got wrong.

Maybe some people picture heaven as a place where all the "right" people celebrate that they made it. But I don't think that's true. I think it will be a place of beautiful humility.

The funny thing is, I'm really looking forward to this aspect of heaven. I can't wait for that crystal-clear awareness of all the opinions and attitudes and ideas and strategies that I had in this life that were quite simply wrong.

No one will be proud. No one will be bragging. We all will want to talk about how wrong we were about so many things and how kind God was to us. I can imagine someone saying, "Seriously, I am the most unworthy person here."

And then someone else will say, "No, friend, it took more grace for me to be here. You need to hear my story."

And we'll say, "No offense, King David, but we've already heard your story. Let somebody else share." (Of course we'll let him share again later.)

At the end of every conversation, we'll agree that when we were back on the old earth, we really had no idea how unmerited that grace really is. We called it grace, but we didn't really think it was totally grace. We thought we'd added just a tad of something good. That we had earned just a bit. We'll realize to our shame that to differing degrees we trusted in our intellect, our morality, the rightness of our doctrine, and our religious performance when all along it was completely grace.

"For by grace you have been saved through faith. And this is not your own doing; it is the gift of God, not a result of works, so that no one may boast" (Ephesians 2:8–9).

Every one of us will have a lot to apologize for.

I estimate that somewhere near the first ten thousand years of heaven will be taken up with the redeemed people of God apologizing to each other for all the ways we judged each other, jostled for position, were proud and divisive and arrogant toward each other. (Of course this is just an estimate; it could be the first twenty thousand years.)

I imagine Paul telling Barnabas he's sorry for splitting up the team over Mark. And admitting to Mark how he should have been more willing to give him another chance. And then all the Christians from first-century Corinth will tell Paul how bad they feel about what a complete pain they were for him.

All the people in churches who split over silly things like organ music will come together and hug each other. The Baptists and Presbyterians will get together, and one side will have to admit to the other side that they were wrong about baptism. And then the side that was right will say they're sorry for their pride and all the snide comments they made. And then there will be no more sides, and the whole thing will be forgotten.

Because of course we'll all be happy to forgive each other. And we'll keep saying, "But God used it for good. We couldn't see it then, but he was at work even in our weakness and sin."

In the meantime, we should strive to hold our beliefs with a charity and kindness that won't embarrass us in heaven.

The air of heaven will blow away the fog that so often clouds our vision in this life. In eternity we'll see the silliness of self-righteousness and quarreling over the nonessentials. But we'll also see with piercing clarity just how essential the essentials really are. We'll see just how precious the truths of the gospel really are.

We will look into each other's eyes, and we won't be able to stop saying, "It was all true! It was all true!" Every word. Every promise.

We'll see that the Cross really conquered death and hell and washed away our sins. We'll see the everlasting reward of believing in Jesus and the eternal hell of rejecting him. We'll look back on our lives and see that God never did forsake us. Not even for a split second. That he was with us every moment—even the darkest moments of despair and seeming hopelessness. We will know in a deeper way than we can now imagine that God truly worked *all* things together for our good. And we'll see that Jesus really did go to prepare a place for us, just as he said.

And everything we did for the sake of Jesus will be so worth it. Every time we stood for truth and looked foolish. Every time we shared the gospel. Every act of service. Every sacrifice.

We will meet men and women from every nation of the old earth who gave their lives in the cause of the gospel—martyrs who died rather than abandon the unchanging truths of the faith. We'll meet people who lost homes and family and whose bodies were whipped and tortured and burned because they refused to renounce the name of Jesus. And we will honor them, and all will see that what they lost and suffered was nothing in comparison to what they gained.

No one will say, "I wish I'd believed less. I wish I'd cared less about the gospel."

Jesus said that people who come to him and hear his words and put them into practice are like a man building a house who dug down deep and laid the foundation on rock. When a flood came and a torrent broke against the house, it couldn't be shaken (Luke 6:46–49, NIV).

As we go about our daily lives—eating, sleeping, studying, working our jobs, falling in love, starting families, and raising children—we all believe specific things about what matters in life, about what our purpose is in this world. In one way or another we all believe something about God.

Our lives are like houses. And each one is built on some foundation of belief. The question is whether what we believe is true—whether it will withstand the flood of suffering in this life, the torrent of death, and the final judgment before our Creator.

Jesus said that an unshakable foundation for life is found only in knowing him, in believing his words and living by his truth. The most important question any of us can ask is, Am I building my life on who Jesus is and what he has done? Is my life built on the rock of a true knowledge of God?

Being grounded on that rock doesn't make you or me better than anyone else. It should make us aware of how dependent we are. It should humble us. The only thing that enables us to stand firm is Jesus and his words. The only thing that enables us to know and dwell with God is the solid rock of the Savior.

The message of Christian orthodoxy isn't that I'm right and someone else is wrong. It's that I am wrong and yet God is filled with grace. I am wrong, and yet God has made a way for me to be forgiven and accepted and loved for eternity. I am wrong, and yet God gave his Son, Jesus, to die in my place and receive my punishment. I am wrong, but through faith in Jesus, I can be made right before a holy God.

This is the gospel. This is the truth that all Christian doctrine celebrates. This is the truth that every follower of Jesus Christ is called to cherish and preserve. Even die for. It is the only truth on which we can build our lives and rest our eternal hope.

ACKNOWLEDGMENTS

A SPECIAL THANKS TO…

Steve and Ken and the team at WaterBrook Multnomah and Random House for their support.

Moby Dick's House of Kabob for feeding me and to Whole Foods and the Kentland's Starbucks for space to write.

Bob and Sharron for making that morning on the beach possible.

The good people of Covenant Life, who make pastoring such a joy. Thank you for the way you support me, encourage me, and pray for me.

All the pastors of Covenant Life for allowing me to invest the time needed to complete this book. Thank you, Kenneth, Grant, and Corby, for all that you carried and led during that time.

All those who read the book and gave me suggestions: Robin, Ken, Greg, Heather, Amy, Josh, Brian, Isaac, and Jeff.

C.J. for the irreplaceable part you played in this story.

Eric for the vision of humble orthodoxy and for prodding me to write.

Justin, who encouraged me three years ago at Together for the Gospel to "write a boring book." Well, here it is, bro! And you were kind enough to read and critique every page. Thank you, Lane, for your gracious support.

John for urging me in Al's basement to turn the humble orthodoxy message into a book.

Mark for lunch and help with the table of contents.

My T5G boys (Collin, Justin, Tullian, and Greg), who listened to me talk endlessly about my writing voice, titles, and blurbs. May God answer our prayers in Asheville.

My editor, David, for allowing me to experiment, for giving me space to write differently, and for always having a vision for the message of this book. To Carol for the line edit.

My assistant, Katherine, for making do without meetings and for so passionately believing in this book.

All the people who prayed for me while I wrote, including my Facebook and Twitter friends. I'm particularly grateful to Mom, Tim, Meg, Linda, Raul, Elsabeth, Trisha, the Covenant Life staff, the Berry family, Donna, and Deborah for consistently telling me that you were praying.

Grandma Harris for trusting Jesus all these years.

My dad for late-night interviews and for letting me share your story.

My children—Emma, Joshua Quinn, and Mary Kate—for being excited about this book, talking to me about titles, celebrating every finished chapter, and asking which one was my favorite.

My sweet wife, Shannon, the love of my life. Thank you for serving me, putting up with me, and caring for our kids day in and day out. Thank you for letting me read you chapters even when you were tired. The book is done, sweetheart! I'm ready to clean the basement and go camping now.

NOTES

Chapter 1: My Rumspringa

1. Velda, quoted in "The Devil's Playground," *21C Magazine,* www.21cmagazine.com/issue1/devils_playground.html.
2. Tom Shachtman, *Rumspringa: To Be or Not to Be Amish* (New York: North Point, 2006), 251.

Chapter 2: In Which I Learn to Dig

1. J. Gresham Machen, *Christianity and Liberalism* (New York: Macmillan, 1923), 29.

Chapter 3: Near but Not in My Pocket

1. Christian Smith with Melinda Lundquist Denton, *Soul Searching: The Religious and Spiritual Lives of American Teenagers* (New York: Oxford University Press, 2005), 163–65.
2. J. I. Packer, *Knowing God* (Downers Grove, IL: InterVarsity, 1973), 83.
3. J. I. Packer, *Concise Theology: A Guide to Historic Christian Beliefs* (Wheaton, IL: Tyndale, 1993), 27.
4. Wayne Grudem, *Bible Doctrine: Essential Teachings of the Christian Faith* (Grand Rapids: Zondervan, 1999), 72.
5. R. C. Sproul, *The Holiness of God* (Wheaton, IL: Tyndale, 2000), 38.
6. I borrowed the microscope-telescope analogy from John Piper's sermon "Passion for the Supremacy of God, Part 1," delivered at

Passion 1997, Desiring God, www.desiringgod.org/Resource Library/ConferenceMessages/ByDate/1997/1906_Passion_for_the _Supremacy_of_God_Part_1/.

Chapter 4: Ripping, Burning, Eating

1. A. J. Jacobs, *The Year of Living Biblically: One Man's Humble Quest to Follow the Bible as Literally as Possible* (New York: Simon and Schuster, 2007), 4.

2. Jacobs, *The Year of Living Biblically,* 9.

3. Sally Lloyd-Jones, *The Jesus Storybook Bible: Every Story Whispers His Name* (Grand Rapids: Zonderkidz, 2007), 14–17.

4. J. I. Packer, *God Has Spoken: Revelation and the Bible* (Downers Grove, IL: InterVarsity, 1979), 50–52.

5. Sinclair B. Ferguson, *Handle with Care! A Guide to Using the Bible* (London: Hodder and Stoughton, 1982), 22.

6. Ferguson, *Handle with Care!,* 28.

7. Wayne Grudem, *Bible Doctrine: Essential Teachings of the Christian Faith* (Grand Rapids: Zondervan, 1999), 41.

8. For further study I suggest reading the chapters on Scripture in a good systematic theology such as Wayne Grudem's *Bible Doctrine.* Or study J. I. Packer's book *"Fundamentalism" and the Word of God,* which lays out a comprehensive statement on the doctrine of Scripture. R. C. Sproul's excellent book *Knowing Scripture* will give you practical tools for interpreting and studying the Bible. And if you wrestle with questions about the reliability of Scripture, read Paul Barnett's *Is the New Testament Reliable?* It's not wrong to have questions. But it is wrong to leave questions unanswered and wallow in doubt when strong, reliable answers are available.

Chapter 5: God with a Bellybutton

1. C. S. Lewis, *Mere Christianity* (New York: Macmillan, 1960), 40–41.

2. The information on the wrong views of Christ's nature is drawn from Wayne Grudem, *Bible Doctrine: Essential Teachings of the Christian Faith* (Grand Rapids: Zondervan, 1999), 241–44.

3. The Chalcedonian Creed states: "We then, following the holy Fathers, all with one consent, teach men to confess one and the same Son, our Lord Jesus Christ, the same perfect in Godhead and also perfect in manhood; truly God and truly man, of a reasonable soul and body; consubstantial with the Father according to the Godhead, and consubstantial with us according to the Manhood; in all things like unto us, without sin; begotten before all ages of the Father according to the Godhead, and in these latter days, for us and for our salvation, born of the Virgin Mary, the Mother of God, according to the Manhood; one and the same Christ, Son, Lord, Only-begotten, to be acknowledged in two natures, inconfusedly, unchangeably, indivisibly, inseparably; the distinction of natures being by no means taken away by the union, but rather the property of each nature being preserved, and concurring in one Person and one Subsistence, not parted or divided into two persons, but one and the same Son, and only begotten, God the Word, the Lord Jesus Christ, as the prophets from the beginning have declared concerning him, and the Lord Jesus Christ himself has taught us, and the Creed of the holy Fathers handed down to us." Taken from "Ancient Creeds," www.monergism .com/thethreshold/articles/onsite/ancientcreeds.html.

4. John M. Frame, *Salvation Belongs to the Lord: An Introduction to Systematic Theology* (Phillipsburg, NJ: P and R Publishing, 2006), 131.

5. Frame, *Salvation Belongs to the Lord,* 130.

6. J. Gresham Machen, *Christianity and Liberalism* (New York: Macmillan, 1923), 96.

7. Machen, *Christianity and Liberalism,* 97.

8. Machen, *Christianity and Liberalism,* 103.

Chapter 6: A Way to Be Good Again

1. J. I. Packer, *Concise Theology: A Guide to Historic Christian Beliefs* (Wheaton, IL: Tyndale, 1993), 134.

2. John R. W. Stott, *The Cross of Christ* (Downers Grove, IL: InterVarsity, 1986), 68.

3. Stott, *The Cross of Christ,* 103.

4. The original version of the story "The Room" (first published in *New Attitude* magazine, April 1995), along with information that clears up questions about its authorship, can be accessed at JoshHarris.com, www.joshharris.com/the_room.php.

5. Marilyn Elias, "A Mind Haunted from Within," *USA Today,* May 8, 2008, Section D, 1–2.

6. Khaled Hosseini, *The Kite Runner* (New York: Riverhead, 2007), 1.

7. Hosseini, *The Kite Runner,* 2.

8. Stott, *The Cross of Christ,* 175.

9. One example of the Muslim version of the story is on www.the modernreligion.com/room.html.

Chapter 7: How Jesus Saved Gregg Eugene Harris

1. Jerry Bridges, from a sermon on Ephesians 4:7–13 entitled "Gifts of Grace to Build the Church" given at Covenant Life, Gaithersburg, MD, on November 23, 2008, www.covlife.org/resources.

2. John Phillips, "San Francisco," copyright © 1967, MCA Music Publishing.

3. John M. Frame, *Salvation Belongs to the Lord: An Introduction to Systematic Theology* (Phillipsburg, NJ: P and R Publishing, 2006), 185.

4. Jerry Bridges, *The Discipline of Grace: God's Role and Our Role in the Pursuit of Holiness* (Colorado Springs: NavPress, 1994), 51.

5. J. I Packer, *Knowing God* (Downers Grove, IL: InterVarsity, 1973), 200.

6. Sinclair B. Ferguson, *Children of the Living God* (Colorado Springs: NavPress, 1987), xi.

Chapter 8: Changed, Changing, to Be Changed

1. "The Ten Commandments," *This American Life,* episode 332, www.thisamericanlife.org/Radio_Episode.aspx?sched=1246.

2. Wayne Grudem, *Bible Doctrine: Essential Teachings of the Christian Faith* (Grand Rapids: Zondervan, 1999), 493.

3. Ted Haggard, "In God They Trust: NBC's Tom Brokaw Goes Inside the World of Christian Evangelicals," October 28, 2005, MSNBC .com, www.msnbc.msn.com/id/9804232/.

4. Robert Murray McCheyne, quoted in John Piper, Justin Taylor, eds., *Suffering and the Sovereignty of God* (Wheaton, IL: Crossway, 2006), 212.

5. Martin Luther, the first of The Ninety-Five Theses written in 1517, quoted in Bruce Demarest, *The Cross and Salvation: The Doctrine of God,* ed. John S. Feinberg (Wheaton, IL: Crossway, 2006), 270.

6. Timothy Keller, "All of Life Is Repentance," www.pcabakersfield .com/articles/all_of_life_is_repentance.pdf.

Chapter 9: I Believe in the Holy Spirit

1. For an example of how misguided this teaching is see 2 Corinthians 12:7–10, where we learn that an ailment Paul faced had nothing to

do with his sin or unbelief. In fact, it was God's purpose to glorify himself through Paul's weakness.

2. John M. Frame, *Salvation Belongs to the Lord: An Introduction to Systematic Theology* (Phillipsburg, NJ: P and R Publishing, 2006), 159.

3. J. I. Packer, *Keep in Step with the Spirit: Finding Fullness in Our Walk with God* (Grand Rapids: Baker, 2005), 11.

4. Daniel B. Wallace and M. James Sawyer, eds., *Who's Afraid of the Holy Spirit? An Investigation into the Ministry of the Spirit of God Today* (Dallas: Biblical Studies Press, 2005), 7.

5. Wallace and Sawyer, *Who's Afraid of the Holy Spirit?* 8.

6. Wallace and Sawyer, *Who's Afraid of the Holy Spirit?* 9.

7. Packer, *Keep in Step with the Spirit,* 57.

Chapter 10: The Invisible Made Visible

1. John M. Frame, *Salvation Belongs to the Lord: An Introduction to Systematic Theology* (Phillipsburg, NJ: P and R Publishing, 2006), 234.

2. John R. W. Stott, *The Message of Ephesians: God's New Society* (Downers Grove, IL: InterVarsity, 1979), 129.

3. Wayne Grudem, quoting John Calvin: "Wherever we see the Word of God purely preached and heard, and the sacraments administered according to Christ's institution, there, it is not to be doubted, a church of God exists." *Bible Doctrine: Essential Teachings of the Christian Faith* (Grand Rapids: Zondervan, 1999), 369.

4. J. I. Packer, *Concise Theology: A Guide to Historic Christian Beliefs* (Wheaton, IL: Tyndale, 1993), 194.

5. John Piper, "Evangelist Bill Piper: Fundamentalist Full of Grace and Joy" (sermon, 2008 Desiring God Conference for Pastors, February 5, 2008), www.desiringgod.org/ResourceLibrary/Biographies/2594 _Evangelist_Bill_Piper_Fundamentalist_Full_of_Grace_and_Joy/.

6. John R. W. Stott, *The Message of the Sermon on the Mount* (Downers Grove, IL: InterVarsity, 1985), 64–65.

7. Dietrich Bonhoeffer, quoted in Stott, *The Message of the Sermon on the Mount,* 62.

Chapter 11: Humble Orthodoxy

1. Timothy Keller, *The Reason for God: Belief in an Age of Skepticism* (New York: Dutton, 2008), 162.

2. I've adapted a quote by Keller in which he addresses the issue of politics: "If we get our very identity, our sense of worth, from our political position, then politics is not really about politics, it is about *us.* Through our cause we are getting a self, our worth. That means we *must* despise and demonize the opposition" (Keller, *The Reason for God,* 168).

3. D. A. Carson, *The Gagging of God: Christianity Confronts Pluralism* (Grand Rapids: Zondervan, 1996), 439.

4. Mark Dever, "Humble Dogmatism," Together for the Gospel, www.t4g.org/2006/02/humble-dogmatism/.

5. Dever, "Humble Dogmatism."

ABOUT THE AUTHOR

JOSHUA HARRIS is a pastor at Covenant Life Church in Gaithersburg, Maryland. He and his wife, Shannon, have three children. This is his fifth book. For information about Josh's work, online sermons, and updates on his speaking schedule, visit:

www.joshharris.com
Twitter: @HarrisJosh
Facebook: www.facebook.com/joshharris.fanpage

Don't Miss These Other
Best-Selling Resources
from *Joshua Harris!*

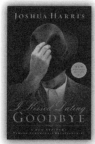

I Kissed Dating Goodbye shows what it means to entrust your love life to God. Joshua Harris shares his story of giving up dating and discovering that God has something even better--a life of sincere love, true purity, and purposeful singleness.

Boy Meets Girl presents a healthy, joyous alternative to recreational dating--biblical courtship. It's romance chaperoned by wisdom, cared for by community, and directed by God's Word. Harris reveals how it worked for him and his wife, and includes inspiring stories from others who've learned to keep God at the center of their relationship.

Lust isn't just a guy problem--it's a human problem. In this "PG-rated" book--straightforward without being graphic--Harris shares his own struggles, speaks to those entrenched in lust or just flirting with temptation, and unveils a plan for fighting back to regain freedom and the joy of holiness.

We are a generation of consumers, independent and critical. We attend church, but we don't want to settle down and truly invest ourselves--we only want to date the church. Is this what God wants for us? Harris calls Christians to stop playing the field and commit, just as Christ is committed to us, His bride. Are you dating the church, or are you committed?